The Charlton Price Guide Canadian Dolls

1st EDITION

By
Evelyn Robson Strahlendorf

W. K. CROSS
Publisher

The Charlton Press
15 BIRCH AVENUE
TORONTO. CANADA M4V 1E1

Canadian Cataloguing in Publication Data

Strahlendorf, Evelyn Robson
The Charlton price guide to Canadian dolls

Includes bibliographical references.
ISBN 0-88968-080-9

1. Dolls--Collectors and collecting--Canada--Catalogs. I. Title.

NK4893.S87 1990   C90-090231-0
                745.592'21'0750971

Charlton International Inc.
15 Birch Avenue,
Toronto, Canada.   ISSN 1180-1778
M4V 1E1   ISBN 0-88968-080-9

Printed in Canada

ABOUT THE AUTHOR

Evelyn Strahlendorf, nee Robson, was born and raised in Hamilton, Ontario. After marrying she moved with her husband Carl to Montreal where they raised four children.

She and her family then spent two years in New Jersey, U.S.A. where Carl was employed. This sojourn in the United States made her aware of the myriad differences in the culture in the two countries.

After moving to Ottawa, with her children well on their way to independence, Evelyn returned to her love of books by joining the National Library as a cataloguer.

She fell in love with doll collecting and began to research Canadian Dolls. It quickly became apparent that there was much work to be done in this field and after three years work Dolls of Canada : a Reference Guide was published in 1986.

Evelyn has since formed a company Distinctive Dolls of Canada Ltd. to promote the making and selling of Canadian collectible dolls.

ACKNOWLEDGEMENTS

First and foremost I would like to thank the five consultants who worked with me on this price guide. For the many hours spent working over lists of dolls and for their intellectual input which I so much appreciated. I couldn't have completed it without their help.
They were chosen as consultants because each one is an acknowledged authority on prices in her own area. Each one is a vendor with years of experience in pricing dolls and in watching the trends in doll popularity that effect the market. They are:

Margaret Hayes, Musqudoboit Harbour, Nova Scotia
Catherine Kerr, Ottawa, Ontario
Marlene Pfeil, Markham, Ontario
Elaine Penn, Saskatoon, Saskatchewan
Marilyn Kilby, Victoria, British Columbia

I would also like to thank Jan Belcher for help with paper dolls; Bruce Crisp for help with translation; Mary Alice Thacker for help with celebrity dolls; Dorothy Steele for help with Inuit and Indian dolls; my daughter Susan for help with editing and Barbara Bickle, Irene Henderson and Gloria Kallis for letters, photographs and discussions that contributed to this book.

Thank you also to the collectors whose dolls are represented and last but not least thank you to my husband Carl who has supported me wholeheartedly in this endeavor.

EDITORIAL

Editor	Jean Dale
Layout	Frank van Lieshout
Cover Doll	Evelyn Robson Strahlendorf

TABLE OF CONTENTS

INTRODUCTION

THE PURPOSE OF THIS BOOK

Is a price guide for Canadian dolls really necessary? In my travels across Canada researching for the book "Dolls of Canada : a Reference Guide", it became evident that there exists a tremendous range in the price of the same doll from one end of the country to the other. It is very disturbing to pay $200.00 for a doll at one doll show and see the same doll in better condition for $100.00 at another show in the next province, and sometimes even in the same city.

Many Canadian collectors have resorted to American price guides, but the market and the dolls are quite different in Canada and it is fruitless to use an American guide for Canadian dolls as so few of our dolls are ever listed there.

A price guide points out the dolls most in demand and shows where the good buys can be found. It is easy to tell where the most demand is because those are the dolls that have gone up in price.

Hopefully, this price guide will give collectors the confidence of knowing the value of the dolls they are buying or selling. This price guide will help to align doll prices across the country. We expect that subsequent editions of this book will reflect this process of alignment and reduce some of the glaring price differences of the past. Future editions will contain dolls previously unreported. Other dolls will be dropped to make space in new editions of this long awaited collectors guide to Canadian doll prices.

Standardising Canadian dolls should help to stabilize the widely fluctuating prices across the country and should make Canadian collections more attractive.

STANDARDS FOR GRADING COMPOSITION DOLLS

Mint Condition

Composition in perfect condition, no flaking or cracks.
Hair still in original set.
Eyes in perfect condition, eyelashes intact.
Original clothing and accessories all there.
Original tags.
Cloth body in perfect condition.

Excellent Condition (Ex.)

Composition in very good condition but could have small wear spot, no crazing or cracks.
All hair present, clean and combed in original style.
Eyes in working order, eyelashes intact. If painted eyes, all eye paint intact.
Has most of original clothing but shoes may be replaced with similar style.
Cloth body clean and intact.

Good Condition (G.)

Composition could be slightly crazed but not bubbled.
Most hair present.
Teeth may be missing.
Eyes in working order but some lashes may be missing.
Should have main piece of original clothing. Some items may be missing.
Clothing may be replaced with exact copy of original clothing or vintage clothing of a similar style.

Cloth body may have small repairs.
May have a missing finger.

Fair Condition (F.)

Composition may be crazed or bubbled.
Some hair present.
Eyes present but could be damaged, some lashes missing.
May have missing fingers or toes.
May not have any original clothing.
May be suitably redressed.
Cloth body may be soiled or repaired.
May be repainted.

STANDARDS FOR GRADING VINYL AND HARD PLASTIC DOLLS

Mint Condition

Face and body in perfect condition.
Hair still in original set.
Eyes and lashes in perfect condition.
Has all the original clothing and accessories.
Has original tags.
Cloth body in perfect condition.
In perfect working order if mechanical.
Accessories complete.

Excellent Condition (Ex.)

Face and body in very good condition but may have very tiny spots. May be
lightly faded. Ears may be discoloured from earrings.
All hair present, clean and combed in original style.
Eyes in working order, lashes or paint intact.
Has most original clothing but shoes or hat may be missing but not both.
Shoes may be replaced with similar style.
Cloth body clean and intact.
Complete with important accessories.

Good Condition (G.)

Face vinyl may have blemished paint. May be marks on the body.
If from the 1950s the face may be discoloured.
Most hair present and not cut.
Eyes in working order but some lashes may be missing.
Should have main piece of original clothing. Some items may be missing.
Clothing may be replaced with exact copies of original clothing or appropriate
 vintage clothing.
Plastic body may have marks, cloth body may have small repairs.
Battery box may need cleaning. Key may be missing.

Fair Condition (F.)

Vinyl face blemished and may have small stains.
Some hair present
Eyes may be damaged, some lashes missing.
May not have any original clothing but dressed in suitable clothing.
Cloth body may be soiled and repaired.
Mechanisms no longer working.

A doll may easily fall between two categories, having some points from a higher category and some from a lower. In this case a price is decided between the two conditions.

USING THIS BOOK

It is helpful to use this book in conjunction with the book "Dolls of Canada : a Reference Guide", because this price guide covers most of the dolls listed there, and uses the same reference numbers.

Dolls in this price guide are divided according to their manufacturers and then listed chronologically. Most dolls are marked by the manufacturer on the back of the head or the nape of the neck. This will help you to readily locate the doll in this price guide. However, because the Eaton's Beauty dolls and the Celebrity and Working dolls were manufactured by various companies, they are not listed by companies but only chronologically.

We have included a short description of each doll and its markings. The pictures are to identify the dolls but the prices are based on the standards. There is an index for dolls' names and an index for reference numbers.

Before looking at the prices, read the standards for the type of doll in which you are interested. Know what we mean when we give a price for a mint doll or for a doll in fair condition. After reading the standards, apply them to the doll that you are interested in pricing. If it is a composition doll and the hair has been played with, it is no longer in mint condition. If the composition is crazed, it is not in excellent condition. Talking dolls are not in excellent condition if they no longer talk.

If you are selling your doll, compare your doll with the standards. Sometimes the condition of the doll will not fit perfectly into one category, so you will have to price it a little higher or a little lower than the category it is closest to. Start with the category closest to the condition of the doll and reduce the price slightly for each defect. Keep in mind that the condition of the doll is strongly reflected in the price of the doll. Just as real estate people say the three things that count when selling a house are location, location, and location, with dolls it is condition, condition, and condition.

If you are buying a doll, compare the doll with the standards for that type of doll. When you find the category the doll is closest to, compare the price asked with the price listed for that particular doll. Remember that if the price for a doll in mint condition seems very high to you, it is because such dolls are rare and they command top dollar.

Also, take into consideration that the dealer usually knows how much demand there is for a doll and that a doll in demand commands a higher price. This book is only a guide and in the end each collector must decide whether a doll is a good buy or not. If you really want a doll, you will probably be willing to pay a little more to get it.

PRICING CANADIAN DOLLS

The prices listed in this book are those normally charged at a doll show or in a store. They are compiled from prices given by the five consultants based on their experience as dealers and from recorded prices from doll shows and advertisements.

These are not prices paid to an owner by a dealer. If you are selling your doll to a dealer, expect to get 40 to 50% less than book value as the dealer has expenses involved in selling dolls and must make a profit in order to stay in business.

One collector selling to another collector often charges less than top dollar as they have not had to advertise or rent a table at a show.

Five factors determine the price of a doll: condition, age, rarity, manufacturer and size. We have not priced the exact doll pictured but what a doll of that type would be worth in mint, excellent, good or fair condition. In some of the newer, less expensive dolls we have not given four prices but only two as there is a smaller range in prices.

Although the mint price may seem high for a composition doll, it should be noted that a composition doll in mint condition is a rare find. Examine a doll that is claimed to be mint carefully before you decide to buy at the top price, as many dolls are called mint but are really only excellent or good. A mint composition doll is a doll that was boxed and left on a shelf and never exposed to heat , cold, sunlight or dampness.

Dolls that are "Mint In the Box" (MIB) are about 10 to 15% higher for vinyl dolls and 40 to 50% higher for composition dolls. The composition dolls in boxes are of course much rarer. For the MIB category the box should be labelled with the manufacturers' name and possibly the name of the doll. A cardboard box with nothing printed on it has very little value.

The classification for "Never Removed From Box" (NRFB) has been popularized in the States mainly because dolls such as Barbie come with many accessories and packing the box is quite complicated. In most cases, however, a vinyl doll is packed very easily and it is impossible to tell if it has ever been out of its box. I don't feel that it has much importance in the value of a doll, except as I mentioned, in the case of a Barbie doll.

Dolls which are unusual such as those with a mechanical action, advertising and celebrity dolls, characters or dolls in costumes such as Mounties or Scottish dolls and black dolls always command a higher price than dolly-faced dolls.

There are fads in the popularity of dolls as in everything else. The hard plastic dolls have recently gone up in price apparently because they are durable. However, vinyl dolls are just as durable and the early models from the 1960's are a very good buy. Many are made of a heavier vinyl than later dolls and are very well made. Dolls of this type are Dee an Cee's GIGI and CHATTY CATHY and Pullan's BEATNIK doll.

Some manufacturers' dolls are more collectable and consequently more expensive than others. Dominion dolls are the oldest commercial dolls and tend to be expensive. Dee an Cee dolls command a higher price because of their quality, Pullan is next in value, probably because many of the Pullan dolls are quite innovative, followed by Reliable, and the last of the big names, Regal. Regal dolls are not as old as the other companies and some are quite cheaply made. Freeman dolls are generally not of high quality, although there are fewer of them and so they are harder to find.

Although they are not made of the fine quality porcelain of European dolls, Canadian bisque dolls are extremely rare and very collectable.

REGIONAL DIFFERENCES

In a country as immense as Canada, there are bound to be regional differences in the pricing and the popularity of certain dolls. The preference for dolls dressed in Indian or Inuit clothing, particularly leather and fur, is stronger in the Prairie provinces. The demand for Eaton's Beauties in the Prairie provinces shows up in higher prices there. Scottish dolls and baby dolls like DREAM BABY are popular in the Maritimes. In Ontario, collectors like unusual dolls such as characters, black dolls, or unusually dressed dolls. A doll like KENNY TOK that has a mechanical feature is much more in demand and is much more expensive in Ontario than in other areas.

The prices can range far and wide on some dolls, but yet are usually within 10% on the ordinary dolly faced dolls. Ontario is the best place to sell your dolls, as the prices are higher there. But if you want to buy dolls, go to the Prairies or the Maritimes. British Columbia seems to steer a middle course: not as high as Ontario but not as low as the Maritimes and the Prairies. Roughly (and we cannot be exact, because what is true for one doll may be different for another), Ontario prices are 40% higher than those of the Prairies and the Maritimes for unusual dolls and character dolls. British Columbia is 10% less than Ontario. For less expensive dolls and dolly-faced dolls, Ontario is only 10% higher than the rest of the country.

For expensive dolls, those over $250.00, the differences are greater: the higher the price, the greater the difference. Some dolls are in fact 150% more in Ontario than in other areas.

This is partly due to demand, for there are more collectors in Ontario trying to find good dolls and that is what pushes up the price.

COLLECTING CANADIAN DOLLS

As we come to know our own music, songs, dance, art and literature, so we should know our own dolls. Dolls are an integral part of our culture, and only by familiarity with dolls made in Canada over the years will we recognize what is a truly Canadian doll.

Some dolls are adaptations of American dolls, it is true. It is possible for a manufacturer in Canada to buy American moulds and to make dolls that are similar to American dolls. However, the Canadian version is usually given a different name and different clothing. In the case of dolls such as CHATTY CATHY or SHIRLEY TEMPLE, the Canadian manufacturer is licensed to make the doll here, and consequently the doll will bear the same name and clothing as the American version.

Dolls such as the BARBARA ANN SCOTT doll, LADDIE, Canadian celebrity dolls and Reliable's Eaton's Beauty dolls are truly Canadian dolls and were not made anywhere else.

There is a growing interest in Canadian dolls, and as the number of collectors in Canada rapidly increases, there will be fewer and fewer old Canadian dolls to go around. A manufacturer in Canada has a winner when 5000 or more dolls of one style are sold. In the States, you must sell at least 50,000 dolls to have reasonable success and 100,000 to have a winner. There are of course millions of collectors in the States and the demand for dolls is very high; consequently, American prices are higher than Canadian prices. This may turn around as Canadian collectors increase in numbers and the few Canadian dolls become harder and harder to find.

For those looking for more information about the original costumes or the history of the Canadian doll industry, see "Dolls of Canada : a Reference Guide", University of Toronto Press.

When neophyte collectors buy dolls they often buy randomly without any particular plan. As their tastes become more sophisticated, they usually choose one type of doll to collect. They may collect only small dolls or only large dolls, baby dolls or lady dolls, bride dolls or black dolls. There are a multitude of choices to make your collection unique.

Most collectors are looking for pretty dolls but there are a number of serious collectors who are willing to pay more to get an unusual doll. A homely doll like PITIFUL PEARL, which was not a popular doll and was sold for only one year, is today a rare doll. Because so few were sold and the doll is quite unusual, it is a valuable addition to a collection.

Doll collecting is an on-going hobby, with the goal being not to just have a sample of the many different dolls available but to upgrade your collection continuously. If you have a doll in excellent condition but it is missing parts of the costume, it is worthwhile to search for the same doll which is not in such good condition but which has the costume intact. Switch the costumes and sell the doll in poorer condition which now has an incomplete costume. The doll you keep will be more valuable because it is now complete. The search for missing items is all part of the fun of collecting.

As we become more and more avid collectors, we are no longer satisfied to have a BARBARA ANN SCOTT doll in our collections but aim to collect a BARBARA ANN SCOTT in every available costume!

The doll prices given in this book are intended as value guides rather than arbitrarily set prices. Each price recorded here is actually a compilation. The retail prices in this book are recorded as accurately as possible but in the case of errors, typographical, clerical or otherwise, the author and publisher assume no responsibility for any loss incurred by users of this book.

INUIT DOLLS

From prehistoric times to the present.

INUIT WOMAN

Date Unknown. 15.25 in. (39 cm). Cloth body. Wooden head with carved features and carved tattoo marks on cheeks. Carved hair. Mark: on foot, 784. Original authentic fur and leather clothing. Large hood to accomodate a baby.
Ref.No.: D of C, AR22, p. 9.

Range: $200.00 - 250.00

WOMAN POWER

Date Unknown. Height, sitting, 8.25 in. (21 cm). Leather body in a sitting position; carved ivory hands. Ivory carved head; eyes painted black. Mark: label, CANADIAN ESKIMO ART; COMMUNITY 757/DNA FRSB./FROBISHER BAY/E564. Authentic sealskin clothing. Umiak is 22.75 in. (58 cm) long with a wooden frame covered in sealskin and includes oars.
Ref.No.: D of C, AZ25, p. 9.

Range: $750.00 - 850.00

INUIT MAN

Date unknown. 17 in. (43 cm). Cloth body. Wooden head with carved features. Authentic sealskin clothing; well made leather mitts and boots.
Ref.No.: D of C, AR19, p. 10.

Range: $225.00 - 275.00

INUIT WOMAN

Date unknown. Inuit woman. 8.25 in. (21 cm). Leather body. Soapstone head; carved features and hair. Doeskin and sealskin clothing. Mark: label, ESKIMO ART, MADE BY AN INUIT AT ESKIMO POINT.
Ref.No.: D of C, AZ32, p. 11.

Range: $250.00 - 300.00

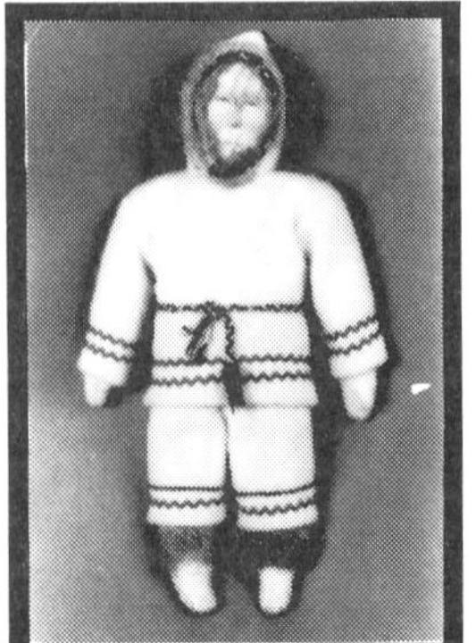

INUIT MAN

Date unknown. Inuit man. 19.75 in. (50 cm). Cloth body. Wooden head; carved features. Unmarked. Dressed in a woollen hooded parka with fur trim, woolen pants, leather and fur mukluks
Ref.No. D of C, AR20, p. 11.

Range: $150.00 - 180.00

INUIT WOMAN

DaLacia Kasudluck. Date unknown. 10 in. (25.5 cm). Cloth body. Soapstone head with carved features and hair. Mark: label, #1073, MADE BY DALACIA KASUDLUCK AT DNOUCDJOVCK. Handmade sealskin pants and parka with large hood to accomodate a baby; leather gloves and boots
Ref.No.: D of C, AE14, p. 11.

Range: $250.00 - 300.00

INUGUGULIAJUIT (THE LITTLE PEOPLE)

La Federation des Cooperative du Nouveau. Date unknown. 4 in. (10 cm). Leather body. Leather head with painted features. Leather and fur clothing are part of doll. Mark: on label, LA FEDERATION DES COOPERATIVE DU NOUVEAU, QUE. LEVIS, QUE., CANADA.
Ref. No.: D of C, BX32, p. 12.

Range: $30.00 - 50.00

INUIT MAN

Date unknown. 9.75 in. (24.5 cm). Cloth body; soapstone mitts and boots. Soapstone head with carved features. Mark: label, ESKIMO/MADE BY AN INUIT AT POND INLET. Dressed in a hooded wool parka trimmed in fur; black pants. *Ref.No.: D of C, AZ33, p. 12.*

Range: $225.00 - 250.00

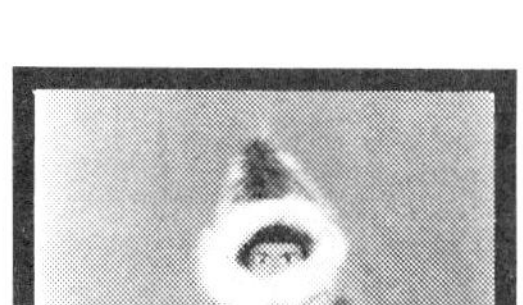

INUIT MAN

Date unknown. 7 in. (17 cm). Cloth body. Plastic shoulderhead; painted eyes; moulded black painted hair. Mark: on foot, LABRADOR. Dressed in a sealskin hooded jacket, cotton pants, leather mukluks and mitts. Made in Labrador. *Ref.No.: D of C, BH7, p. 12.*

Range: $40.00 - 60.00

INUIT MAN

ca.1966. 11 in. (28 cm). Cloth body. Bone head with carved features. Unmarked. Dressed in an embroidered white parka trimmed around hood with white fur cloth, wolverine mitts, navy blue sailcloth pants, leather mukluks. Made by an Inuit on Baffin Island. *Ref.No.: D of C, CB15, p. 13.*

Range: $225.00 - 260.00

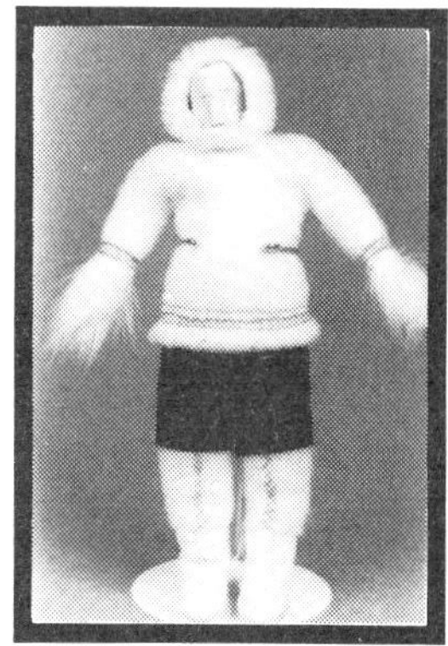

CLYDE RIVER INUIT

Ootoovah Tigullaraq. Ca.1970. 16 in. (40.5 cm). One piece cloth body. Cloth head with attached nose; painted features. Completely dressed in baby sealskin and leather boots. Mark: label, ESKIMO ART, HANDMADE BY OOTOOVAH TIGULLARAQ FROM CLYDE RIVER. *Ref. No.: D of C, AB1A, p. 13.*

Range: $230.00 - 280.00

BONE PLAY DOLLS

1970. 3.50 in. (9 cm), 4.75 in. (12 cm), 5.25 in. (13.5 cm).
Holes drilled in the bone, arms, and legs; attached with strong
thread. Largest doll has been carved to suggest clothing.
Ref.No.: D of C, BC7, p. 13.

Left: $7.50 ; Centre: $ 8.50 ; Right: $19.00.

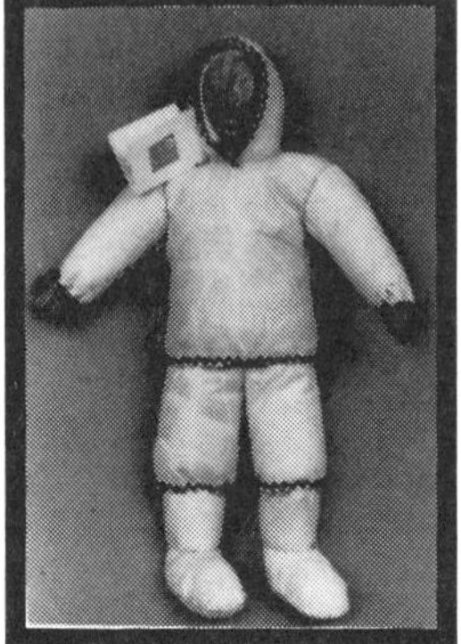

INUIT MAN

Esau Ulayok. 1976. 13 in. (33 cm). Cloth body; soapstone
head with carved features. Clothing made of caribou turned
inside out and trimmed with rickrack. Mark: label, MADE BY
ESAU ULAYOK FROM ESKIMO POINT.
Ref.No.: D of C, CP29, p. 14.

Range: $250.00 - 280.00

INUIT MAN

Allikie Eeshieiut A-K. Ca.1976. 13 in. (33 cm). Cotton head
with embroidered features; wool hair. Felt hands. Authentic
fur and leather clothing, felt and fur boots, and leather mitts.
Handmade by Allikie Eeshieiut A-K from Frobisher Bay.
Ref.No.: D of C, BH5, p. 14.

Range: $220.00 - 250.00

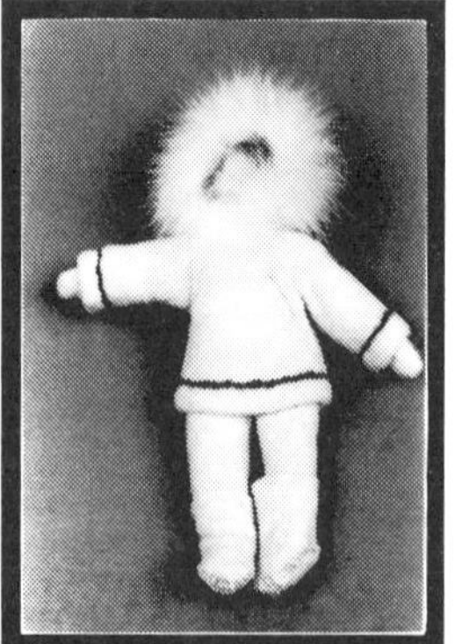

INUIT MAN

Noleeant. 1977. 5.75 in. (15 cm). Cloth body. Leather head;
no features; wool hair. Mark: label, NOLEEANT OF SPENCE
BAY/63Y9210. Handmade leather clothing; fur trimmed
hood.
Ref.No.: D of C, AR18, p. 14.

Range: $60.00 - 75.00

INUIT MAN

Jimmy Jacobson. 1977. 12 in. (30.5 cm). Whalebone body. Stone head and carved features. Mark: label, JIMMY JACOBSON FROM TUKTOYAKTUK, N.W.T. Dressed in fox, seal, and rabbit furs.
Ref.No.: D of C, BZ13, p. 15.

Range: $250.00 - 300.00

INUIT WOMAN

Emily Katiak. 1977. 13 in. (33 cm). Cloth body. Canvas head embroidered features; black wool hair. Mark: label, MADE BY EMILY KATIAK FROM COPPERMINE, N.W.T. Cotton print overdress, felt underskirt, trimmed with rabbit fur, dark red satin pants, navy felt mukluks with rawhide bottoms, fur mitts, fastened by a braided and tasselled holder, and hood with wolf fur trim.
Ref.No.: D of C, CE2, p. 15.

Range: $200.00 - 220.00

INDIAN DOLLS

From prehistoric times to the present.

PLAINS INDIAN

Indian. 1939. 19 in. (48.5 cm). Cloth body. Leather head; beaded eyes; horsehair braids; beaded mouth. Unmarked. Dressed in handmade buckskin clothing trimmed with beaded patterns, feather headdress, beaded leather shoes. *Ref.No.: D of C, BZ14, p. 21.*

Range: $150.00 - 200.00

SIX NATIONS INDIAN

1947. 6.25 in. (16 cm). Cloth body. Cloth head; features drawn in ink; black human hair braids. Unmarked. Handmade leather clothing.
Ref.No.: D of C, BM30, p. 21.

Range: $65.00 - 85.00

INDIAN FAMILY

Katie Scow. ca.1950. Father, 11 in. (28 cm); mother, 9 in. 23 cm); boy, 8 in. (20.5 cm); girl, 7 in, (17 cm). Cloth bodies and heads; embroidered features; wool hair. Mark: on mother's cape, K.C.
Ref.No.: D of C, BZ12, p. 22.

Range: $300.00 - 350.00

BROKEN NOSE

Owa'nyudane' and Gana'gweya'hon. 1960. 7 in. (17 cm). Cornhusk body. Carved wooden mask over face; long grey hair. Mark: on the bottom, IROQRAFTS/SIX NATION RESERVE. Dressed in wool, leather with bead trim clothing.

Ref.No.: D of C, AZ36, p. 22.

Range: $55.00 - 75.00

EAGLE DANCER

Six Nations Indian. 1960. 4 in. (10 cm). Cornhusk body. Head is that of a bird, arms are covered by the wings, eyes are beads. Unmarked.
Ref.No.: D of C, BC5, p. 22.

Range: $75.00 - 95.00

INDIAN MAIDEN

ca.1970. 7.75 in. (10.5 cm). Brown hard plastic teen body, jointed shoulderd and neck. Hard plastic head; brown sleep eyes, moulded lashes; black mohair braids; closed mouth. Unmarked. Dressed in beaded leather suit by Indians. Wears feather headdress and carries a bow.
Ref.No. : D of C, BP11, p. 23.

Range: $15.00 - 20.00

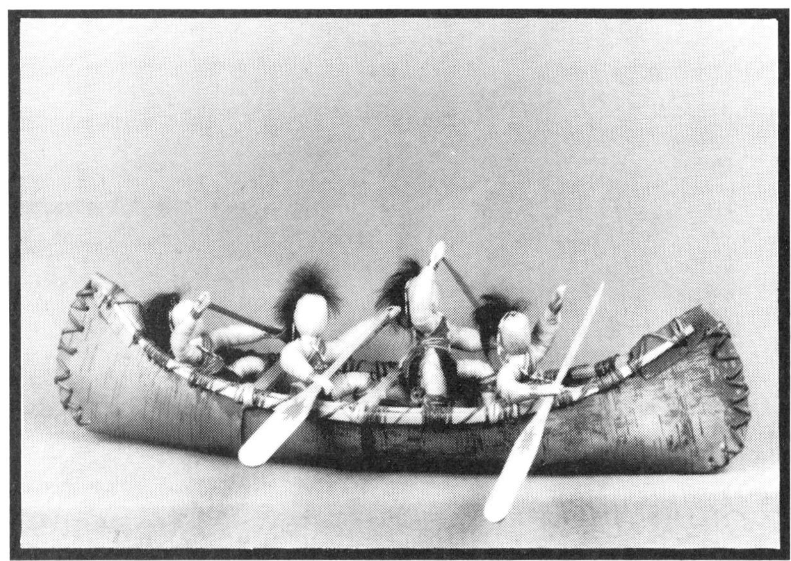

IROQUOIS WARRIORS

Six Nations Indians. 1970. Height, 5.5 in. (14 cm) x 22.5 in. (57 cm). Cornhusk bodies; no features; synthetic black hair. Unmarked. Dressed in wool, leather, and beads.
Ref.No.: D of C, AZ27, p. 24.

Range: $125.00 - 150.00

HOOP DANCER

Rhea Skye. 1975. 8 in. (20.5 cm). Cornhusk body and head; no features; black wool braids. Mark: label, RHEA SKYE/MOHAWK INDIAN/RICE LAKE RESERVE. Dressed in leather trimmed with beads.
Ref.No.: D of C, AZ34, p. 24.

Range: $ 70.00 - 85.00

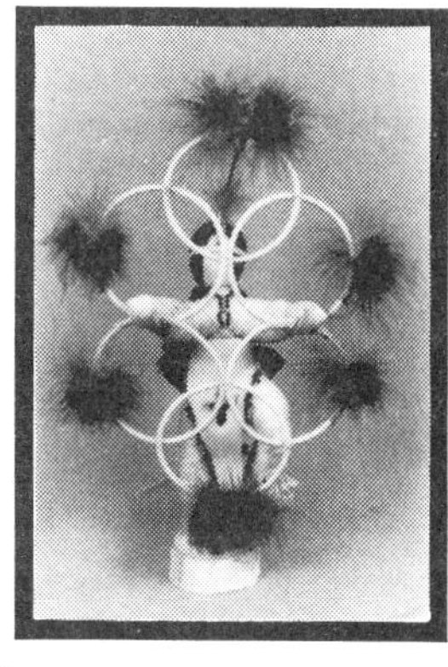

BLACKFOOT MEDICINE MAN

Indian. 1974. 10 in. (25.5 cm). Cloth body with wire armature. Leather head; beaded eyes and mouth; black braids. Unmarked. Dressed in handmade beaded leather clothing, fur headdress and carrying leather medicine bag.
Ref.No.: D of C, BX31, p. 24.

Range: $80.00 - 110.00

GASESA

Owa'nyudane and Ginada'y'asas. Date unknown. (one of the host of supernaturals dedicated to the healing of certain illnesses). 7.5 in. (18 cm). Cornhusk body. Face covered with a cornhusk mask. Mark: on bottom, IROQRAFTS/SIX NATION RESERVE. Original label. Dressed in wool and beaded leather, carrying stick.
Ref.No.: D of C, AZ36A, p. 25.

Range: $ 55.00 - 75.00

MOHAWK INDIAN

1975. 9 in. (23 cm). Cornhusk body and head; no features; black wool braids. Unmarked. Dressed in beaded leather, carrying shield and spear. Made at the Rice Lake Reserve, Ontario.
Ref.No.: D of C, AZ35, p. 25.

Range: $65.00 - 85.00

INDIAN MAIDEN

ca.1975. 7.5 in. (19 cm). Brown hard plastic teen body, jointed shoulders and neck. Hard plastic head; brown sleep eyes, moulded lashes; black synthetic hair; closed mouth. Unmarked. Dressed by Indians in leather and fur.
Ref.No.: D of C, BP14, p. 25.

Range: $15.00 - 20.00

FALSE FACE SOCIETY DOLL

Six Nations Indian. 1977. 3.25 in. (8 cm) x 5.25 in. (13 cm). Cornhusk body. Black mask face with carved features, red painted mouth; black hair possibly dyed moss. Unmarked.
Ref.No.: D of C, BY6, p. 26.

Range: $45.00 - 65.00

LACROSSE PLAYER

Owa"ny udani' and Negi"yend'gowa. Date unknown. 7 in. (17 cm). Cornhusk body and head; no features on the face; black hair. Mark: on bottom, IROQRAFTS/SIX NATION RESERVE. Original label. Dressed in wool, leather, and beads and carrying a lacrosse racquet.
Ref.No.: D of C, BC3, p. 26.

Range: $45.00 - 65.00

SIX NATIONS INDIAN

Date unknown. Height, 4 in. (10 cm).Cornhusk body. Carved wooden mask; long grey hair. Mark: label. Dressed in leather and wool.
Ref.No.: D of C, BC4, p. 26.

Range: $45.00 - 65.00

SALICH BUTTON BLANKET DOLL

Joyce Willie. 1980. 18 in. (45.5 cm). Cloth body. Cloth head; embroidered features; black wool hair. Unmarked. Southern Kwagiutl button blanket and headdress.
Ref.No.: D of C, CA39, p. 28.

Range: $225.00 - 275.00

PLAINS INDIAN

Regal. Ca.1980. 31 in. (79 cm). Plastic body, jointed hips, shoulders, and neck. Vinyl head; brown sleep eyes, lashes, painted lower lashes; rooted dark brown curls; closed mouth. Mark: on head, REGAL TOY LTD./MADE IN CANADA. Dressed by a Canadian Indian, Muriel Cuthbert of Wetaskiwin, Alberta. In a white buckskin dress, beaded belt, earrings and headband. Carrying a beaded leather bag.
Ref.No.: D of C, CO27A, p. 29.

Range: $125.00 - 150.00

SIX NATIONS INDIAN

Ken and Rye Skye. 1980. 6.50 in. (16.5 cm). Cornhusk body. Apple head; eyes look like seeds; wool hair. Unmarked. Doll is sitting on a stump which bears a label, KEN AND RYE SKYE/SIX NATION INDIAN/INDIANS A. Handmade leather clothing, trimmed with beads.
Ref.No.: D of C, BM28, p. 27.

Range: $60.00 - 75.00

CORNHUSK DANCER

Ontario Ojibwa Indian. 1983. 8 in. (20.5 cm). Dancing figure made of cornhusk; black wool braids. Mark: label, ONTARIO OJIBWA/CORNHUSK DANCER. Dressed in wool and leathher with leather shoes, carrying axe.
Ref.No.: D of C, CM6, p. 29.

Range: $30.00 - 45.00

COWICHAN DOLL

Reliable. 1985. 18 in. (45.5 cm). Brown plastic body, jointed hips, shoulders, and neck. Vinyl head; brown sleep eyes, lashes, painted lower lashes; rooted straight black hair; closed mouth. Mark: on head RELIABLE TOYS CO. LTD./C MADE IN CANADA; on body, RELIABLE (in script); label, Handknit Cowichan Indian sweater by S. Betts.
Ref.No.: D of C, CM7, p. 31.

Range: $60.00 - 85.00

MOHAWK WARRIOR

Cindy and Isabelle Skye. 1986. 23 in. (58.5 cm). Cornhusk one-piece body, fingers individually wrapped in tiny strips of cornhusk. Cornhusk head, no features. Synthetic black hair in braids. Unmarked. Dressed in leather pants, fringed and beaded; leather apron, bead trim; leather vest, shell trimmed; cotton shirt; leather moccasins, beaded and fur trimmed.
Ref.No.: D of C, CT1, p. 31.

Range: $200.00 - 250.00

EATON'S BEAUTY DOLLS
1900 -

The Eaton's Beauty dolls are not priced based on the condition of the doll in the photograph, but based on the standards for Eaton's Beauties. For a doll to be mint, it must have the original ribbon, a replacement ribbon has no value, although it may look nice in your collection. Having the original ribbon increases the value of the doll by about $100.00.

April Katz and Dorothy Churchill's dolls must have been bought only at Eaton's to be considered of any value. The value of Eaton's Beauty dolls by these two artists is because they are part of a series. These dolls were sold as limited editions and so there are few of them and they are hard to obtain. Eaton's ships only one of a series to the Maritimes and this is snapped up quickly. Ottawa receives only five and it is almost impossible to buy one.

GRADING STANDARDS FOR EATON'S BEAUTY DOLLS

MINT

> Includes the original printed ribbon.
> Has original underwear and socks and shoes.
> Hair in the original set.
> Head in perfect condition, no flakes, chips, cracks.
> Body in perfect condition.
> Eyes in good working order.
> May have appropriate old clothing.

EXCELLENT

> Has original underwear and socks and shoes.
> Hair may be combed but not thin.
> Bisque head not cracked or chipped, painted bisque.
> Head may have worn spots.
> Body may show signs of wear, but not broken.
> If kid body, no replaced parts, may be mended.
> Eyes in working order.

GOOD

> Underwear, or socks and shoes may be missing.
> Bisque head may have a hairline crack.
> Painted bisque may be dirty and worn.
> Hair may be worn or replaced with mohair or human
> hair wig. Synthetic wigs not acceptable.
> May need restringing.
> Eyes may need resetting.
> Kid body may have replaced arms but body not completely replaced

FAIR

> Has no original clothing.
> Eyes may be broken and need replacing.
> Bisque head may have hairline cracks or chips.
> Body in need of repair.
> Needs new wig.
> May have broken fingers.
> Teeth may be missing.

ARMAND MARSEILLE

ca.1900. 24 in. (62 cm). Kid leather body, upper arms and upper legs, bisque forearms, papier-mache ball-jointed lower legs. Bisque shoulderhead; blue glass sleep eyes, lashes, painted upper and lower lashes; blond mohair wig; open mouth showing teeth. Mark: on head 370/AM 3 DEP.
Ref.No.: D of C, CF2, p. 67.

Note: Regional price differences. Higher prices in B.C.

Mint $750.00   Ex. $550.00   G. $425.00   F. $350.00

J.D. KESTNER

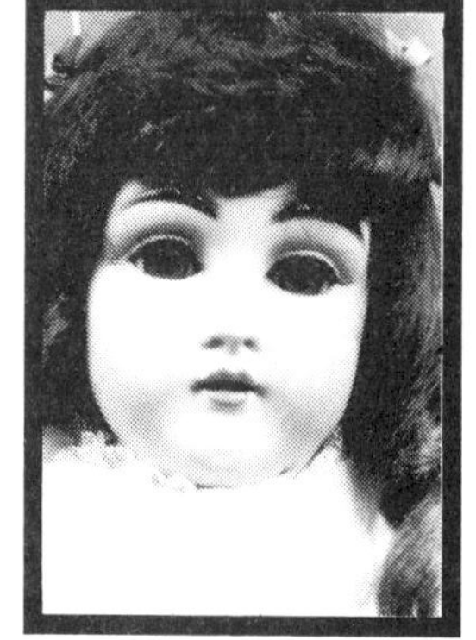

1905. 26 in. (66 cm). Kid leather body, gusset hip and knee joints, bisque replaced forearms, kid upper arms. Bisque head; replaced blue glass sleep eyes, eyelashes, painted upper and lower lashes; replaced dark brown wig; open mouth showing two teeth. Mark: on head, DEP 15413.
Ref.No. D of C, CH22, p. 68.

Note: Regional price differences. Higher prices in B.C.

Mint $900.00   Ex. $725.00   G. $550.00   F. $450.00

ARMAND MARSEILLE

1908. 21.5 in. (55 cm). Papier-mache bodies, wooden stick upper arms and upper legs, composition forearms and lower legs, ball-jointed; bisque socket heads, one has fixed blue glass eyes and the other has brown glass sleep eyes, lashes, painted upper and lower lashes; blond mohair wigs in ringlets; open mouths showing four teeth. Mark: on heads, ARMAND MARSEILLE/MADE IN GERMANY/390/A8M.
Ref.No.: D of C, CW6, p. 69.

Mint $625.00   Ex. $500.00   G. $400.00   F. $300.00

The doll prices given in this book are intended as value guides rather than arbitrarily set prices. Each price recorded here is actually a compilation. The retail prices in this book are recorded as accurately as possible but in the case of errors, typographical, clerical or otherwise, the author and publisher assume no responsibility for any loss incurred by users of this book.

SCHOENAU & HOFFMEISTER

1909. 18 in. (45.5 cm). Papier-mache fully ball-jointed body with wooden forearms. Bisque head with a slight sheen; blue glass sleep eyes, lashes, painted upper and lower lashes; brown mohair wig; open mouth showing teeth. Mark: on head, S (a star with PB in the centre) H/1909/1 1/2/GERMANY/.
Ref.No.: D of C, BS2A, p. 69.

Mint $625.00   Ex. $540.00   G. $495.00   F. $400.00

SCHOENAU & HOFFMEISTER

1909. 21 in. (53.5 cm). Papier-mache fully ball-jointed body. Bisque head; glass sleep eyes, lashes, painted upper and lower lashes; brown human hair wig; open mouth showing two teeth. Mark: on head S (star with PB in centre) H/ 1909 /3 1/2 / GERMANY.
Ref.No.: D of C, CH18, p. 70.

Note: Regional price differences. Higher prices in Prairies.

Mint $725.00   Ex. $650.00   G. $550.00   F. $440.00

CUNO & OTTO DRESSEL

1909-10. 19.75 in. (50 cm). Papier-mache fully ball-jointed body with red Holtz Masse stamp. Bisque head; blue glass sleep eyes, eyelashes, painted upper and lower lashes; brown mohair wig with curled bangs; open mouth, showing teeth. Mark: on head, C/3.
Ref.No.: D of C, BT17, p. 70.

Note: Regional price differences. Higher prices in Prairies and B.C.

Mint $700.00   Ex. $650.00   G. $600.00   F. $550.00

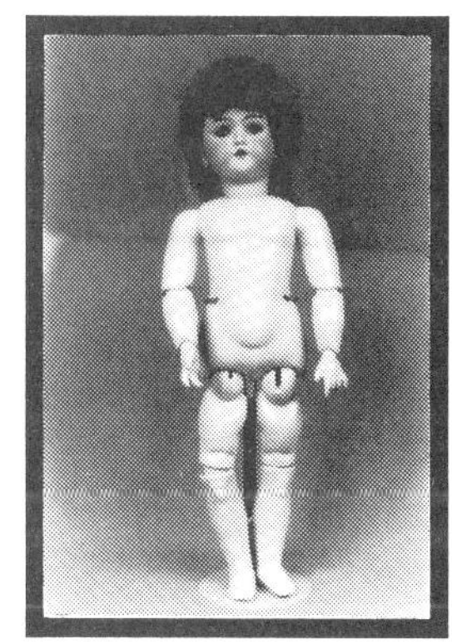

CUNO & OTTO DRESSEL

1909-10. 21 in. (53.5 cm). Papier-mache fully ball-jointed body. Bisque head; brown glass sleep eyes, lashes, painted upper and lower lashes; long blond wig with bangs; open mouth showing two teeth. Mark: on head, C/4; oval hole in the back of head.
Ref.No.: D of C, CH26, p. 71.

Mint $750.00   Ex. $700.00   G. $650.00   F. $575.00

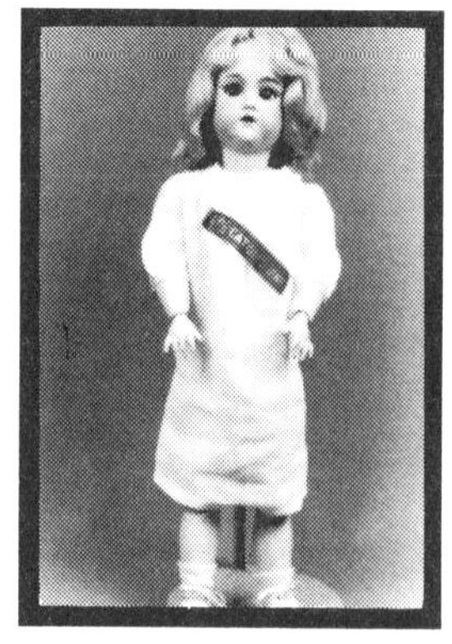

CUNO & OTTO DRESSEL

1910. 20 in. (51 cm). Papier-mache fully ball-jointed body. Bisque head, dimpled chin; blue glass sleep eyes, painted upper and lower lashes; blond mohair wig; open mouth showing teeth. Mark: on head, C/3, two small holes above mark, hole above each ear; on body, red Holtz Masse mark. Photograph courtesy of Brooks-Kennedy Studio, St. Catharines, Ont.
Ref.No.: D of C, XH16, no. 72.

Mint $700.00   Ex. $650.00   G. $600.00   F. $550.00

CUNO AND OTTO DRESSEL

1911. 19.5 in. (49.5 cm). Fully ball-jointed papier-mache body. Bisque head, dimpled chin; blue glass sleep eyes, painted upper and lower lashes; blond mohair wig; open mouth showing four teeth. Mark: head, GERMANY/C/3.
Ref.No.: D of C, BH25, p. 70.

Note: Regional price differences.

Mint $700.00   Ex. $650.00   G. $600.00   F. $550.00

CUNO & OTTO DRESSEL

1911-12. 19 in. (48.5 cm). Papier-mache fully ball-jointed body. Bisque head; stationary brown glass eyes; light brown wig; open mouth showing four teeth. Mark: on head, GERMANY/C/3.
Ref.No.: D of C, CH31, p. 72.

Mint $700.00   Ex. $650.00   G. $600.00   F. $550.00

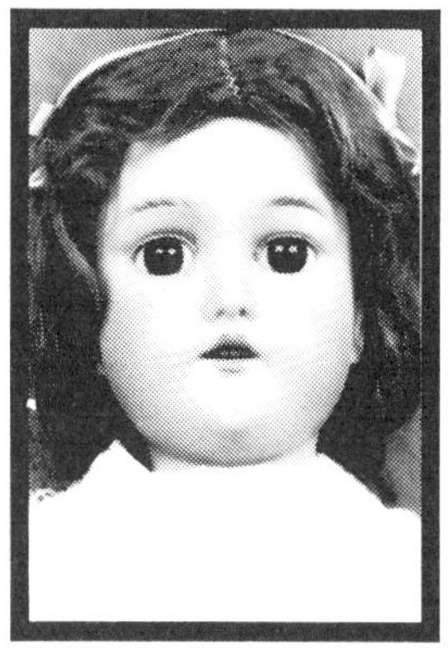

ARMAND MARSEILLE

1912-13. 19.75 in. (50 cm). Composition fully ball-jointed body. Bisque head, dimpled chin; brown glass sleep eyes, lashes, painted upper and lower lashes; long light brown mohair wig; open mouth showing teeth. Mark: on head, ARMAND MARSEILLE/GERMANY/390/A4M.
Ref.No.: D of C, BT8A, p. 73.

Mint $625.00   Ex. $500.00   G. $425.00   F. $325.00

ARMAND MARSEILLE

1914-15. 25 in. (63.5 cm). Composition fully ball-jointed body. Bisque head, dimpled chin; blue glass sleep eyes, lashes, painted upper and lower lashes; replaced human hair wig, original was brown mohair; open mouth, showing four teeth. Mark: MADE IN GERMANY/ARMAND MARSEILLE/390/A 8 M.
Ref.No.: D of C, CJ19, p. 73.

Mint $750.00   Ex. $650.00   G. $450.00   F. $375.00

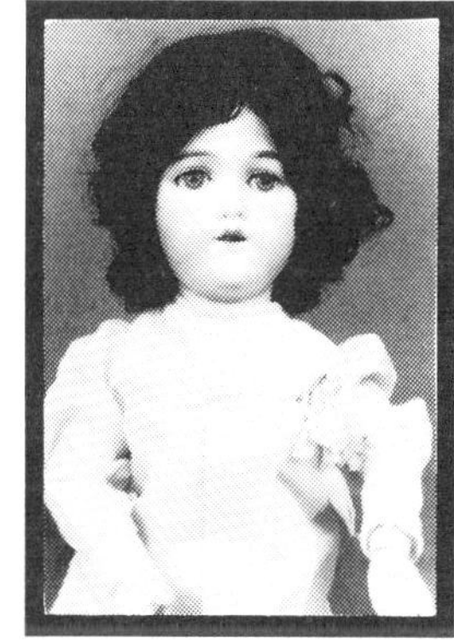

ARMAND MARSEILLE

1914. 22.5 in. (57 cm). Papier-mache fully ball-jointed body. Bisque head; Blue glass sleep eyes, painted upper and lower lashes; light brown mohair wig; open mouth showing four teeth. Mark: on head, ARMAND MARSEILLE/MADE IN GERMANY/390/A4M.
Ref.No.: D of C, BP19, p. 73.

Mint $675.00   Ex. $575.00   G. $450.00   F. $375.00

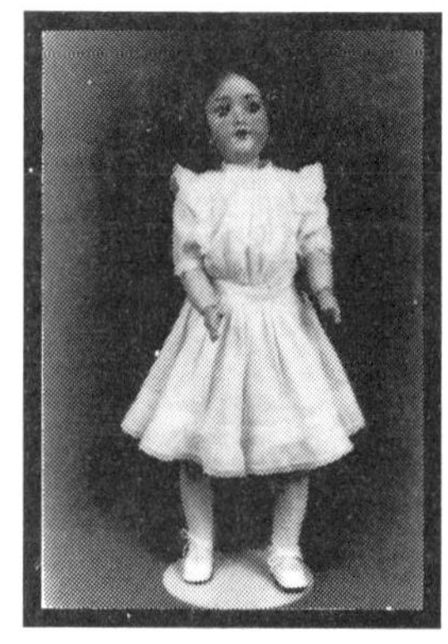

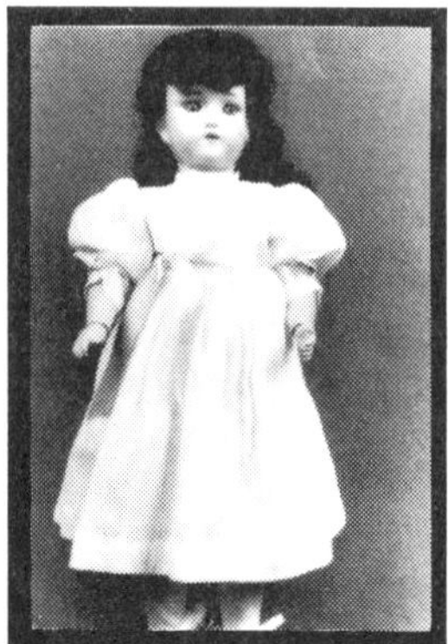

DOMINION TOY

19l5. 20 in. (50.5 cm). Composition hands, trunk and legs, wooden arms, fully ball-jointed. Composition head, open crown; light blue tin sleep eyes, repainted face, painted lashes, red dots in eye corners, nostril dots; replaced wig (original was mohair), closed mouth. Mark: on body, MADE IN CANADA (in an arch over) DTMC.
Ref.No.: D of C, CL22, p. 74.

Mint $450.00   Ex. $350.00   G. $300.00   F. $200.00

S.F.B.J.

ca.1922. Eaton Special Doll (not an Eaton's Beauty) 20 in. (51 cm). Papier-mache body, fully-jointed, wooden arms with French joints, composition hands, composition legs with French joints. Bisque head; all black glass sleep eyes, painted upper and lower lashes; dark brown human hair wig; open mouth showing four porcelain teeth. Mark: on head, S.F.B.J./60/PARIS.
Ref.No.: D of C, CW5, p. 74.

Mint $900.00   Ex. $825.00   G. $725.00   F. $650.00

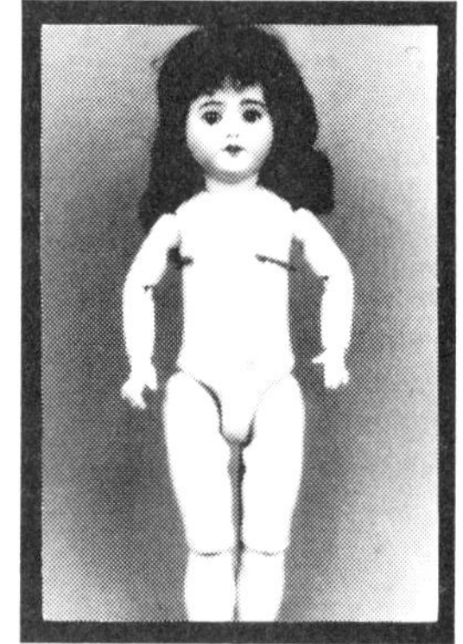

S.F.B.J.

1922-23. Eaton Special Doll (not an Eaton's Beauty). 19 in. (48.5 cm). Composition fully-jointed French body marked with the S.F.B.J. mark. Bisque head; blue glass sleep eyes, lashes; light brown human hair wig; open mouth, four moulded porcelain teeth. Mark: on head, 22/D/S.F.B.J./60/PARIS/3.
Ref.No.: D of C, BH26, p. 75.

Mint $900.00   Ex. $825.00   G. $725.00   F. $650.00

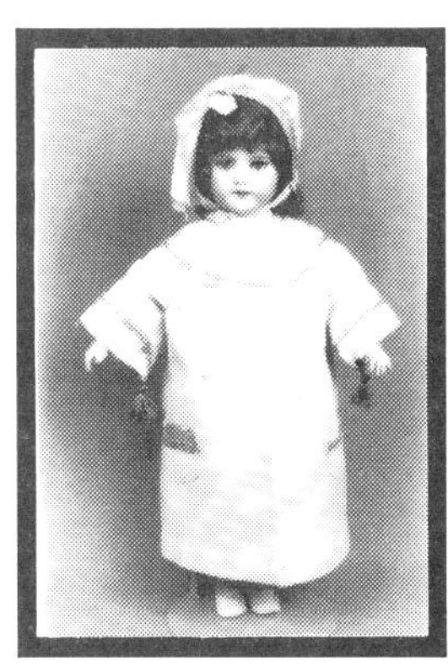

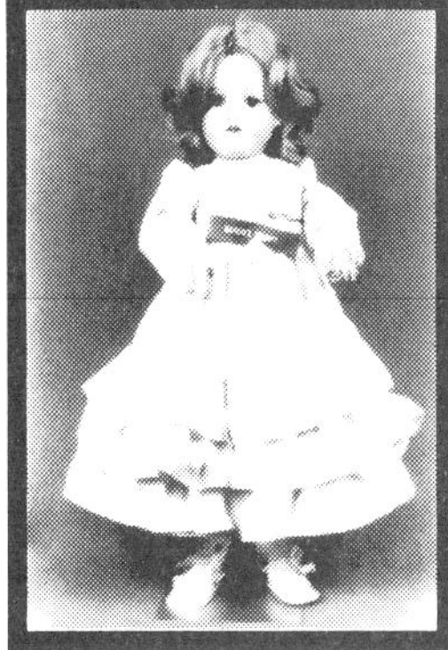

ARMAND MARSEILLE

1924. 21 in. (53.5 cm). Composition fully ball-jointed body. Bisque head; brown glass sleep eyes, eyelashes, painted upper and lower lashes; replaced blond wig; open mouth, showing two teeth. Mark: on head, ARMAND MARSEILLE/390N/GERMANY/A 6 M. Replaced ribbon.
Ref.No.: D of C, AP31, p. 75.

Mint $675.00   Ex. $550.00   G. $450.00   F. $350.00

ARMAND MARSEILLE

1924. 21.25 in. (54 cm). Composition fully ball-jointed body. Bisque head; blue glass sleep eyes, lashes, painted upper and lower lashes; blond mohair wig; open mouth showing teeth. Mark: on head, ARMAND MARSEILLE/GERMANY/390/A4M. Photograph neg. no. 79-1624 courtesy of National Museums of Canada, National Museum of Man.
Ref.No.: D of C, BQ24A, p. 75.

Mint $650.00   Ex. $550.00   G. $475.00   F. $325.00

ARMAND MARSEILLE

1925. 19 in. (48.5 cm). Composition fully ball-jointed body. Bisque head; brown glass sleep eyes, painted upper and lower lashes; long blond mohair wig with bangs; open mouth showing four teeth. Mark: on head, MADE IN GERMANY/390/ A 2 L/2 M.
Ref.No.: D of C, BH27, p. 76.

Mint $625.00   Ex. $525.00   G. $450.00   F.   350.00

ARMAND MARSEILLE

1927. 22 in. (56 cm). Composition fully ball-jointed body. Bisque head; blue glass stationary eyes (originally were sleep eyes), painted uppers and lowers; brown mohair wig; open mouth showing four teeth. Mark: on head, ARMAND MARSEILLE/GERMANY/390/A 4 M.
Ref.No.: D of C, CE34, p. 76.

Mint $650.00   Ex. $550.00   G. $475.00   F. $350.00

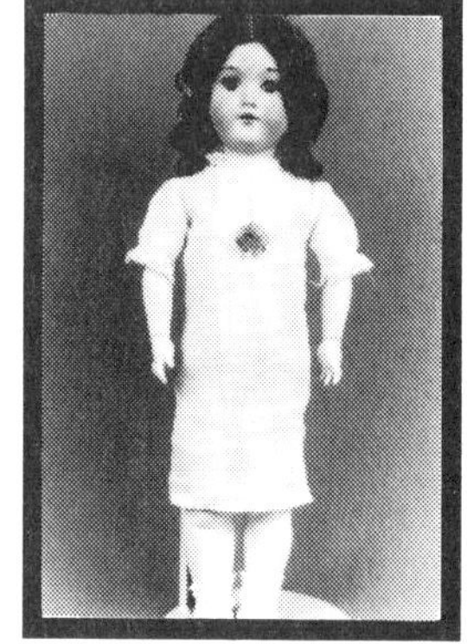

ARMAND MARSEILLE

1927-28. Fully jointed Doll (not an Eaton's Beauty). 19.5 in. (49.5 cm). Composition fully ball-jointed body. Bisque head; blue glass sleep eyes, lashes, painted upper and lower lashes; brown mohair wig; open mouth showing four teeth. Mark: on head, ARMAND MARSEILLE/GERMANY/390/A 3 M.
Ref.No.: D of C, BY14, p. 76.

Mint $600.00   Ex. $525.00   G. $450.00   F. $325.00

BIG SISTER

Cuno & Otto Dressel. 1927. 29 in. (74 cm). Composition fully ball-jointed body. Bisque head, highly coloured; blue glass sleep eyes, lashes, painted upper and lower lashes; brown human hair wig; open mouth showing four teeth and felt tongue. Mark: on head, CUNO & OTTO DRESSEL/GERMANY.
Ref.No.: D of C, CH32, p. 77.

Note: Regional price differences. Higher prices in Prairies and B.C.

Mint $1,100.00 Ex. $950.00   G. $875.00   F. $625.00

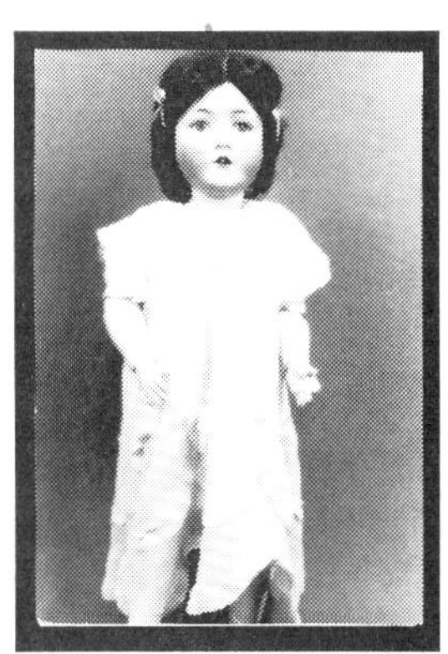

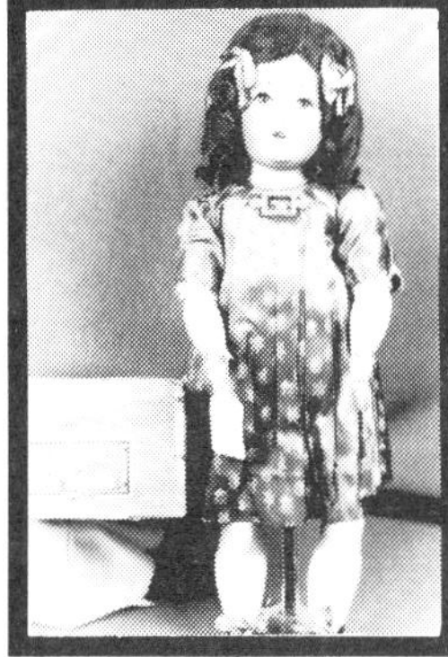

CUNO & OTTO DRESSEL

1929-30. 25 in. (63.5 cm). Composition fully ball-jointed body. Bisque head; grey-blue glass sleep eyes, lashes, painted upper and lower lashes; original brown wig; open mouth showing four teeth. Mark: on head, 6/CUNNO & OTTO DRESSEL/GERMANY.
Ref.No.: D of C, CA18, p. 78.

Note: Regional price differences. Higher prices in B.C.

Mint $900.00   Ex. $800.00   G. $725.00   F. $675.00

ARMAND MARSEILLE

1934. 20 in. (50.5 cm). Papier-mache, straight limbed, jointed hips, shoulders, and neck. Painted bisque head; blue glass sleep eyes, lashes, eyeshadow above eyes; blond mohair wig. Mark: on head, ARMAND MARSEILLE in an arch over 390/ A 2 1/2 M.
Ref.No.: D of C, CJ17, p. 78.

Note: Regional price differences.

Mint $575.00   Ex. $475.00   G. $400.00   F. $300.00

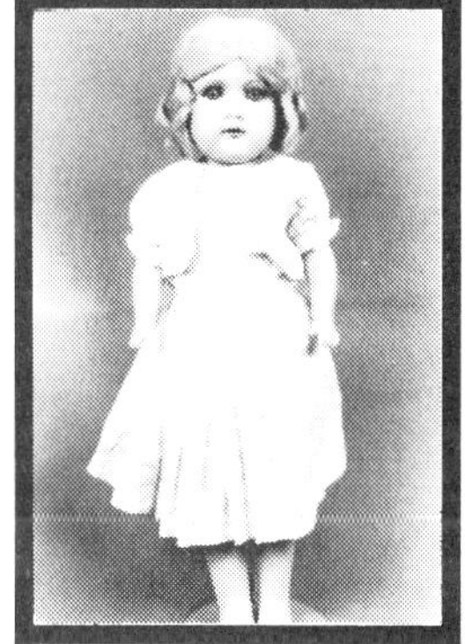

ARMAND MARSEILLE

1935-36. 19 in. (51 cm). Papier-mache, straight limbed, jointed hips, shoulders, and neck. Painted bisque head; brown glass sleep eyes, lashes, eyeshadow above the eyes; brown mohair wig; closed mouth. Mark: on head, A 449 M/GERMANY/0 1/2. Replaced ribbon.
Ref.No.: D of C, BH23, p. 79.

Mint $575.00   Ex. $475.00   G. $400.00   F. $300.00

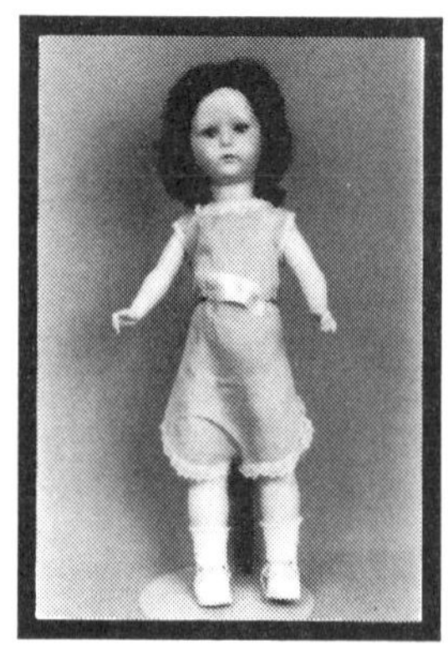

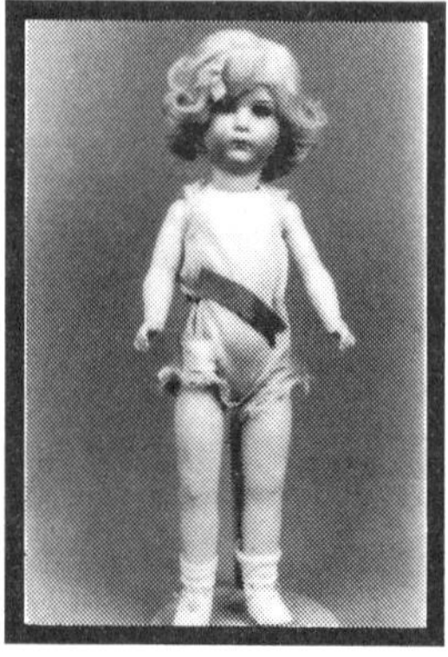

ARMAND MARSEILLE

1935-36. 20 in. (50.5 cm). Papier-mache, straight limbed, jointed hips, shoulders, and neck. Painted bisque head; blue glass sleep eyes, lashes, eyeshadow above and below the eyes; blond mohair wig, original blue hair-ribbon; closed mouth. Mark: on head, A 449 M/GERMANY/0 1/2. ORIGINAL EATON'S BEAUTY RIBBON.
Ref.No.: D of C, CH24, p. 79.

Mint $575.00   Ex. $475.00   G. $400.00   F. $300.00

ARMAND MARSEILLE

1936-37. 19 in. (43.5 cm). Papier-mache, straight limbed, jointed at hips, shoulder, and head. Painted bisque head; brown glass sleep eyes, lashes, painted upper lashes; brown mohair wig; open mouth showing four teeth. Mark: on head, ARMAND MARSEILLE/GERMANY/390/A 2 1/2 M.
Ref.No.: D of C, BH24, p. 80.

Mint $575.00   Ex. $475.00   G. $400.00   F. $300.00

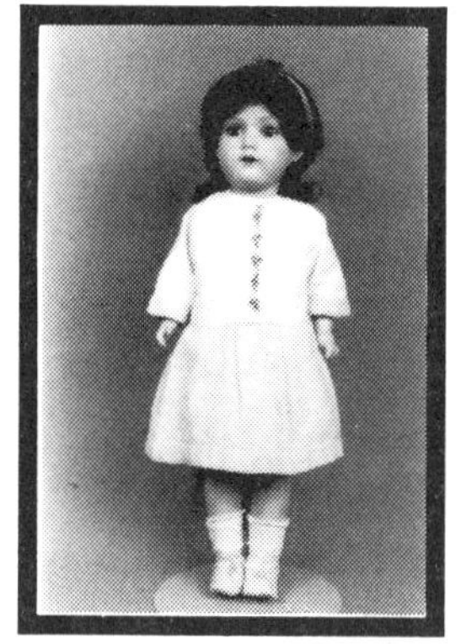

OLD FASHIONED BEAUTY

Armand Marseille. 1939-40. (Not an Eaton's Beauty). 16 in. (40.5 cm). Composition (cardboard and plaster, painted), straight limbed, jointed hips, shoulders, and neck. Painted bisque head; brown glass sleep eyes, lashes, eyeshadow above eyes; blond mohair wig in ringlets; open mouth showing four teeth. Mark: on head, GERMANY/390/A 2 1/2 M.
Ref.No.: D of C, CJ20, p. 80.

Mint $450.00   Ex. $350.00   G. $300.00   F. $250.00

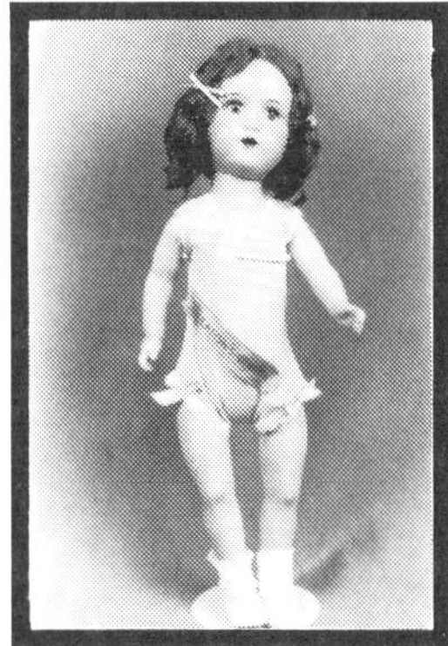

RELIABLE - 1940-1941

1940-41. 18 in. (45.5 cm). Composition, straight limbed, jointed hips, shoulders, and neck. Composition head; blue lithographed metal sleep eyes, lashes; light brown mohair wig; open mouth showing teeth. Mark: on head, RELIABLE/MADE IN CANADA.
Ref.No.: D of C, CR18, p. 81.

Mint $375.00   Ex. $300.00   G. $225.00   F. $100.00

RELIABLE - 1941-1942

1941-42. 18.5 in. (47 cm). Composition straight limbed, jointed hips, shoulders, and neck. Composition head; blue lithographed metal sleep eyes, lashes; blond mohair wig; open mouth showing teeth. Mark: on head, RELIABLE/MADE IN CANADA.
Ref.No.: D of C, CP2, p. 81.

Mint $400.00   Ex. $300.00   G. $225.00   F. $100.00

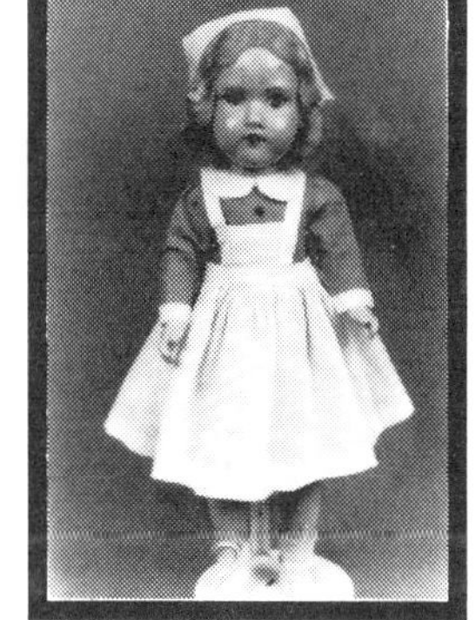

RELIABLE - 1942-1943

1942-43. 19 in. (48 cm). Composition, straight limbed, jointed hips, shoulders, and neck. Composition head; blue lithographed metal sleep eyes, lashes; light brown mohair wig; open mouth showing teeth. Mark: on head, RELIABLE/MADE IN CANADA.
Ref.No.: D of C, BC13, p. 81.

Mint $400.00   Ex. $300.00   G. $225.00   F. $100.00

RODDY

1958-59. Feature Value Doll (not an Eaton's Beauty). 13 in. (33 cm). Hard plastic walking doll, jointed hips, shoulders, and neck. Hard plastic head; blue sleep eyes, moulded lashes; auburn synthetic wig with bangs; closed mouth. Mark: on body, RODDY/MADE IN ENGLAND.
Ref.No.: D of C, BS10, p. 82.

Mint   **$95.00**   **Ex.**   **$75.00**   **G.**   **$50.00**   **F.**   **$35.00**

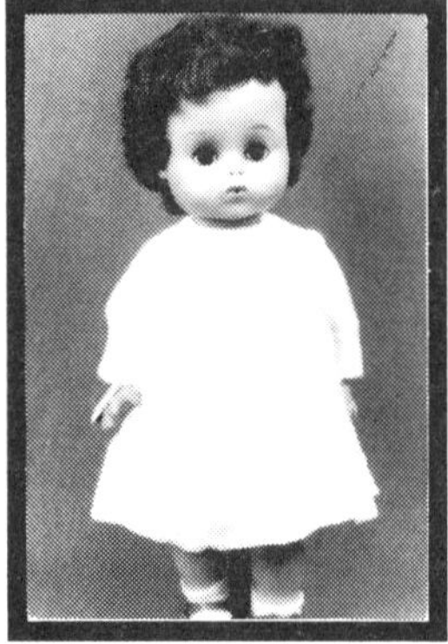

DEE AN CEE - 1960

1960. 18 in. (46 cm). Plastic toddler, jointed hips, shoulders, and neck. Vinyl head; brown sleep eyes, lashes, painted lower lashes; rooted brown curly hair; open mouth nurser. Mark: on head, 1960/EATON BEAUTY BY DEE & CEE, on body 2.
Ref.No.: D of C, CA29, p. 82.

Mint   **$175.00**   **Ex.**   **$125.00**   **G.**   **$75.00**   **F.**   **G45.00**

REGAL - 1963

1963. 21 in. (53.5 cm). Plastic body, jointed hips, shoulders, and neck. Vinyl head, blue sleep eyes, lashes, painted lower lashes, rooted blond saran curly hair, open mouth nurser. Mark: on head, REGAL/MADE IN CANADA.
Ref.No.: D of C, CP4, p. 82.

Mint   **$125.00**   **Ex.**   **$65.00**   **G.**   **$50.00**   **F.**   **$30.00**

REGAL - 1964

1964. 21 in. (53 cm). Plastic body, jointed hips, shoulders, and neck. Vinyl head; blue sleep eyes, lashes, painted lower lashes; rooted brown curls; open mouth nurser. Mark: on head, REGAL, on body, REGAL.
Ref.No.: D of C, BQ11, p. 83.

Mint   **$125.00**   **Ex.**   **$65.00**   **G.**   **$50.00**   **F.**   **$30.00**

RELIABLE - 1965

1965. 18 in. (45.5 cm). One piece Vinyl-flex stuffed body. Vinyl head; blue plastic sleep eyes, lashes, painted lower lashes; rooted brown saran hair; closed watermelon mouth. Mark: on head, RELIABLE/MADE IN CANADA.
Ref.No.: D of C, BZ15, p. 83.

Mint. $110.00   Ex. $85.00   G. $65.00   F. $45.00

DOROTHY CHURCHILL - 1978

1978. 18 in. (45.5 cm). Fully jointed composition body. Bisque head; blue stationary eyes, lashes, painted upper and lower lashes; brown wig; open mouth showing teeth and tongue. Mark: on head, 47 of 100/E (inside a diamond) DOROTHY CHURCHILL.
Ref.No.: D of C, CV12, p. 83.

Mint $450.00   Ex. $350.00   G. $200.00   F. $150.00

DOROTHY CHURCHILL - 1980

1980. 20 in. (51 cm). Fully jointed composition body. Bisque head; stationary blue eyes, lashes, painted upper and lower lashes; long brown hair wig; open mouth, showing teeth and tongue. Mark: on head, DOROTHY 1980/CHURCHILL E (inside a diamond) 162.
Ref.No.: D of C, CV10, p. 84.

Mint $450.00   Ex. $350.00   G. $200.00   F. $150.00

DOROTHY CHURCHILL - 1981

1981. 18 in. (45.5 cm). Ball-jointed composition body. Bisque head; stationary brown glass eyes, lashes and painted upper and lower lashes; human hair wig in ringlets; closed mouth. Mark: on head, DOROTHY CHURCHILL, a capital E inside a diamond, 79/1981. Coat with Eaton Beauty label inside. Limited edition of 200.
Ref.No.: D of C, CG35, p. 84.

Mint $450.00   Ex. $350.00   G. $200.00   F.   150.00

GAIL KAREN

April Katz. 1983. 17 in. (43 cm). All bisque, jointed hips, shoulders, and neck. Bisque head; stationary brown eyes, painted upper and lower lashes. Blond wig in long ringlets; closed mouth. Mark: on head, APRIL KATZ #60/CANADA/1983; card bearing artist's signature. Limited edition of 200.
Ref.No.: D of C, AP5, p. 85.

Mint $450.00   Ex. $350.00   G. $200.00   F. $150.00

APRIL KATZ

1984. 17 in. (43 cm). All bisque body, jointed hips, shoulders, and neck. Bisque head; brown glass stationary eyes, painted upper and lower lashes; long black hair in ringlets; closed mouth. Mark: on head, 1984 EATON BEAUTY/APRIL KATZ (in script) #250. Made from Steiner mould, SGDG/Paris. Limited Edition of 250.
Ref.No.: D of C, CY1, p. 85.

Mint $450.00   Ex. $350.00   G. $200.00   F. $150.00

LOUISETTE

April Katz. 1989. 16 in. (41 cm). Cloth body, porcelain arms, legs and shoulderplate. Bisque head; stationary blue glass eyes, painted upper and lower lashes. Dark brown upswept wig; closed mouth. Mark: on head, APRIL KATZ/1989/134 OF 250. On Tag: LOUISETTE/1989/EATON BEAUTY/LIMITED EDITION/250/APRIL KATZ.
Ref.No.: PGE1

Mint $400.00   Ex. $325.00   G. $200.00   F. $150.00

CANADIAN CELEBRITY DOLLS

Canadian Celebrity dolls are made to honour a Canadian. They may or may not be made in Canada.

DIONNE QUINTUPLETS

Madame Alexander. 1934. 10 in. (25.5 cm). Composition bent-limb baby body, jointed hips, shoulders, and neck. Composition head; brown sleep eyes, lashes, painted lower lashes; brown moulded hair; closed mouth. Mark: on head, DIONNE/ALEXANDER; on body, MADAME ALEXANDER.
Ref.No.: D of C, BT1A, p. 86.

Mint set $2,200.00 - 2,500.00
Ex. $ 350.00 - 400.00 each

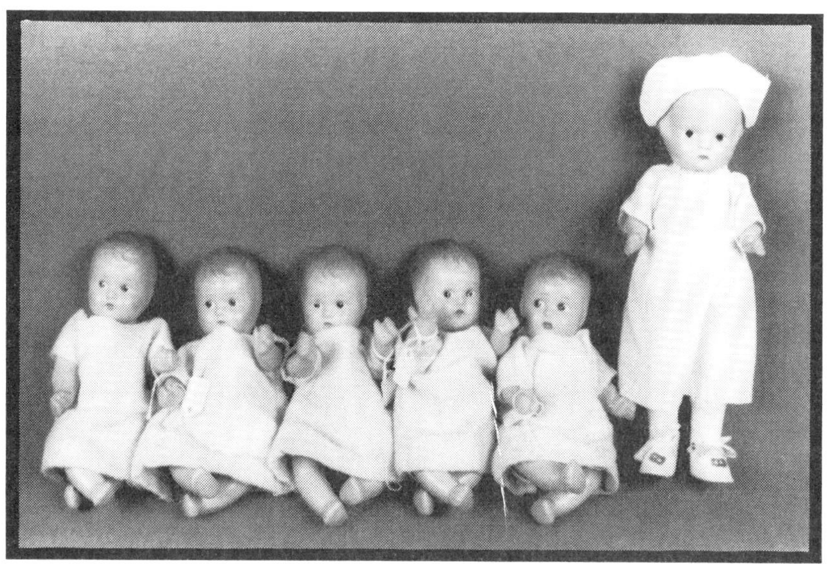

DIONNE QUINTUPLETS

Superior. Ca.1934. Babies, 7 in. (17 cm); nurse, 10 in.(25.5 cm). Composition bent-limb baby bodies, jointed hips, shoulders, and neck. Nurse ie straight limbed. Composition heads; babies, brown painted side-glancing eyes; nurse, black painted side-glancing eyes; light brown moulded hair; closed mouths. Mark: babies, on head, SUPERIOR; nurse, unmarked. *Ref.No.: D of C, CE21, p. 87.*

Mint set $1,400.00

DIONNE QUINTUPLETS

Madame Alexander. 1935. 7.5 in. (18 cm). Composition bent-limb baby bodies, jointed hips, shoulders, and neck. Composition head; brown painted side-glancing eyes, painted upper lashes; brown moulded hair; closed mouth. Mark: on head, ALEXANDER; on back, ALEXANDER.
Ref.No.: D of C, BW11, p. 89.

Mint set, teeter-totter and box   **$3,500.00**
Ex.   **$250.00 - 300.00 each**

Dolls that are "Mint In the Box" (MIB) are about 10 to 15% higher for vinyl dolls and 40 to 50% higher for composition dolls. The composition dolls in boxes are of course much rarer. For the MIB category the box should be labelled with the manufacturers' name and possibly the name of the doll. A cardboard box with nothing printed on it has very little value.

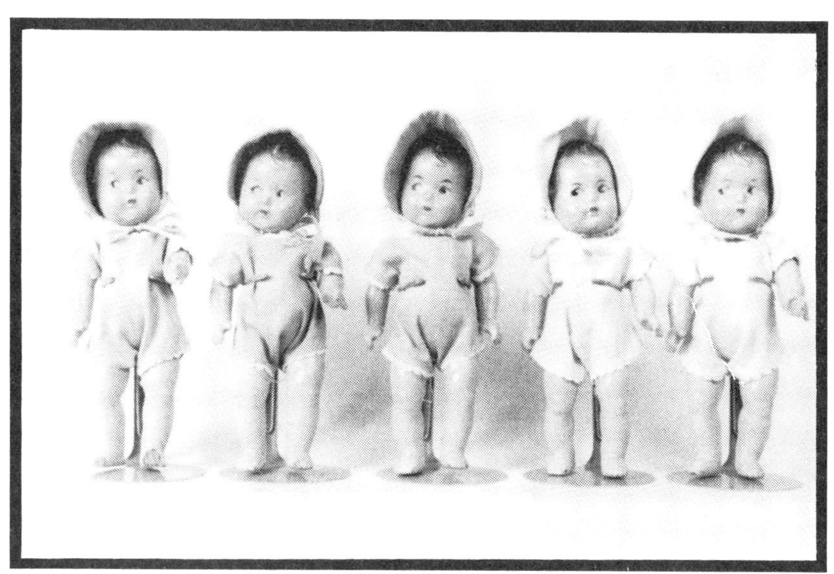

DIONNE QUINTUPLETS

Madame Alexander. 1935. 7.5 in. (18 cm). Composition bodies, jointed hips, shoulders, and neck. Composition head; brown painted side-glancing eyes, painted upper lashes; brown moulded hair; closed mouth. Mark: on head, ALEXANDER; on body, ALEXANDER.
Ref.No.: D of C, AB2, p. 90.

Ex. set $1,750.00
Ex. sold separately $250.00 - 300.00

DIONNE QUINTUPLETS

Madame Alexander. 1936. 16 in. (40.5 cm). Composition bodies, jointed hips, shoulders, and neck. Composition head; brown glassene eyes, lashes, painted lower lashes; brown human hair wigs; closed mouth. Mark: on body, ALEXANDER.
Ref.No.: D of C, BW8, p. 89.

This set is rarely seen.

Mint set $4,500.00 - 5,500.00
Ex. sold separately $625.00 - 750.00

BARBARA ANN SCOTT

Reliable. 1948. 15 in. (38 cm). Composition body, jointed hips, shoulders, and neck. Composition head; blue sleep eyes, lashes; painted lower lashes and brows; honey blond mohair wig; open smiling mouth showing teeth. Mark: on head, RELIABLE/MADE IN CANADA. Lace costume.
Ref.No.: D of C, AM24, p. 90.

Note: Prices vary widely.

Mint $375.00   Ex. $275.00   G. $200.00   F. $100.00

BARBARA ANN SCOTT

Reliable. 1949. 15 in. (38 cm). Composition body, jointed hips, shoulders, and neck. Composition head; blue sleep eyes, lashes, painted lower lashes, brows painted in separate strokes; blond mohair wig; open mouth, smiling and showing teeth. Mark: on head, RELIABLE/MADE IN CANADA. Blue costume trimmed in maribou.
Ref.No.: D of C, AP8, p. 91.

Mint $375.00   Ex. $275.00   G. $200.00   F. $100.00

BARBARA ANN SCOTT

Reliable. 1950. 15 in. (38 cm). Composition body, jointed hips, shoulders, and neck. Composition head; blue sleep eyes, lashes, painted lower lashes and brows; honey blond saran wig; open smiling mouth showing teeth. Mark: on head, RELIABLE/MADE IN CANADA. Original tag. Velveteen skating costume trimmed with maribou.
Ref.No.: D of C, AW21, p. 91.

Mint $375.00   Ex. $275.00   G. $200.00   F. $100.00

BARBARA ANN SCOTT

Reliable. 1951. 15 in. (38 cm). Composition body, jointed hips, shoulders, and neck. Composition head; blue sleep eyes, lashes, painted brows; honey blond mohair wig; open smiling mouth showing teeth. Mark: on head, RELIABLE/MADE IN CANADA. Blue and gold skating costume with maribou trim.
Ref.No.: D of C, CA23, p. 92.

Mint $375.00   Ex. $275.00   G. $200.00   F. $100.00

MARILYN BELL

Dee an Cee. 1954. 16 in. (40.5 cm). One piece Skintex body. Vinyl head; blue sleep eyes, lashes, painted lower lashes; rooted blond curls; open-closed smiling mouth showing painted teeth. Mark: on head, MARILYN BELL/D&C TOY CO./1954. Swimsuit and robe.
Ref.No.: D of C, AP29A, p. 93.

Ex. $125.00   G. $75.00   F. $45.00

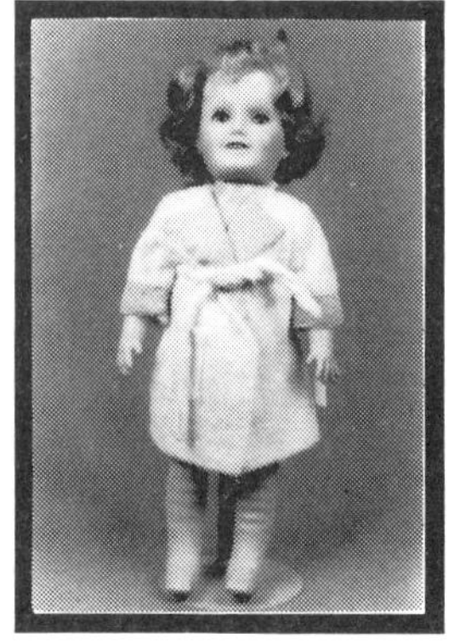

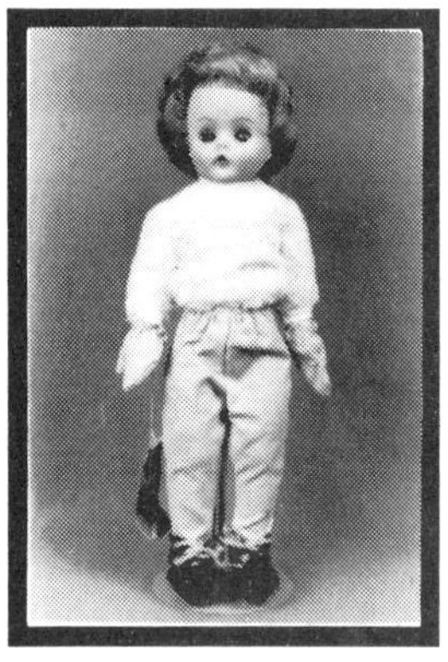

ANNE HEGGTVEIT

Reliable. 1961. 16 in. (40.5 cm). Plastic body and legs, vinyl arms, jointed hips, shoulders, and neck. Vinyl head; blue sleep eyes, lashes, painted lower lashes; rooted blond saran hair; closed mouth. Mark: on body, RELIABLE/CANADA. Original tag, Canadian Olympic Ski Champion/Anne Heggtveit Doll. Made by/Reliable in Canada.
Ref.No.: D of C, BQ1, p. 92.

Note: This is a common doll without the costume.

Mint $125.00   Ex. $95.00   G. $45.00   F. $25.00

KAREN MAGNUSSEN

Regal. 1974. 18 in. (45.5 cm). Plastic body, jointed hips, shoulders, and neck. Vinyl head; blue sleep eyes, lashes, eyeshadow; rooted blond curls; closed mouth. Mark: on head, REGAL TOY/MADE IN CANADA; on body, REGAL/CANADA/PAT. PEND.; dress tag, KAREN MAGNUSSEN, Made by REGAL TOY LTD. CANADA Original skating dress.
Ref.No.: D of C, CD16, p. 93.

Note: This is a common doll without the costume.

Mint $85.00   Ex. $75.00   G. $35.00   F. $20.00

BOBBY ORR

Regal. 1975. 12 in. (30.5 cm). Plastic body, jointed hips, waist, shoulders, and neck. Vinyl head; blue painted eyes; brown moulded hair; open-closed mouth smiling, showing painted teeth. Mark: on body, MADE IN/HONG KONG. Original Boston Bruins uniform.
Ref.No.: D of C, CF16, p. 94.

Mint $75.00   Ex. $50.00   G. $35.00   F.   20.00

THE GREAT GRETSKY

Mattel. 1983. 12 in. (30.5 cm). Plastic body, jointed hips, waist, shoulders, and neck. Vinyl head; painted blue eyes; blond moulded hair; open-closed mouth showing teeth. Mark: on body, MATTEL INC. 1983/TAIWAN.
Ref.No.: D of C, CS14A, p. 95.

Mint $65.00   Ex. $50.00   G. $25.00   F. $15.00

THE WORKING DOLL

A working doll is a doll that has a purpose other than as a toy, such as, an advertising doll, display doll, or one that represents an organization. Since the costume often creates the character, the clothing is very important.

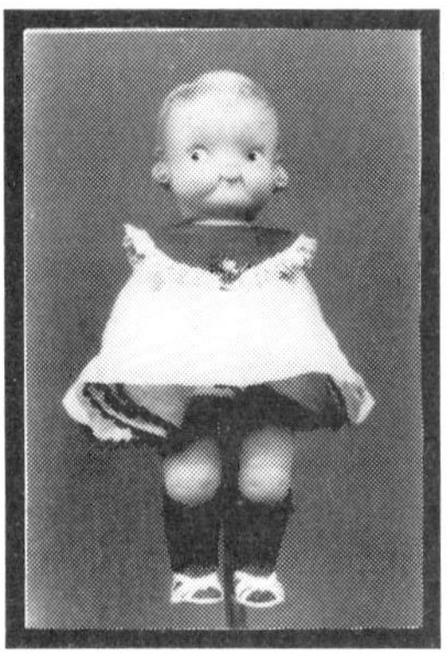

CAMPBELL SOUP KID

Reliable. ca.1954. 10 in. (25.5 cm). One piece vinyl body, jointed neck. Vinyl head; black painted side-glancing eyes, painted upper lashes; light brown moulded hair; closed watermelon mouth. Mark: on head, CAMPBELLS.
Ref.No.: D of C, BM33, p. 99.

Mint $75.00   Ex. $55.00   G. $35.00   F. $20.00

CAMPBELL SOUP KID

Reliable. ca.1962. 10 in. (25.5 cm). One piece vinyl body, jointed at neck. Vinyl head; black painted side-glancing eyes, painted upper lashes; brown moulded hair; closed watermelon mouth. Mark: on head, CAMPBELL/RELIABLE/MADE IN CANADA/10.
Ref.No.: D of C, CF8, p. 99.

Mint $75.00   Ex. $75.00   G. $35.00   F. $20.00

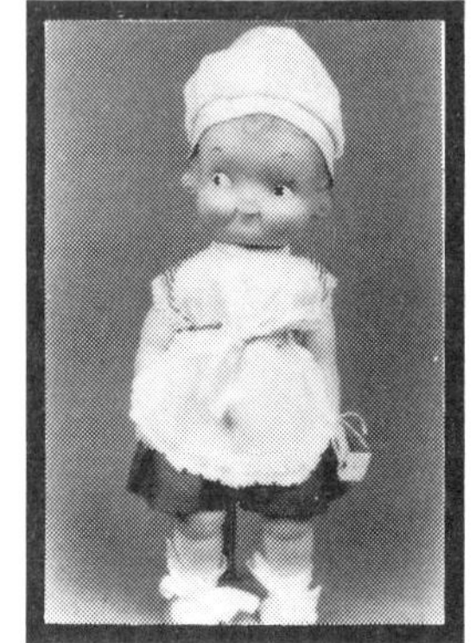

CAMPBELL SOUP DOLL

Regal. ca.1975. 18 in. (45.5 cm). Plastic body, jointed hips, shoulders, and neck. Vinyl head; brown sleep eyes, lashes, three painted upper lashes; rooted black hair in braids and bangs; closed smiling mouth. Mark: on head, REGAL TOY LTD./MADE IN CANADA/166 E.
Ref.No.: D of C, BX11, p. 100.

Mint $75.00   Ex. $55.00   G. $45.00   F. $25.00

GERBER BABY

Viceroy. 1955. 12 in. (30.5 cm). All rubber bent-limb baby body, jointed hips, shoulders and neck. Rubber head with dimples; inset blue plastic eyes; detailed moulded hair; open-mouth nurser. Mark: on body,A VICEROY/SUNRUCO DOLL/MADE IN CANADA/Patent Pending.
Ref.No.: D of C, BN4, p. 100.

Mint $80.00   Ex. $55.00   G. $45.00   F. $25.00

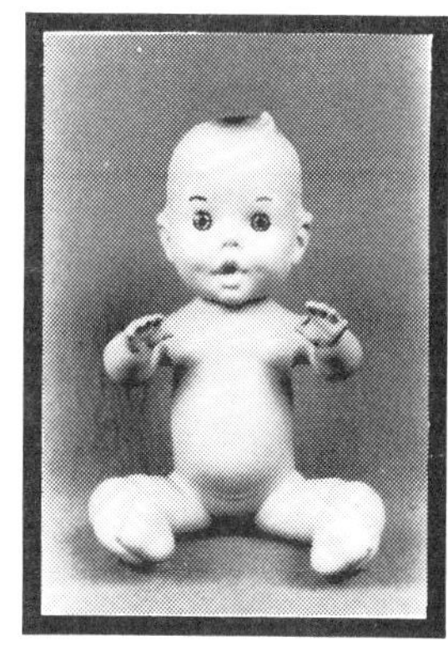

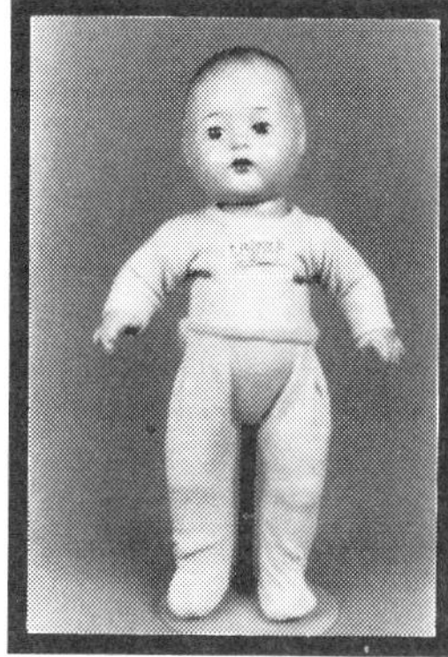

DR. DENTON DOLL

Unknown. ca.1938. 17 in. (43 cm). Composition body, jointed hips, shoulders, and neck. Composition head; brown sleep eyes, lashes, painted lower lashes; brown moulded hair, closed mouth. Unmarked. Original two piece blue sleepers with label marked, No./5/DR. DENTON 34/INCH/TWO-PIECE SLEEPER/Pat. IN CANADA DEC.8,1925/MADE BY/MERCURY MILLS LTD.
Ref.No.: D of C, CD24, p. 101.

Mint $100.00   Ex. $80.00   G. $45.00   F. $25.00

KATIE-CURAD

Reliable. ca.1970. 17 in. (43 cm). Plastic teen body, jointed hips, shoulders, and neck. Vinyl head; sleep eyes, lashes, painted lower lashes; rooted blond curls; closed mouth. Mark: on head, RELIABLE (in script); on body, RELIABLE (in script) /MADE IN CANADA.
Ref.No.: D of C, BH19, p. 101.

Mint $75.00   Ex. $55.00   G. $30.00   F. $20.00

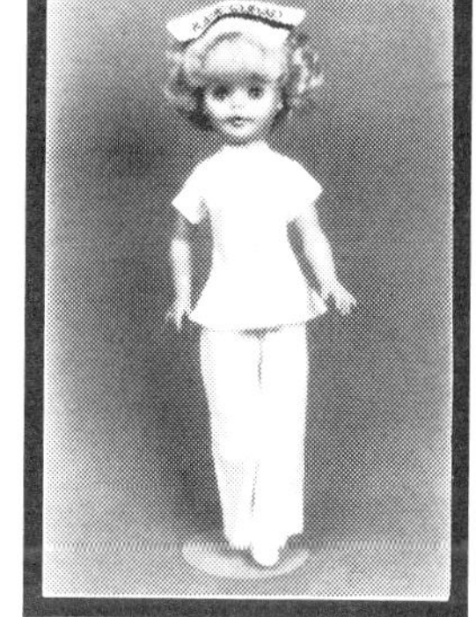

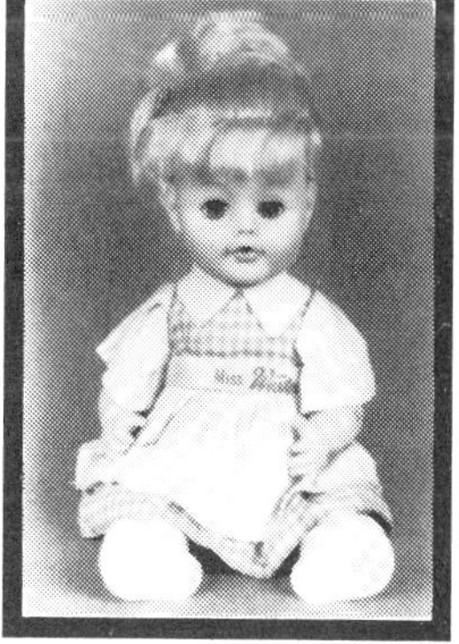

MISS WESTON

Reliable. ca.1975. 14 in. (35.5 cm). Plastic body and legs, vinyl arms, jointed hips, shoulders, and neck. Vinyl head; blue sleep eyes, lashes, painted lower lashes; rooted blond hair in ponytail and bangs; open-mouth nurser. Mark: on head, RELIABLE/MADE IN CANADA.
Ref.No.: D of C, CA16, p. 101.

Mint $55.00   Ex. $40.00   G. $25.00   F. $15.00

NUN

Reliable. ca.1942. 19 in. (45.5 cm). Composition body, jointed hips, shoulders, and neck. Composition head; blue stencilled metal eyes, lashes; no hair; open mouth showing teeth. Mark: on head, RELIABLE/MADE IN CANADA. Original nun's costume, fine brown wool habit, cream linen cape, cotton wimple, leather sandals. Wearing a tiny rosary made in France.
Ref.No.: D of C, BO1, p. 103.

Mint $250.00   Ex. $200.00   G. $125.00   F.$75.00

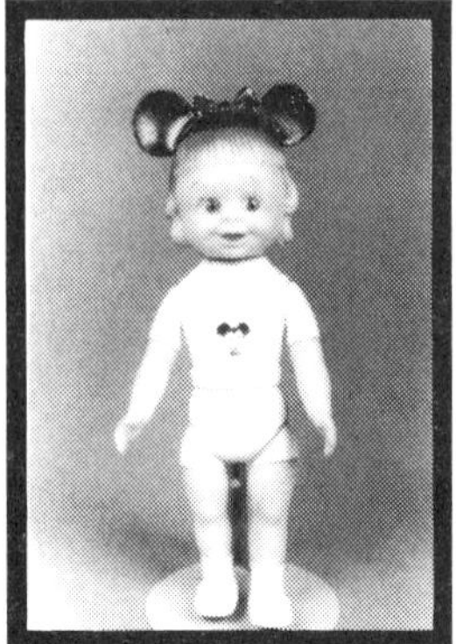

MOUSEKETEER

Reliable. ca.1955. 11 in. (28 cm). Vinyl body, jointed hips, shoulders, and neck. Vinyl head with mouse ears and bow moulded to the head; inset blue plastic side-glancing eyes, painted upper lashes; brown moulded hair; open-closed smiling mouth. Mark: on head, RELIABLE.
Ref.No.: D of C, CH5, p. 102.

Mint $75.00   Ex. $55.00   G. $35.00   F. $25.00

YOUNG OLYMPIANS OF CANADA

Reliable. 1958. 11 in. (28 cm). Hard plastic teen body, jointed shoulders and neck. Hard plastic head; blue sleep eyes, moulded lashes; blond mohair wig; closed mouth. Mark: on back, RELIABLE/PAT. 1958. Original ski suit with label on the chest, skis and poles. Original medal, YOUNG OLYMPIANS OF CANADA. JEUNES OLYMPIENS DU CANADA.
Ref.No.: D of C, BN9, p. 103.

Mint $40.00   Ex. $30.00   G. $20.00   F. $10.00

CANADIAN GIRL GUIDE

Beau Sol. 1980. 12 in. (30.5 cm). Cloth body and head. Embroidered features; wool hair. Unmarked.
Ref.No.: D of C, BN19, p. 104.

Mint $30.00 **Ex.** $25.00 **G.** $15.00 **F.** $8.00

CANADIAN PAPER DOLLS

Canadian made paper dolls are hard to find.

HAROLD AND HIS PLAYMATES

Canadian Home Journal. 1929. By Grace G. Drayton, from the Canadian Home Journal, June 1929.
Ref.No.: D of C, XH3, p. 111.

Uncut: $18.00 - 20.00

TOMMY'S EARLY SUMMER WARDROBE

Canadian Home Journal. 1930. By Mae Browne, from the Canadian Home Journal, May 1930.
Ref.No.: D of C, XH2, p. 112.

Uncut: $18.00 - 20.00

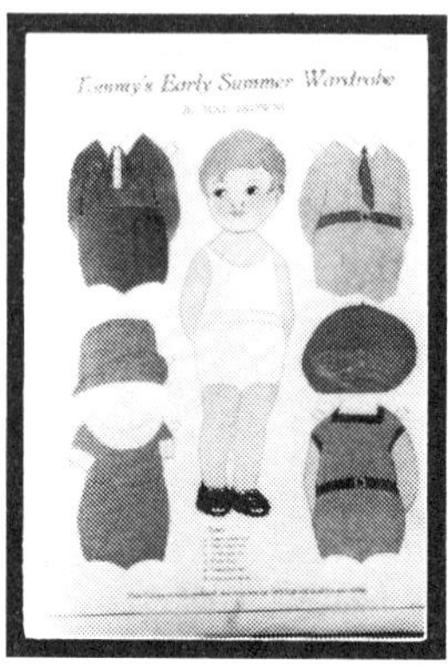

MARY LOU'S COUSIN ANN

Canadian Home Journal. 1932. By Lydia Fraser, from the Canadian Home Journal, Jan. 1932.
Ref.No.: D of C, XH5, p. 112.

Uncut: $14.00 - 16.00

MARY LOU'S COUSIN ANN

Canadian Home Journal. 1933. By Lydia Fraser, from the Canadian Home Journal, Nov. 1933.
Ref.No.: D of C, XH4, p. 112.

Uncut: $14.00 - 16.00

MISS MUFFET

Unknown. ca.1960. 31 in. (79 cm). Cardboard doll, three dresses, and a coat.
Ref.No.: D of C, CC22, p. 113.

Uncut: $12.00 - 15.00

1835 CUTOUT DOLL

Billings Estate. ca.1980. 8.5 x 14 in. (21.5 x 35.5 cm). Doll and typical clothing worn in 1835 described in English and French. Illustrated by Kay Irvine.
Ref.No.: D of C, BO50, p. 113.

Uncut: $0.50 - 1.00

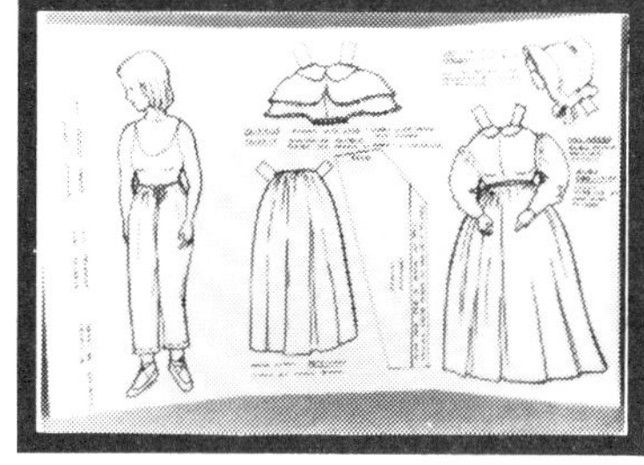

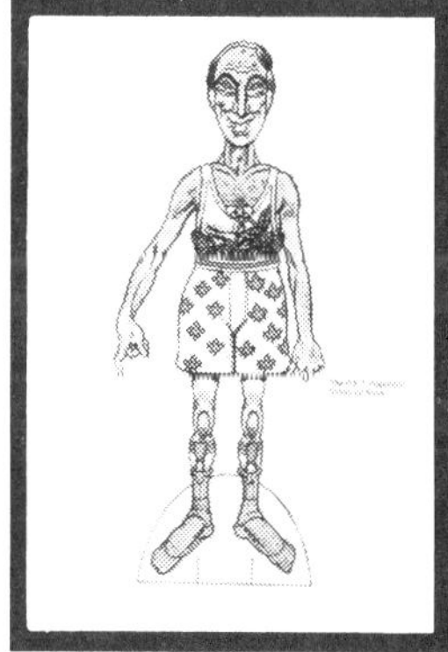

THE P.E.T. PAPERDOLL DRESS-UP BOOK

Graham Pilsworth. 1982. 9 x 12 in. (23 x 30.5 cm). Published by Key Porter Books Limited, Toronto, Ont.
Ref.No.: D of C, AF18, p. 114. See also Figs. AE20, AE21, and AE23.

Uncut: $15.00 book

NATIVE DOLL

Carmen Vair. 1984. One sheet, 11.5 x 17.5 in. (29.5 x 44 cm). The doll illustrates the cloth dolls made by Carmen Vair and shows the many items of clothing that her dolls wear. Illustrated by Fran Tyrer.
Ref.No.: D of C, BV18, p. 115.

Uncut: $10.00 - 12.00

COMMERCIAL DOLLS OF THE TWENTIETH CENTURY

BEAVER DOLL AND TOY CO.
1917 -

BEAVER

ca.1917. 18 in. (45.5 cm). Excelsior stuffed body and legs, composition forearms. Composition shoulderhead; blue sleep eyes, painted upper and lower lashes; human hair wig over moulded hair; open mouth with two replaced teeth. Unmarked. Original box: Beaver Doll And Toy Co. A rare doll. *Ref.No.: D of C, CX10, p. 121.*

Mint $200.00   Ex. $175.00   G. $150.00   F. $125.

BERT PERLMAN INC. (KEHAGIAS)
1985 - 1986

ARTIST

Kehagias. 1985. 9.5 in. (24 cm). Plastic body, vinyl arms and legs, jointed hips, shoulders, and neck. Vinyl head; blue sleep eyes, lashes; long black rooted hair; closed mouth. Mark: on body, KEHAGIAS/MADE IN/CANADA. Wrist label KEHAGIAS/RELIABLE TOY CO. LTD.
Ref.No.: D of C, CN7, p. 122.

Mint $40.00   Ex. $35.00   G. $25.00   F. $20.00

BEAUTY QUEEN

Kehagias. 1985. 9.5 in. (24 cm). Plastic body, vinyl arms and legs, jointed hips, shoulders, and neck. Vinyl head; blue sleep eyes, lashes; long blond rooted curly hair; closed mouth. Mark: on body, Kehagias/MADE IN/CANADA. Wrist label Kehagias/RELIABLE TOY CO./TORONTO,CANADA.
Ref.No.: D of C, CN3A, p. 122.

Mint $40.00   Ex. $35.00   G. $30.00   F. $20.00

HEATHER

Kehagias. 1985. Cloth body, vinyl arms and legs. Vinyl head; blue sleep eyes, lashes; slightly moulded light brown hair; closed mouth. Marks: the same as ADAM.
Ref.No.: D of C, XH24, p. 123.

Mint $50.00   Ex. $40.00   G. $30.00   F. $20.00

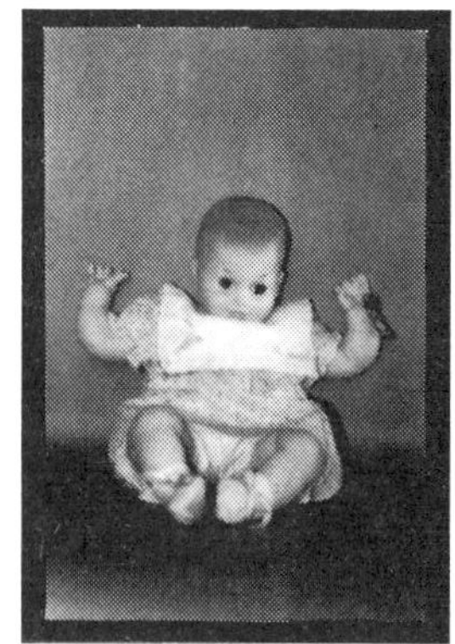

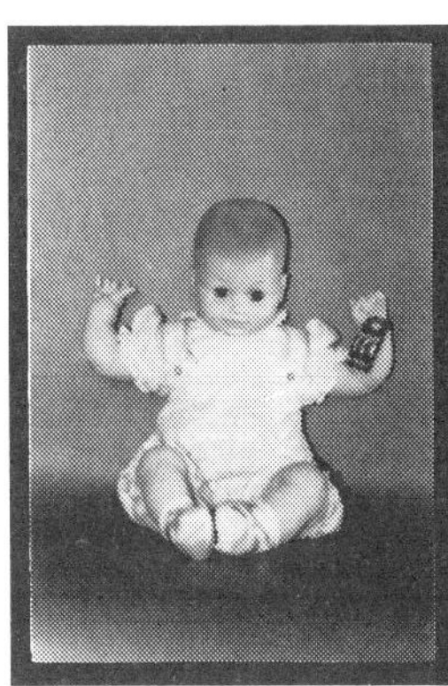

ADAM

Kehagias. 1985. 21 in. (53.5 cm). Cloth body, vinyl arms and legs. Vinyl head; blue sleep eyes, lashes; slightly moulded light brown hair; closed mouth. Mark: on head, RELIABLE (in script)/MADE IN CANADA ; tag on body, MADE BY ONT. REG. NO. 63A 3438/RELIABLE TOY CO. LTD. TORONTO, CANADA; tag on arm, KEHAGIAS /RELIABLE TOY CO. LTD/LTEE /TORONTO, CANADA.
Ref.No.: D of C, XH23, p. 123.

Mint $50.00   Ex. $40.00   G. $30.00   F. $20.00

KEHAGIAS

1985. 12 in. (30.5 cm). Vinyl one-piece bent-limb baby body. Vinyl head; blue painted side-glancing eyes; light brown moulded hair; open mouth nurser. Unmarked. Original box, KEHAGIAS/RELIABLE TOY CO./MADE IN CANADA.
Ref.no.: D of C, CS15A, p. 123.

Mint $25.00   Ex. $20.00   G. $15.00   F. $10.00

THE BISCO DOLL CO.
1917 - 1920

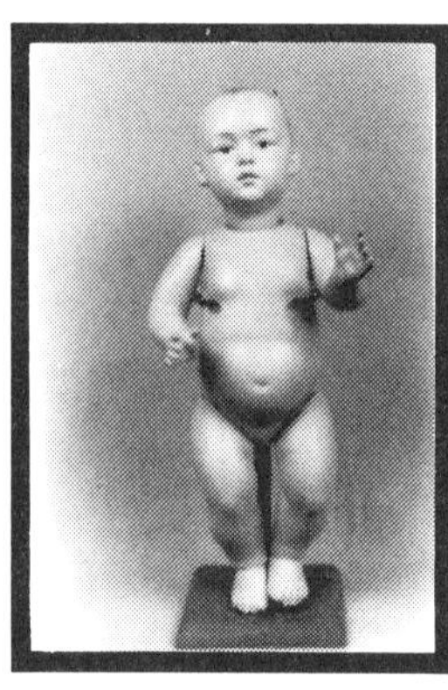

BISCO

1918. 16.5 in. (42 cm). All painted bisque, bent-limb body, jointed hips, shoulders, and neck. Painted bisque socket head, blue painted intaglio eyes with highlights, black line over eye; nostril dots; light brown moulded hair; open-closed mouth painted soft pink with fine outline in dark pink. Mark: on head and body. The Bisco Baby is a rare Canadian doll. *Ref.No.: D of C, CW9, p. 124.*

Mint $500.00   Ex. $400.00   G. $325.00   F. $225.00

CHEERIO TOY COMPANY
1939 - 1966

CHEERIO

ca.1950. 8 in. (20.5 cm). One piece hard plastic doll. Blue painted side-glancing eyes, light brown moulded hair; closed mouth. Mark: on body, CHEERIO/MADE IN CANADA.
Ref.No.: D of C, BW20, p. 125.

Mint $35.00 **Ex.** $30.00 **G.** $20.00 **F.** $15.00

CLS

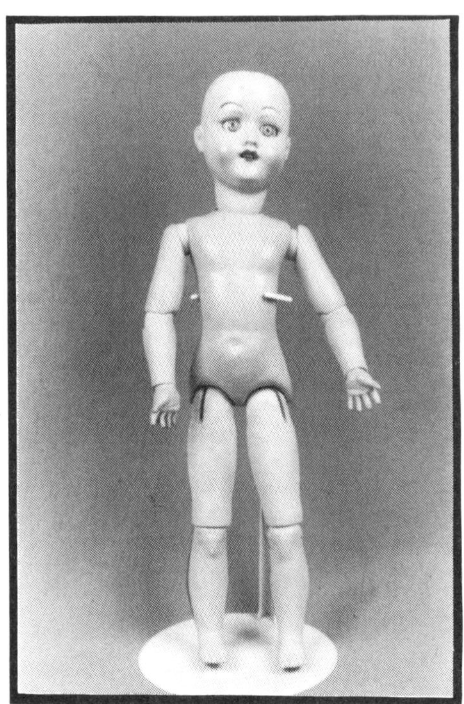

CLS

Date unknown. 19.5 in. (49.5 cm). Composition body, forearms, hands, and lower legs; wooden upper arms and upper legs. French knee joints, German ball-jointed elbows. Painted bisque head; blue glass sleep eyes; painted upper and lower lashes; brown horsehair wig; open mouth showing four teeth. Mark: on head, incised, CLS trademark with TORONTO/CANADA.
Ref.No.: D of C, CP22, CP28, p. 126, 127. A rare doll.

Mint $600.00   Ex. $500.00   G. $400.00   F. $300.00

DEE an CEE TOY COMPANY LTD.1938-1964

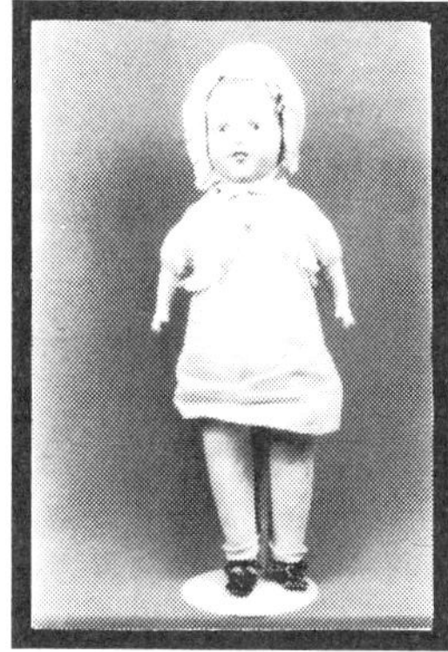

DEE AN CEE - 1938

ca.1938. 24 in. (61 cm). Cloth body, composition arms and legs. Composition shoulderhead, blue sleep eyes, lashes; moulded hair, light brown; closed mouth. Mark: on shoulderplate, A/DEE & CEE TOY.
Ref.No.D of C; CE8 p. 131

Mint $200.00   Ex. $170.00   G. $110.00   F. $70.00

BETTY

ca.1938. 15 in. (38 cm). Cloth body, upper arms and legs, composition forearms. Composition shoulderhead; blue painted eyes; moulded hair, painted reddish blond; closed mouth. Unmarked.
Ref.No. D of C; BN15 p. 131

Mint $125.00   Ex. $90.00   G. $50.00   F. $25.00

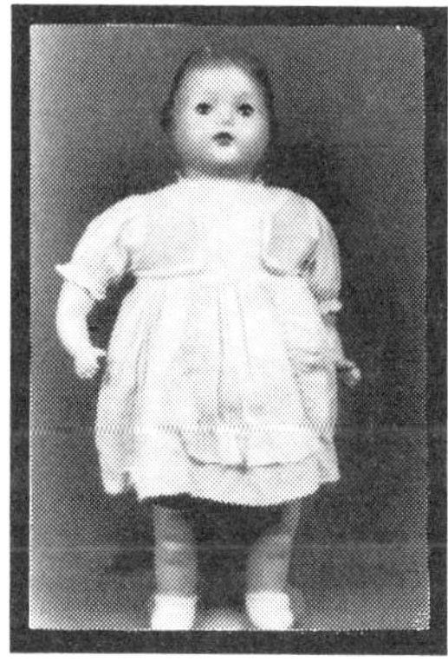

DEE AN CEE - 1938

ca.1938. 27.5 in. (71 cm). Excelsior stuffed cloth body, legs, and upper arms, composition forearms. Composition shoulderhead; painted blue eyes, long painted upper lashes; moulded hair, painted brown; open-closed mouth showing two painted teeth. Mark: on shoulderplate, DEE AN CEE/MADE IN CANADA.
Ref.No. D of C; BF36 p. 131

Mint $185.00   Ex. $160.00   G. $90.00   F. $60.00

DEE AN CEE - 1939 - 17 in.

ca.1939. 17 in. (43 cm). Cloth body, composition forearms and bent-limb legs. Composition shoulderhead; blue tin sleep eyes, painted upper lashes; moulded hair; closed mouth. Mark: on shoulderplate, DEE & CEE TOY CO./MADE IN CANADA.
Ref.No. D of C; CW25 p. 132

Mint $125.00   Ex. $90.00   G. $50.00   F. $25.00

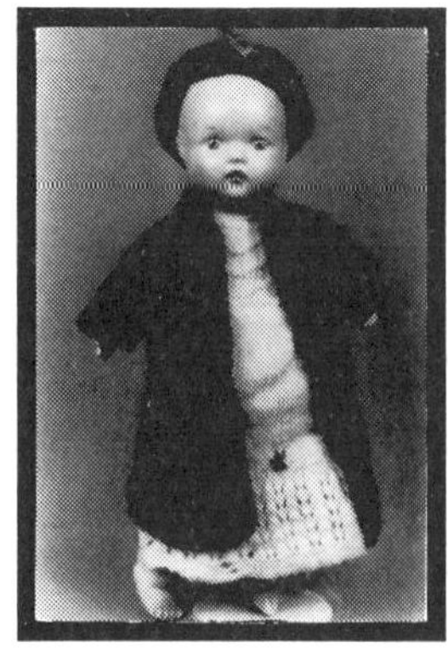

SNUGGLES - 23 in.

ca.1939. 23 in (58.5 cm). Cloth body, composition forearms and straight legs. Composition shoulderhead; blue metal sleep eyes, lashes, painted lower lashes; reddish brown moulded hair, closed mouth. Mark: label on the dress, SNUGGLES/DEE AN CEE TOY/MADE IN CANADA.
Ref.No. D of C; CN23 p. 132

Mint $250.00   Ex. $180.00   G. $110.00   F.$60.00

KNOCKABOUT DOLL

ca.1939. 15 in. (38 cm). Cloth body and legs, composition forearms. Composition shoulderhead; painted brown side-glancing eyes; moulded short brown hair; closed mouth. Mark: on shoulderplate, DEE AN CEE/MADE IN/CANADA. (The N in AN and IN are backward).
Ref.No. D of C; AM19 p. 132

Mint $100.00   Ex. $75.00   G. $40.00   F. $25.00

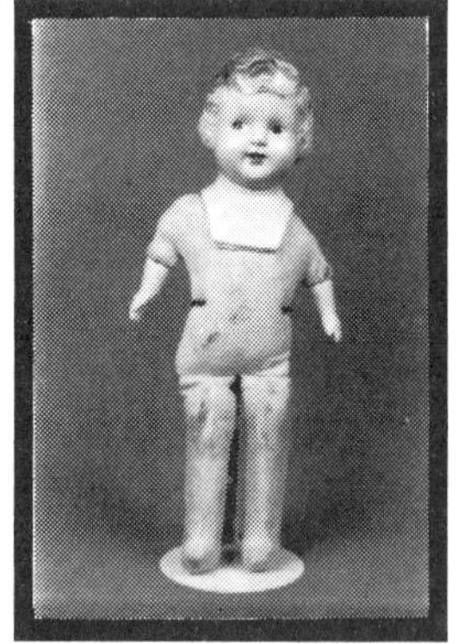

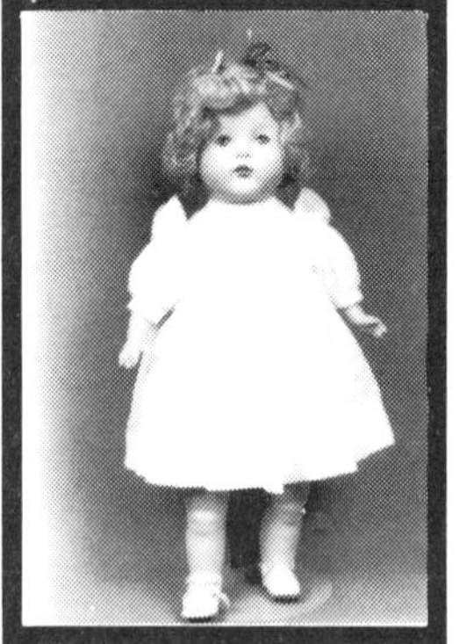

SNUGGLES - 22 in. Closed Mouth

ca.1940. 22 in. (56 cm). Cloth body, composition forearms and straight legs. Composition shoulderhead; blue tin sleep eyes, lashes, painted lower lashes; blond mohair wig; closed mouth.
Ref.No. D of C; BJ4 p. 133

Mint $265.00   Ex. $195.00   G. $150.00   F. $85.00

DEE AN CEE - 1940 - 11.5 in.

ca.1940. ll.5 in. (29.5 cm). Dark brown composition bent-limb baby, head and trunk one piece, jointed hip and shoulders. Painted side-glancing black eyes, moulded black hair plus wool top-knots, closed mouth. Mark: on back, DEE AN CEE/CANADA.
Ref.No. D of C; CC14 p. 133

Mint $95.00   Ex. $75.00   G. $45.00   F. $20.00

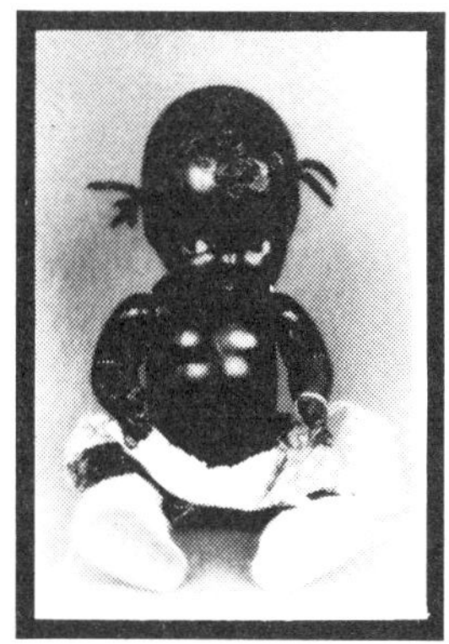

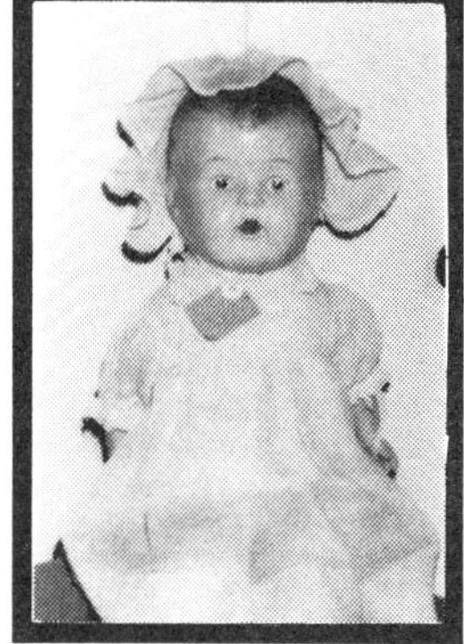

DEE AN CEE - 1940 - 24 in.

ca.1940. 24 in. (61 cm). Excelsior stuffed cloth body and legs, composition arms. Composition shoulderhead; blue painted eyes; reddish blond moulded hair; closed mouth.
Ref.No. D of C; CT16 p. 133

Mint $125.00   Ex. $90.00   G. $50.00   F. $25.00

DRINKING BABY

ca.1941. 12 in. (30.5 cm). Composition bent-limb body, jointed hips, shoulders, and neck. Composition head; brown painted eyes, black line over eye; moulded brown hair; metal mouth nurser. Mark: on body, DEE AN CEE/CANADA.
Ref.No. D of C; DA1 p. 134

Mint $90.00   Ex. $70.00   G. $40.00   F. $20.00

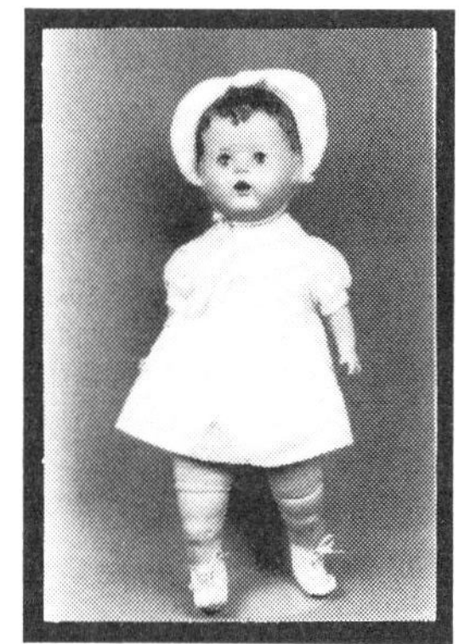

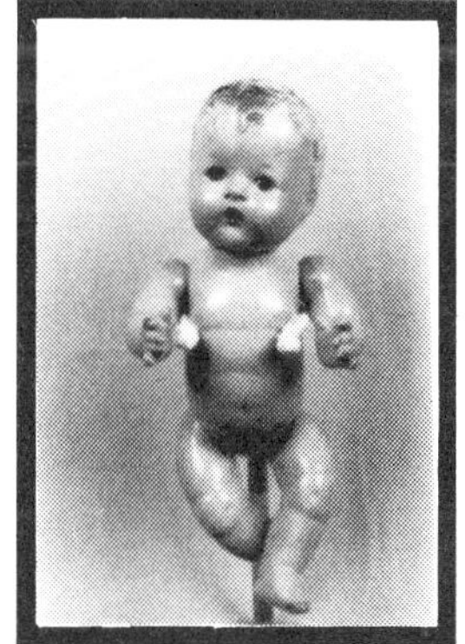

SNUGGLES - 22 in. Open Mouth

ca.1942. 22 in. (56 cm). Cloth body, composition forearms and straight legs. Composition shoulderhead; blue tin sleep eyes, lashes, painted lower lashes; moulded black hair; open mouth showing two inset teeth and red tongue.
Ref.No. D of C; BJ3 p. 134

Mint $250.00   Ex. $200.00   G. $120.00   F. $65.00

CRYING BABY

1944. 21 in. (53.5 cm). Cloth body, with crier, composition forearms and straight legs. Composition head; blue painted eyes, long painted upper lashes; brown moulded hair; open-closed mouth showing two painted teeth. Unmarked.
Ref.No. BJ10 p. 135

Mint $225.00   Ex. $190.00   G. $120.00   F. $75.00

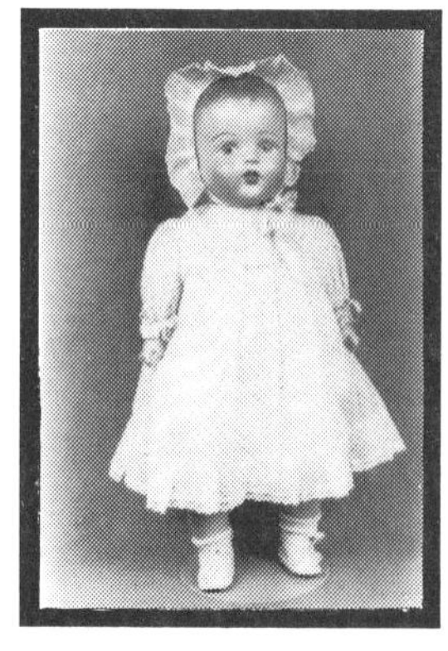

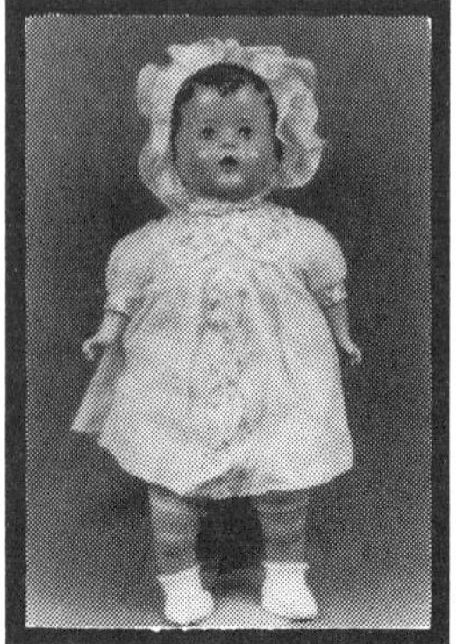

LITTLE DARLING - Blue Tin Eyes

ca.1944. 24 in. (61 cm). Cloth body, composition forearms and straight legs. Composition head; blue tin sleep eyes, lashes, painted lower lashes; moulded brown hair; open mouth showing two teeth. Mark: on shoulderplate, DEE CEE TOY/MADE IN CANADA.
Ref.No. D of C; CI15 p. 135

Mint $250.00   Ex. $200.00   G. $120.00   F. $65.00

LITTLE DARLING - Blue Eyes

ca.1945. 24 in. (61 cm). Cloth body, composition forearms and straight legs. Composition head; blue sleep eyes, lashes, painted lower lashes; moulded brown hair; open mouth showing two teeth. Mark: on shoulderplate, DEE & CEE TOY CO./MADE IN CANADA.
Ref.No. D of C; BF31 p. 136

Mint $250.00   Ex. $200.00   G. $120.00   F.$65.00

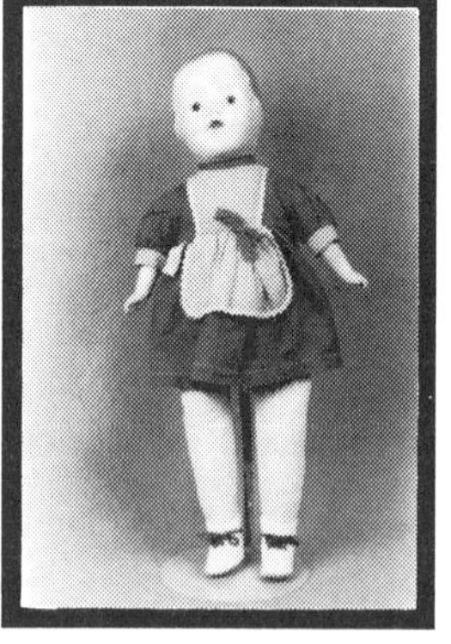

BETTY

ca.1945. 23 in. (58 cm). Excelsior stuffed cloth body, legs, and upper arms; composition forearms. Composition shoulderhead; painted brown eyes; moulded strawberry blond hair. Mark: Unmarked.
Ref.No. D of C; BC18 p. 136

Mint $125.00   Ex. $90.00   G. $50.00   F. $30.00

DEE AN CEE - 1946

ca.1946. 14 in. (35.5 cm). Composition body, jointed hips, shoulders, and neck. Composition head; blue sleep eyes, lashes, painted lower lashes; blond mohair wig; closed rosebud mouth. Mark: on back, DEE AN CEE/CANADA
Ref.No. D of C; CE31 p. 136

Mint $140.00   Ex. $105.00   G. $75.00   F. $40.00

SNUGGLES - 18in.

ca.1947. 18 in. (45.5 cm). Cloth body, composition hands and straight legs. Composition head; brown sleep eyes, lashes, painted lower lashes; moulded brown hair; closed mouth. Mark: on head, DEE & CEE DOLL.
Ref.No. D of C; CI4 p. 137

Mint $160.00   Ex. $120.00   G. $85.00   F. $50.00

SWEETUMS

1948. 14 in. (35.5 cm). Cloth body with crier, Skintex arms and legs. Composition shoulderhead. Eyes painted blue. Moulded hair, painted strawberry blond. Closed mouth.
Ref.No. D of C; BC19 p. 137

Mint $95.00   Ex. $75.00   G. $50.00   F. $25.00

CHERUB SMILE-N-CRY DOLL

1948. 13.5 in. (34.5 cm). Cloth body, legs and upper arms, composition forearms. Composition two-face head, one face smiling and one crying; painted blue side-glancing eyes; bald head; closed mouth on one face, open-closed mouth on the other.
Ref.No. D of C; CC11 p. 138

Note: This doll is much more in demand in some areas than others. Price varies widely.

Mint $250.00   Ex. $190.00   G. $125.00   F. $60.00

SNUGGLES - 22 in.

ca.1949. 22 in. (56 cm). Cloth body, composition forearms and straight legs. Composition shoulderhead; blue tin sleep eyes, lashes, eyeshadow, painted lower lashes; blond mohair wig; open mouth showing two teeth and tongue.
Ref.No. D of C; CX18 p. 139

Mint $265.00   Ex. $210.00   G. $125.00   F. $85.00

BETTY

1949. 18 in. (45.5 cm). Excelsior stuffed cloth body, legs and upper arms, composition forearms. Composition shoulderhead; blue painted eyes; moulded reddish-brown hair; closed mouth. Mark: on shoulderplate, A/DEE & CEE TOY.
Ref.No. D of C; CE29 p. 139

Mint $140.00   Ex. $95.00   G. $55.00   F. $35.00

DEE AN CEE - 1950

ca.1950. 26 in. (66 cm). One piece Skintex body, swivel neck. Vinyl head; blue sleep eyes, lashes; light brown moulded hair; open-closed mouth, moulded tongue. Mark: on head, DEE & CEE.
Ref.No. D of C; CB21 p. 139

Mint $100.00   Ex. $75.00   G. $40.00   F. $20.00

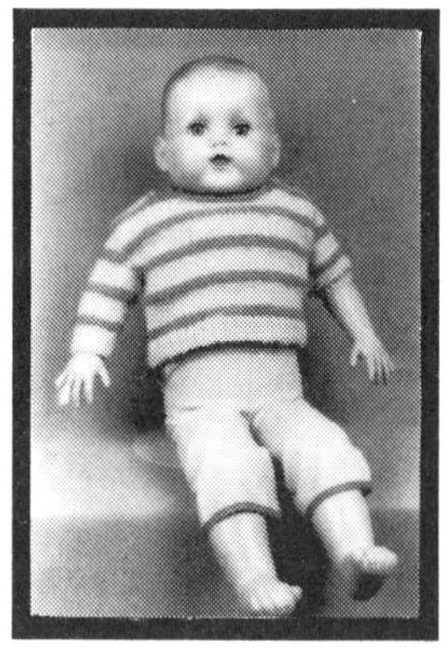

DEE AN CEE - 1952

ca.1952. 25 in. (63.5 cm). One piece Skintex body. Vinyl head; blue sleep eyes, lashes, painted lower lashes; rooted blond saran hair with bangs; closed mouth. Mark: on head, DC.
Ref.No. D of C; CF12 p. 140

Mint $85.00   Ex. $75.00   G. $55.00   F. $25.00

HONEY BEA

ca.1954. 15 in. (38 cm). One piece Flexee-vinyl body, dimpled knees. Vinyl head; brown sleep eyes, lashes, painted lower lashes; rooted saran ponytail and bangs; closed mouth. Mark: on head, DEE & CEE. Wearing roller-skates.
Ref.No. D of C; CB32 p. 140

Mint $70.00 **Ex.** $45.00 **G.** $35.00 **F.** $20.00

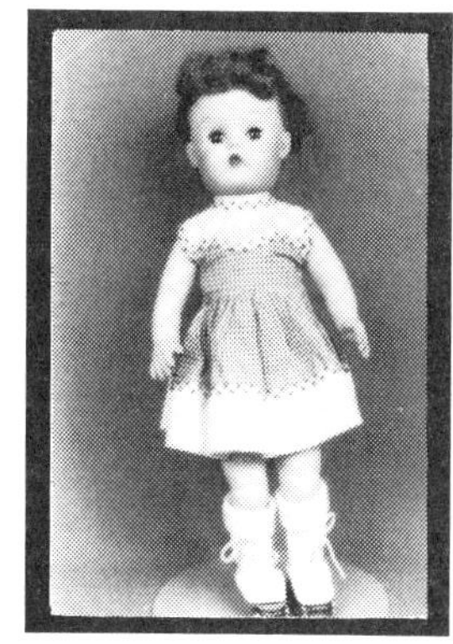

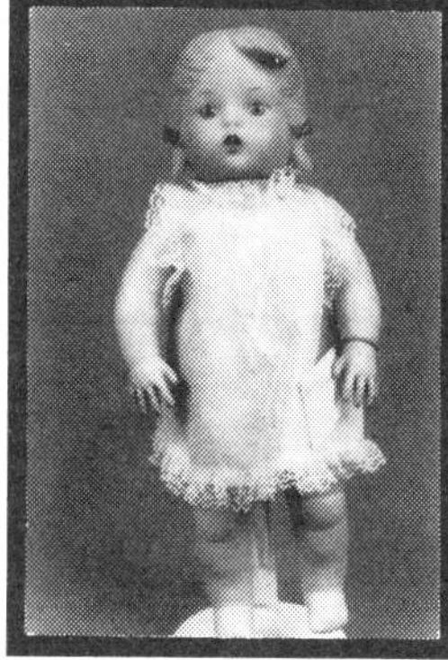

HEIDI

1954. 13 in. (33 cm). One piece stuffed Skintex body. Vinyl head; inset plastic eyes; moulded hair in braids, painted yellow with red barretts; open-closed mouth, painted teeth. Mark: on head, DEE CEE.
Ref.No. D of C; CG23 p. 140

Mint $55.00 **Ex.** $45.00 **G.** $35.00 **F.** $25.00

BRIDE DOLL

1955. 17 in. (43.5 cm). One piece Flexee-vinyl body. Vinyl head; blue sleep eyes, lashes, painted lower lashes; rooted blond saran hair; closed mouth. Unmarked.
Ref. no. D of C; CI10 p. 141

Mint $65.00 **Ex.** $55.00 **G.** $45.00 **F.** $25.00

KOWEEKA BABY

ca.1955. 10.5 in. (26.5 cm). Stuffed cloth body in a sitting position. Vinyl face from the KOWEEKA mould; painted black eyes; black synthetic hair; open-closed smiling mouth, showing teeth. Unmarked.
Ref.No. D of C; BU3, p. 141

Mint $60.00 **Ex.** $40.00 **G.** $30.00 **F.** $20.00

MANDY

1956. 14 in. (35.5 cm). One piece stuffed Skintex brown body. Vinyl head; black painted eyes, ethnic features; heavily detailed moulded hair in braids at the back and painted black; open-closed mouth, painted teeth. Mark: on head, DEE & CEE.
Ref.No. D of C; CF31 p. 141

Mint $85.00   Ex. $70.00   G. $45.00   F. $20.00

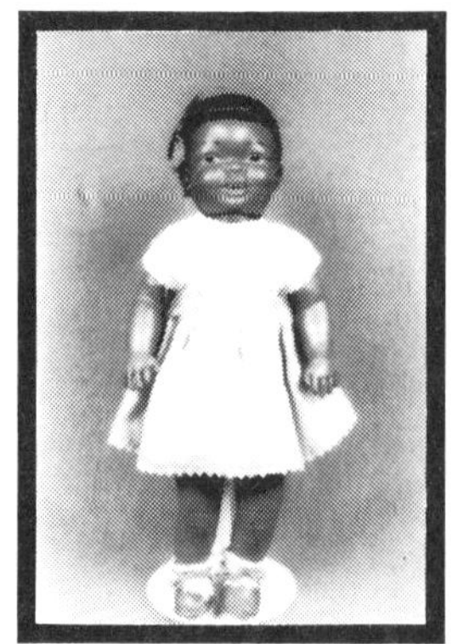

56

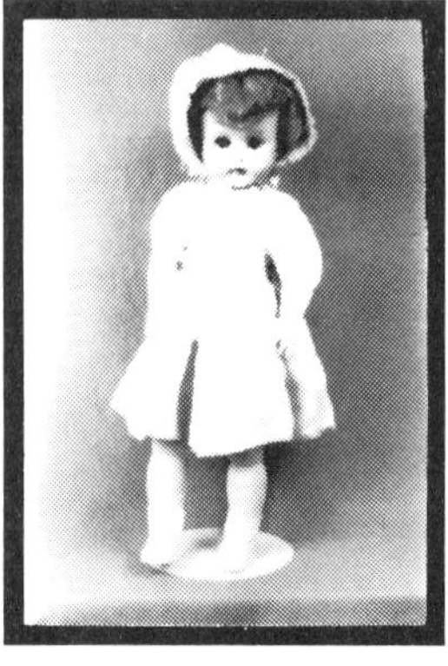

CAROL

1957. 25 in. (63.5 cm). One piece stuffed Flexee-vinyl body. Vinyl head; blue sleep eyes, lashes, painted lower lashes; rooted honey blond saran hair; closed mouth. Mark: on head, DC.
Ref.No. D of C; BC15 p. 142

Mint $65.00   Ex. $55.00   G. $40.00   F. $30.00

TINY TEARS

1958. 13 in. (33 cm). Vinyl bent-limb baby, jointed hips, shoulderss and neck; with crier. Vinyl head. Brown sleep eyes, eyelashes. Rooted brown curls. She was also sold with moulded hair. Open mouth nurser. Unmarked.
Ref.No. D of C; BF30 p. 142

Note: Price varies widely.

Mint $125.00   Ex. $100.00   G. $60.00   F. $25.00

CINDY IN HER SUNDAY BEST

1958. 17 in. (43.5 cm). Plastic body, jointed hips, waist, shoulders, and neck. Vinyl head; blue sleep eyes, lashes, painted lower lashes; rooted honey blond saran curls; closed mouth. Mark: on head, D & C; on body, DEE AN CEE.
Ref.No. D of C; CF30 p. 143

Mint $50.00   Ex. $40.00   G. $25.00   F. $15.00

DEE AN CEE - 1958

ca.1958. 22 in. (56 cm). Hard plastic body, jointed hips, shoulders, and neck. Hard plastic head; blue sleep eyes, lashes, painted lower lashes; moulded hair, painted light brown; open mouth showing two inset teeth and tongue. Mark: on body, D&C.
Ref.No. D of C; BY16 p. 144

Mint $175.00   Ex. $150.00   G. $95.00   F. $75.00

Note: Appears on new issue Canadian postage stamps June 8th, 1990.

LOVABLE FAMILY, CINDY, PENNY, and BABY SISTER

1959. CINDY has a plastic body with jointed hips, waist, shoulders, and neck. Vinyl head, sleep eyes, lashes and painted lower lashes; rooted blond hair; closed mouth. PENNY has a vinyl body; jointed hips, shoulders, and neck. Vinyl head; sleep eyes, lashes; rooted Buster Brown hair; closed mouth. BABY SISTER has one piece vinyl body.
Ref.No. D of C; CX19 p. 143

Mint $175.00   Ex. $125.00   G. $80.00   F. $60.00

DREAM BABY

1959. 16 in. (40.5 cm). Plastic body, jointed hips, shoulders, and neck. Vinyl head; blue sleep eyes, lashes, painted lower lashes; rooted short curly brown hair; closed mouth. Mark: on head, DEE CEE; on body, DEE AN CEE.
Ref.No. D of C; AE10 p. 143

Mint $45.00   Ex. $35.00   G. $25.00   F. $15.00

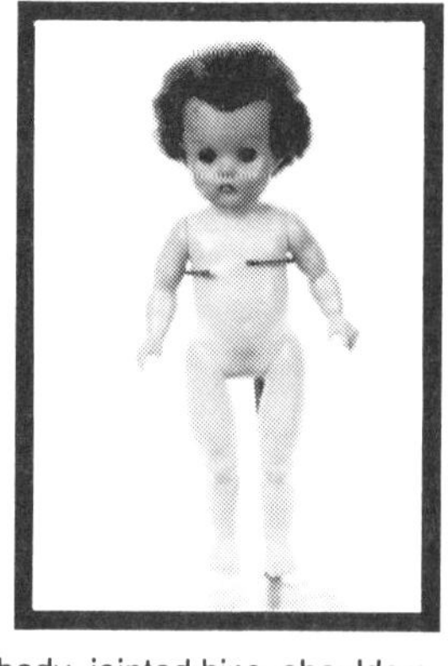

KELLY IN PIGTAILS

1959. 16 in. (40.5 cm). Plastic body, jointed hips, shoulders, and neck. Vinyl head; blue sleep eyes, lashes, painted lower lashes; rooted blond saran hair in pigtails with bangs; closed mouth. Mark: on head, 3; on body, D&C.
Ref.No. D of C; CR10 p. 144

Mint $55.00   Ex. $45.00   G. $35.00   F. $20.00

BABY SUE

1959. 24 in. (61 cm). Plastic baby body, jointed hips, shoulders, and neck. Vinyl head; brown sleep eyes, lashes, painted lower lashes; rooted auburn short curls; open mouth nurser. Mark: on body, DEE AN CEE.
Ref.No. D of C; BX5 p. 144

Mint $65.00   Ex. $55.00   G. $40.00   F. $25.00

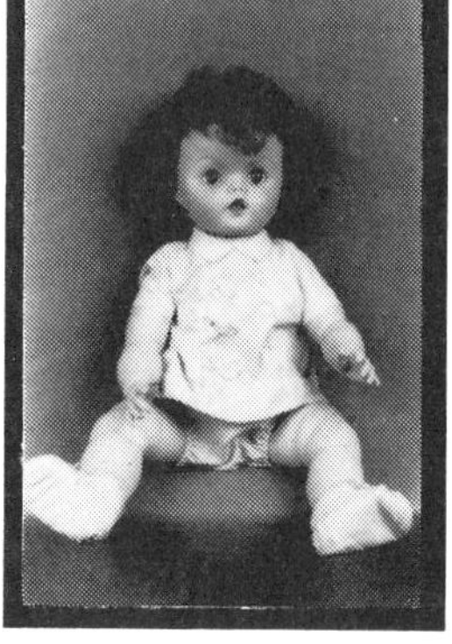

KELLY

1959. 15 in. (38 cm). Plastic body, jointed hips, shoulders, and neck. Vinyl head; blue sleep eyes, lashes, painted lower lashes; rooted blond saran curls; closed mouth. Mark: on head, MADE IN CANADA/DEE AN CEE.
Ref.No. D of C; CB14 p. 145

Mint $45.00   Ex. $35.00   G. $25.00   F. $15.00

DREAM BABY

1959. 18 in.(46 cm). Plastic body, jointed hips, shoulders, and neck. Vinyl head; blue sleep eyes, lashes, painted lower lashes; rooted curly brown hair; closed mouth. Mark: on head, DEE AN CEE. Made with a very thick heavy plastic.
Ref.No. D of C; AM23 p. 145

Mint $60.00   Ex. $45.00   G. $35.00   F. $25.00

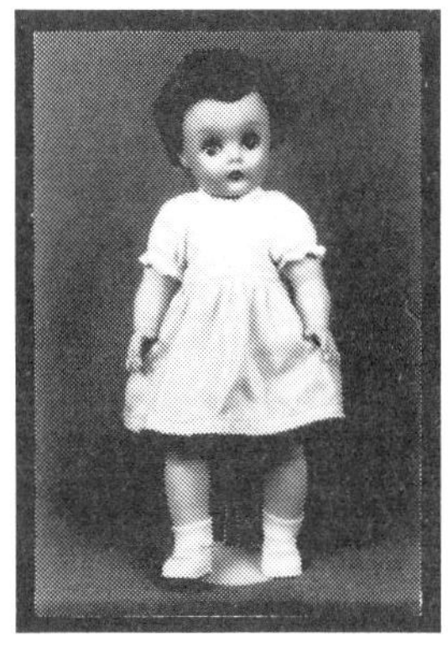

HONEY BEA

1959. 18 in. (45.5 cm). Plastic body, jointed hips, shoulders, and neck. Vinyl head; brown sleep eyes, lashes, painted lower lashes; rooted, saran, brown ponytail and bangs; closed mouth. Mark: on head, DEE AN CEE.
Ref.No. D of C; BS12 p. 146

Mint $95.00   Ex. $75.00   G. $55.00   F. $30.00

BONNIE - 19 in.

1959. 19 in. (48.5 cm). One piece stuffed Flexee-vinyl. Vinyl head; blue sleep eyes, lashes; rooted blond saran hair; closed mouth. Mark: on head, DEE AN CEE.
Ref.No. D of C; CF29 p. 145

Mint $55.00   Ex. $45.00   G. $35.00   F. $25.00

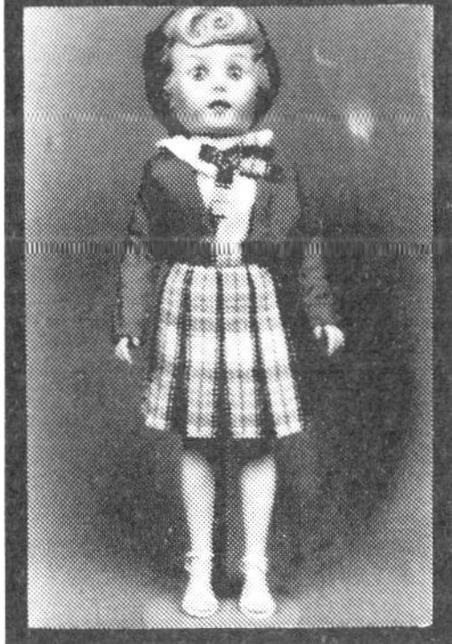

BONNIE - 17 in.

1959. 17 in. (43 cm). One piece stuffed vinyl body. Vinyl head; inset blue eyes; deeply moulded hair; closed mouth. Mark: on head, DEE & CEE.
Ref.No. D of C; CW31 p. 146

Mint $75.00   Ex. $60.00   G. $35.00   F. $25.00

NANETTE BRIDESMAID

1959. 19 in. (48.5 cm). Hard plastic teen body, jointed hips, waist, shoulders, and neck. Vinyl head; brown sleep eyes, lashes, painted lower lashes; rooted brown saran curls; closed mouth. Unmarked.
Ref.No. D of C; BQ15 p. 147

Mint $75.00   Ex. $60.00   G. $35.00   F. $25.00

SWEET SUE FORMAL

1959. l8 in. (45.5 cm). Plastic body, jointed waist, hips, shoulders, and neck. Vinyl head; blue sleep eyes, lashes, painted lower lashes; rooted saran hair in a ponytail with bangs; closed mouth. Mark: on head, DEE CEE
Ref.No. D of C; BZ28 p. 147

Mint $85.00   Ex. $65.00   G. $40.00   F. $30.00

MARGO

1959. 24 in. (61 cm). One-piece Flexee-vinyl body. Vinyl head; blue sleep eyes, lashes, painted lower lashes; rooted blond curls; closed mouth.
Ref.No. D of C; CT14 p. 147

Mint $65.00   Ex. $50.00   G. $40.00   F. $25.00

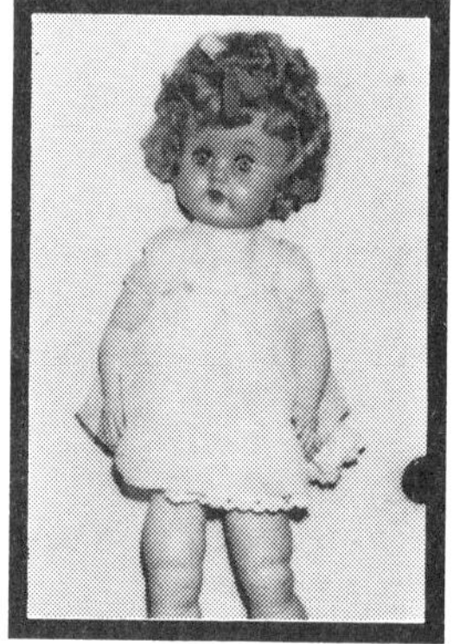

CINDY BRIDE

1959. 17 in. (43.5 cm). Plastic body, jointed hips, waist, shoulders, and neck, wearing nail polish. Vinyl head; pierced ears and pearl earrings; blue sleep eyes, lashes, painted lower lashes; rooted short blond saran hair; closed mouth. Mark: on head, D&C; on body, DEE AN CEE.
Ref.No. D of C; BX16 p. 148

Mint $85.00   Ex. $65.00   G. $40.00   F $30.00

KOWEEKA

ca.1960. 15 in. (38 cm). Brown plastic body, jointed hips, shoulders, and neck. Vinyl head; painted black eyes; rooted straight black hair; open-closed mouth, smiling and showing painted teeth. Mark: on head, KOWEEKA [c]/HUDSONS BAY CO.; on body, MADE IN CANADA/DEE AND CEE.
Ref.No. D of C; CX14 p. 149

Mint $115.00   Ex. $85.00   G. $65.00   F. $45.00

POLLYANNA

1960. 31 in. (79 cm). Plastic teen-aged girl, jointed hips, shoulders, and neck. Vinyl head; blue sleep eyes, lashes, distinctive black lashes painted at outside of upper eyelids; rooted blond saran hair with bangs; open-closed mouth, smiling and showing painted teeth. Mark: on head WALT DISNEY/PROD./MFR. BY DEE AN CEE/NF; on body, DEE AN CEE.
Ref.No. D of C; CS22A p. 150

Mint $150.00   Ex. $125.00   G. $85.00   F. $55.00

DRINK 'N WET BABY - Moulded Hair

1960. 19 in. (47 cm). Plastic baby body, jointed hips, shoulders, and neck. Vinyl head; blue sleep eyes, lashes, painted lower lashes; moulded light brown hair; open mouth nurser. Mark: on head, DEE CEE.
Ref.No. D of C; CD8 p. 148

Mint $35.00   Ex. $30.00   G. $25.00   F. $15.00

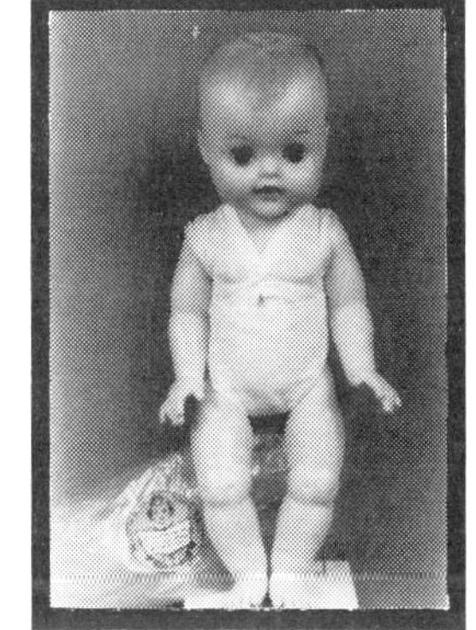

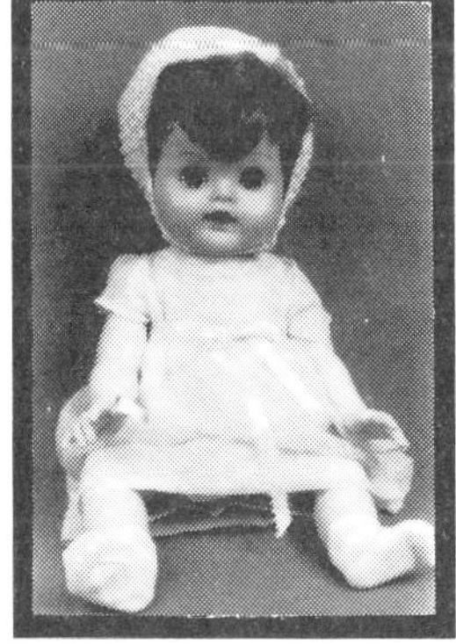

DRINK 'N WET BABY - Saran Hair

1960. 19 in. (47 cm). Plastic baby body, jointed hips, shoulders, and neck. Vinyl head; blue sleep eyes, lashes, painted lower lashes; brown rooted saran curly hair; open mouth nurser. Mark: on head, DEE CEE.
Ref.No. D of C; CG19 p. 149

Mint $55.00   Ex. $45.00   G. $30.00   F. $20.00

KELLY

1960. 18 in. (45.5 cm). Plastic body, jointed hips, shoulders, and neck. Vinyl head; blue sleep eyes, lashes and painted lower lashes; rooted blond saran hair; closed mouth. Mark: on head, DEE AN CEE.
Ref.No. D of C; CI9 p. 151

Mint $75.00   Ex. $60.00   G. $35.00   F. $25.00

WILLY

1960. 16 in. (40.5 cm). Plastic body, jointed hips, shoulders, and neck. Vinyl head; blue sleep eyes, lashes, painted lower lashes; well defined moulded hair, painted black; closed mouth. Mark: on body, DEE AN CEE.
Ref.No. D of C; CW22 p. 153

Mint $60.00   Ex. $45.00   G. $35.00   F. $20.00

MARYBEL THE DOLL THAT GETS WELL

1960. 15 in. (38 cm). Plastic body and legs, vinyl arms. Vinyl head; blue sleep eyes, lashes; rooted blond saran hair; closed mouth. Mark: on head, DEE CEE; on body, D&C.
Ref.No. D of C; CG4 p. 152

Note: Mint must have crutches, arm and leg casts.

Mint $125.00   Ex. $80.00   G. $40.00   F. $20.00

PATTY KAY

1960. 30 in. (76.5 cm). Plastic body, jointed hips, shoulders, and neck. Vinyl head with dimpled cheeks and chin; brown sleep eyes, lashes, painted lower lashes, repainted brows; rooted brown curly hair; open-closed mouth with four moulded teeth, two up and two down. Mark: on head, DEE CEE.
Ref.No. D of C; CB5 p. 152

Mint $80.00   Ex. $65.00   G. $40.00   F. $25.00

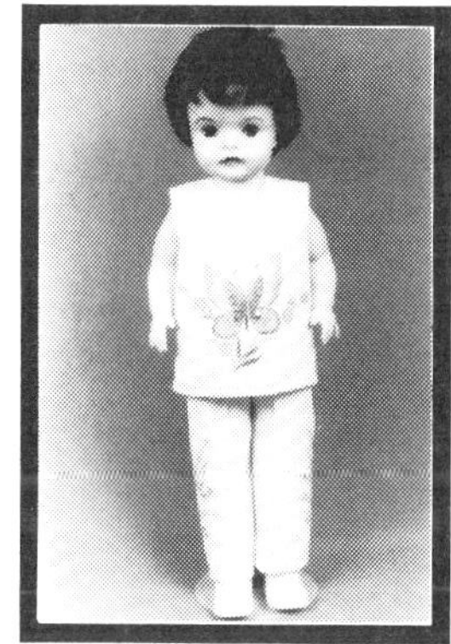

GIGI

1960. 20.5 in. (52 cm.). Plastic body, jointed hips, shoulders, and neck. Vinyl head; green sleep eyes, lashes; long red saran hair with bangs; smiling closed mouth. Mark: on body, D & C.
Ref.No.: DB4.

Mint $100.00   Ex. $80.00   G. $50.00   F. $30.00

KELLY

1960. 16 in. (40.5 cm). Plastic body, jointed hips, shoulders, and neck. Vinyl head; brown sleep eyes, lashes, painted lower lashes; rooted short curly brown saran hair; closed mouthh. Mark: on head, D&C/3; on body, 165-5/D&C.
Ref.No. D of C; AM21 p. 151

Mint $75.00   Ex. $50.00   G. $35.00   F. $25.00

CALYPSO JILL - 14in.

1960. 14 in. (35.5 cm). Plastic body, jointed hips, shoulders, and neck. Vinyl head; moulded eyes painted black; black moulded hair in pigtails and bangs; mouth open-closed. Mark: on head, DEE CEE.
Ref.No. D of C; CR21 p. 148

Mint $100.00   Ex. $85.00   G. $70.00   F. $50.00

DRINK 'N WET BABY - 1961

1961. 20 in. (50.5 cm). Brown plastic body, jointed hips, shoulders, and neck. Vinyl head; brown sleep eyes, lashes, painted lower lashes; rooted short curly hair; open mouth nurser. Mark: on body, 20-638.
Ref.No. D of C; CJ4 p. 153

Mint $70.00   Ex. $50.00   G. $35.00   F. $25.00

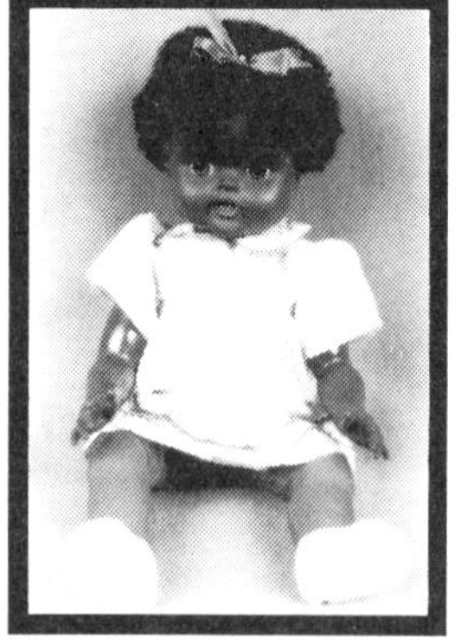

CALYPSO BILL - 16 in.

1961. 16 in. (40.5 cm). Brown plastic body, jointed hips, shoulders, and neck. Vinyl head; painted black eyes; moulded black curly hair; open-closed mouth showing six painted teeth. Mark: DEE CEE.
Ref.No. D of C; CD19 p. 154

Mint $110.00   Ex. $90.00   G. $75.00   F. $50.00

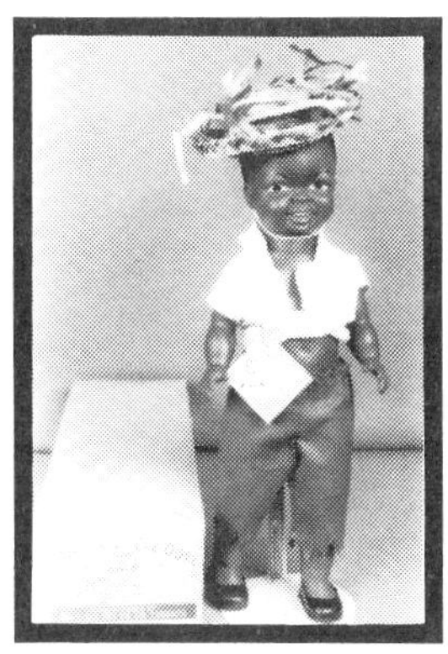

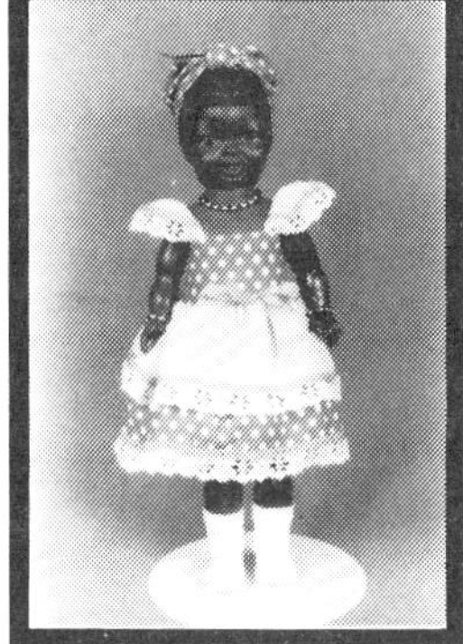

CALYPSO JILL - 16 in.

1961. 16 in. (40.5 cm). Brown plastic body, jointed hips, shoulders, and neck. Vinyl head; painted black eyes; well defined moulded hair with bangs and pigtails in black; open-closed mouth, smiling and showing painted teeth. Mark: on body, DEE AN CEE.
Ref.No. D of C; CS9 p. 154

Mint $110.00   Ex. $90.00   G. $75.00   F. $50.00

LULUBELLE

1961. 20 in. (51 cm). Brown plastic body, jointed hips, shoulders, and neck. Vinyl head; golden brown sleep eyes, lashes; rooted black curly hair; open mouth nurser. Mark: on head, DEE AN CEE; on body, DEE AN CEE.
Ref.No. D of C; CW22A p. 154

Mint $65.00   Ex. $50.00   G. $40.00   F. $25.00

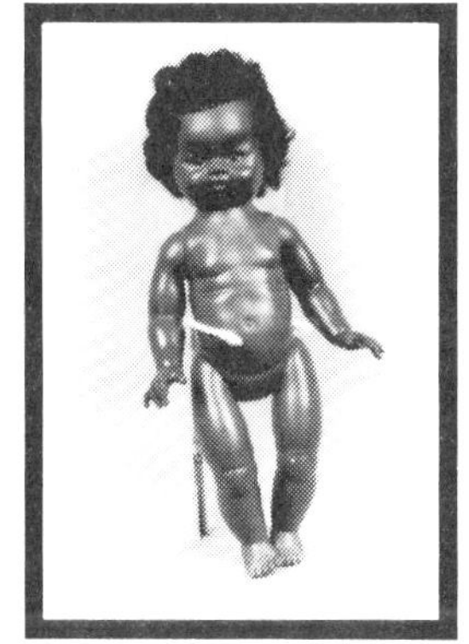

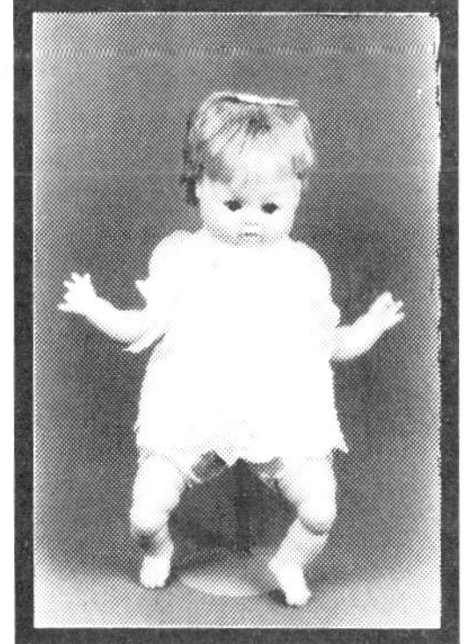

DREAM BABY - 17 in.

1961. 17 in. (43 cm). Cloth body, vinyl bent-limb arms and legs. Vinyl head; chubby face, blue sleep eyes, lashes, rooted straight blond hair over moulded hair; open-closed mouth. Mark: on head, DEE AN CEE.
Ref.No. D of C; BN32 p. 155

Mint $50.00   Ex. $45.00   G. $35.00   F. $25.00

DREAM BABY - 18 in. Cloth

1961. 18 in. (45.5 cm). Cloth body, vinyl bent-limb arms and legs. Vinyl head; painted blue eyes; rooted straight saran hair; closed mouth. Mark: on head. DEE CEE.
Ref.No. D of. C; CW10 p. 155

Mint $75.00 Ex. $50.00 G. $35.00 F. $25.00

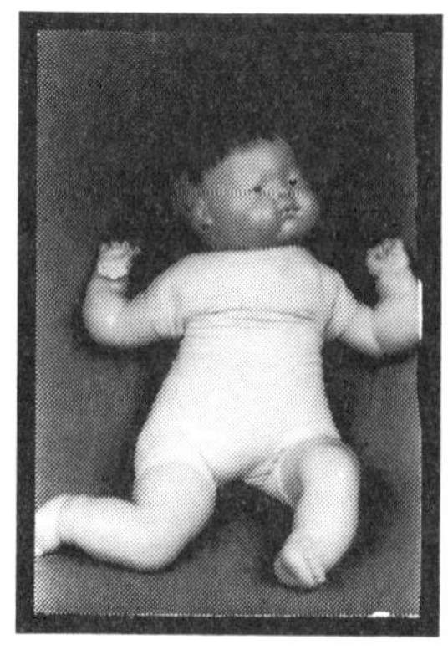

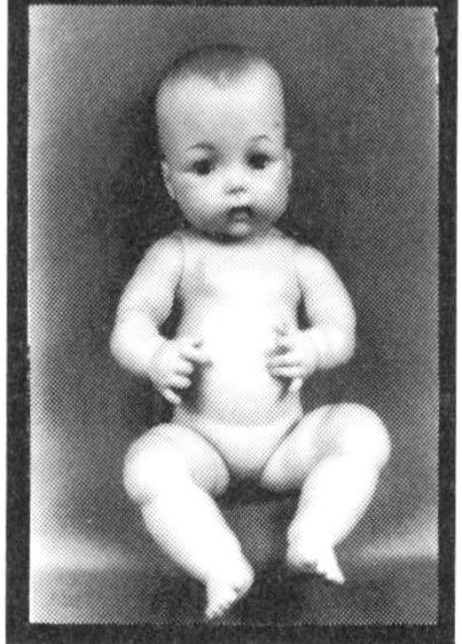

DREAM BABY - 19 in. Vinyl

1961. 19 in. (47 cm). Vinyl bent-limb baby body, jointed hips, shoulders, and neck. Vinyl head; blue sleep eyes, lashes and painted lower lashes; reddish brown moulded hair; open mouth nurser. Mark: on head, DEE CEE/1961; on body, DC.
Ref.No. D of C; BX6 p. 155

Mint $65.00 Ex. $50.00 G. $40.00 F. $30.00

DREAM BABY - 18 in. Vinyl

1961. 18 in. (45.5 cm). Vinyl bent-limb baby body, jointed hips, shoulders, and head. Vinyl head; blue sleep eyes, lashes, painted lower lashes; rooted brown straight hair over moulded hair; open mouth nurser. Mark: on head, DEE CEE; on body, DEE CEE.
Ref.No. D of C; CA36 p. 156

Mint $75.00 Ex. $60.00 G. $45.00 F. $35.00

CINDY

1961. 17 in. (43 cm). Plastic teen body, jointed hips, waist, shoulders, and neck. Vinyl head; brown sleep eyes, lashes, painted lower lashes; rooted brown hair; closed mouth.
Ref.No. D of C; CT23 p. 157

Mint $75.00 Ex. $55.00 G. $35.00 F. $25.00

MOON BABY - 18 in.

1961. 18 in. (45.5 cm). Plastic body vinyl bent-limb arms and legs, jointed hips, shoulders, and neck. Vinyl head; large blue sleep eyes, long dark lashes; rooted blond saran hair; open mouth nurser. Mark: on head, DEE CEE.
Ref.No. D of C; CD3 p. 156

Mint $80.00   **Ex.** $60.00   **G.** $40.00   **F.** $25.00

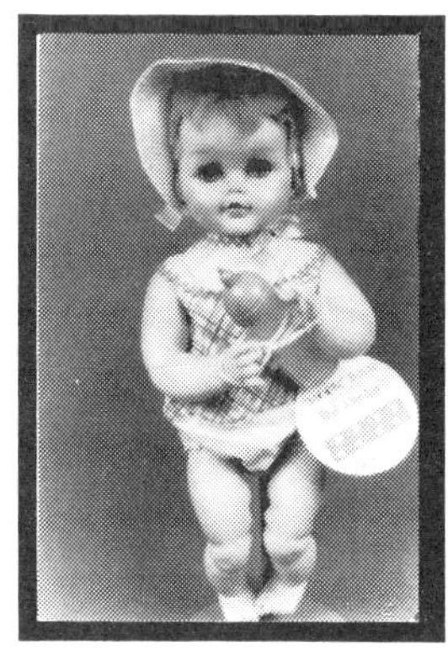

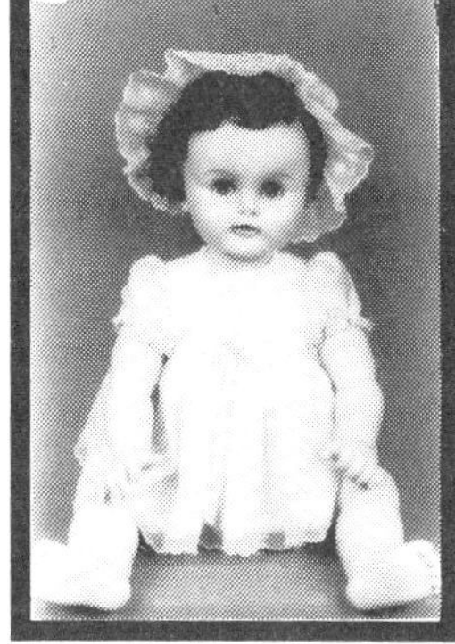

MOON BABY - 28 in.

1961. 28 in. (71.5 cm). Plastic bent-limb baby body, jointed hips, shoulders, and neck, with a crier in the body. Vinyl head; blue sleep eyes, lashes, painted lower lashes; rooted saran black hair in a baby feather cut; open mouth nurser. Mark: on head, Dee Cee.
Ref.No. D of C; BZ21 p. 157

Mint $100.00   **Ex.** $80.00   **G.** $60.00   **F.** $40.00

WILLY THE SAILOR

1961. 16 in. (40.5 cm). Plastic body, jointed hips, shoulders, and neck. Vinyl head; blue sleep eyes, lashes, painted lower lashes; moulded hair, painted black; closed mouth. Original label, DEE AND CEE/QUALITY ABOVE ALL.
Ref.No. D of C; BQ6 p. 157

Mint $75.00   **Ex.** $60.00   **G.** $35.00   **F.** $20.00

WILLY THE MOUNTIE

1961. 16 in. (40.5 cm). Plastic body, jointed hips, shoulders, and neck. Vinyl head; blue sleep eyes, lashes, painted lower lashes; moulded black hair; closed mouth.
Ref.No. D of C; BQ21 p. 158

Mint $80.00   **Ex.** $65.00   **G.** $35.00   **F.** $20.00

MARYBEL THE GET WELL DOLL

1961. 15 in. (38 cm). Plastic body and legs, vinyl arms. Vinyl head; blue sleep eyes, lashes, painted lower lashes; rooted brown saran hair; open mouth nurser. Mark: on head, DEE CEE; on body, D&C.
Ref.No. D of C; CF32 p. 158

Mint $125.00   Ex. $80.00   G. $40.00   F. $20.00

Note: Mint must have original crutches, arm and leg casts.

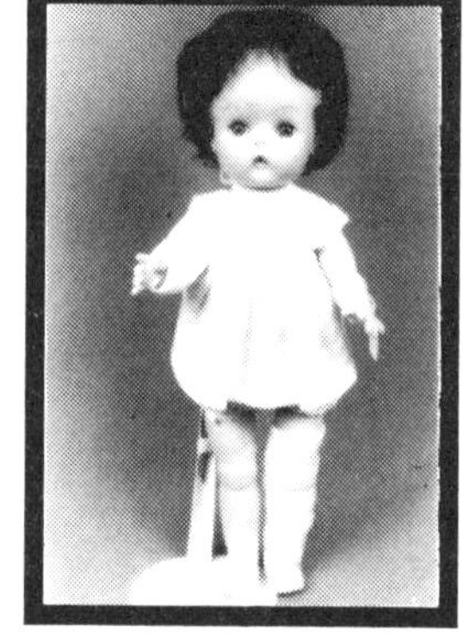

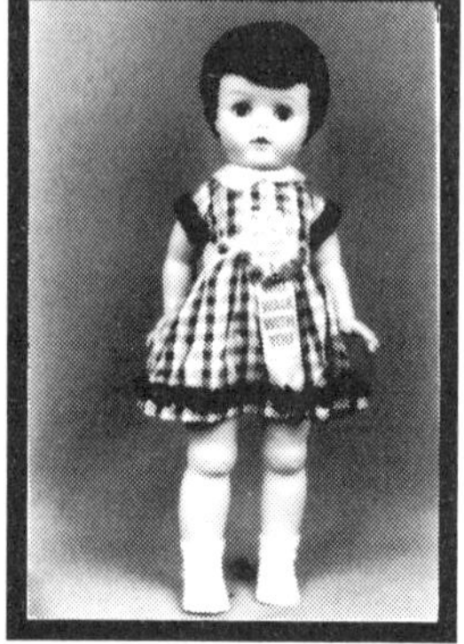

KELLY

1961. 22 in. (56 cm). Plastic body, jointed hips, shoulders, and neck. Vinyl head. Brown sleep eyes, eyelashes; painted lower lashes. Rooted dark brown short curls. Open-closed mouth. Mark: on head, D&C.
Ref.No. D of C; BS32 p. 158

Mint $75.00   Ex. $50.00   G. $35.00   F. $25.00

CHATTY CATHY

1961. 20 in. (50 cm). Hard plastic body, jointed hips, shoulders, and neck; holes in the front for speaker and pullring in the back to operate talking device. Vinyl head; blue sleep eyes, lashes, freckles; rooted blond saran hair with bangs; open-closed mouth showing two teeth. Mark: on body, CHATTY CATHY/c1961 CHATTY BABY/c1961/BY MATTEL INC./U.S. PAT. 3,017,187/OTHER U.S. &/FOREIGN PATS. PEND./PAT. IN CANADA 1962.
Ref.No. D of C; BU5 p. 159

Mint $150.00 talking   Ex. $105.00 talking
G. $80.00 not talking F. $ $ 45.00 not talking

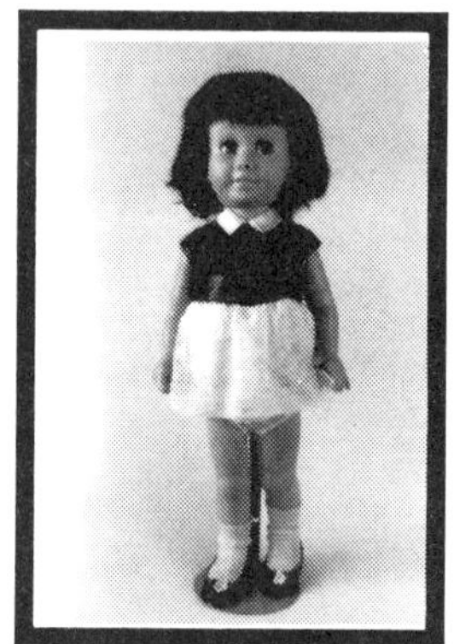

DREAM BABY - 18 in. Moulded Hair

ca.1962. 18 in. (45.5 cm). Cloth body, vinyl bent-limb arms and legs; Vinyl head; blue sleep eyes, lashes; light-brown slightly moulded hair; open-closed mouth. Mark: on head, DEE AN CEE/MADE IN CANADA.
Ref.No. D of C; CD25 p. 159

Mint $60.00 Ex. $45.00 G. $35.00 F. $25.00

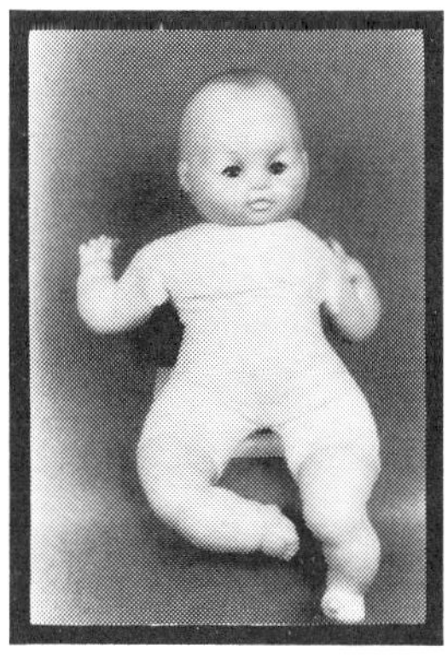

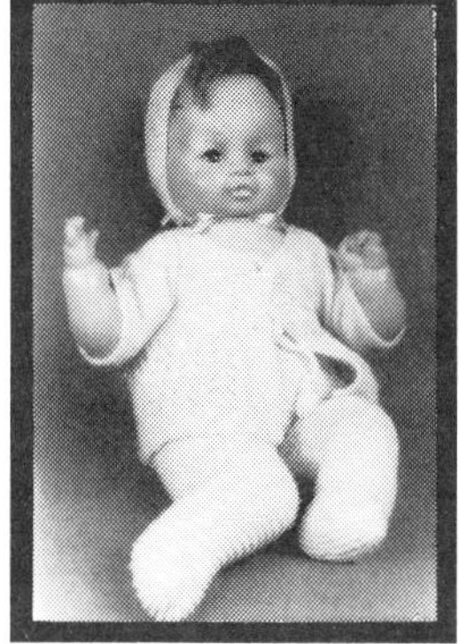

DREAM BABY - 18 in. Blond Hair

ca.1962. 18 in. (45.5 cm). Pink cloth body, vinyl bent-limb arms and legs, swivel neck. Vinyl head; blue sleep eyes, lashes; rooted blond straight hair; open-closed mouth, moulded tongue. Mark: on head, DEE AN CEE/MADE IN CANADA.
Ref.No. D of C; CB17 p. 159

Mint $65.00 Ex. $50.00 G. $40.00 F. $30.00

TINY CHATTY BABY

1962. 15 in. (38 cm). Plastic body, jointed hips, shoulders, and neck, pullring at shoulder. Vinyl head; blue sleep eyes, lashes; rooted straight brown hair; open-closed mouth showing two moulded teeth.
Ref.No. D of C; CX16 p. 160

Mint $125.00 talking   Ex. $95.00 talking
G. $50.00 not talking F. $30.00 not talking

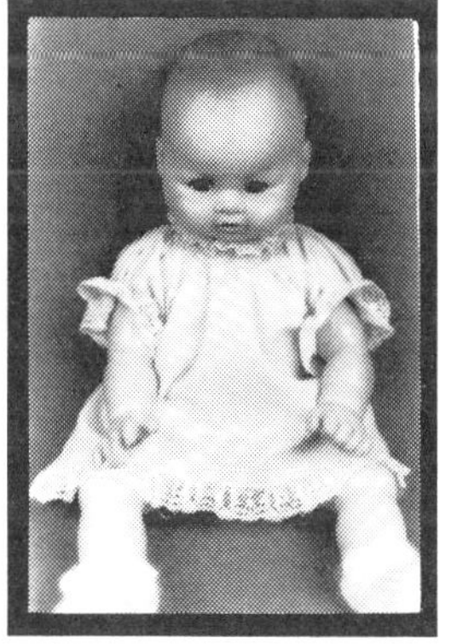

DEE AN CEE - 1962

ca.1962. 19 in. (47 cm). Plastic bent-limb baby body, jointed hips, shoulders, and neck. Blue sleep eyes, lashes; light brown moulded hair; open mouth nurser. Mark: on head, DEE AN CEE.
Ref.No. D of C; CP5 p. 160

Mint $65.00 Ex. $50.00 G. $40.00 F. $30.00

CINDY BRIDE

ca.1962. 17 in. (43 cm). Plastic teen body, jointed hips, shoulders, and neck. Vinyl head, holes for earrings; brown sleep eyes, lashes, painted lower lashes; rooted blond saran hair; closed mouth. Mark: D & C.
Ref.No. D of C; CF21 p. 161

Mint $50.00   Ex. $40.00   G. $35.00   F. $25.00

DEE AN CEE -1962

ca.1962. 17 in. (43 cm). Plastic teen body, jointed hips, shoulders, and neck. Vinyl head; blue sleep eyes, lashes; rooted blond saran hair; closed mouth. Mark: D & C.
Ref.No. D of C; CF25 p. 161

Mint $80.00   Ex. $60.00   G. $35.00   F. $25.00

KOOKIE

ca.1963. 25 in. (64 cm). Black cloth body, legs and upper arms, pink cloth forearms. Vinyl head; brown sleep eyes, lashes, eyeshadow and extra heavy upper lashes, painted lower lashes; rooted long black hair; open-closed mouth. Mark: on head, DEE CEE.
Ref.No. D of C; BU17 p. 161

Mint $65.00   Ex. $55.00   G. $30.00   F. $20.00

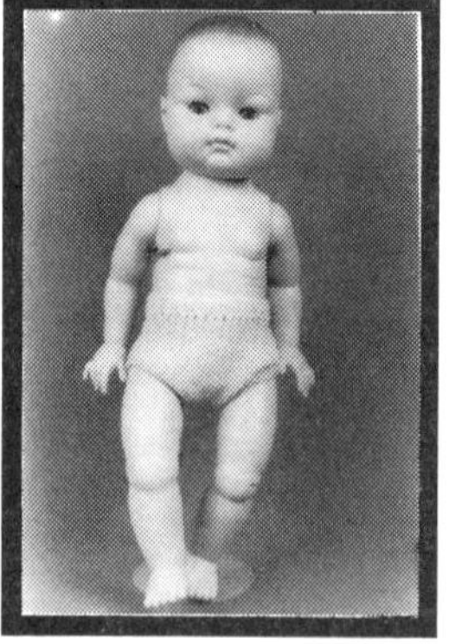

DEE AN CEE - 1963 - 19 in.

ca.1963. 19 in. (47 cm). Plastic body, jointed hips, shoulders, and neck. Vinyl head; blue sleep eyes, lashes; light brown slightly moulded hair; closed mouth. Mark: on head, DEE AN CEE CANADA; on body, MADE IN CANADA DEE AN CEE.
Ref.No. D of C; CD9 p. 160

Mint $50.00   Ex. $40.00   G. $30.00   F. $20.00

DEE AN CEE - 1963 - 20 in.

ca.1963. 20 in. (51 cm). Plastic body, jointed hips, shoulders, and neck. Vinyl head; blue sleep eyes, lashes; rooted brown saran curly hair; closed mouth. Mark: on head, DEE CEE/CANADA/20; on body, MADE IN CANADA/DEE AN CEE.
Ref.No. D of C; CL26 p. 162

Mint $45.00   Ex. $35.00   G. $25.00   F. $15.00

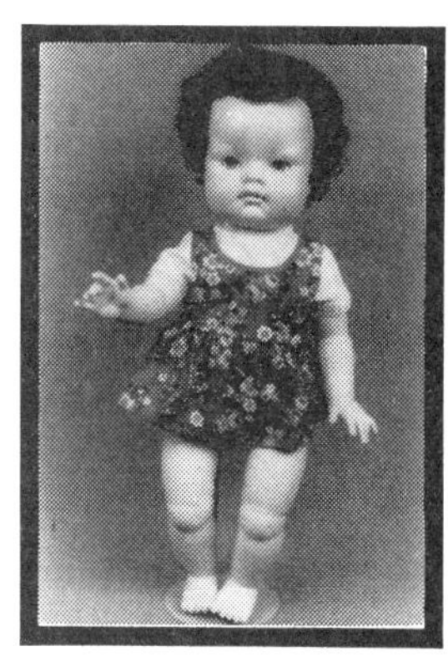

MARY McCLARY

ca.1963. 17 in. (43 cm). Plastic teen body, jointed hips, waist, shoulders, and neck. Vinyl head; blue sleep eyes, lashes, tiny painted lower lashes, three long upper lashes at outside edges of eyes; rooted brown saran hair with blond streak at the front; closed mouth. Mark: on head, DEE & CEE; on body, DEE AN CEE.
Ref.No. D of C; BX13 p. 162

Mint $85.00   Ex. $65.00   G. $40.00   F. $30.00

BABY PATTABURP

ca.1963. 17 in. (43 cm). Cloth body, vinyl arms and legs. Vinyl head; blue sleep eyes, lashes; rooted straight blond hair; open-closed mouth. Mark: on head, DEE AN CEE; label on body, MATTEL.
Ref.No.: DH6 p. 162

Mint $65.00   Ex. $50.00   G. $40.00   F. $25.00

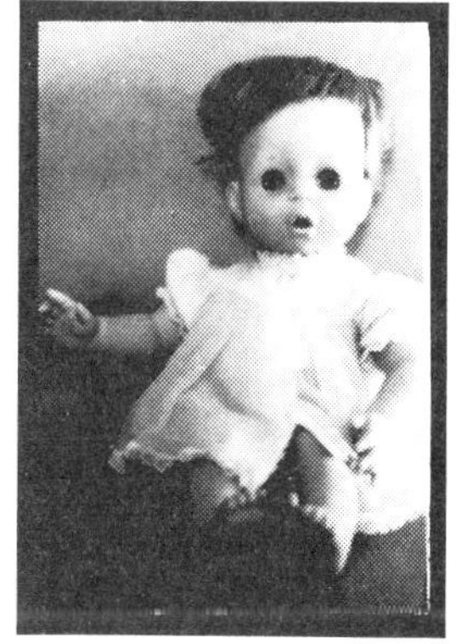

DEE AN CEE - 1963

ca.1963. 12 in. (30 cm). Brown plastic body and legs, vinyl arms, upturned hands. Brown vinyl head; inset brown plastic eyes, moulded lashes, painted lower lashes; rooted light brown hair; open-closed mouth. Mark: on head, DEE CEE/MADE IN CANADA.
Ref.No. D of C; CJ11 p. 163

Mint $45.00   Ex. $35.00   G. $20.00   F. $10.00

DEE AN CEE - 1963

ca.1963. 12 in. (30 cm). Plastic body, jointed hips, shoulders, and neck. Vinyl head; fixed blue plastic eyes, moulded lashes; rooted brown curls; open-closed mouth. Mark: on head, DEE CEE/MADE IN/CANADA.
Ref.No. D of C; CJ10 p. 163

Mint $35.00   Ex. $25.00   G. $20.00   F. $10.00

DEE AN CEE - 1963

ca.1963. 11.5 in. (29 cm). Brown plastic body, vinyl arms, upturned hands, jointed hips, shoulders, and neck. Vinyl head; fixed brown eyes, plastic lashes, painted lower lashes; rooted straight black hair; open-closed mouth. Mark: on head, DEE CEE/MADE IN CANADA; on body, DEE & CEE/MADE IN CANADA.
Ref.No. D of C; BU31 p. 163

Mint $45.00   Ex. $35.00   G. $20.00   F. $10.00

DEE AN CEE - 1964

1964. 15 in. (38 cm). Plastic body, jointed hips, shoulders, and neck. Vinyl head; blue side-glancing sleep eyes, lashes; rooted long blond hair; closed pouty mouth. Mark: on head, DEE & CEE/MADE IN CANADA/1964.
Ref.No. D of C; BX10 p. 164

Mint $55.00   Ex. $40.00   G. $30.00   F. $20.00

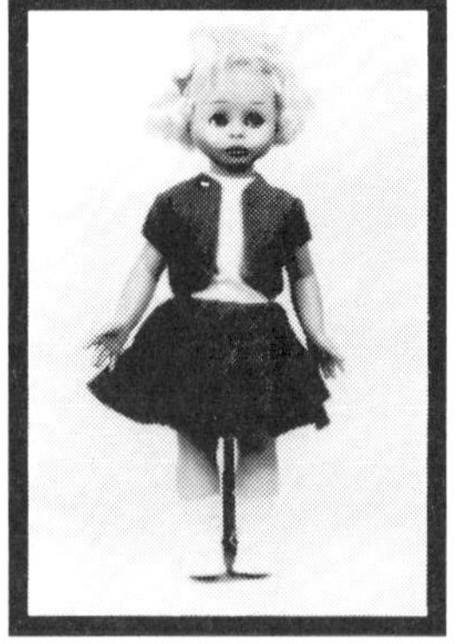

DEE AN CEE - 1964

1964. 15 in. (38 cm). Plastic body and legs, vinyl arms, jointed hips, shoulders, and neck. Vinyl head; blue side-glancing sleep eyes, lashes; rooted platinum blond saran hair; closed pouty mouth. Mark: on head, DEE & CEE/MADE IN CANADA/COPYRIGHT 1964.
Ref.No. D of C; AN5 p. 164

Mint $55.00   Ex. $40.00   G. $30.00   F. $20.00

DISTINCTIVE DOLLS OF CANADA LTD.
1987 -

After doing Sir John in vinyl in 1988 D.D.C. began working with Star Doll of Toronto to make a line of collectable dolls that are made in Canada. In 1989 they co-produced Elizabeth Manley in vinyl.

SIR JOHN A. MACDONALD

1988. 18 in. (46 cm). Vinyl body, jointed hips, shoulders and neck. Vinyl head; blue painted eyes; grey moulded curly hair; closed mouth. Mark: on head, Macdonald/Yvonne Richardon/1987 Canada ; on back, Macdonald/Yvonne Richardson/1987 Canada/Distinctive Dolls/ of Canada Ltd/logo. Dressed in white cotton shirt, lined cream wool pants and vest, black wool coat, tie, moulded boots and pocket watch. Includes medallion with the company logo and tag on his wrist.
Ref.No.: DM6 and DM 7.

Mint $180.00   Ex. $150.00   G. $100.00   F. $80.00

DOMINION TOY MANUFACTURING COMPANY LIMITED
1911 - 1932

Canada's earliest known commercial doll maker. Dominion dolls are very collectable.

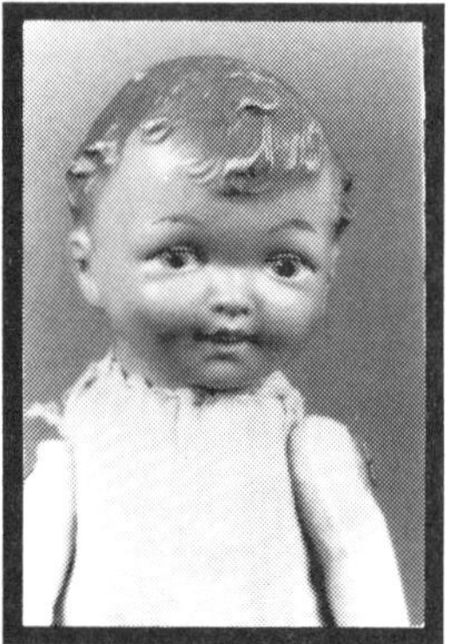

DOMINION - 1911

ca.1911. 19 in. (49 cm). Excelsior stuffed cloth body, legs and upper arms; composition forearms. Composition head; painted blue eyes with highlights and a fine black line over the eye; deeply moulded hair, painted light brown; open-closed mouth showing two moulded teeth. Unmarked.
Ref.No.: D of C, BW34, p. 166.

Mint $250.00   Ex. $200.00   G. $150.00   F. $85.00

DOMINION - 1911

ca.1911. 16.5 in. (42 cm). Excelsior stuffed cloth body, legs and upper arms; composition gauntlet hands. Composition shoulderhead with small round shoulderplate; eyes painted blue with a fine black line over each eye; deeply moulded hair, painted brown; closed mouth. Unmarked.
Ref.No.: D of C, BX34, p. 167.

Mint $225.00   Ex. $185.00   G. $140.00   F. $75.00

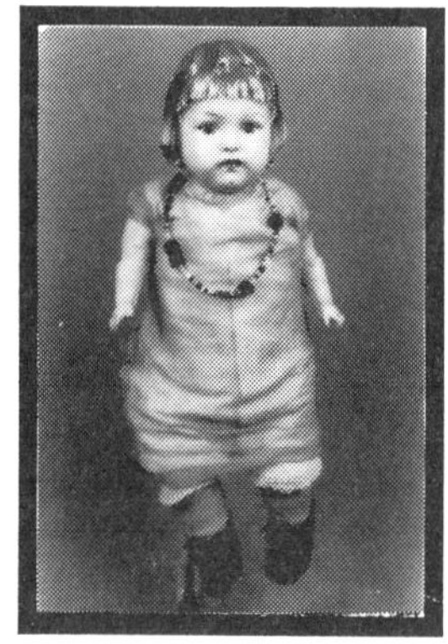

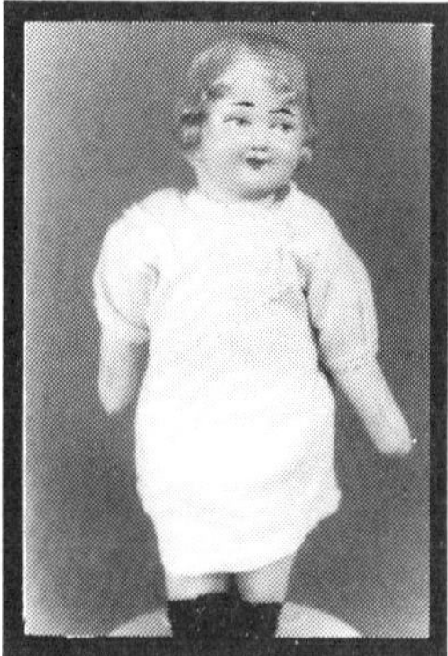

DOMINON - 1911

ca.1911. 9 in. (23 cm). Excelsior stuffed cloth body, legs and arms, jointed hips and shoulders with metal discs; one arm is longer than the other. Blue side-glancing painted eyes, black line over eye; light brown moulded hair with moulded headband; closed mouth. Mark: Original label with the Dominion shield marked, DOMINION/BRAND/DOLLS & TOYS/MADE IN CANADA.
Ref.No.: D of C, CN19, p. 167.

Mint $150.00   Ex. $125.00   G. $100.00   F. $65.00

DOMINON - 1912

ca.1912. 29 in. (73.5 cm). Excelsior stuffed cloth body and legs, composition gauntlet hands, jointed hips and shoulders with metal discs. Composition flange head; blue intaglio eyes, fine black line over eye; deeply moulded light brown hair; closed smiling mouth. Unmarked.
Ref.No.: D of C, CB24, p. 167.

Mint $285.00   Ex. $250.00   G. $195.00   F. $120.00

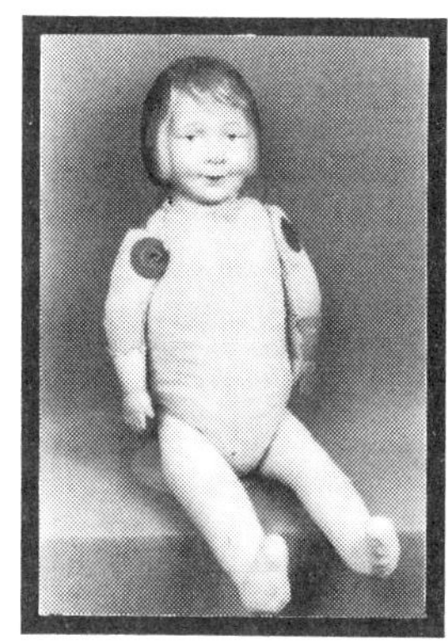

DOMINION - 1913

ca.1913. l7 in. (44.5 cm). Excelsior stuffed cloth body, legs and upper arms; composition gauntlet hands. Composition head; painted blue side-glancing eyes; moulded hair with moulded hole for a ribbon, painted brown; closed mouth. Unmarked.
Ref.No.: D of C, Cl8, p. 168.

Mint $145.00   Ex. $115.00   G. $85.00   F. $60.00

DOMINION - 1915

ca.1915. 13.75 in. (35 cm). Excelsior stuffed cloth body, legs and forearms; composition lower arms; feet are stitched on black fabric. Composition shoulderhead; painted eyes; moulded hair, painted strawberry blond; closed mouth, painted orange-red. Unmarked.
Ref.No.: D of C, BF5, p. 169.

Mint $200.00   Ex. $150.00   G. $95.00   F. $60.00

TIPPERARY TOMMY

ca.1915. 14 in. (36 cm). Cloth body with composition hands and boots. Composition head; painted blue eyes with a fine black line over each eye; moulded hair, painted light brown; closed mouth, painted red. Unmarked.
Ref.No.: D of C, AP9, p. 168.

Mint $225.00   Ex. $195.00   G. $110.00   F. $85.00

DOMINION - 1916

ca.1916. 25 in. (63.5 cm). All composition bent-limb baby. Composition head; painted blue eyes with a fine black line over each eye, and painted lashes; moulded hair. Unmarked.
Ref.No.: D of C, CD7, p. 169.

Mint $250.00   Ex. $220.00   G. $185.00   F. $130.00

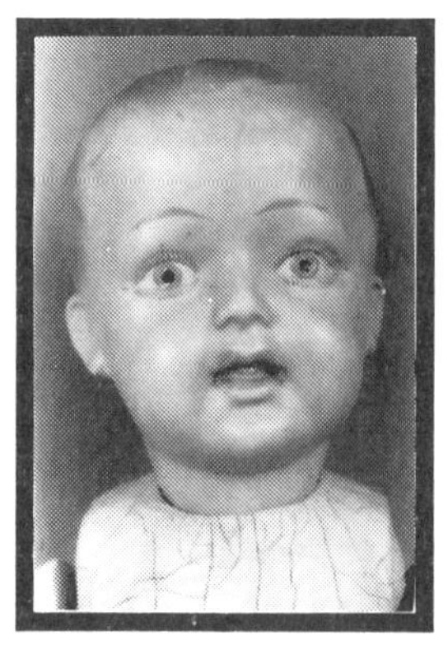

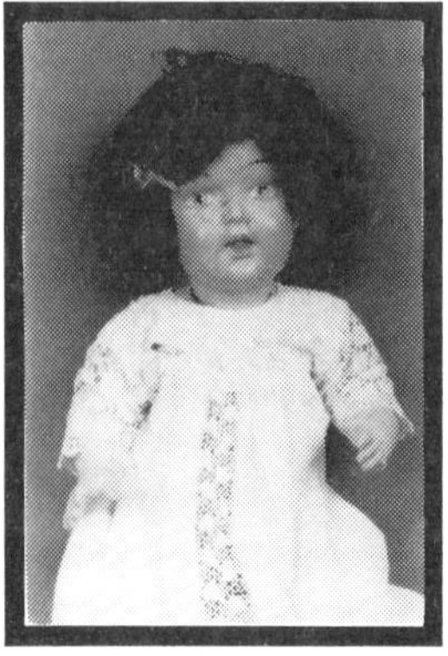

DOMINION - 1916

ca.1916. 23 in. (58.5 cm). All composition bent-limb baby. Composition head; painted blue eyes, fine black line over the eye, and painted lashes; original brown mohair wig; open-closed mouth with two painted teeth. Mark: a shield on the body with D.T.M.C. in it.
Ref.No.: D of C, CF5, p. 169.

Mint $275.00   Ex. $230.00   G. $175.00   F. $110.00

DOMINION - 1917

ca.1917. 14 in. (35.5 cm). All composition bent-limb baby. Composition head; painted intaglio violet eyes with a fine black line over each eye, and painted lashes; moulded light brown hair; closed mouth. Mark: a shield on the body with D.T.M.C./MADE IN CANADA in it.
Ref.No.: D of C, CL6, p. 171.

Mint $225.00   Ex. $175.00   G. $125.00   F. $75.00

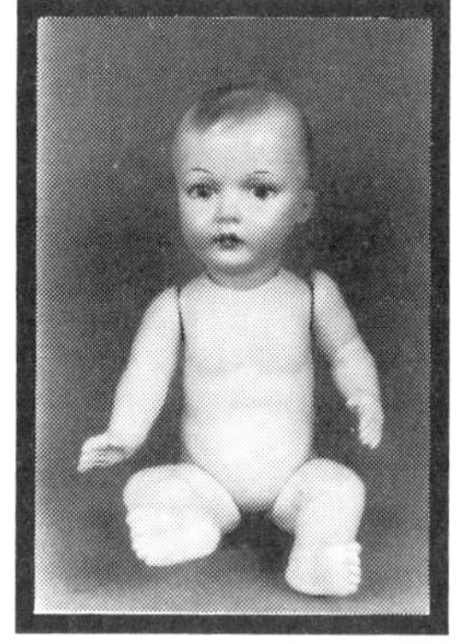

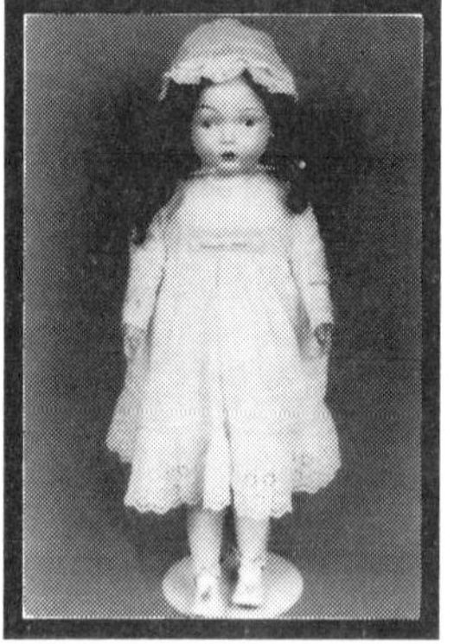

DOLLY WALKER

ca.1918. 28 in. (71.5 cm). Cardboard body with composition forearms, wooden upper arms and wooden legs, jointed with hinges. Composition shoulderhead; painted blue eyes; fine black line over eye; nostril dots; moulded hair, painted light brown plus a human hair wig which is not attached to the head. Closed mouth. Mark: D.T.M.C./MADE IN CANADA.
Ref.No.: D of C, CA8, p. 170.

Mint $750.00   Ex. $500.00   G. $325.00   F. $225.00

DOMINION - 1919

ca.1919. 14 in. (35.5 cm). Cloth body, legs and forearms; composition lower arms. Composition shoulder head; painted blue eyes; painted long upper lashes; moulded hair painted light brown; closed mouth painted red. Mark: D.T.CO. on shoulderplate.
Ref.No.: D of C, BH32, p.171.

Mint. $150.00   Ex. $120.00   G. $95.00   F. $60.00

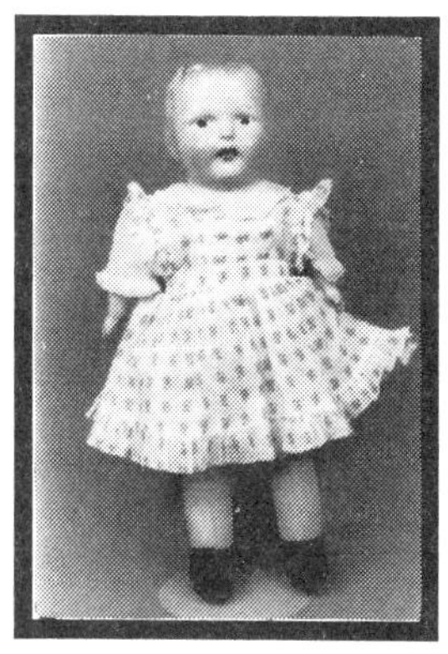

DOMINION -1920

ca.1920. 19 in. (48.5 cm). Excelsior stuffed cloth body and upper arms; bent-limb legs; composition gauntlet hands. Composition head with open crown and wooden pate; grey tin sleep eyes, painted lashes; original blond mohair wig; open mouth. Mark: MADE IN CANADA/D.T.M.C. on the body.
Ref.No.: D of C, CL27, p. 172.

Mint $250.00   Ex. $215.00   G. $175.00   F. $130.00

DOMINION - 1920

ca.1920. 19.5 in. (49.5 cm). Cloth body, legs and forearms; composition lower arms. Composition shoulder head; painted blue eyes, painted long upper lashes; original blond wig; closed mouth painted red. Mark: D.T.C. on shoulderplate.
Ref.No. : D of C, AP19, p. 172.

Mint $250.00   Ex. $215.00   G. $175.00   F. $110.00

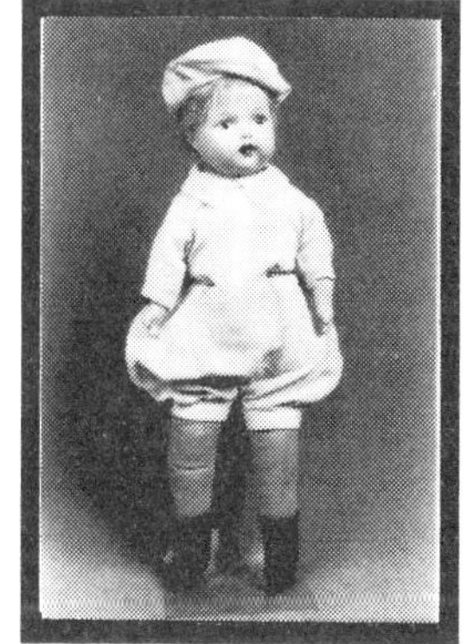

ALICE

ca.1922. 20 in. (51 cm). Excelsior stuffed cloth body and legs, composition gauntlet hands. Composition shoulderhead; blue painted eyes, long painted upper lashes; blond mohair wig over moulded hair; closed mouth. Mark: on head, D.T.C.
Ref.No.: D of C, CN27, p. 172.

Mint $220.00   Ex. $160.00   G. $115.00   F. $70.00

DOMINION - 1923

ca.1923. 20.5 in. (52 cm). Fully ball-jointed composition body with wooden arms. Composition head; light green celluloid sleep eyes; painted upper and lower lashes with red dots in the corners; open-closed mouth with four painted teeth. Mark: on the body, MADE IN CANADA/D.T.M.C.
Ref.No.: D of C, CA31, p. 173.

Mint $325.00   Ex. $275.00   G. $185.00   F. $140.00

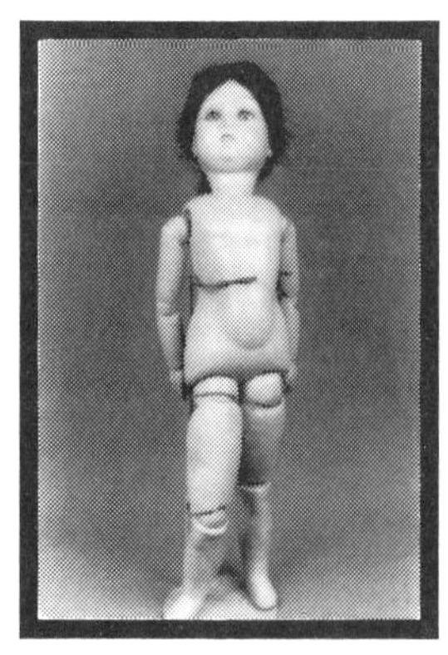

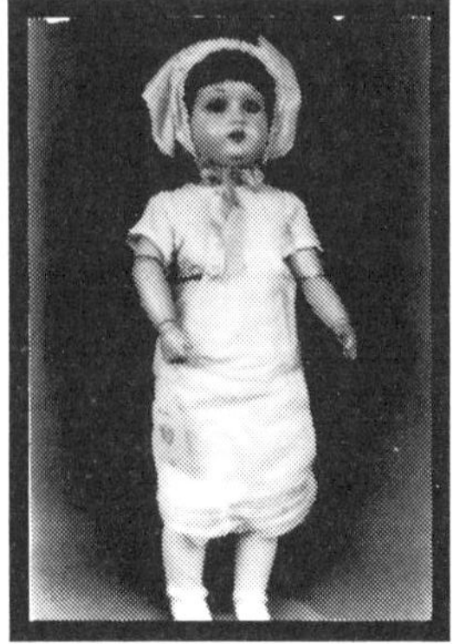

DOMINION -1924

ca.1924. 19 in. (48.5 cm). Fully ball-jointed composition body with wooden arms and composition legs. Composition head; grey-blue celluloid sleep eyes, painted upper and lower lashes; original brown mohair wig; open mouth with teeth missing. Mark: on the body; a shield with D.T.M.C./MADE IN CANADA in it.
Ref.No.: D of C, CC8, p. 173.

Mint $300.00   Ex. $260.00   G.   180.00   F.   140.00

KUDLEE BABY

ca.1924. 18 in. (45.5 cm). Kapok stuffed cloth body and legs, composition gauntlet hands. Composition shoulderhead; celluloid sleep eyes; moulded hair; open-closed mouth, tongue painted darker than the lips. Mark: on shoulderplate, DTMCo.; original label, KUDLEE/BABY/Kapok filled/MADE IN CANADA/BY/DOMINION TOY CO. LTD./TORONTO.
Ref.No.: D of C, CN28, p. 174.

Mint $275.00   Ex. $250.00   G. $195.00   F. $130.00

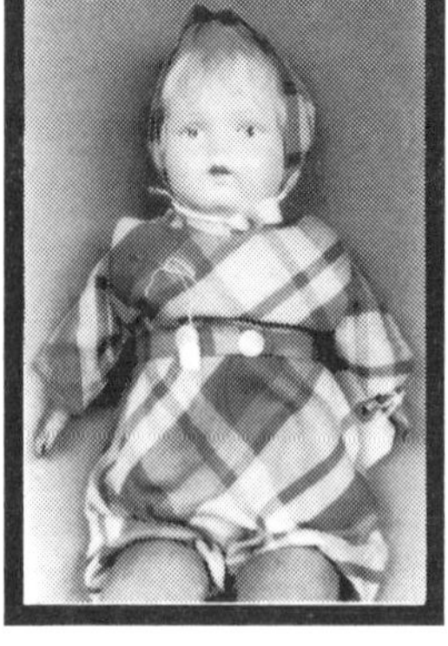

DOMINION - 1924

ca.1924. 21 in. (53.5 cm). Excelsior stuffed body, legs and upper arms, composition forearms, crier in the body. Composition shoulderhead; painted blue eyes with fine black line over each eye, painted upper lashes; blond mohair wig; closed mouth. Mark: D.T.C. on shoulderplate.
Ref.No.: D of C, CF4, p. 174.

Mint $195.00   Ex. $150.00   G. $125.00   F $75.00

DOMINION - 1926

ca.1926. 14 in. (35.5 cm). All composition bent-limb baby. Composition open crown head; blue celluloid sleep eyes with painted lashes; blond mohair wig; open-closed mouth showing two painted teeth. Mark: MADE IN CANADA/D.T.M.C. on the body.
Ref.No.: D of C, CD33, p.175.

Mint $250.00   Ex. $215.00   G. $175.00   F. $130.00

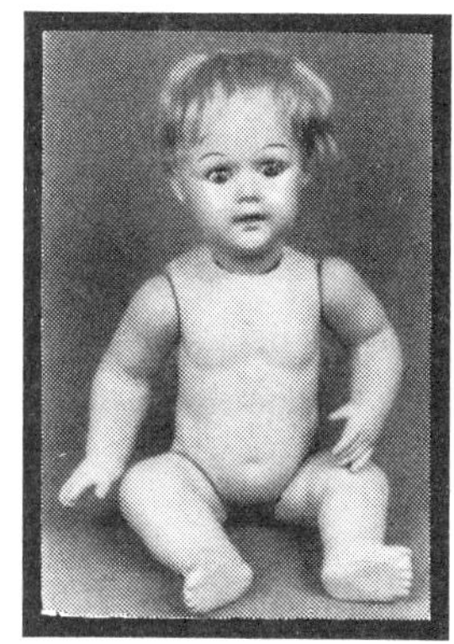

DOMINION - 1926

ca.1926. 27 in. (69 cm). Cloth body very long and slender. Composition head; brown painted side-glancing eyes with highlights; a fine black line around the eye with painted upper and lower lashes; grey eye shadow and a fine black line above the eye; brows are a series of separate strokes; closed mouth and nostril dots; black synthetic wig. Mark: D.T.C.
Ref.No.: D of C, CC5, p. 175.

Mint $275.00   Ex. $225.00   G. $175.00   F. $90.00

DOMINION -1926

ca.1926. 26 in. (66 cm). Long slender cloth body. Composition head; black painted eye with black eyeliner; light brown synthetic hair; closed mouth. Mark: on head, D.T.C.
Ref.No.: D of C, CQ12, p. 175.

Mint $260.00   Ex. $210.00   G. $160.00   F. $75.00

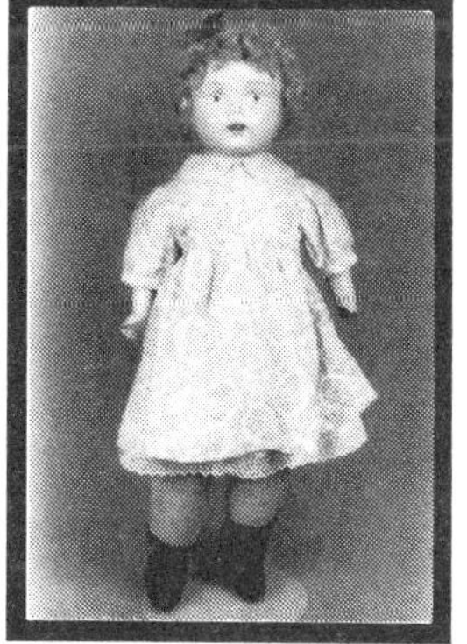

DOMINION - 1926

ca.1926. 20 in. (51 cm). Excelsior stuffed cloth body, legs and upper arms; composition forearms. Composition shoulderhead; painted blue eyes; painted upper lashes; blond mohair wig; open mouth with two teeth. Mark: D.T. CO. on shoulderplate.
Ref.No.: D of C, BZ7, p. 176.

Mint $225.00   Ex. $160.00   G. $115.00   F. $75.00

DOMINION - 1926

ca.1926. 23 in. (58.5 cm). Excelsior stuffed cloth body, legs, and upper arms; composition three-quarter arms. The cloth on the legs is pink. Composition shoulderhead; blue celluloid sleep eyes; lashes; painted upper and lower lashes; blond mohair wig; open mouth showing two inset teeth and tongue. Mark: D.T.M.C. on shoulderplate.
Ref.No.: D of C, CL25, p. 176.

Mint $240.00   Ex. $200.00   G. $160.00   F. $100.00

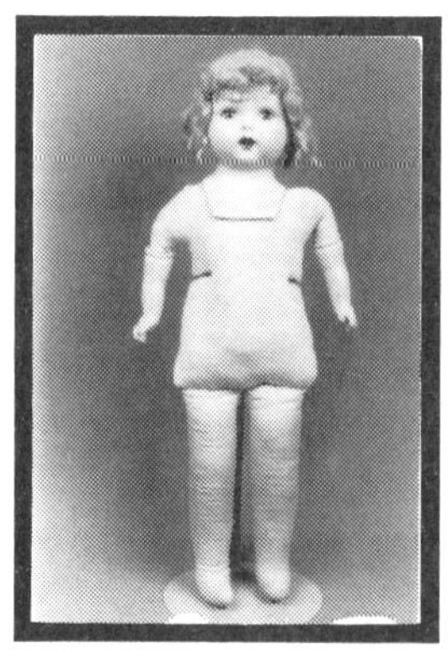

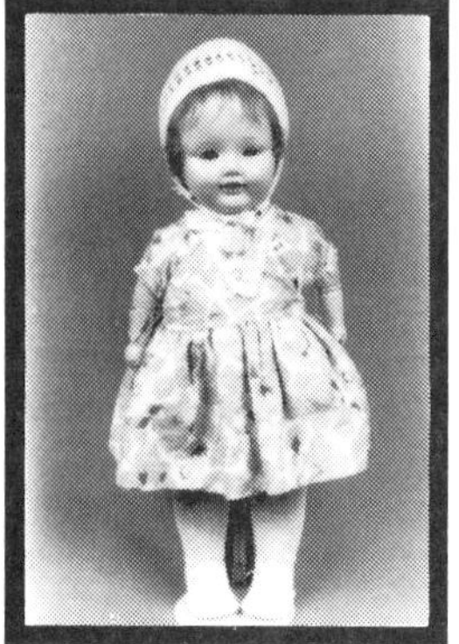

DOMINION - 1927

ca.1927. 20 in. (51 cm). Excelsior stuffed cloth body, legs and upper arms; composition forearms. Composition shoulderhead; blue tin sleep eyes, lashes, painted lower lashes; original mohair wig; open mouth showing replaced teeth and tongue. Mark: Unmarked.
Ref.No.: D of C, CM8, p. 176.

Mint $225.00   Ex. $160.00   G. $125.00   G. $85.00

DOMINION - 1927

ca.1927. 27 in. (69 cm). Cloth body; very long and slender. Composition head; painted black eyes with highlights; grey eyeshadow and a black line outlining the eye; brown mohair wig; closed mouth. Mark: D.T.C. on head.
Ref.No.: D of C, CC6, p. 177.

Mint $275.00   Ex. $225.00   G. $175.00   F. $90.00

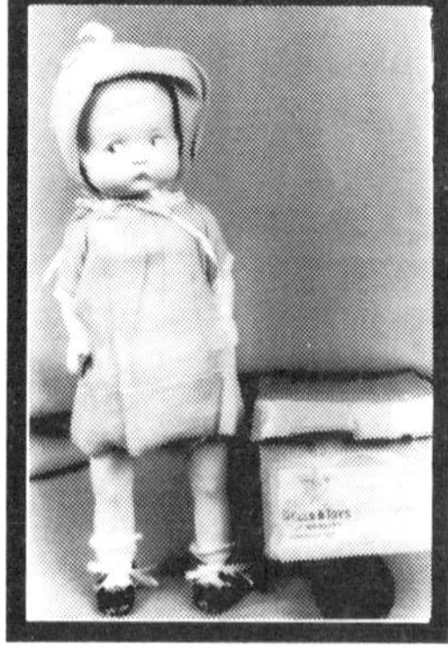

PANSY

ca.1928. 14.5 in. (37 cm). Excelsior stuffed cloth body, composition arms and legs that are attached to the body with a heavy wire going through the limb and the body and through the other limb. Composition shoulderhead; painted blue side-glancing eyes; painted upper lashes; fine black line over the eye; moulded reddish gold hair; closed mouth. Mark: Unmarked.
Ref.No.: D of C, CM9, p. 177.

Mint $250.00   Ex. $225.00   G. $175.00   F. $90.00

DOMINION - 1928

ca.1928. 27.5 in. (70 cm). Cloth body, upper arms and upper legs; composition forearms and long straight lower legs; crier in the body. Composition shoulder head; blue sleep celluloid eyes, painted upper and lower lashes; blond mohair wig with bangs; open mouth showing teeth and tongue. Mark: D.T.C. on shoulderplate.
Ref.No.: D of C, BT24, p. 177.

Mint $300.00   Ex. $250.00   G. $175.00   F. $140.00

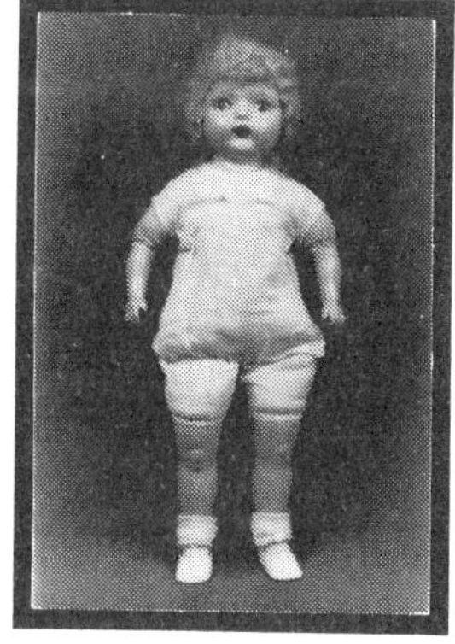

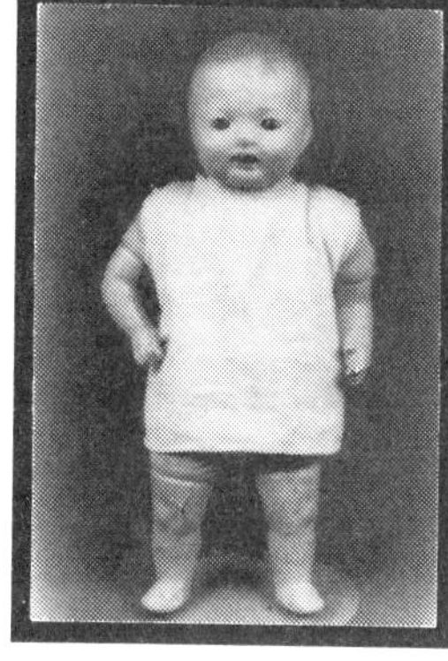

DOMINION - 1929

ca.1929. 17 in. (43 cm). Cloth body, upper arms and upper legs, composition bent-limb arms and straight legs. Composition shoulderhead with dimpled cheeks; blue celluloid sleep eyes; lashes; painted upper lashes; moulded hair painted blond; open mouth showing two inset teeth and tongue. Mark: D.T.M.C. on shoulderplate.
Ref.No: D of C, BY12, p. 178.

Mint $275.00   Ex. $195.00   G. $150.00   F. $120.00

The doll prices given in this book are intended as value guides rather than arbitrarily set prices. Each price recorded here is actually a compilation. The retail prices in this book are recorded as accurately as possible but in the case of errors, typographical, clerical or otherwise, the author and publisher assume no responsibility for any loss incurred by users of this book.

EARLE PULLAN COMPANY LIMITED
1945-1967

The Pullan company is noted for their innovative dolls. Composition Pullan dolls are hard to find.

BIRTH CERTIFICATE DOLL

1947. 20 in. (51 cm.). All composition baby, jointed hips, shoulders, and neck. Composition head; blue sleep eyes, lashes, painted upper lashes; blond wig; closed mouth. Unmarked.
Ref.No.: D of C, PU13, p. 183

Mint $200.00   Ex. $145.00   G. $85.00   F. $45.00

PULLAN - 1947

19 in. (49 cm). All composition, jointed hips, shoulders, and neck. Composition head; blue sleep eyes, lashes, painted lower lashes; original light brown mohair wig with bangs; closed painted rosebud mouth. Mark: on head, PULLAN on body, PULLAN.
Ref.No.: D of C, BH16,p. 183

Mint $200.00   Ex. $145.00   G. $85.00   F. $40.00

BABY JASPER

1948. 10 in. (25 cm). All composition dark brown bent-limb baby, jointed hips, shoulders, and neck. Composition head; eyes painted black, side glancing; moulded hair painted black; closed mouth painted red. Mark: on body, A PULLAN DOLL.
Ref.No.: D of C, BM35, p. 184

Mint $95.00   Ex. $75.00   G. $45.00   F. $25.00

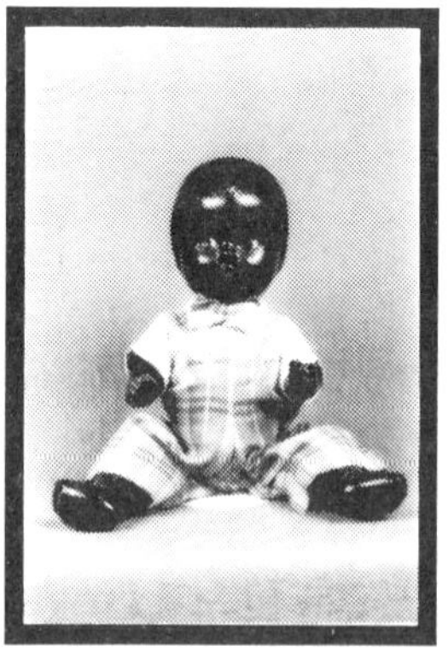

DINKY DRINKY

1948. 10 in. (25 cm). All composition baby, jointed hips and shoulders. Composition one piece head and body; eyes painted black, side glancing; moulded hair painted reddish brown; metal ring in mouth painted red. Mark: on body, PULLAN DOLL.
Ref.No.: D of C, BW28, p. 184

Mint $65.00 Ex. $45.00 G. $30.00 F. $20.00

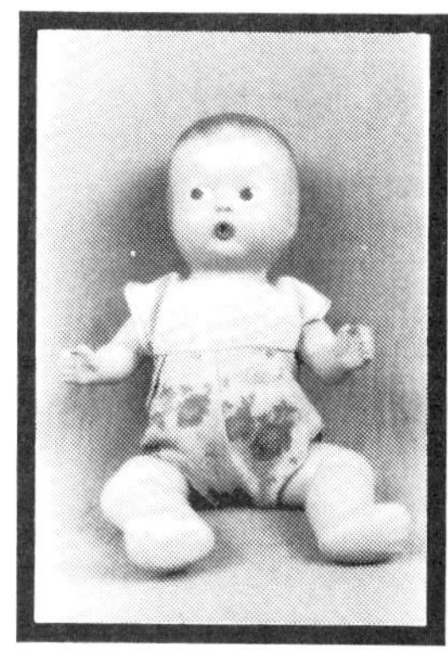

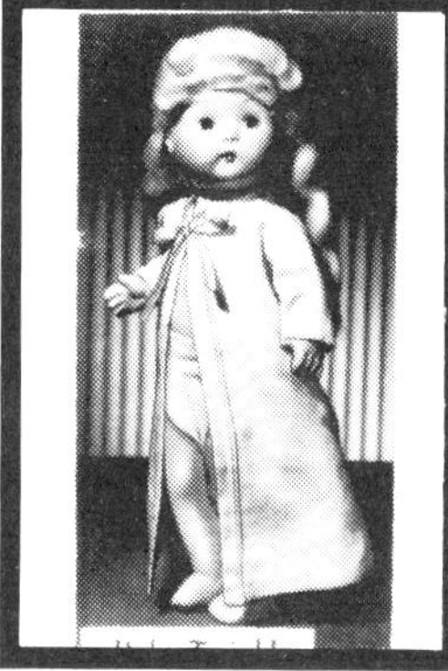

BABY TWINKLE

1948. 14.5 in. (37 cm). All composition, jointed hips, shoulders, and neck. Composition head; sleep eyes, lashes, painted upper lashes; knee-length blond wig; closed mouth.
Ref.No.: D of C, PU12, p. 184

Mint $150.00 Ex. $95.00 G. $60.00 F. $35.00

BABY PULLAN

1948. 10 in. (25 cm). All composition baby, jointed hips and shoulders. Composition one piece head and body; painted blue eyes, side-glancing; moulded hair painted reddish brown; closed mouth painted red. Mark: on body, PULLAN DOLL.
Ref.No.: D of C, BW27, p. 185

Mint $55.00 Ex. $40.00 G. $30.00 F. $20.00

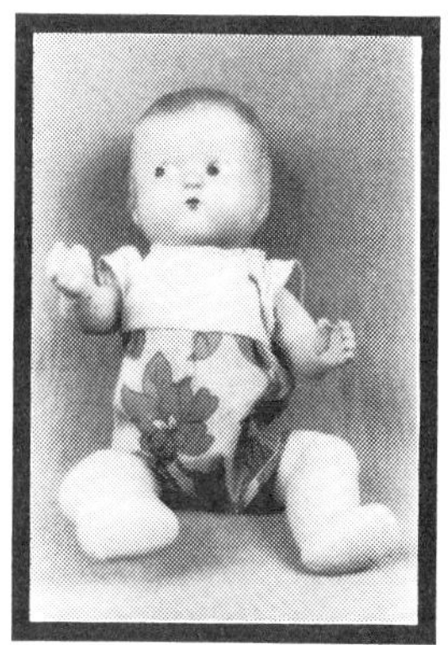

MISS PULLAN

1948. 20 in. (51 cm). All composition, jointed hips, shoulders, and neck. Composition head; sleep eyes, lashes; mohair wig; closed mouth
Ref.No.: D of C, PU11, p. 185

Mint $240.00 Ex. $185.00 G. $105.00 F. $60.00

LITTLE LULU - Cloth Body

1949. 14 in. (35.5 cm). Cloth body. Swivel type cloth head; black painted eyes; black wig with red hairbow; watermelon mouth. Unmarked.
Ref.No.: D of C, PU10, p. 185

Mint $200.00   Ex. $150.00   G. $120.00   F. $75.00

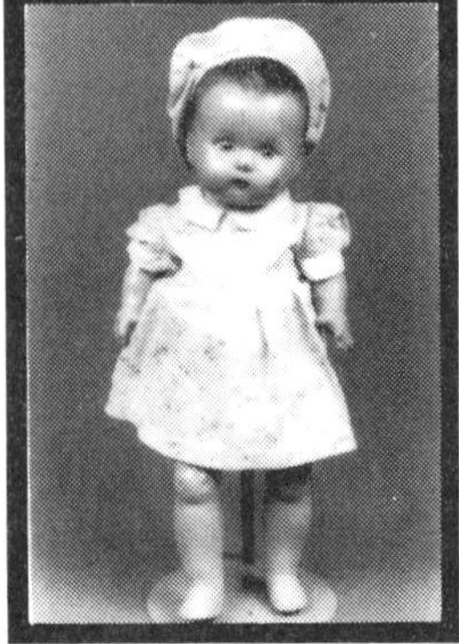

BETTY

1949. 20 in. (50.5 cm). All-composition toddler, jointed hips, shoulders, and neck. Composition head; blue painted eyes, painted upper lashes; moulded hair painted light brown; closed mouth. Mark: on head, PULLAN.
Ref.No.: D of C, CG12, p. 186

Mint $125.00   Ex. $90.00   G. $60.00   F. $30.00

SHIRLEY

1949. 14 in. (35.5 cm). All-composition toddler, jointed hips, shoulders, and neck. Composition head; brown sleep eyes, lashes, lowers painted reddish brown; original blond wig in braids; closed rosebud mouth. Mark: on head, PULLAN DOLL; on body, PULLAN DOLL.
Ref.No.: D of C, CA35, p. 186

Mint $135.00   Ex. $105.00   G. $70.00   F. $35.00

WEDDING DOLL

1950. 20 in. (51 cm). All composition, jointed hips, shoulders, and neck. Composition head; sleep eyes, lashes, painted lower lashes; brown wig; closed mouth. Unmarked.
Ref.No.: D of C, PL31, p. 186

Mint $160.00   Ex. $120.00   G. $75.00   F. $35.00

JACK and JILL

1950. 14 in. (35.5 cm). All composition, jointed hips, shoulders, and neck. Composition head; sleep eyes, lashes, painted lower lashes; moulded light brown hair; closed mouth. Unmarked.
Ref.No.: D of C, PL32, p. 187

JACK
Mint **$95.00** **Ex.** **$75.00** **G.** **$50.00** **F.** **$35.00**

JILL
Mint **$95.00** **Ex.** **$75.00** **G.** **$50.00** **F.** **$35.00**

SKATING QUEEN

1950. 18 in. (45.5 cm). All composition jointed hips, shoulders, and neck. Composition head; sleep eyes, lashes, painted lower lashes; blond wig; closed mouth. Unmarked.
Ref.No.: D of C, PU5, p. 187

Mint **$150.00** **Ex.** **$125.00** **G.** **$85.00** **F.** **$55.00**

WALKING DOLL

1951. 20 in. (50.5 cm). All composition child, jointed hips, shoulders, and neck. Composition head; brown sleep eyes, lashes; blond mohair wig; closed mouth painted red. Mark: on body, PULLAN.
Ref.No.: D of C, AZ4, p. 188

Mint **$225.00** **Ex.** **$170.00** **G.** **$90.00** **F.** **$60.00**

ALICE IN WONDERLAND

1951. 17 in. (43 cm). All composition, jointed hips, shoulders, and neck. Composition head; sleep eyes, lashes, painted lower lashes; long blond hair; open mouth showing teeth. Unmarked.
Ref.No.: D of C, PU8, p. 188

Mint **$175.00** **Ex.** **$150.00** **G.** **$85.00** **F.** **$65.00**

LOIS

1951. 17 in. (43 cm). All composition, jointed hips, shoulders, and neck. Composition head; sleep eyes, lashes, painted lower lashes; blond saran wig; closed mouth. Unmarked.
Ref.No.: D of C, PU7, p. 187

Mint $165.00   Ex. $150.00   G. $85.00   F. $65.00

SWEETIE

1951. 17in. and 21 in. (43cm and 53.5 cm). Cloth body, crier, stuffed rubber arms and legs. Composition head; sleep eyes, lashes; curled wig; closed mouth. Unmarked.
Ref.No.: D of C, PU6, p. 188

Mint $125.00   Ex. $95.00   G. $50.00   F. $30.00

LITTLE LULU - Composition

1951. 14 in. (35.5 cm). All composition, jointed hips, shoulders, and neck. Composition head; oval eyes painted all black; moulded hair painted black, red ribbon stapled on head; watermelon mouth painted red. Mark: on head, PULLAN DOLL.
Ref.No.: D of C, AW28, p. 189

Mint $225.00   Ex. $185.00   G. $110.00   F. $65.00

GIANT SQUEEZE ME DOLLS

1952. 28 in. (71.5 cm). One piece rubber latex stuffed with foam rubber. Hard plastic head; sleep eyes, lashes, painted lowers; moulded hair; open mouth, inset plastic teeth.
Ref.No.: D of C, PU4 & PU3, p. 189

GIRL
Mint $150.00   Ex. $110.00   G. $75.00   F. $50.00
BOY
Mint $150.00   Ex. $110.00   G. $75.00   F. $50.00

BABY LOVIE

1953. 25 in. (63.5 cm). Cloth body, crier, stuffed rubber arms and legs. Composition head; sleep eyes, lashes; curled mohair wig; closed mouth. Unmarked.
Ref.No.: D of C, PU1, p. 190

Mint $135.00   Ex. $100.00   G. $55.00   F. $35.00

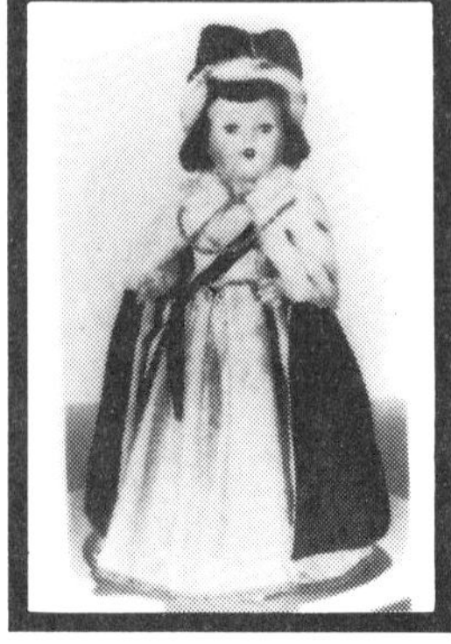

CORONATION DOLL

1953. All composition, jointed hips, shoulders, and neck. Composition head; sleep eyes, lashes; brown wig; open mouth showing teeth. Unmarked.
Ref.No.: D of C, PU2, p. 189

Mint $250.00   Ex. $185.00   G. $95.00   F. $45.00

LUCILLE

1954. 17 in., 19 in. and 23 in. (43 cm., 48.5cm. and 58.5 cm.). Cloth body with crier, stuffed rubber arms and legs. Vinyl head; sleep eyes, lashes; deeply moulded blond hair; open-closed mouth. Unmarked.
Ref.No.: D of C, PL36, p. 190

Mint $120.00   Ex. $85.00   G. $45.00   F. $30.00

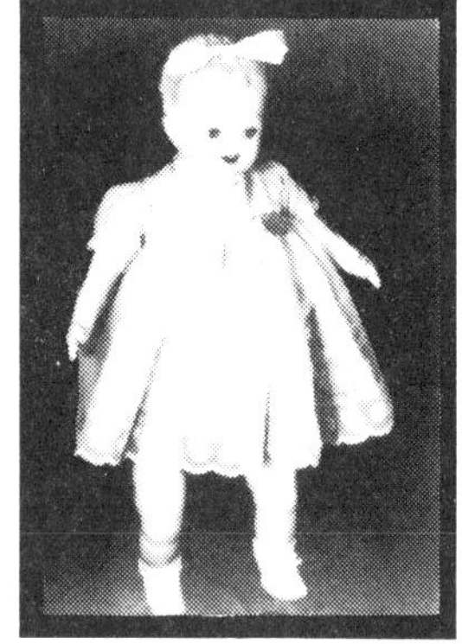

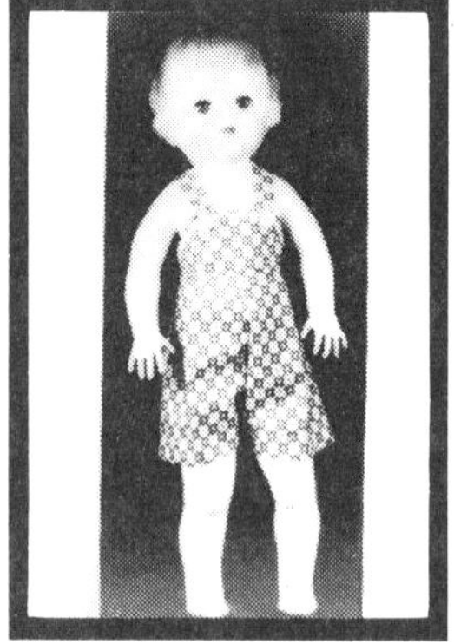

SUNSHINE TWIN

1954. 25 in. (63.5 cm). One-piece stuffed rubber, with cryer. Vinyl head; sleep eyes, lashes; deeply moulded light brown hair; closed mouth. Unmarked.
Ref.No.: D of C, PL37, p. 191

Mint $120.00   Ex. $85.00   G. $45.00   F. $25.00

SUNSHINE TWIN

1954. 25 in. (63.5 cm). One-piece stuffed rubber body, squeeze voice. Vinyl head; sleep eyes, lashes; deeply moulded light brown hair; open-closed mouth. Unmarked.
Ref.No.: D of C, PU0, p. 191

Mint $120.00   Ex. $85.00   G. $45.00   F. $25.00

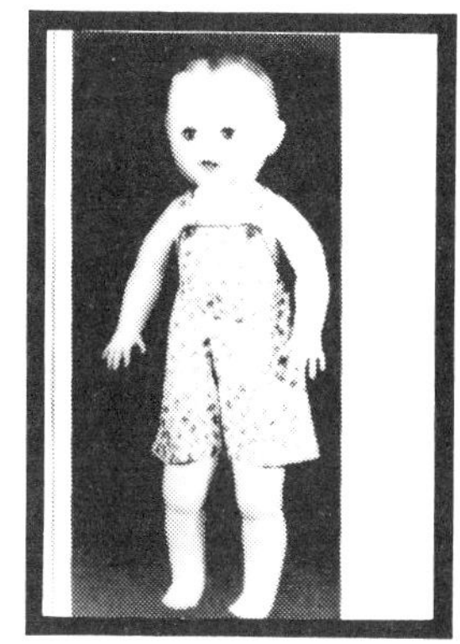

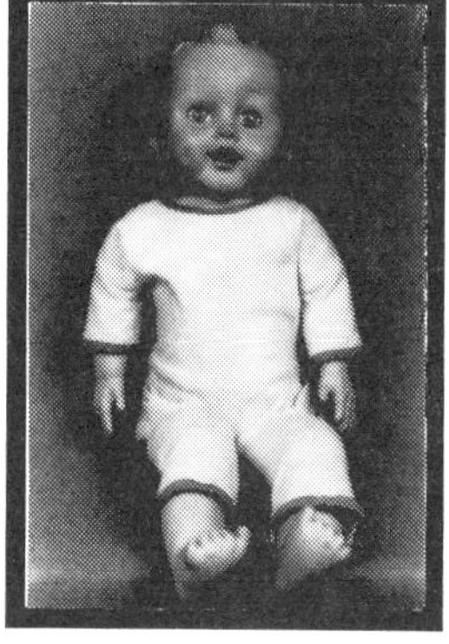

BILLY

1954. 20 in. (51 cm). One piece latex rubber body. Vinyl head with dimples; hazel sleep eyes with lashes and painted lower lashes; deeply moulded hair with a curl in the front, light brown; open-closed mouth. Mark: on head; PULLAN.
Ref.No.: D of C, CW8, p. 190

Mint $90.00   Ex. $60.00   G. $35.00   F. $20.00

BEDTIME BUNTING

1955. 20 in. and 22 in. (51 cm and 56 cm). Latex body with squeeze voice. Vinyl head; sleep eyes, lashes; moulded light brown hair; open-closed mouth. Unmarked.
Ref.No.: D of C, PL34, p. 191

Mint $95.00   Ex. $65.00   G. $35.00   F. $20.00

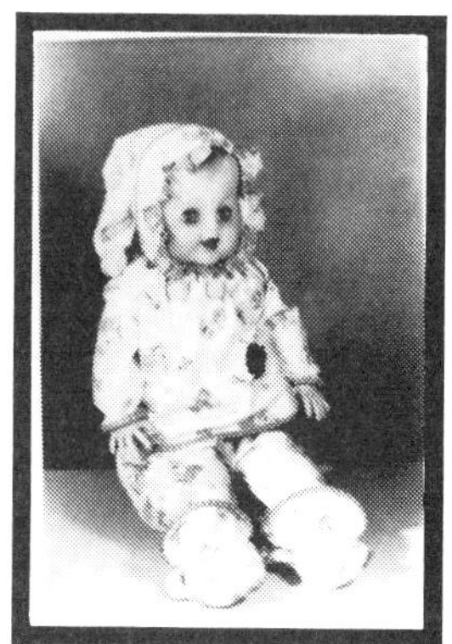

OVERALLS BABY

1955. 20 in. (50.5 cm). Latex body and legs, squeeze voice, vinyl arms. Vinyl head; sleep eyes, lashes; moulded light brown hair; open-closed mouth. Unmarked.
Ref.No.: D of C, PL35, p. 191

Mint $95.00   Ex. $65.00   G. $35.00   F. $20.00

CANDY

1956. 17 in. (43 cm). One-piece vinyl skin body with wire armature inside to enable the doll to assume any position. Vinyl head; sleep eyes, lashes, painted lower lashes; brown rooted saran hair; mouth open-closed. Unmarked.
Ref.No.: D of C, PL28, p. 192

Mint $75.00   Ex. $60.00   G. $35.00   F. $20.00

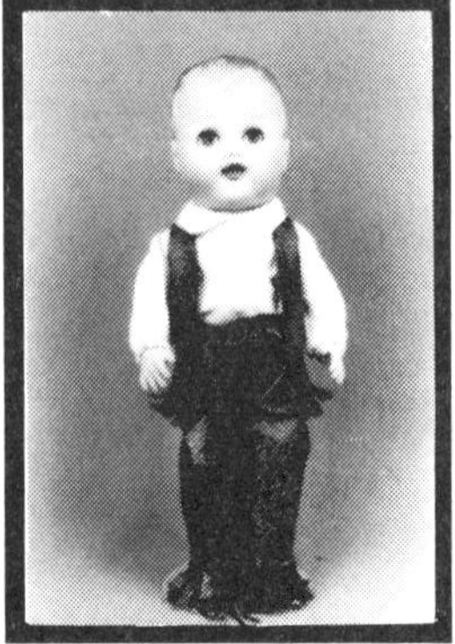

PULLAN - 1956

15 in. (38 cm). One piece vinyl body, jointed neck. Vinyl head; blue sleep eyes, lashes, painted lower lashes; very detailed moulded hair painted brown; open-closed mouth. Mark: on head, PULLAN.
Ref.No.: D of C, BN25, p. 192

Mint $50.00   Ex. $40.00   G. $25.00   F. $15.00

MINDY

1957. 15 in. (38 cm). One piece doll with brown vinyl skin with flexiwire armature. Brown vinyl head; painted eyes; black heavily detailed moulded hair in braids; open-closed mouth. Umarked.
Ref.No.: D of C, PL30, p. 192

Mint $125.00   Ex. $95.00   G. $75.00   F. $45.00

SKISUIT DOLL

1957. 17 in. and 24 in. (43 cm and 61 cm). One-piece vinyl body with flexiwire, squeeze voice. Vinyl head; sleep eyes, lashes; rooted curly saran hair; open-closed mouth. Unmarked.
Ref.No.: D of C, PL24, p. 193

24 in. Size
Mint $75.00   Ex. $60.00   G. $35.00   F. $20.00

17 in. Size
Mint $65.00   Ex. $50.00   G. $30.00   F. $15.00

BABY BUNTING

1957. 22 in. (56 cm). Vinyl body with flexiwire, squeeze voice. Vinyl head; sleep eyes, lashes; rooted curly saran hair; open-closed mouth. Unmarked.
Ref.No.: D of C, PL25, p. 193

Mint $75.00   Ex. $60.00   G. $35.00   F. $20.00

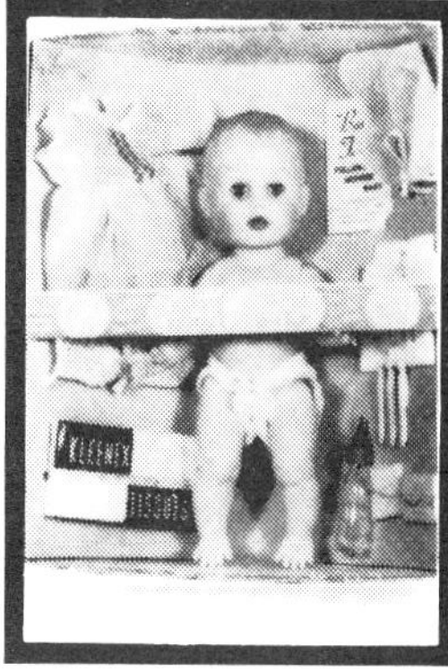

BABY TEARS

1957. 14 in. and 16 in. (35.5cm and 40.5 cm). Plastic body, jointed hips, shoulders, and neck. Vinyl head; sleep eyes, lashes, moulded hair, open mouth nurser.
Ref.No.: D of C, PL27, p. 193

MOULDED HAIR:
Mint $60.00   Ex. $40.00   G. $25.00   F. $15.00

ROOTED HAIR:
Mint $70.00   Ex. $45.00   G. $25.00   F. $15.00

BALLERINA

1957. 17 in. (43 cm). Vinyl body with wire in the legs to allow the doll to assume any position. Vinyl head; sleep eyes, lashes; rooted saran hair in chignon style; closed mouth. Unmarked.
Ref.No.: D of C, PL29, p. 194

Mint $95.00   Ex. $65.00   G. $35.00   F. $20.00

CINDY

1957. 14 in. (35.5 cm). One piece doll with brown vinyl skin, jointed neck. Vinyl head; brown sleep eyes, lashes, painted lower lashes; very curly rooted black hair; closed mouth. Mark: on head, PULLAN 2; on body, A; on foot, V-15-2.
Ref.No.: D of C, CH9, p. 194

Mint $80.00   Ex. $60.00   G. $30.00   F. $20.00

BRIDE

1958. 17 in. (43 cm). Plastic teen body, jointed hips, shoulders, and neck. Vinyl head, earrings; blue sleep eyes, lashes; rooted saran blond hair; closed mouth. Mark: PULLAN.
Ref.No.: D of C, CT21, p. 194

Mint $75.00   Ex. $50.00   G. $35.00   F. $20.00

94

MOTHER and FAMILY

1958. Mother, 21 in. (53.5 cm), daughter, 12 in. (30.5 cm), son, 10 in. (25.5 cm), baby, 8 in. (20.5 cm). Mother: vinyl body, jointed shoulders and neck. Vinyl head; sleep eyes, lashes; rooted saran curls; closed mouth. Daughter: vinyl body; vinyl head; glassine eyes; rooted hair; closed mouth. Son: vinyl body and head with freckles; painted side-glancing eyes; moulded hair; closed smiling mouth. Baby: vinyl body and head; painted eyes; moulded hair. Unmarked.

Ref.No.: D of C, PL26, p. 196

Mint $200.00   Ex. $170.00   G. $95.00   F. $65.00

RAGS to RICHES DOLL

1958. 21 in. (50.5 cm). Plastic teen body and legs, vinyl arms, jointed shoulders and neck. Vinyl head; blue sleep eyes, lashes; rooted reddish-brown long saran hair with bangs and originally worn in a ponytail; closed mouth painted red. Mark: on neck, PULLAN; on back, A; sole of left foot 16; sole of right foot VH3-21.
Ref.No.: D of C, BF33, p. 196

Mint $75.00   Ex. $55.00   G. $35.00   F. $20.00

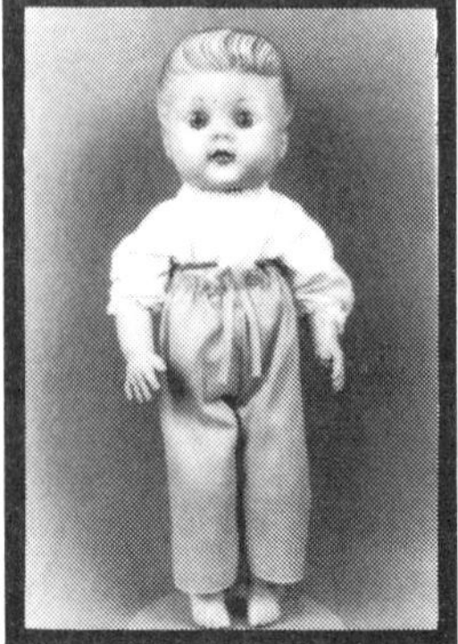

BABS

1957. 15 in. (38 cm). One piece vinyl body. Vinyl head; fixed brown eyes; deeply moulded hair in a ponytail; closed mouth. Mark: on head, PULLAN.
Ref.No.: D of C, CO20 & CO21, p. 195

Mint $60.00   Ex. $40.00   G. $30.00   F. $20.00

ORIENTAL PRINCESS

1958. 20 in. (50.5 cm). Plastic teen doll, jointed at waist, elbows, knees, hips, shoulders, and ankles. Vinyl head with pierced ears, earrings; blue sleep eyes, lashes, painted lower lashes; rooted long black saran hair worn up in a roll; closed mouth. Mark: on head, PULLAN.
Ref.No.: D of C, CG17, p. 196

Mint $95.00   Ex. $75.00   G. $45.00   F. $25.00

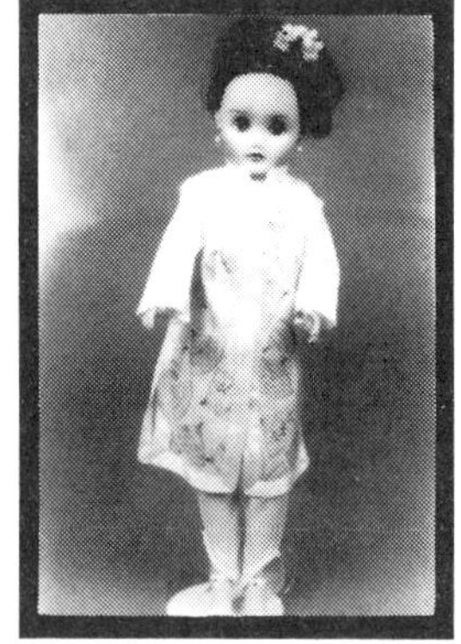

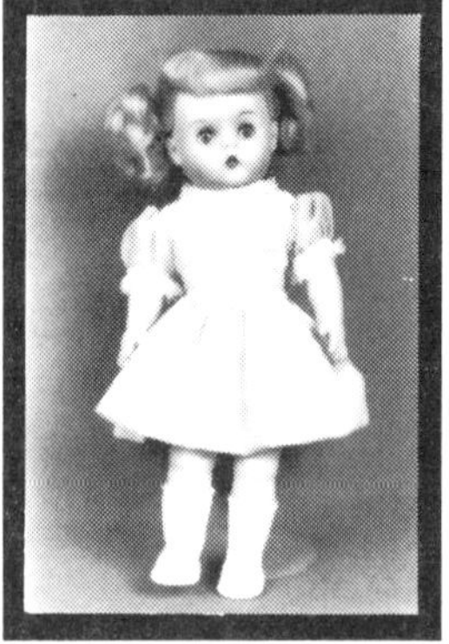

DREAM DOLL

1958. 16 in. (40.5 cm). One piece body, soft vinyl skin stuffed with foam, jointed neck. Vinyl head; blue sleep eyes, lashes, painted lower lashes; rooted blond saran hair; closed mouth painted red. Mark: on head, PULLAN.
Ref.No.: D of C, BH14, p. 197

Mint $55.00   Ex. $45.00   G.   35.00   F. $20.00

BABY PRINCESS

1959. 23 in. (57 cm). Plastic baby body, jointed hips, shoulders, and neck. Vinyl head; sleep eyes, lashes; rooted blond saran curls with long forehead curl; open mouth nurser. Unmarked.
Ref.No.: D of C, PL2, p. 197

Mint $75.00   Ex. $50.00   G. $40.00   F. $25.00

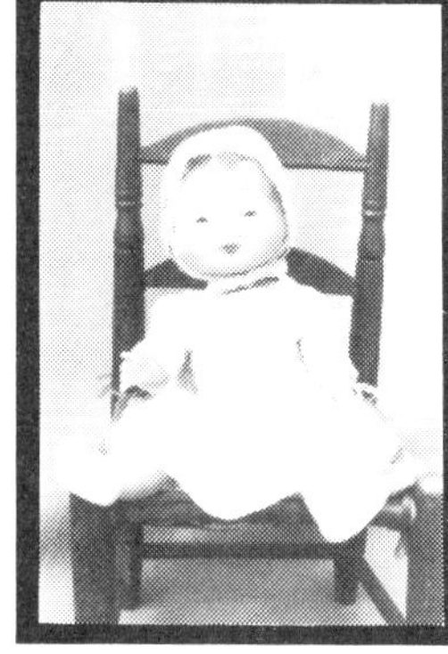

PULLAN

1959. 12.5 in. (32 cm). Plastic body, jointed hips, shoulder, and neck. Vinyl head; blue inset eyes; rooted reddish-blond straight hair; closed mouth painted red. Mark: on head, PULLAN.
Ref.No.: D of C, BJ23, p. 197

Mint $75.00   Ex. $55.00   G. $40.00   F. $25.00

BRIDE

1959. 15 in. (37 cm). Plastic body, jointed hips, shoulders, and neck. Vinyl head; blue sleep eyes, lashes, painted lower lashes; rooted brown curled hair; closed mouth. Mark: on head, PULLAN; wearing original label.
Ref.No.: D of C, BX8, p. 198.

Mint $80.00   Ex. $55.00   G. $35.00   F. $25.00

ANNETTE

1959. 15 in. (38 cm). Plastic body, jointed hips, shoulders, and head. Vinyl head; blue sleep eyes, lashes, three painted upper lashes; rooted short blond hair with bangs; closed mouth. Mark: on head, PULLAN.
Ref.No.: D of C, BZ23, p. 198

Mint $75.00   Ex. $60.00   G. $35.00   F. $20.00

MISS LUCKY GREEN

1960. 15 in. (38 cm). Plastic body, jointed hips, shoulders, and neck. Vinyl head; blue sleep eyes, lashes, painted lower lashes; rooted honey blond saran hair in ponytail and bangs; closed mouth. Mark: on head, PULLAN.
Ref.No.: D of C, CP20, p. 199

Mint $85.00   Ex. $60.00   G. $40.00   F. $25.00

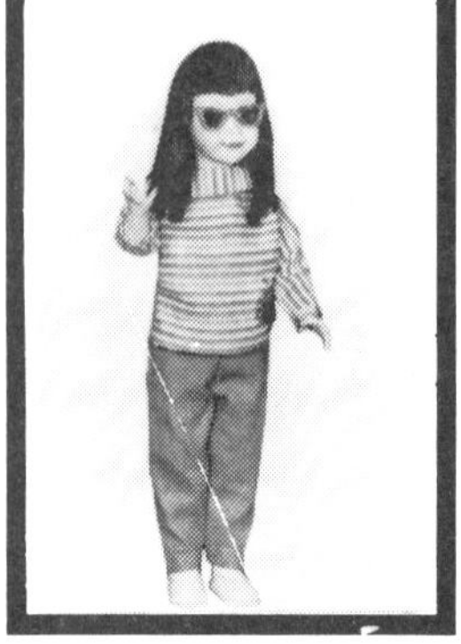

BEATNIK DOLL

1960. 21 in. (53.5 cm). Plastic, jointed hips, shoulders, and neck. Vinyl head. Sleep eyes. Rooted long straight black saran hair. Mouth closed, smiling. Unmarked.
Ref.No.: D of C, PL6, p. 198

Mint $115.00   Ex. $90.00   G. $65.00   F. $35.00

WENDY ANN - 35 in.

1960. 35 in. (89 cm). Plastic body, jointed hips, shoulders, and neck. Vinyl head; sleep eyes, lashes; rooted curly saran hair; closed mouth. Unmarked.
Ref.No.: D of C, PL4, p. 199

Mint $135.00   Ex. $95.00   G. $60.00   F. $40.00

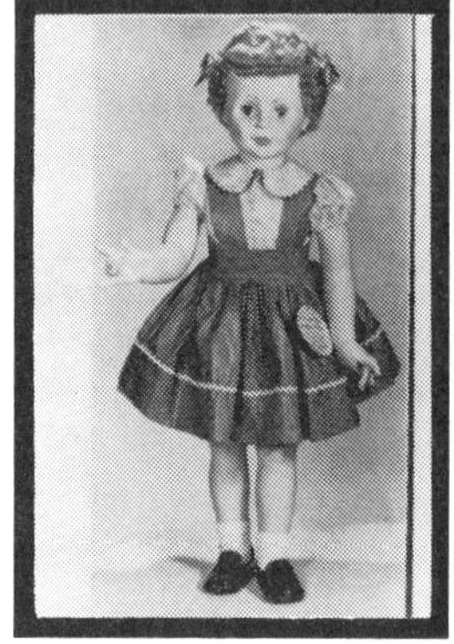

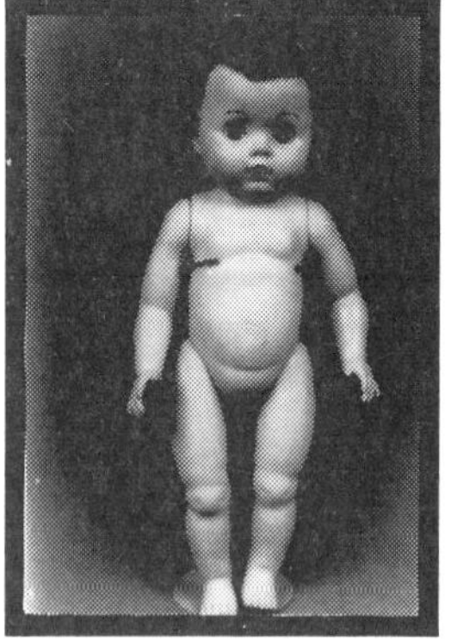

JILL

1961. 20 in. (51 cm). Plastic toddler, jointed hips, shoulders, and neck; vinyl head; blue plastic sleep eyes, lashes, painted lower lashes; rooted light brown curls; open mouth nurser. Mark: on head, PULLAN; on body, PULLAN.
Ref.No.: D of C, CW14, p. 199

Mint $65.00   Ex. $45.00   G. $35.00   F. $25.00

LOIS

1961. 32 in. (81 cm). Plastic body, jointed hips, shoulders, and neck. Vinyl head; sleep eyes, lashes, rooted curly saran hair; closed mouth. Unmarked.
Ref.No.: D of C, PL15, p. 200

Mint $120.00   Ex. $85.00   G. $55.00   F. $45.00

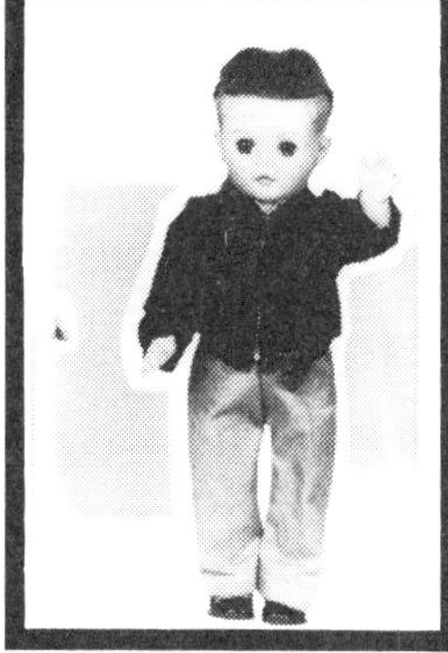

BOBBY

1961. 20 in. (51 cm). Plastic body, jointed hips, shoulders, and neck. Vinyl head; sleep eyes, lashes; moulded light brown hair; closed mouth. Unmarked.
Ref.No.: D of C, PL16, p. 200

Mint $75.00   Ex. $50.00   G. $40.00   F. $25.00

LITTLE MISTER BAD BOY

1961. 16 in. (40.5 cm). Plastic body, vinyl arms, jointed hips, shoulders, and neck. Hard vinyl head; blue sleep eyes, lashes, painted lower lashes; well defined moulded hair painted brown; closed mouth painted red. Mark: on head, PULLAN.
Ref.No.: D of C, BN26, p. 200

Mint $85.00   Ex. $60.00   G. $50.00   F. $20.00

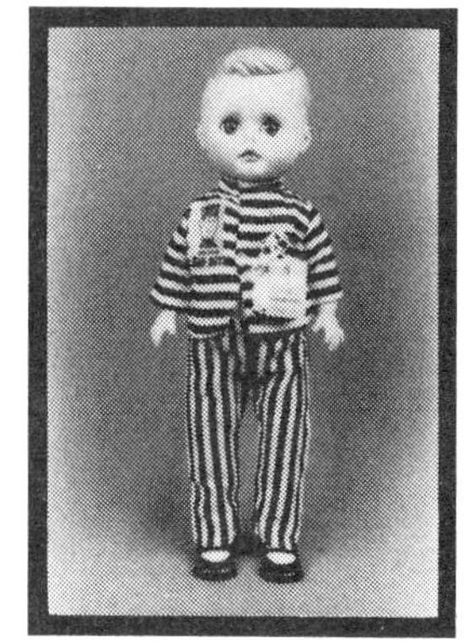

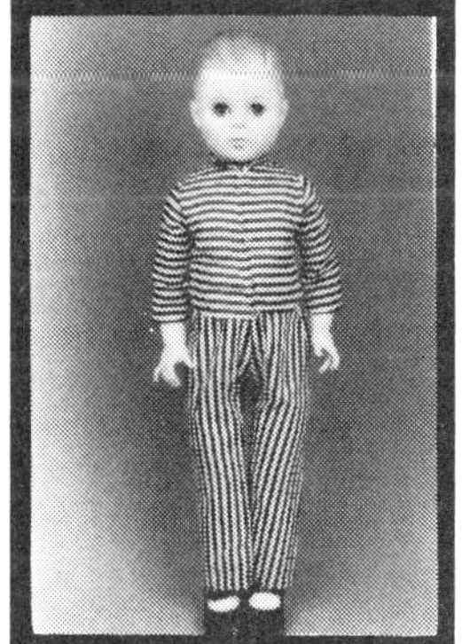

LITTLE MISTER BAD BOY

1961. 30 in. (76.5 cm). Plastic body, jointed hips, shoulders, and head. Hard vinyl head; blue sleep eyes, lashes; moulded light brown hair; closed mouth. Mark: on head, PULLAN.
Ref.No.: D of C; BZ19 p. 201

Mint $140.00   Ex. $105.00   G. $70.00   F. $40.00

BOBBY

1961. l5 in. (38 cm). Plastic body, jointed hips, shoulders, and neck. Hard vinyl head; blue sleep eyes, lashes, painted lower lashes; well defined moulded hair painted light brown; closed mouth. Mark: on head, PULLAN; on body, PULLAN.
Ref.No.: D of C, BN30, p. 202

Mint $55.00 Ex. $45.00 G. $30.00 F. $20.00

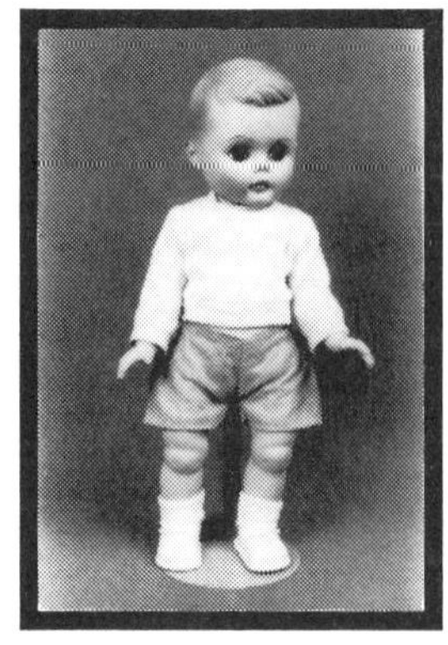

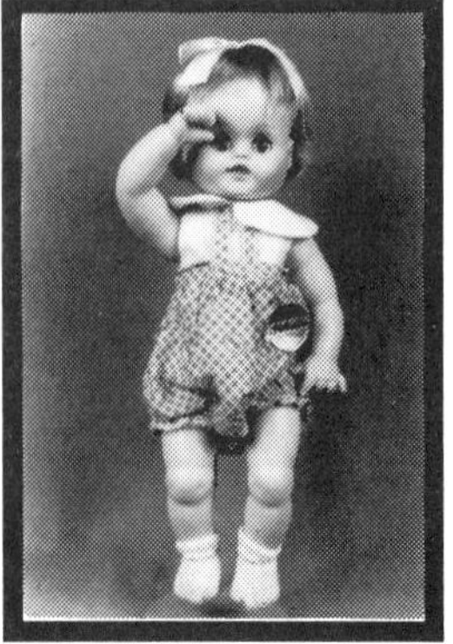

DOLLY POP

1961. 15.5 in. (40 cm). Plastic toddler, jointed hips, shoulders, and neck; spring in the right hand to bring a lollipop to her mouth. Vinyl head; blue sleep eyes, lashes, painted lower lashes; rooted straight blond hair over moulded hair; open mouth nurser. Mark: on head, PULLAN.
Ref.No.: D of C, BQ20, p. 202

Note: Prices for working order.

Mint $85.00 Ex. $70.00 G. $35.00 F. $25.00

CLEOPATRA

1962. 22 in. (56 cm). Plastic, jointed hips, shoulders, and neck. Vinyl head; painted eyes with eyeshadow and eyeliner; rooted extra long black saran hair; closed mouth. Unmarked.
Ref.No.: D of C, PL8, p. 202.

Note: This is a scarce doll.

Mint $125.00 Ex. $105.00 G. $75.00 F. $45.00

ANGEL FACE

1962. 14 in. (37 cm). Plastic toddler, jointed hips, shoulders, and neck. Vinyl head; blue sleep eyes, lashes; rooted brown curls with bangs; open mouth nurser. Mark: on head, PULLAN.
Ref.No.: D of C, BN16, p. 203

Mint $50.00 Ex. $40.00 G. $30.00 F. $20.00

VALERIE

1962. 23 in. (58 cm). Plastic body, jointed hips, shoulders, and neck. Vinyl head; blue sleep eyes, lashes, painted lower lashes; rooted short blond hair; closed mouth. Mark: on head, PULLAN/MADE IN CANADA.
Ref.No.: D of C, AM34, p. 203

Mint $65.00   Ex. $45.00   G. $35.00   F. $25.00

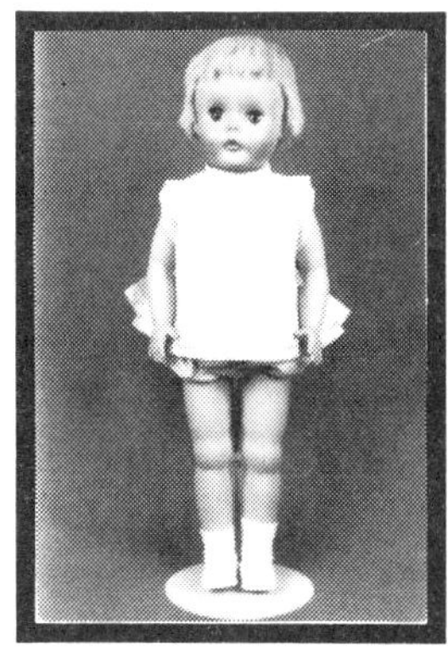

ESKIMO

1962. 16 in. (40.5 cm). Plastic body and legs, vinyl arms, jointed hips, shoulders, and neck. Vinyl head; inset brown plastic eyes; rooted short straight black hair; closed mouth. Mark: on head, PULLAN.
Ref.No.: D of C, BZ32, p. 204

Mint $75.00   Ex. $55.00   G. $45.00   F. $30.00

WENDY ANN

1963. 36 in. (91.5 cm). Plastic body, jointed hips, shoulders, and neck. Vinyl head; sleep eyes, lashes; rooted long blond straight hair; closed mouth. Unmarked.

Ref.No.: D. of C, PL11, p. 204

Mint $135.00   Ex. $95.00   G. $60.00   F. $40.00

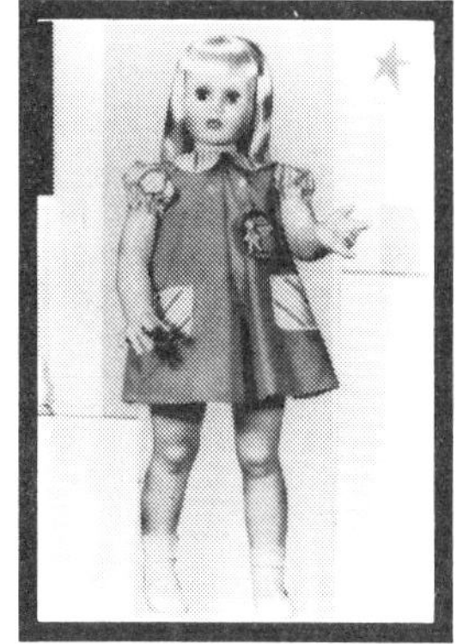

FRITZ and FREDA

1963. 13 in. (33 cm). Plastic bodies, jointed hips, shoulders, and neck. Vinyl head; painted eyes; deeply moulded painted hair; closed mouth. Unmarked.

Ref.No.: D. of C, PL13, p 206

SINGLE:
Mint $80.00 Ex. $60.00 G. $40.00 F. $30.00

PAIR:
Mint $175.00 Ex. $130.00 G. $90.00 F. $70.00

POOR PITIFUL PEARL

1963. 16 in. (40.5 cm). Plastic body and legs, vinyl arms, jointed hips, shoulders, and neck. Vinyl head with freckles; brown sleep eyes, lashes and painted upper lashes; rooted long blond hair; watermelon mouth. Mark: on head, PULLAN. *Ref.No.: D of C, BF4, p. 205.*

Note: Hard to find as few were made.

Mint $95.00   **Ex.** $75.00   **G.** $60.00   **F.** $40.00

LANA LEE

1963. 16 in. (40.5 cm). Plastic body, jointed hips, shoulders, and neck. Vinyl head; blue sleep eyes, lashes, painted lashes at outside upper edge of eye; rooted blond hair; watermelon mouth. Mark: on head, PULLAN/MADE IN CANADA. *Ref.No.: D of C, CI6, p. 205*

Mint $65.00   **Ex.** $45.00   **G.** $35.00   **F.** $25.00

LOUIE

1963. 12 in. (30.5 cm). Plastic jointed hips, shoulders, and neck. Vinyl head; painted side-glancing eyes; rooted red saran curls; closed watermelon mouth. Umarked. *Ref.No.: D of C, PL10, p. 206*

Mint $50.00   **Ex.** $40.00   **G.** $30.00   **F.** $25.00

PEACHES

1964. 12 in. (30.5 cm). Plastic body and legs, vinyl arms, jointed hips, shoulders and neck. Vinyl head, glassine fixed eyes, moulded lashes; rooted brown hair; open closed mouth. Unmarked. *Ref.No.: D of C, PL12, p. 207*

Mint $40.00   **Ex.** $30.00   **G.** $20.00   **F.** $10.00

VIC and VICKY

1964. 10 in. (23 cm). Plastic toddlers, vinyl arms, jointed hips, shoulders, and neck. Vinyl head; painted side-glancing blue eyes, painted lashes. Boy has rooted strawberry blond hair, girl has rooted blond hair. Open-closed mouth. Mark: on head, PULLAN, MADE IN CANADA.
Ref.No.: D of C, BN14, p. 207

PAIR:
Mint $80.00   **Ex.** $60.00   **G.** $40.00   **F.** $30.00
SINGLE
Mint $35.00   **Ex.** $25.00   **G.** $15.00   **F.** $10.00

MARLANE

1964. 12 in. (30 cm). Plastic teen body and legs, vinyl arms, jointed hips, shoulders, and neck. Vinyl head; painted side-glancing eyes, painted upper lashes; rooted straight red saran hair; closed mouth. Mark: on head, PULLAN.
Ref.No.: D of C, CF27, p. 208

Mint $35.00   **Ex.** $25.00   **G.** $15.00   **F.** $8.00

BOXER

1965. 12 in. (30.5 cm). Plastic, jointed hips, shoulders, and neck. Vinyl head; painted side-glancing eyes with one permanently black eye; rooted light brown hair; closed watermelon mouth. Unmarked.
Ref.No.: D of C, PL23, p. 208.

Note: Not many were made.

Mint $55.00 Ex. $45.00 G. $35.00 F. $20.00

PRETTY PENNY

1965. 30 in. (76.5 cm). Plastic, jointed hips, shoulders, and neck. Vinyl head; sleep eyes, lashes, eyeshadow; rooted long straight saran hair with bangs; open-closed mouth. Unmarked.
Ref.No.: D of C, PL21, p. 208

Mint $90.00 Ex. $70.00 G. $50.00 F. $30.00

MISS MARJIE

1965. 12 in. (30 cm). Plastic body, vinyl arms, jointed hips, shoulders, and neck. Vinyl head; painted side-glancing eyes; rooted blond curly hair with a "growing" section on top; closed mouth. Mark: on head, MARGIE.
Ref.No.: D of C, BN33, p. 209

Mint $40.00 Ex. $30.00 G. $20.00 F. $10.00

PEACHES INDIAN GIRL

1965. 12 in. (30 cm). Brown plastic body and legs, vinyl arms wit upturned hands, jointed hips, shoulders, and neck. Vinyl head; brown sleep eyes, plastic lashes; incised brows; rooted straight black saran hair; open-closed mouth. Mark: on head, PULLAN/MADE IN CANADA; on body, PULLAN.
Ref.No.: D of C, CH12, p. 209.

Mint $45.00 Ex. $35.00 G. $25.00 F. $15.00

PROSPECTOR

1966. 14 in. (35.5 cm). Cloth body formed by clothing, vinyl arms, vinyl boots. Cloth head with vinyl face; black painted eyes; grey fake fur hair, beard is rooted into face; smiling watermelon mouth. Mark: tag on body, EARLE PULLAN CO. LTD./TORONTO, CANADA.
Ref.No.: D of C, XH26, p. 209

Mint $40.00   Ex. $30.00   G. $25.00   F. $15.00

TWINKLE ESKIMO

1966. 10 in. (25.5 cm). Vinyl body, jointed hips, shoulders, and neck. Vinyl head; painted black side-glancing eyes; rooted straight black hair; closed mouth. Unmarked.
Ref.No.: D of C, PL20, p. 210

Mint $35.00   Ex. $25.00   G. $20.00   F. $10.00

SUZANNE

1966. 17 in. (43 cm). Plastic body with vinyl arms, jointed hips, shoulders, and neck. Vinyl head; sleep eyes, lashes; rooted red saran hair; closed mouth. Unmarked.
Ref.No.: D of C, PL18, p. 210

Mint $50.00   Ex.$40.00   G. $30.00   F. $20.00

SUZANNE

1966. 16 in. (40.5 cm). Plastic body, jointed hips, shoulders, and neck. Vinyl head; blue sleep eyes, lashes, painted lower lashes; rooted platinum blond long straight saran hair; closed mouth. Mark: on head, PULLAN.

Ref.No.: D. of C, CO17, p. 210

Mint $50.00   Ex. $40.00   G. $30.00   F. $20.00

WENDY ANN - 36 in.

1962. 36 in. (91.5 cm). Plastic body, jointed hips, shoulders and neck. Vinyl head; blue sleep eyes, lashes, painted lower lashes; honey blond saran curly hair with bangs; closed mouth. Unmarked.
Ref.No.: D of C, CZ10, p. 203

Mint $135.00   Ex. $95.00   G. $60.00   F. $40.00

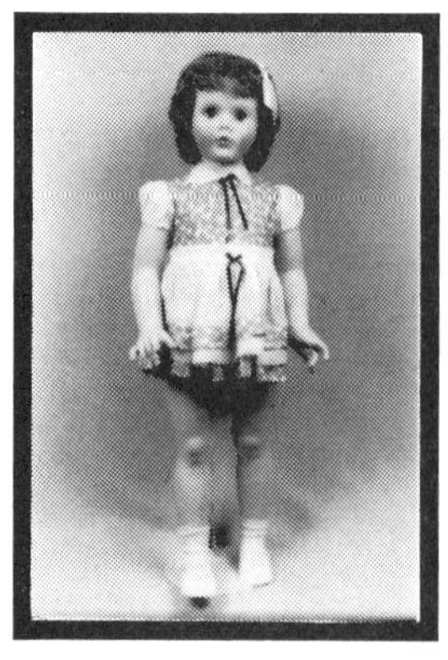

CINDY

1961. 20 in. (50.5 cm). Brown plastic body, jointed hips, shoulders and neck. Brown vinyl head; brown sleep eyes, lashes; rooted black curly hair; open mouth nurser. Unmarked:
Ref.No.: D of C, PL17, p. 201.

Mint $115.00   Ex. $85.00   G. $65.00   F. $35.00

BABY TALKS

1961. 20 in. (50.5 cm). Vinyl body, jointed hips, shoulders and neck. Vinyl head; inset plastic eyes; rooted saran hair; open mouth. BABY TALKS has a special six read voice mechanism that allows her to chuckle, goo, and giggle by squeezing her tummy and moving her to and fro. Unmarked.
Ref.No.: D of C, PL14, p. 201.

Mint $95.00   Ex. $75.00   G. $55.00   F. $35.00

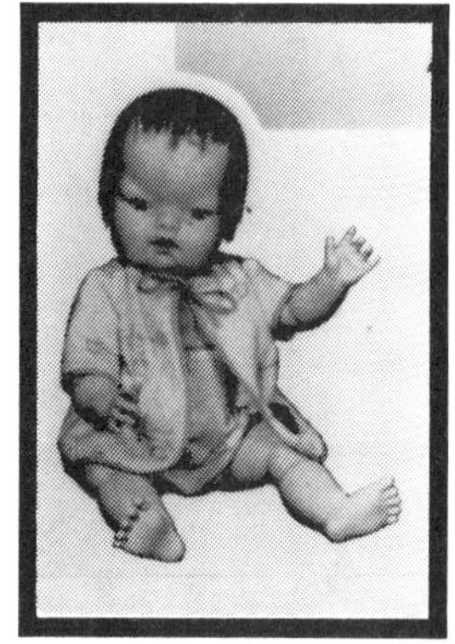

FREDA

1963. 13 in. (38 cm). Plastic body and legs, vinyl arms. Vinyl head; brown painted eyes; hair moulded into bangs and braids with bows, painted light brown; open-closed mouth showing two painted teeth. Mark: on head, PULLAN.
Ref.No.: D of C, CF22, p. 206.

Mint $80.00   Ex. $60.00   G. $40.00   F. $30.00

THE FLORENTINE STATUARY COMPANY
1917 - 1932

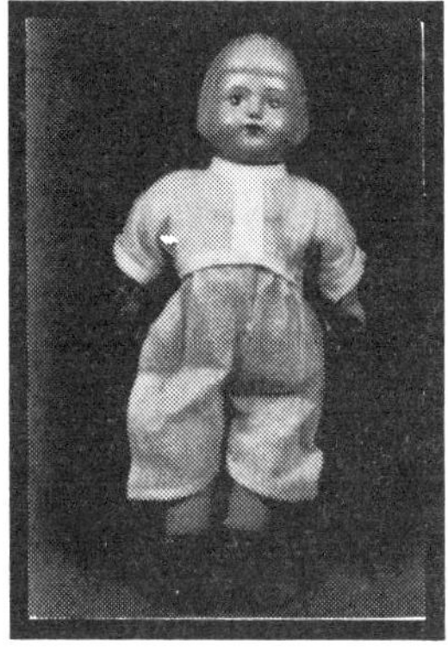

FLORENTINE - 1918

ca.1918. 12.5 in. (31 cm) Cloth body, legs and upper arms, wooden forearms and hands, painted pink. Composition shoulderhead; painted blue eyes with a fine black line over the eyes, painted brows; moulded Buster Brown hair, painted brown; closed mouth painted red, nostril dots. Mark: on shoulderplate, FLORENTINE/TORONTO.
Ref.No.: D of C, AM26, p. 211.

Mint $175.00   Ex. $150.00   G. $85.00   F. $50.00

INDIAN

ca.1918. 17 in. (43 cm). Excelsior stuffed cloth body and legs, composition gauntlet hand. Brown composition shoulderhead; black painted eyes with highlights, black line over eye; black human hair wig; closed mouth. Mark: on shoulderplate, FLORENTINE/TORONTO.
Ref.No.: D of C, CN11, p. 212.

Note: A rare doll.

Mint $300.00   Ex. $250.00   G. $175.00   F. $75.00

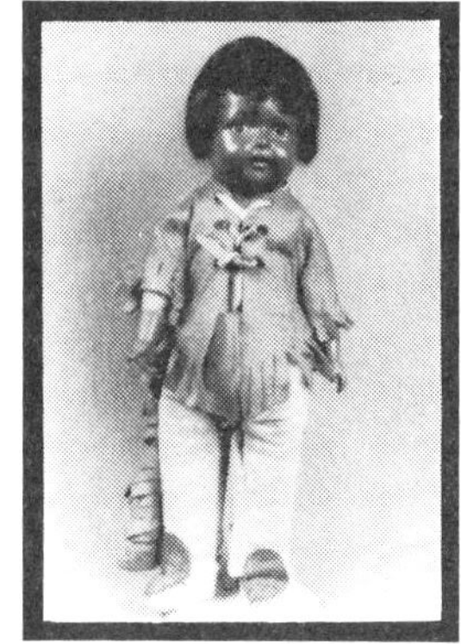

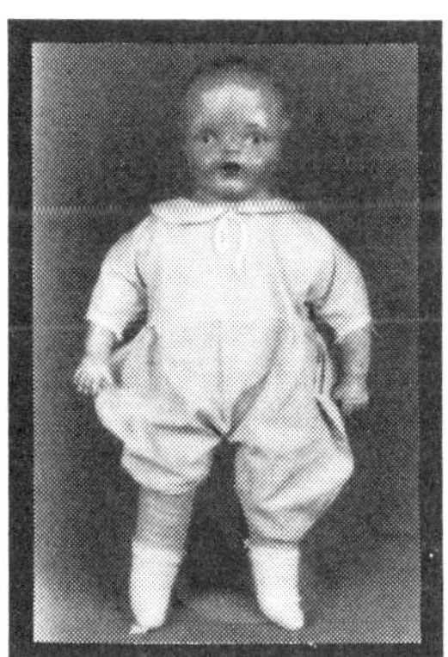

FLORENTINE - 1920

ca.1920. 22 in. (56 cm). Cloth body and legs, composition forearms. Composition shoulderhead; blue painted eyes, black line over eye, upper painted lashes; blond moulded hair; closed mouth. Unmarked.
Ref.No.: D of C, BZ8, p. 213.

Mint $225.00   Ex. $150.00   G. $110.00   F. $85.00

FLORENTINE - 1925

ca.1925. 24 in. (60 cm). Cloth body with composition arms and legs. Composition shoulderhead; blue sleep eyes, painted lashes and brows; original blond wig; open mouth, showing teeth and tongue. Mark: on shoulderplate, FLORENTINE/TORONTO.
Ref.No.: D of C, AP21, p. 214.

Mint $300.00   Ex. $250.00   G. $175.00   F. $85.00

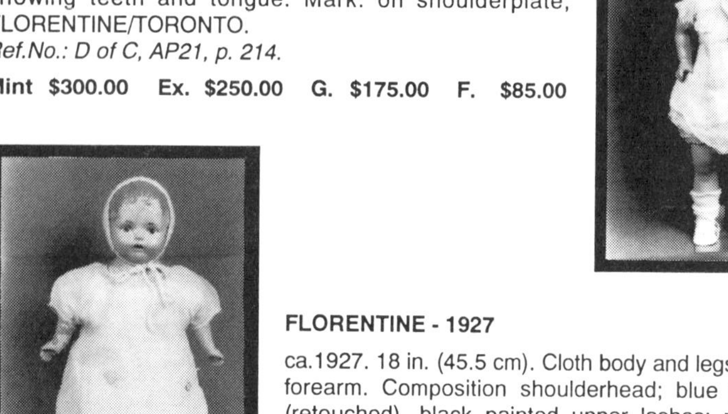

FLORENTINE - 1927

ca.1927. 18 in. (45.5 cm). Cloth body and legs, composition forearm. Composition shoulderhead; blue painted eyes (retouched), black painted upper lashes; moulded hair; open-closed mouth. Mark: on shoulderplate, FLORENTINE/TORONTO.
Ref.No.: D of C, CR16, p. 214.

Mint $150.00   Ex. $120.00   G. $95.00   F. $55.00

FREEMAN TOY COMPANY
1943 - 1952

Freeman Toy Company produced a low quality doll. The Company ceased operation with the introduction of vinyl technology.

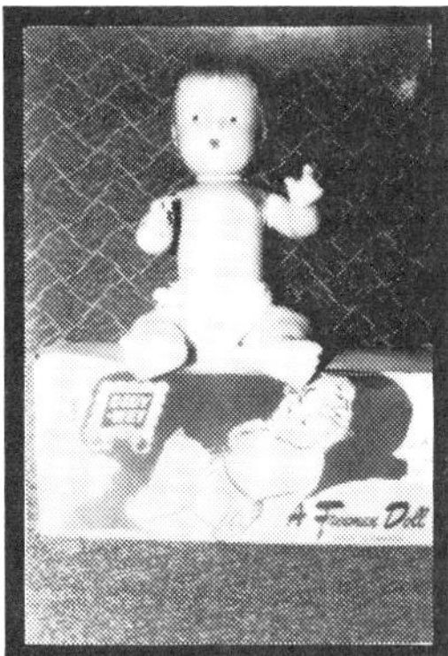

DIDY-WET

ca.1945. All composition bent-limb baby, jointed hips, shoulders and neck. Composition head; painted eyes; moulded hair; open-mouth nurser. Unmarked.
Ref.No.: D of C, CZ2, p. 215.

Mint $120.00   Ex. $75.00   G. $65.00   F. $35.00

FREEMAN - 1944

ca.1944. 20 in. (51 cm). Cloth body, composition forearms and straight legs. Composition head; blue painted eyes, painted lower lashes, upper eyeshadow; black moulded hair; closed mouth. Unmarked.
Ref.No.: D of C, CL31, p. 216.

Mint $150.00   Ex. $105.00   G. $80.00   F. $50.00

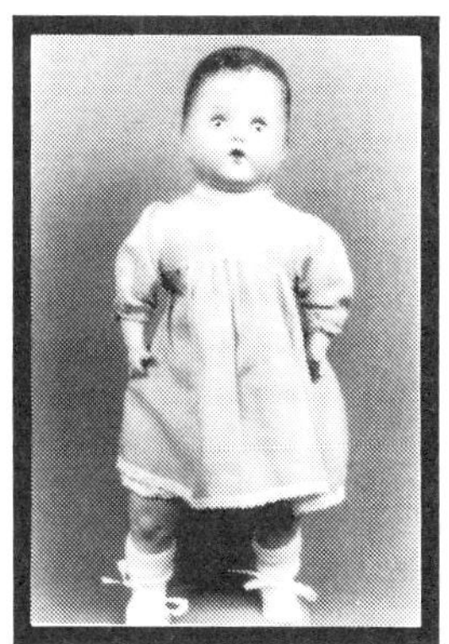

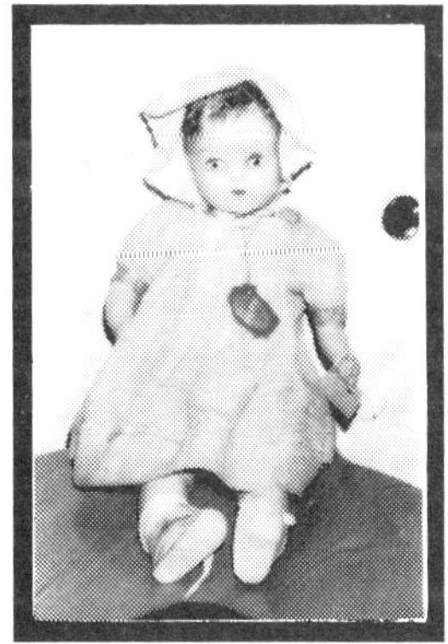

FREEMAN - 1946

ca.1946. 25 in. (63.5 cm). Cloth body, composition arms and legs. Composition head; painted blue eyes, eyeshadow, painted lower lashes; moulded brown hair; closed mouth. Original Tag: A GENUINE FREEMAN DOLL/MADE IN CANADA.
Ref.No.: D of C, CT20, p.216.

Mint $160.00   Ex. $115.00   G. $90.00   F. $60.00

FREEMAN - 1946

ca.1946. 19 in. (48.5 cm). Cloth body, composition forearms and straight legs. Composition head; blue painted eyes, painted lower lashes, upper eyeshadow; brown moulded hair; closed mouth. Unmarked.
Ref.No.: D of C, CA27, p. 216.

Mint $150.00   Ex. $105.00   G. $80.00   F. $50.00

FREEMAN - 1947

ca.1947. 24 in. (61 cm). Cloth body, composition forearms, straight legs. Composition head; blue painted eyes, painted lower lashes, upper eyeshadow; brown moulded hair; closed mouth. Original Tag: A/GENUINE/FREEMAN DOLL (in script)/MADE IN CANADA.
Ref.No.: D of C, CA33, p. 217.

Mint $160.00   Ex. $115.00   G. $90.00   F. $60.00

FREEMAN - 1948

ca.1948. 16 in. (41 cm). Composition body, jointed hips, shoulders, and neck. Composition head; blue sleep eyes, lashes, painted lower lashes; brown mohair wig in braids with curly bangs; closed mouth. Mark: on body, FREEMAN TOY/TORONTO, CANADA.
Ref.No.: D of C, AP11, p. 217.

Mint $175.00   Ex. $130.00   G. $85.00   F. $55.00

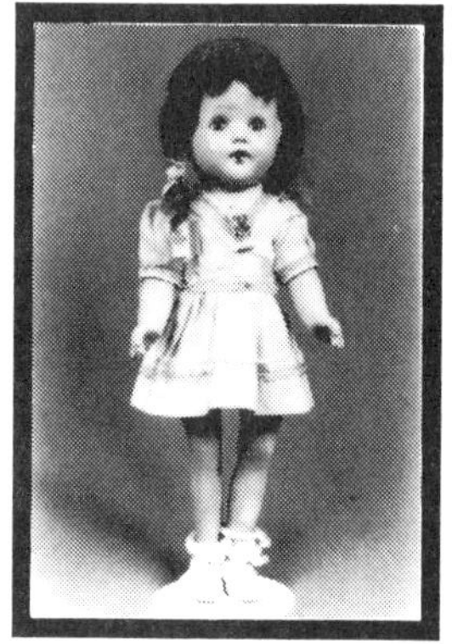

FREEMAN - 1948

ca.1948. 22 in. (56 cm). Cloth body, composition arms and legs. Composition flange head; painted blue eyes, eyeshadow, painted lower lashes; moulded dark brown hair; closed mouth. Original label: A GENUINE/FREEMAN DOLL/MADE IN CANADA.
Ref.No.: D of C, CT6, p. 217.

Mint $155.00   Ex. $120.00   G. $95.00   F. $60.00

FREEMAN - 1950

ca.1950. 24 in. (62 cm). Cloth body, composition hands and legs. Composition head; blue sleep eyes, lashes, painted lower lashes; blond mohair wig with curly bangs; open mouth showing two teeth and tongue. Original Tag: A FREEMAN/DOLL/MADE IN CANADA/FREEMAN TOY COMPANY/TORONTO.

Ref.No.: D of C, AZ5, p. 218.

Mint $300.00   Ex. $250.00   G. $150.00   F. $90.00

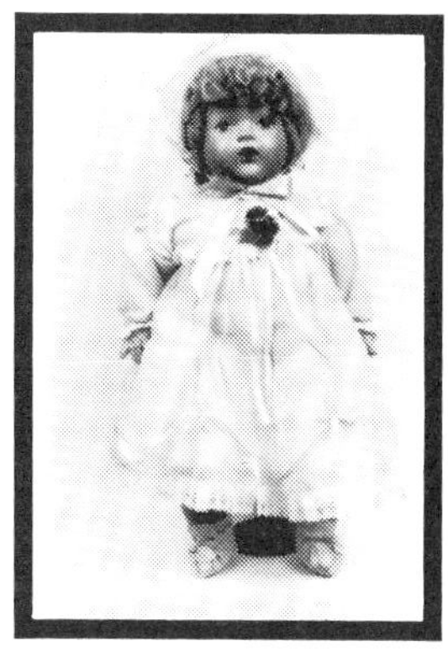

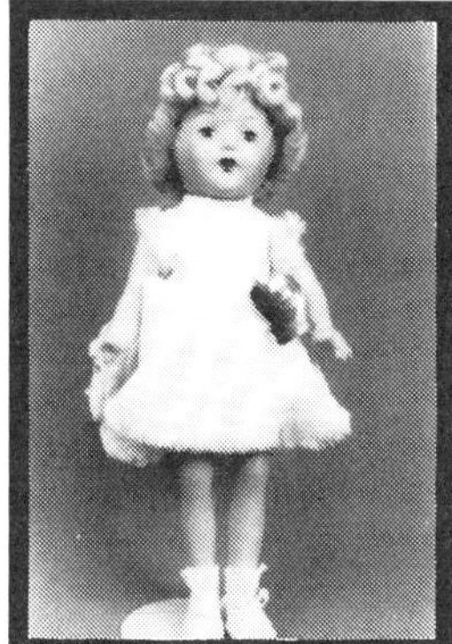

FREEMAN - 1951

ca.1951. 17 in. (43 cm). Composition body, jointed hips, shoulders, and neck. Composition head; blue sleep eyes, lashes, painted lower lashes; blond mohair wig; closed mouth. Mark: on head, FREEMAN TOY/TORONTO. Original label, A FREEMAN DOLL/MADE IN/CANADA/FREEMAN TOY COMPANY/TORONTO.

Ref.No.: D of C, CN34, p. 218.

Mint $185.00   Ex. $140.00   G. $95.00   F. $65.00

GILTOY COMPANY
ca1945

This Company was located in Montreal and operated between 1945 and 1950.

GILTOY

ca.1945. 14 in. (35.5 cm). Composition body, jointed hips, shoulders and neck. Composition head; blue painted side-glancing eyes; brown moulded hair; closed mouth. Mark: on body W.O.L. Original label, GILTOY/OUR TRADEMARK IS/YOUR GUARANTEE/FOR QUALITY AND/WORKMANSHIP.
Ref.No.: D of C, CN24, p. 219.

Mint $175.00   Ex. $125.00   G. $85.00   F. $60.00

GOODTIME TOYS
1970 - 1977

This was a short-lived company whose dolls cannot be identified without the box.

FASHION DOLL

Goodtime Toys, ca1975. 20 in. (51 cm). Plastic teen body, jointed hips, shoulders, and neck. Vinyl head; blue sleep eyes, lashes, eyeshadow; rooted platinum long hair on the side and short on top; closed mouth. Mark: on head, 14R. *Ref.No.: D of C, BX15, p. 219.*

Mint   **$45.00**   **Ex.**   **$35.00**   **G.**   **$25.00**   **F.**   **$15.00**

INDIEN ART et ESKIMO de la MAURICE INC.
1979 -

This company specializes in dolls for the tourist trade.

OTTER BELT

1982. 12 in. (30.5 cm). Brown moulded one piece body made of an unbreakable latex mixture. Painted designs on face and arms. Black painted eyes, wool braids, closed mouth. Mark: on label, INDIEN ART ESKIMO/OTTER BELT.
Ref.No.: D of C, AO22, p. 220.

Mint $95.00 **Ex.** $75.00 **G.** $55.00 **F.** $35.00

INDIAN CHILD

1983. 4 in. (10 cm). Brown one piece moulded body. Black painted side-glancing eyes, black moulded hair, closed mouth. Mark: label, Indien Art Eskimo.

Ref.No.: D of C, AP4, p. 220.

Mint $25.00   **Ex.** $20.00   **G.** $12.00   **F.** $8.00

MEGGAN'S DOLL HOUSE
1972 -

Meggan's Doll House is owned by Heather Anne and Jim Moriarty. Although the business has been established since 1972, it wasn't until 1987 that it really took off in a big way. The factory, which produces over 400 porcelain doll per month, is located in Smith Falls, Ont. The artistic control is in Heather Anne's hands and the marketing is taken care of by Jim.

Meggan's dolls have a fine smooth bisque finish and the painting is very well done. The workshop employs about twelve people who are obviously very well trained in their craft. These dolls are an excellent buy for the money.

Walt Disney World in Orlando, Florida invited Meggan's to show and sell their porcelain dolls at Disney's eight-day World Doll and Teddy Bear Convention in 1989. Meggan's dolls were a sell-out and they have been invited back for the 1990 show.

The Japanese government selected Meggan's to participate in a travelling trade show in Japan in 1989 and in 1990 Meggan's will be at the famous Nuremburg Toy Fair. Meggan's Doll House is putting Canada on the map as a porcelain doll maker.

Meggan's have a line of Classics, which are limited edition dolls. Then there is Meggan's Collectibles which has a line of twenty-two dolls and these are unlimited.

A new line began in 1989 of dolls made from original moulds especially for Meggan's. These will be in Limited editions of 200 and the moulds will be destroyed when these are sold.

EMILY

1989. (Classic) 20 in. (52 cm). All porcelain. Moments of Childhood Series. Edition of 300. Dressed in a nightie and slippers.
Ref.No.: PGA14.

Mint: $250.00

SARAH

1989. (Classic) 18 in. (46 cm). Edition of 100. Lace trimmed blouse and skirt with matching hat. Carrying a basket.
Ref.No.: PGA13.

Mint: $220.00

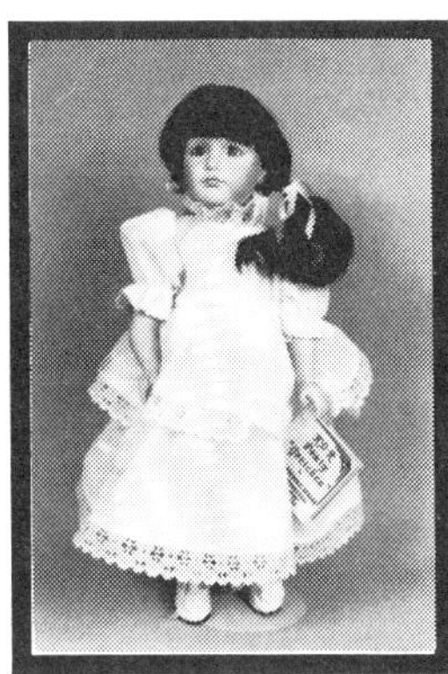

GRETCHEN

1989. (Meggan's Collectibles). 17 in. (43.5 cm). All porcelain.
Lace trimmed dress, socks and shoes.
Ref.No.: PGA15.

Mint: $140.00

VICTORIA ANNE

1989. (Original). 20 in. (51 cm). Cloth body, porcelain hands
and feet. Limited edition of 200. Rose dress, flowered apron,
socks and shoes.
Ref.No.: PGA11.

Mint: $225.00

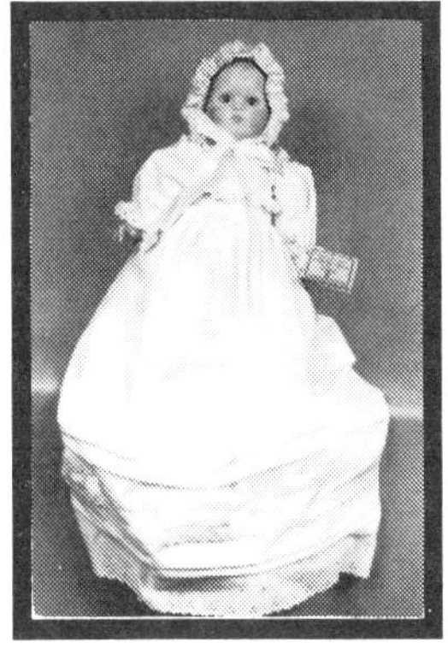

ANITA MARIE

1989. (Original). 17 in. (43.5 cm). Cloth body, porcelain hands
and feet. White gown and bonnet.
Ref.No.: PGA16.

Mint: $250.00

MIGHTY STAR COMPANY LIMITED
1977 -

Mighty Star no longer make dolls in Canada although a few are dressed here.

MIGHTY STAR

ca.1978. 23 in. (58.5 cm). Plastic body, jointed hips, shoulders, and neck. Vinyl head; blue sleep eyes, lashes; rooted blond hair with side braids; closed mouth. Mark: on head, DOLL/c1965 CANADA.
Ref.No.: D of C, CG25, p. 221.

Mint $40.00   Ex. $30.00   G. $20.00   F. $15.00

MIGHTY STAR

1980. 19 in. (48.5 cm). Plastic teen body and legs, jointed hips, shoulders, and neck. Vinyl head; blue sleep eyes, lashes; rooted long blond hair with bangs; closed mouth. Mark: on head, 14R.
Ref.No.: D of C, CG6, p. 221.

Mint $45.00   Ex. $35.00   G. $25.00   F. $15.00

MIGHTY STAR

1981. 20 in. (51 cm). Plastic teen body, jointed hips, shoulders, and neck. Vinyl head; brown sleep eyes, lashes, painted lower lashes; rooted long brown curls with bangs; closed mouth. Mark:unmarked.
Ref.No.: D of C, AO8, p. 221.

Mint $35.00   Ex. $30.00   G. $25.00   F. $15.00

COUNTRY CUZZINS

1981. 24 in. (61 cm). Cloth body, arms and legs, vinyl hands. Vinyl head; blue sleep eyes, lashes; rooted long curly blond hair; closed mouth. Mark: on head, 4/MIGHTY STAR/CANADA. Original overalls, shirt and hat.
Ref.No.: D of C, CG7, p. 222.

Mint $55.00   Ex. $45.00   G. $30.00   F. $18.00

MIGHTY STAR - 20 in.

1981. 20 in. (51 cm). Plastic teen body, jointed hips, shoulders, and neck. Vinyl head; blue sleep eyes, lashes, painted lower lashes; rooted blond with bangs; closed mouth. Mark: on head, 14R.
Ref.No.: D of C, AO7, p. 222.

Mint $40.00   Ex. $35.00   G. $25.00   F. $15.00

MIGHTY STAR - 18 in.

1982. 18 in. (45.5 cm). Plastic body, jointed hips, shoulders, and neck. Vinyl head; blue sleep eyes, lashes, blue eyeshadow; rooted brown curls with bangs; closed mouth. Mark: on head, 5.
Ref.No.: D of C, AP3, p. 222.

Mint $35.00   Ex. $25.00   G. $20.00   F. $15.00

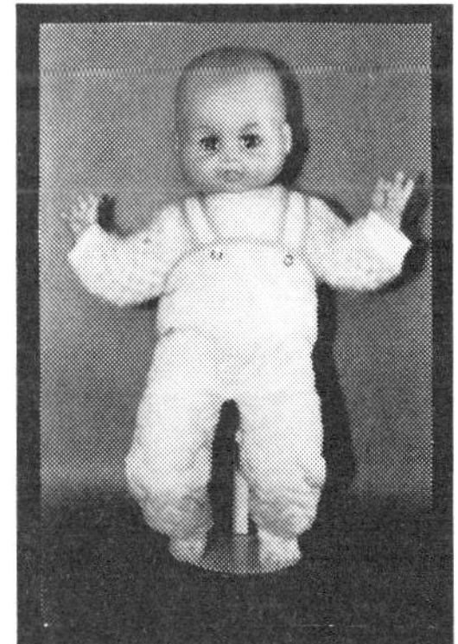

BABY CRISSIE

1982. 18 in. (45.5 cm). Cloth body with crier, vinyl arms and legs. Vinyl head ; blue sleep eyes, lashes; slightly moulded light brown hair; open-closed mouth. Mark: on head, STAR/09094/PLATED MOULDS INC./C1961.; on body, MADE BY ONT. REG. NO. 71B7816/MIGHTY STAR LTD.-DOLL DIVISION.
Ref.No.: D of C, XH27, p. 223.

Mint $35.00   Ex. $30.00   G. $20.00   F. $15.00

BABY WETSY

1982. 16 in. (40.5 cm). Plastic body and legs, vinyl arms, jointed hips, shoulders, and neck. Vinyl head; blue sleep eyes, lashes; rooted brown curls; open mouth nurser. Unmarked.
Ref.No.: D of C, CG5, p. 223.

Mint $25.00   Ex. $20.00   G. $15.00   F. $10.00

CANADA GIRL

1983. 12 in. (30.5 cm). Plastic body, jointed hips, shoulders, and neck. Vinyl head; blue sleep eyes, lashes; rooted blond short curls; open-closed mouth. Mark: on head, STAR DOLL.
Ref.No.: D of C, AA18, p. 223.

Mint $30.00 Ex. $25.00 G. $15.00 F. $10.00

NOMA TOYS LTD.
1945 - 1948

Noma Toys only made dolls for a three year period in their history.

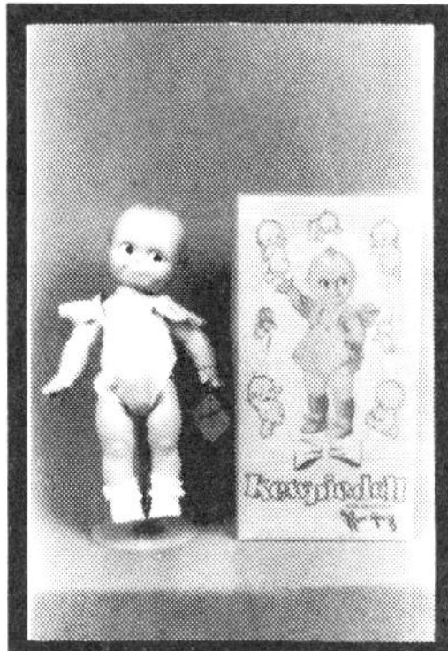

KEWPIE DOLL

1945. 13 in. (33 cm). Composition body, jointed hips, shoulders, and neck. Composition head; black painted side-glancing eyes; distinctive kewpie-style moulded hair; closed watermelon mouth. Unmarked doll.
Ref.No.: D of C, BF25, p. 224.

Mint $225.00   Ex. $160.00   G. $120.00   F. $95.00

SCOOTLES

1947. 13 in. (33 cm). Composition body, jointed hips, shoulders, and neck. Composition head dimpled cheeks and chin, nostril dots; blue painted eyes, painted upper lashes; reddish moulded curls; closed watermelon mouth. Mark: Unmarked.
Ref.No.: D of C, CD15, p. 224.

Mint $350.00   Ex. $300.00   G. $200.00   F. $100.00

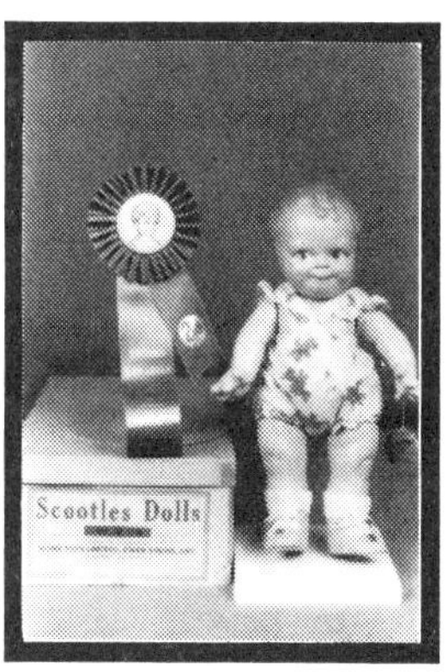

OIL PATCH KIDS
ca1985

Little is known about this company. The dolls seemed to be available only in the west.

OIL PATCH KID

1985. 10 in. (25.5 cm). Cloth body. Vinyl head with freckles ; blue stencilled eyes; rooted black wool hair; closed watermelon mouth. Mark: no mark on doll; original Well licence. Comes with plastic oil barrel and black velvet Oil Patch Pet with eyes and feet.
Ref.No.: D of C, CR12, p. 225.

Mint **$35.00** **Ex.** **$25.00** **G.** **$15.00** **F.** **$10.00**

PERFECT DOLL COMPANY
1948

Perfect Doll lasted only one year which makes their dolls quite rare.

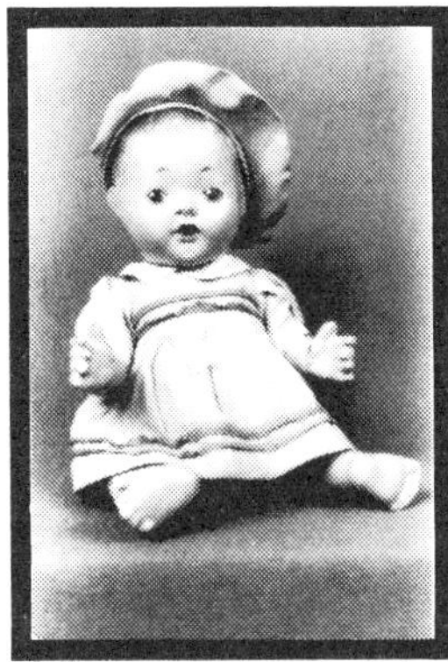

PERFECT

1948. 12 in. (30.5 cm). Composition bent-limb baby body. Composition head; blue painted eyes with fine black line and highlights; brown moulded hair; closed mouth. Mark: on head, PERFECT/MADE IN CANADA.
Ref.No.: D of C, AP32, p. 225.

Note: A rare doll.

Mint $150.00   Ex. $120.00   G. $85.00   F. $65.00

REGAL TOY COMPANY
1959-1984

Regal Toy Company was established in 1959, well after the plastics era had begun. All Regal dolls are plastic or plastic and cloth.

Regal dolls had a distinctly Canadian flavour.

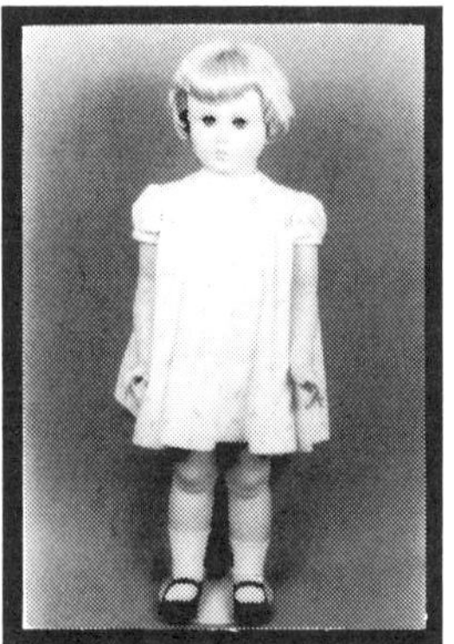

LITTLE PRINCESS WALKER

1961. 36 in. (91.5 cm). Plastic body, jointed hips, shoulders, and neck. Vinyl head; blue sleep eyes, lashes, painted lower lashes; rooted blond saran hair; closed mouth. Unmarked.
Ref.No.: D of C, CS25A, p. 228.

Mint $140.00   Ex. $105.00   G. $50.00   F. $35.00

WALKING PLAY PAL

1962. 23 in. (58.5 cm). Plastic body, jointed hips, shoulders, and neck. Vinyl head; blue sleep eyes, lashes, painted lower lashes; rooted light brown curls over moulded hair; open mouth nurser. Mark: on head REGAL TOY/CANADA; on body, REGAL (in script)/CANADA.
Ref.No.: D of C, CD17, p. 228.

Mint $75.00   Ex. $45.00   G. $25.00   F. $20.00

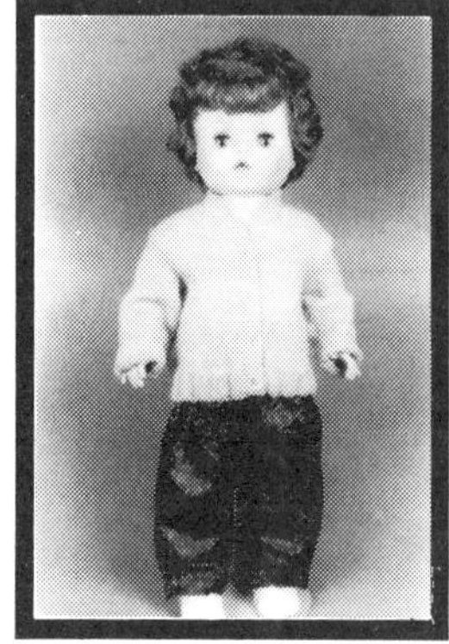

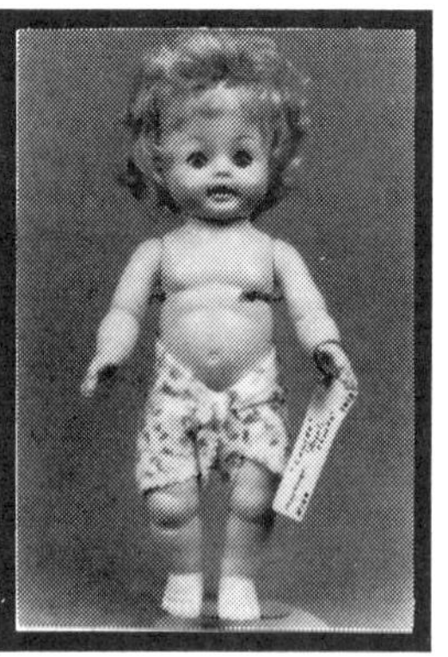

TEAR DROPS

1962. 12 in. (30.5 cm). Plastic body, jointed hips, shoulders, and neck. Vinyl head; blue sleep eyes, lashes, painted lower lashes; rooted saran curls; open mouth nurser. Mark: on head, REGAL TOY/MADE IN CANADA; on body, REGAL/CANADA.
Ref.No.: D of C, CG29, p. 229.

Mint $55.00   Ex. $5.00   G. $20.00   F. $10.00

BOUDOIR DOLL

1962, 15 in. (38 cm). Plastic body and legs, vinyl arms, jointed hips, shoulders, and neck. Vinyl head; blue sleep eyes, lashes, painted lower lashes; rooted long grey hair with bangs; closed mouth. Mark: on head, a crown over REGAL TOY/MADE IN CANADA.
Ref.No.: D of C, AP27, p. 229.

Mint $50.00   Ex. $35.00   G. $20.00   F. $10.00

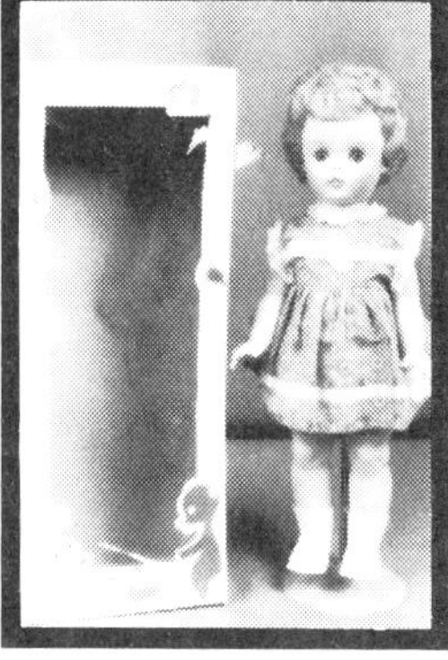

PENNY

1962. 17 in. (43 cm). Plastic body, jointed hips, shoulders, and neck. Vinyl head; blue sleep eyes, lashes, painted lower lashes; rooted blond curly saran hair; closed mouth. Mark: on head, REGAL TOY.
Ref.No.: D of C, CI11, p. 229.

Mint $45.00   Ex. $30.00   G. $20.00   F $10.00

GAIL

1962. 13 in. (33 cm). Plastic body, jointed hips, shoulders, and neck. Vinyl head; blue plastic sleep eyes, lashes; rooted dark brown saran curly hair; closed mouth. Mark: on head, a crown over REGAL TOY/MADE IN CANADA; on body, REGAL/CANADA.
Ref.No.: D of C, CG8, p. 228.

Mint $45.00   Ex. $30.00   G. $20.00   F. $10.00

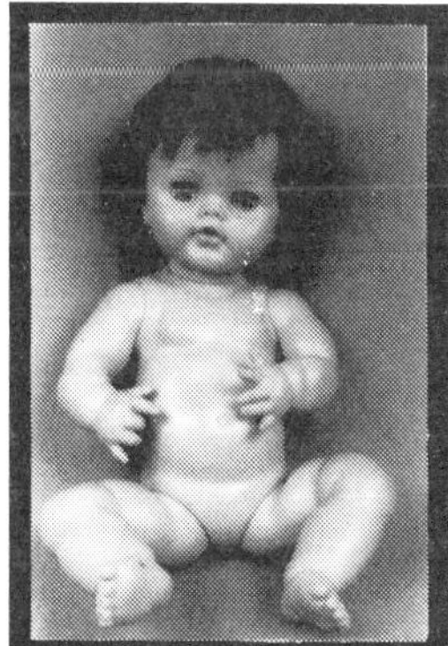

BABY DEAR

ca. 1963. 20 in. (51 cm). Plastic bent-limb baby body, jointed hips, shoulders, and neck. Vinyl head; blue sleep eyes, lashes; rooted dark brown hair; open mouth nurser. Mark: on head, a crown over REGAL TOY/MADE IN CANADA; same on body.
Ref.No.: D of C, CE7, p. 230.

Mint $50.00   Ex. $35.00   G. $20.00   F. $15.00

REGAL - 1963

ca.1963. 21 in. (53.5 cm). Plastic body, jointed hips, shoulders, and neck. Vinyl head; brown sleep eyes, lashes; rooted brown curls; open-closed mouth. Mark: on body, REGAL/CANADA.
Ref.No.: D of C, CJ13, p. 230.

Mint $45.00   Ex. $30.00   G. $20.00   F. $15.00

GAIL

1962. 16 in. (40.5 cm). Plastic body, jointed hips, shoulders, and neck. Vinyl head; blue sleep eyes, lashes, painted lower lashes; rooted blond hair with bangs; closed mouth. Mark: on head, REGAL TOY/MADE IN CANADA.
Ref.No.: D of C, CS7, p. 230.

Mint $45.00   Ex. $25.00   G. $15.00   F. $8.00

BABY DEAR

1963, 20 in. (51 cm). Plastic body, vinyl bent-limb arms and legs, jointed hips, shoulders, and neck. Vinyl head; blue sleep eyes, lashes, painted lower lashes; rooted brown curls; open-closed mouth. Mark: on head, REGAL TOY/MADE IN CANADA.
Ref.No.: D of C, CO1A, p. 231.

Mint: $50.00   Ex. $40.00   G. $25.00   F. $20.00

KIMMIE ESKIMO

1964. 10 in. (25.5 cm). Brown plastic body, jointed hips, shoulders, and neck. Vinyl head; painted black side-glancing eyes, painted upper lashes; rooted straight black hair; closed watermelon mouth. Mark: on head, REGAL/MADE IN CANADA.
Ref.No.: D of C, CW23A, p. 231.

Mint $35.00   Ex. $25.00   G. $15.00   F. $8.00

BABY KIMMIE

1964. 9 in. (23 cm). Vinyl bent-limb baby body, jointed hips, shoulders, and neck. Vinyl head; black painted side-glancing eyes, three painted upper lashes; rooted black straight hair; closed mouth. Mark: on head, REGAL TOY/MADE IN CANADA; on body, REGAL TOY/MADE IN CANADA/9-G.
Ref.No.: D of C, CW20, p. 231.

Mint $30.00   Ex. $25.00   G. $20.00   F. $10.00

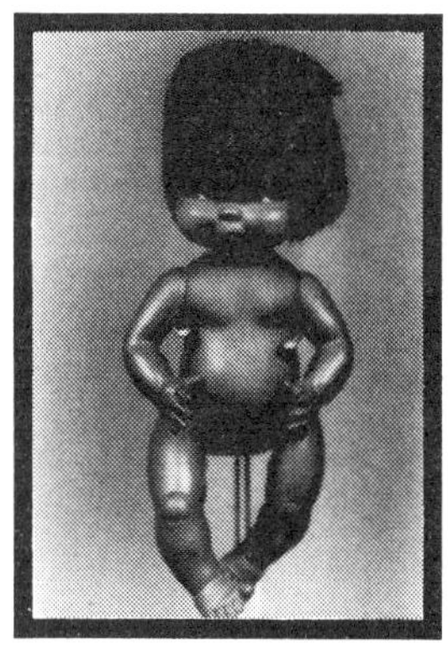

CANDY

1964. 24 in. (61 cm). Plastic body, jointed hips, shoulders, and neck. Vinyl head; brown sleep eyes, lashes, painted lower lashes; rooted long blond nylon hair with bangs; closed mouth. Mark: on head, REGAL TOY/MADE IN CANADA. Unusually well-dressed.
Ref.No.: D of C, BM1, p. 232.

Mint $75.00   Ex. $45.00   G. $25.00   F. $20.00

KIMMIE - 12 in.

1965. 12 in. (30.5 cm). Brown plastic body and legs, vinyl arms, jointed hips, shoulders, and neck. Brown vinyl head; moulded black three-dimensional side-glancing eyes; rooted black hair; closed watermelon mouth. Mark: on head, REGAL/MADE IN CANADA.
Ref.No.: D of C, CH11, p. 232.

Mint $45.00   Ex. $30.00   G. $20.00   F. $10.00

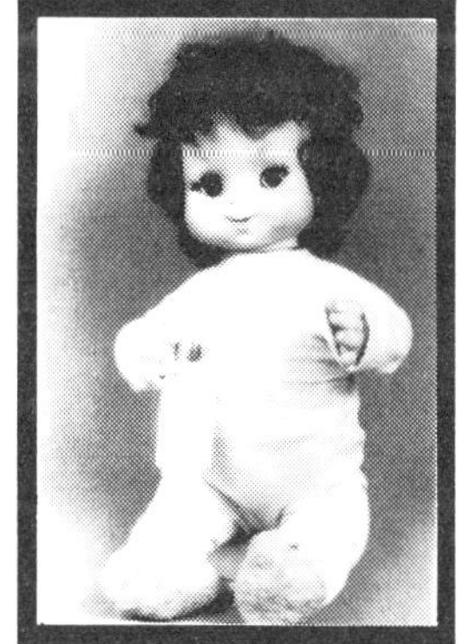

SNUGGLES - 18 in.

ca. 1966. 18 in. (45.5 cm). Moulded foam plastic on a wire frame, vinyl forearms. Vinyl swivel head; dark brown sleep eyes, three outer lashes; rooted dark brown hair; closed watermelon mouth. Mark: on head, REGAL TOY/MADE IN CANADA.
Ref.No.: D of C, CH7, p. 232.

Mint $35.00   Ex. $25.00   G. $20.00   F. $10.00

TRESSY

1967. 12 in. (30.5 cm). Plastic teen body and legs, vinyl arms, jointed hips, shoulders, and neck. Vinyl head; blue painted side-glancing eyes; rooted brown saran hair with hair "growing" out of the top of her head with a key supplied to wind it back in; closed mouth. Mark: on head, REGAL.
Ref.No.: D of C, BZ30, p. 233.

Mint **$40.00** **Ex.** **$25.00** **G.** **$15.00** **F.** **$10.00**

CANDY WALKER

1967. 25 in. (63.5 cm). Plastic body, jointed hips, shoulders, and neck. Vinyl head; blue sleep eyes, lashes, painted lower lashes; rooted blond nylon hair; closed mouth. Mark: REGAL TOY/MADE IN CANADA.
Ref.No.: D of C, CI7, p. 233.

Mint **$70.00** **Ex** **$40.00** **G.** **$20.00** **F.** **$15.00**

INDIAN PRINCESS

ca. 1968. 13 in. (33 cm). Brown plastic body, jointed hips, shoulders, and neck. Vinyl head; brown plastic sleep eyes, lashes, four upper lashes; rooted black long straight hair; closed mouth. Mark: on head, c REGAL TOY/MADE IN CANADA.
Ref.No.: D of C, CJ27, p. 233.

Mint **$50.00** **Ex.** **$40.00** **G.** **$20.00** **F.** **$10.00**

REGAL - 1968

ca.1968. 23 in. (58.5 cm). Cloth body, vinyl arms and legs. Vinyl head; blue sleep eyes, lashes and three painted outer lashes; rooted blond hair; closed smiling mouth. Mark: on head, REGAL TOY LTD./MADE IN CANADA/19c68.
Ref.No.: D of C, CG3, p. 234.

Mint **$55.00** **Ex.** **$45.00** **G.** **$35.00** **F.** **$25.00**

DRINK and WET BABY DEAR

1969. 18 in. (45.5 cm). Plastic body and legs, vinyl arms, jointed hips, shoulders, and neck. Vinyl head; blue sleep eyes, lashes, three upper lashes; rooted brown curly hair; open mouth nurser. Mark: on body, REGAL/CANADA.
Ref.No.: D of C, AN35, p. 234.

Mint $25.00   Ex. $20.00   G. $15.00   F. $10.00

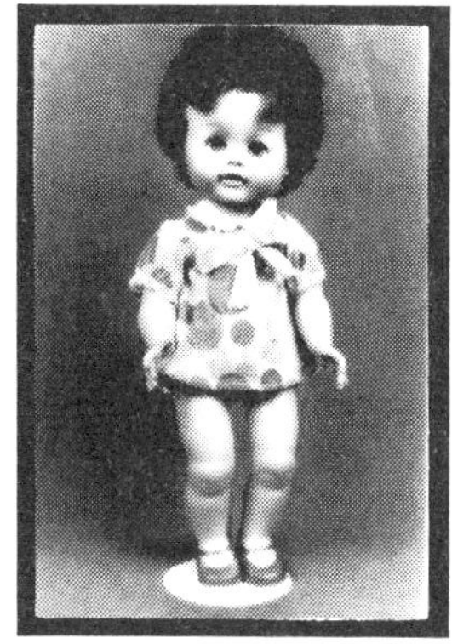

KIMMIE - 10 in.

ca. 1970, 10 in. (25.5 cm). Plastic body, jointed hips, shoulders, and neck. Vinyl head with freckles; blue stencilled side-glancing eyes, painted upper lashes; rooted short blond curly hair; closed watermelon mouth. Mark: on head, REGAL/MADE IN CANADA.
Ref.No.: D of C, CS6, p. 234.

Mint $20.00   Ex. $15.00   G. $10.00   F. $8.00

SNUGGLES - 20 in.

1970, 20 in. (51 cm). Cloth body, vinyl three-quarter arms and legs. Vinyl head; blue stencilled eyes and upper lashes; blond rooted hair; open-closed mouth. Mark: on head, REGAL TOY/MADE IN CANADA.
Ref.No.: D of C, CF20, p. 235.

Mint $40.00   Ex. $30.00   G. $20.00   F. $15.00

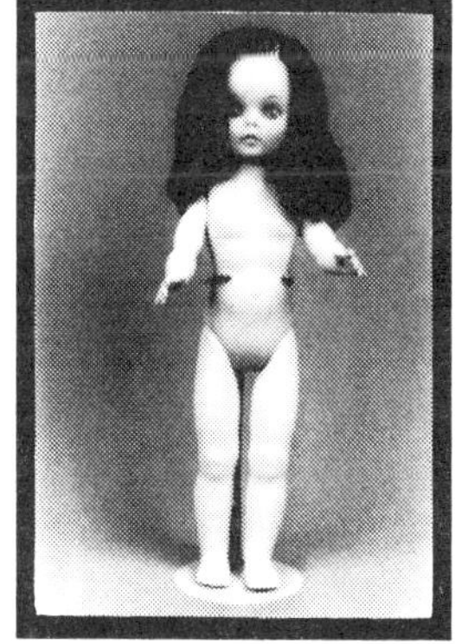

VICKI WALKER

ca. 1970, 18 in. (45.5 cm). Plastic body, jointed hips, shoulders, and neck. Vinyl head; blue sleep eyes, originally had lashes, three painted upper lashes on the outside of the eye; rooted long black hair; closed mouth. Mark: on head, REGAL/MADE IN/CANADA; on body, REGAL/CANADA.
Ref.No.: D of C, AN31, p. 235.

Mint $30.00   Ex. $25.00   G. $20.00   F. $10.00

BABY BROTHER and BABY SISTER - 17 in.

1970, 17 in. (43 cm). Plastic bent-limb baby bodies, anatomically correct, jointed hips, shoulders, and neck. Vinyl head; blue plastic sleep eyes, lashes, three painted upper lashes; rooted nylon hair; open-closed mouth. Mark: on head, REGAL TOY CO. LTD./MADE IN CANADA.
Ref.No.: D of C, BN10, p. 235.

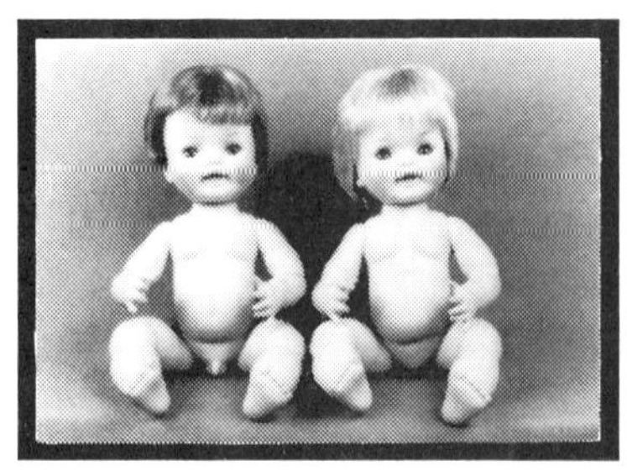

GIRL:

Mint	$35.00	**Ex.**	$25.00
G.	$20.00	**F.**	$15.00

BOY:

Mint	$45.00	**Ex.**	$25.00
G.	$25.00	**F.**	$15.00

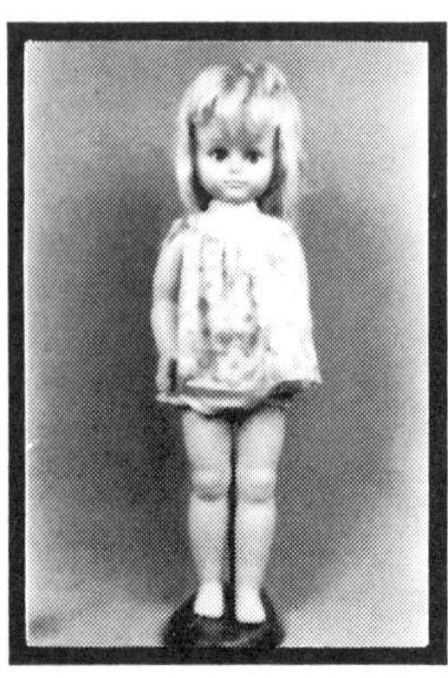

WENDY WALKER - 1970

ca. 1970, 24 in. (61 cm). Plastic body, jointed hips, shoulders, and neck. Vinyl head; brown sleep eyes, lashes; rooted blond nylon hair; closed mouth. Mark: on head, REGAL TOY LTD./MADE IN CANADA/249T.
Ref.No.: D of C, BL7, p. 236.

Mint $35.00   Ex. $25.00   G. $20.00   F. $10.00

ESKIMO TODDLER

1971, 18 in. (45.5 cm). Plastic body, jointed hips, shoulders, and neck. Vinyl head; brown sleep eyes, lashes, painted upper lashes at outside of eyes; rooted black nylon hair; closed mouth.
Ref.No.: D of C, BF26, p. 236.

Mint $30.00   Ex. $25.00   G. $15.00   F. $10.00

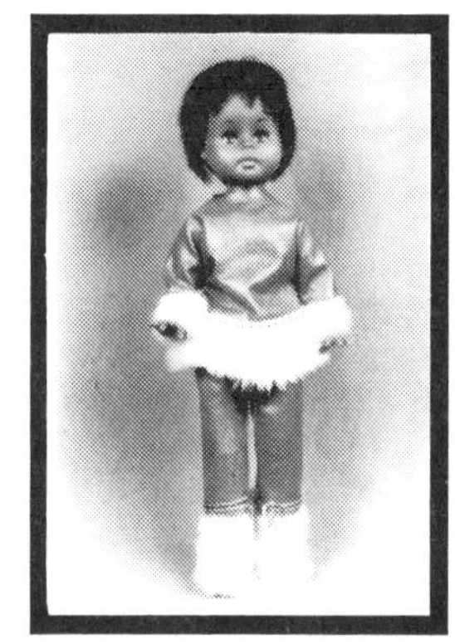

BABY BROTHER and
BABY SISTER - 12 in.

1971, 12 in. (30.5 cm). Plastic bent-limb baby bodies, anatomically correct, jointed hips, shoulders, and neck. Vinyl heads; blue plastic sleep eyes, lashes, three painted lashes on upper outside of eyes; rooted blond saran hair; open-closed mouth. Mark: on head, REGAL TOY LTD./MADE IN CANADA/129G.
Ref.No.: D of C, BN7, p. 236.

GIRL:

Mint	$30.00	Ex.	$20.00
G	$15.00	F.	$10.00

BOY:

Mint	$35.00	Ex.	$20.00
G.	$20.00	F.	$15.00

BABY SOFTINA

1973, 14 in. (35.5 cm). One piece vinyl body. Vinyl head; blue stencilled eyes and upper lashes; rooted auburn nylon hair; open-closed mouth. Mark: on head, 21/140 SPE/REGAL; on body, 1423 REGAL/12.
Ref.No.: D of C, CG31, p. 237.

Mint $15.00 **Ex.** $10.00 **G.** $8.00 **F.** N/C

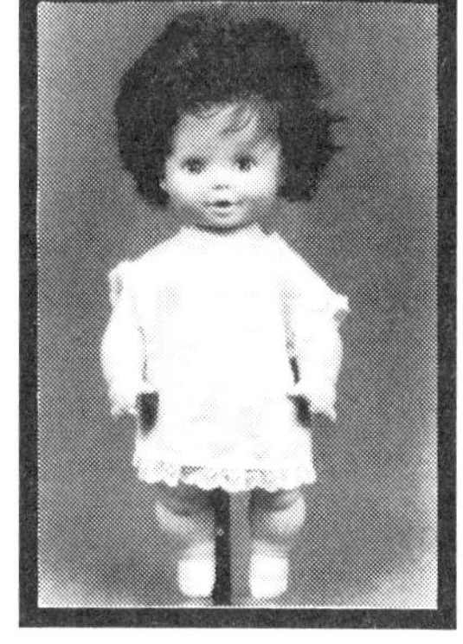

BONNIE and RONNIE RAG DOLLS

1973, 20 in. (51 cm). Cloth body and legs, vinyl hands. Vinyl head with freckles; blue sleep eyes, three painted upper lashes; rooted nylon hair; closed watermelon mouth. Mark: REGAL TOY Co./MADE IN CANADA/30 c (in a circle) O8.
Ref.No.: D of C, BZ9, p. 237.

Note: Ronnie is scarcer.

BONNIE

Mint	$50.00	Ex.	$40.00	G.	$30.00	F.	$20.00

RONNIE:

Mint	$65.00	Ex.	$50.00	G.	$40.00	F.	$25.00

WENDY WALKER - 30 in.

1973, 30 in. (76.5 cm). Plastic body, jointed hips, shoulders, and neck. Vinyl head; blue sleep eyes, lashes, painted lower lashes; rooted blond hair; closed mouth. Mark: on head, REGAL TOY LTD./MADE IN CANADA; on body, REGAL/CANADA.
Ref.No.: D of C, CS24A, p. 237.

Mint $35.00   Ex. $20.00   G. $15.00   F. $10.00

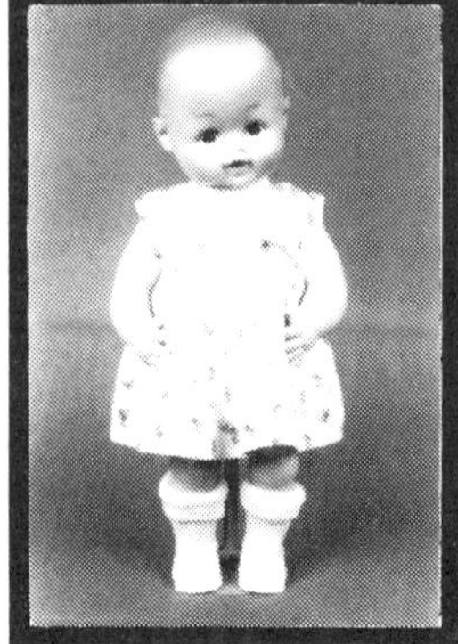

DRINK and WET BABY - 1973

1973, 14 in. (35.5 cm). Plastic body, jointed hips, shoulders, and neck. Vinyl head; stencilled blue eyes, upper lashes; reddish brown moulded hair; open mouth nurser. Mark: on head, REGAL TOY/MADE IN CANADA/141 B P.E.
Ref.No.: D of C, AM17, p. 238.

Mint $15.00   Ex. $12.00   G. $10.00

RENEE TODDLER

1974, 18 in. (45.5 cm). Plastic body, jointed hips, shoulders, and neck. Vinyl head; blue plastic sleep eyes, lashes, painted lower lashes; rooted auburn nylon hair; closed mouth. Mark: on head, REGAL/MADE IN CANADA.
Ref.No.: D of C, CS12, p. 238.

Mint $20.00   Ex. $15.00   G. $10.00

GRANNY

ca. 1974, (called BUTTONS in D of C), 15 in. (38 cm). Plastic body, jointed hips, shoulders, and neck. Vinyl head with glasses painted on her face; stencilled blue eyes and upper lashes; rooted streaked black and white nylon hair; open-closed mouth. Mark: on head, 11/REGAL TOY LTD./MADE IN CANADA/151 P TE.
Ref.No.: D of C, BM36, p. 239.

Note: Granny originally had a baby granddaughter and wore a mob cap.

Mint $30.00   Ex. $20.00   G. $15.00   F. $8.00

BUTTONS

ca. 1975, 15 in. (38 cm). Plastic body jointed hips, shoulders, and neck. Vinyl head; blue stencilled eyes and upper lashes; rooted nylon streaked auburn hair; open-closed mouth. Mark: on head, REGAL TOY LTD./MADE IN CANADA/1817 TPE; on body, REGAL/CANADA.
Ref.No.: D of C, AM28, p. 239.

Mint $20.00   Ex. $15.00   G. $10.00   F. $8.00

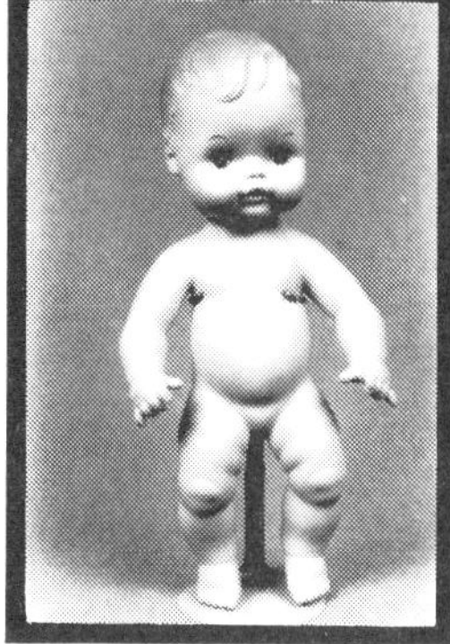

HUG-A-BYE BABY - 10 in.

1975, 10 in. (25.5 cm). One piece vinyl body. Vinyl head; stencilled blue eyes, upper lashes; reddish brown moulded hair; open-closed mouth. Mark: on head, REGAL TOY LTD./MADE IN CANADA/10 B 3 P5.
Ref.No.: D of C, AN10, p. 239.

Mint $15.00   Ex. $10.00   G. $5.00

HUG-A-BYE BABY - 14 in. Moulded Hair

1975, 14 in. (35.5 cm). One piece vinyl body. Vinyl head; stencilled blue eyes, upper lashes; reddish brown moulded hair; open-closed mouth. Mark: on head, REGAL TOY/MADE IN CANADA/141 B P.E.
Ref.No.: D of C, AN15, p. 240.

Mint $15.00   Ex. $10.00   G. $5.00

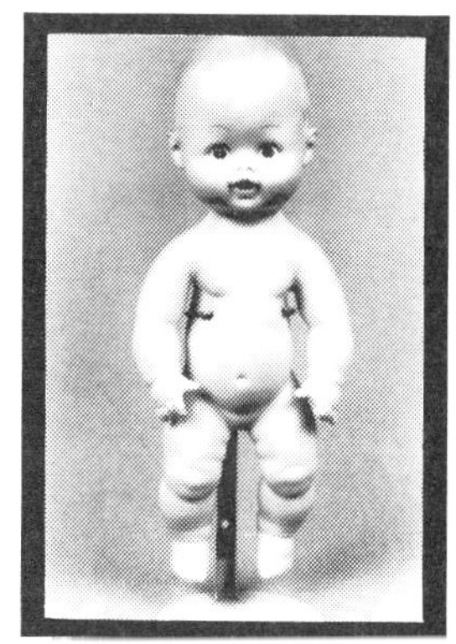

WENDY WALKER - 24 in.

ca. 1975, 24 in. (61 cm). Plastic body, jointed hips, shoulders, and neck. Vinyl head; blue sleep eyes, lashes, painted lower lashes; rooted long blond nylon hair; closed mouth. Mark: on head, REGAL TOY LTD./MADE IN CANADA/249T; on body, REGAL/CANADA/PAT. PEND.
Ref.No.: D of C, AO5, p. 240.

Mint $25.00   Ex. $20.00   G. $15.00   F. $10.00

INDIAN GIRL

ca. 1975, 18 in. (45.5 cm). Brown plastic body, jointed hips, shoulders, and neck. Vinyl head; brown sleep eyes, lashes, three painted upper lashes; rooted black hair; closed mouth. Mark: on head, REGAL TOY/MADE IN CANADA.
Ref.No.: D of C, AO25, p. 240.

Mint $30.00 **Ex.** $20.00 **G.** $15.00 **F.** $10.00

HIGHLAND LASS

1975, 16 in. (40.5 cm). Plastic body and legs, vinyl arms, jointed hips, shoulders, and neck. Vinyl head; blue stencilled eyes, painted upper lashes; rooted long blond hair; open-closed mouth. Mark: on head, REGAL TOY LTD./MADE IN CANADA/151 TPE.
Ref.No.: D of C, BP3, p. 241.

Mint $40.00 **Ex.** $25.00 **G.** $15.00 **F.** $10.00

HUG-A-BYE

1975, 16.5 in. (42 cm). Body and head are one-piece vinyl. Blue painted side-glancing eyes, three painted upper lashes; light brown moulded hair; watermelon mouth. Mark: on body, 163/REGAL/MADE IN CANADA.
Ref.No.: D of C, CS14, p. 241.

Note: Often mistaken for a Campbell's Soup doll.

Mint $30.00 **Ex.** $20.00 **G.** $15.00 **F.** $10.00

WENDY WALKER

1975, 24 in. (61 cm). Plastic body, jointed hips, shoulders, and neck. Vinyl head; plastic sleep eyes, lashes, painted lower lashes; rooted blond curls with bangs; closed mouth. Mark: on head, 249T.
Ref.No.: D of C, BF13, p. 241.

Mint $30.00 **Ex.** $25.00 **G.** $20.00 **F.** $10.00

BUTTONS

1975, 15 in. (38 cm). Plastic body, jointed hips, shoulders, and neck. Vinyl head; blue stencilled eyes, painted upper lashes, upper eyeshadow; rooted long blond hair with bangs; closed mouth. Mark: REGAL.
Ref.No.: D of C, BX14, p. 242.

Mint $25.00   Ex. $20.00   G. $15.00   F. $8.00

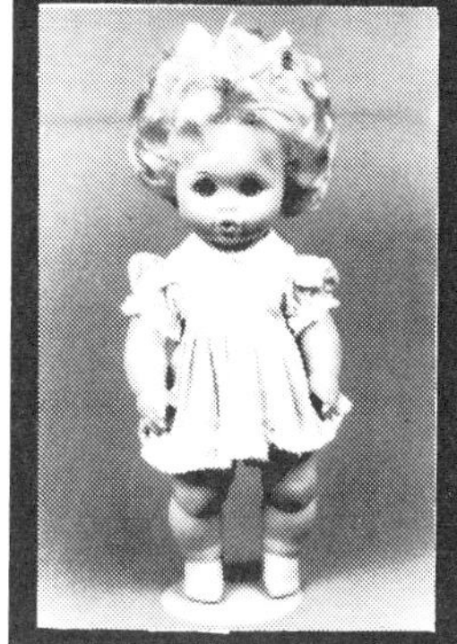

LUV & KISSES

1976, 16 in. (40.5 cm). One piece vinyl body. Vinyl head; blue sleep eyes, eyelashes, painted brows; rooted blond curls; open mouth. Makes a kissing sound when the leg is pressed. Mark: REGAL/MADE IN CANADA/166K; on body, 1616/REGAL TOY/MADE IN CANADA.
Ref.No.: D of C, AN17, p. 242.

Mint: $30.00   Ex. $25.00   G. $20.00   F. $10.00

OFFICIAL CANADIAN OLYMPIC HOSTESS

1976, 15 in. (38 cm). Plastic body and legs, vinyl arms, jointed hips, shoulders, and neck. Vinyl head; stencilled blue eyes and upper lashes; rooted blond hair with bangs; closed mouth. Mark: on head, REGAL TOY LTD./MADE IN CANADA/151 T PE.
Ref.No.: D of C, AZ18, p. 242.

Note: Becomes a common doll without the costume.

15 inch size
Mint $55.00   EX. $30.00   G. $15.00   F. $10.00
30 inch size
Mint $100.00   Ex. $65.00   G $45.00   F. $25.00

Dolls that are "Mint In the Box" (MIB) are about 10 to 15% higher for vinyl dolls and 40 to 50% higher for composition dolls. The composition dolls in boxes are of course much rarer. For the MIB category the box should be labelled with the manufacturers' name and possibly the name of the doll. A cardboard box with nothing printed on it has very little value.

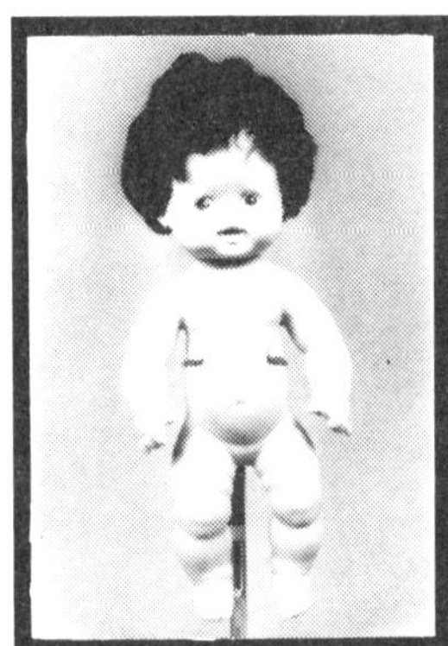

HUG-A-BYE BABY - 14 in. Rooted Black Curls

1976, 14 in. (35.5 cm). One piece vinyl body. Vinyl head; blue stencilled eyes and upper lashes; rooted black curls; open-closed mouth. Mark: on head, REGAL TOY/MADE IN CANADA/141 B P.E.
Ref.No.: D of C, AN20, p. 243.

Mint $20.00   Ex. $15.00   G. $10.00   F. $5.00

REGAL - 1976

ca.1976. 18 in. (45.5 cm). Cloth body, vinyl bent-limb arms and legs. Vinyl head; brown sleep eyes, lashes; rooted black hair; closed watermelon mouth.Mark: on head, REGAL/MADE IN CANADA.
Ref.No.: D of C, CH10, p. 243.

Note: A very unusual doll. Not shown in the catalogue.

Mint $75.00   Ex. $60.00   G. $45.00   F. $25.00

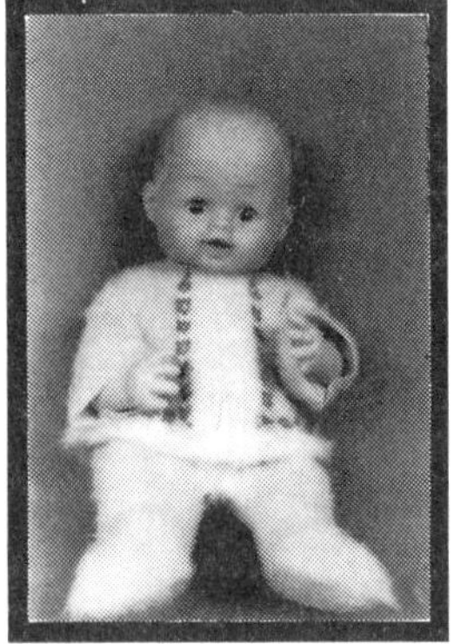

DRINK and WET BABY - 1976 - 14 in.

1976, 14 in. (35.5 cm). Plastic body, jointed hips, shoulders, and neck. Vinyl head; blue stencilled eyes, painted upper lashes; reddish brown moulded hair; open mouth nurser. Mark: on head, REGAL TOY/MADE IN CANADA/141B P.E.
Ref.No.: D of C, CE10, p. 243.

Mint $20.00   Ex. $15.00   G. $10.00   F. $5.00

REGAL - 1976

ca.1976. 15 in. (38 cm). Cotton print body, cloth head. Blue painted side-glancing eyes, painted upper lashes; yellow wool hair; painted smiling mouth. Mark: label on side, REGAL TOY LIMITED. Music box inside plays Brahms Lullaby.
Ref.No.: D of C, BX20, p. 244.

Note: Not listed in the catalogue. Mint condition must have working music box.

Mint: $30.00   Ex. $20.00   G. $15.00   F. $8.00

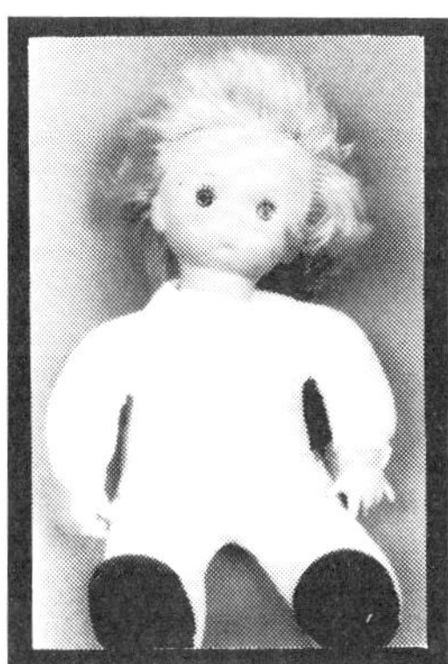

POPPI

1976, 17 in. (43 cm). Pink cotton body, vinyl hands, black cotton sewn on shoes. Vinyl head; stencilled blue side-glancing eyes and upper lashes; rooted blond hair; closed epouting mouth. Mark: on head, REGAL TOY/CANADA.
Ref.No.: D of C, CE11, p. 244.

Mint $12.00   Ex. $8.00   G. $5.00

RENEE BOUDOIR

1977, 18 in. (45.5 cm). Plastic body, jointed hips, shoulders, and neck. Vinyl head; blue plastic sleep eyes, lashes, painted upper lashes on outside of eye; rooted long blond hair; closed mouth. Mark: on head, REGAL TOY/MADE IN CANADA ; on body, REGAL/CANADA/PAT. PEND.
Ref.No.: D of C, CG22, p. 244.

Mint $30.00   Ex. $20.00   G $15.00   F. $10.00

SUCK-A-THUMB

1977, 16 in. (40.5 cm). Cloth body and legs, vinyl hands. Vinyl head with freckles; black painted eyes with highlights, painted upper and lower lashes; rooted auburn hair; open-closed mouth, shaped to hold her thumb. Mark: on head, 30TS6/REGAL/CANADA.
Ref.No.: D of C, CD2, p. 245.

Mint $20.00   Ex. $10.00   G. $8.00   F. $5.00

BABY DRINK and WET

1978, 21 in. (53.5 cm). Plastic body and legs, vinyl arms. Vinyl head; blue plastic sleep eyes, lashes, painted lower lashes; reddish blond moulded hair; open mouth nurser. Mark: on body, REGAL (in script)/CANADA; on hip, REGAL/CANADA.
Ref.No.: D of C, CE15, p. 245.

Mint $25.00   Ex. $15.00   G. $10.00   F. $8.00

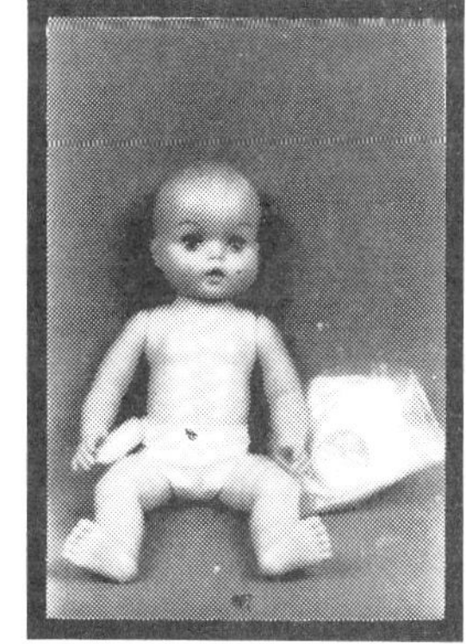

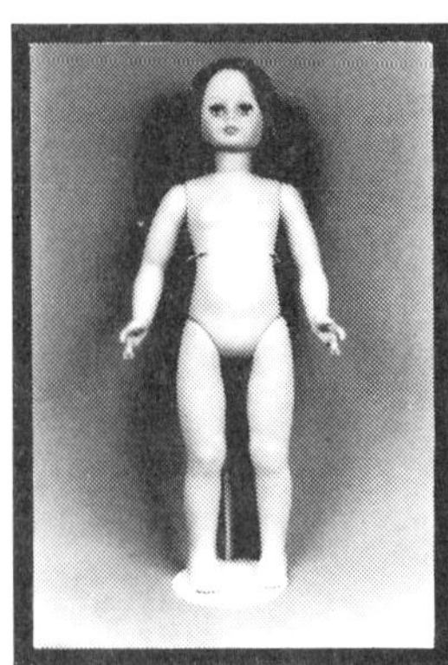

WENDY WALKER - 32 in.

1979, 32 in. (81.5 cm). Plastic body; jointed hips, shoulders, and neck. Vinyl head; blue plastic sleep eyes, lashes, painted lower lashes; rooted nylon long auburn hair; closed mouth. Mark: on head, 3280/20 EYE/C REGAL TOY LTD./MADE IN CANADA; on body, REGAL/CANADA/PAT. PEND.
Ref.No.: D of C, AO2, p. 245.

Mint $40.00   Ex. $30.00   G.$25.00   F. $20.00

LAFFY CATHY

1979, 17 in. (43 cm). Plastic bent-limb body with on-off switch for battery operated laughing mechanism; jointed hips, shoulders, and neck. Vinyl head; blue sleep eyes, lashes, three painted upper lashes on the outside of eyes; rooted straight auburn hair; open-closed mouth. Mark: on head, REGAL TOY CO. LTD./MADE IN CANADA.
Ref.No.: D of C, BN24, p. 246.

Note: Mint must include wand

Mint $ 50.00   Ex. $35.00   G. $25.00

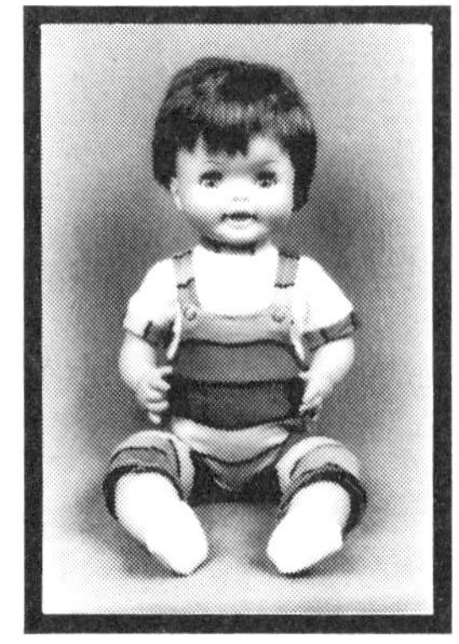

COLOURFUL CANDY

1979, 20 in. (51 cm). Plastic teen body, jointed hips, shoulders, and neck. Vinyl head; blue stencilled eyes with black line over eye, painted upper lashes; rooted blond curls; open-closed mouth. Mark: on head, 5/REGAL TOY LTD./MADE IN CANADA/151 TPE.
Ref.No.: D of C, CI31, p. 246.

Mint $35.00   Ex. $20.00   G. $15.00   F. $10.00

LA COLLECTION REGAL SERIES - 1979

1979, 20 in. (51 cm). Plastic teen body and legs, vinyl arms, jointed hips, shoulders, and neck. Vinyl head; blue sleep eyes, lashes, blue eyeshadow; rooted blond curls; open-closed mouth. Mark: on head, REGAL TOY/CANADA/207 T.
Ref.No.: D of C, Cl18, p. 246.

Mint $35.00   Ex. $25.00   G. $20.00   F. $10.00

LA COLLECTION REGAL SERIES - 1979

1979, 20 in. (51 cm). Plastic teen body, jointed hips, shoulders, and neck. Vinyl head; blue sleep eyes, lashes, blue eyeshadow; rooted blond curly hair; open-closed mouth. Mark: REGAL TOY/CANADA/207F.
Ref.No.: D of C, Cl19, p. 247.

Mint $35.00   Ex. $25.00   G. $20.00   F. $10.00

WENDY WALKER - 1979

1979, 24 in. (61 cm). Plastic body, jointed hips, shoulders, and neck. Vinyl head; blue sleep eyes, lashes, eyeshadow; rooted blond hair; closed mouth. Mark: on head, REGAL TOY CO./MADE IN CANADA/219T.
Ref.No.: D of C, BS36, p. 247.

Mint $25.00   Ex. $20.00   G. $15.00   F. $10.00

LA COLLECTION REGAL SERIES - 1980

ca. 1980, 20 in. (51 cm). Plastic teen body and legs, vinyl arms, jointed hips, shoulders, and neck. Vinyl head; blue sleep eyes, lashes, blue eyeshadow; rooted blond hair; open-closed mouth.
Ref.No.: D of C, Cl17, p. 247.

Mint $35.00   Ex. $25.00   G. $20.00   F. $10.00

RUFFLES and BOWS

1980, La Collection Regal Series. 18 in. (45.5 cm). Cloth body, vinyl arms and legs. Vinyl head; blue plastic sleep eyes, lashes; rooted straight blond hair; closed mouth. Mark: on head, REGAL TOY/M '1' C/200 M8.
Ref.No.: D of C, CI16, p. 248.

Mint $35.00   Ex. $25.00   G. $20.00   F. $15.00

ESKIMO

1981, 19 in. (48.5 cm). Brown plastic body, jointed hips, shoulders, and neck. Brown vinyl head; stencilled brown eyes, painted upper lashes; rooted straight black hair; closed mouth. Mark: on head 3604/174 PE/REGAL/MADE IN CANADA; on body, REGAL/CANADA/PAT. PEND.
Ref.No.: D of C, AO33, p. 248.

Mint $30.00   Ex. $20.00   G. $15.00   F. $10.00

PRETTY BABY

1981, La Collection Regal Series. 18.5 in. (47 cm). Cloth body, bent-limb vinyl arms and legs. Vinyl head; blue sleep eyes, lashes; rooted straight blond hair over moulded hair; closed mouth. Mark, on head, G/200 BE/REGAL/CANADA.
Ref.No.: D of C, BU35, p. 249.

Mint $35.00   Ex. $25.00   G. $20.00   F. $15.00

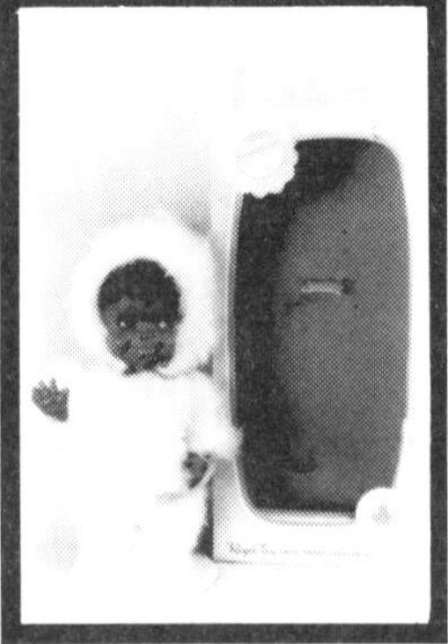

KIMMIE - 1981

ca. 1981, 12 in. (30.5 cm). Brown plastic body, vinyl arms and legs, jointed hips, shoulders and neck. Vinyl head; three dimensional black side-glancing eyes; rooted straight black hair; watermelon mouth. Mark: on body, REGAL (in script)/CANADA.
Ref.No.: D of C, CY10, p. 249.

Mint $45.00   Ex. $30.00   G.   20.00   F. $15.00

RELIABLE TOY COMPANY LIMITED
1920 -

Reliable Toy Company was bought in 1988 by Allied Plastics. A division of the comapny is still called Reliable and is making a small line of dolls. They are mainly concentrating on wheeled plastic toys.

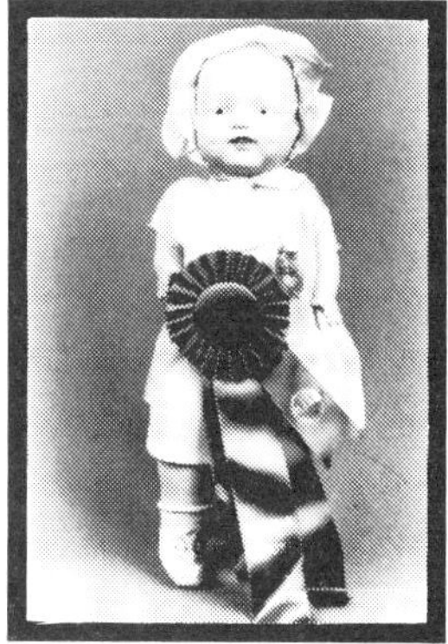

BABY BUBBLES

1929. 18 in. (45.5 cm). Cloth body and legs, composition arms. Composition head; painted blue eyes, upper lashes and brows; moulded hair, painted blond, open-closed mouth showing two painted teeth. Unmarked.
Ref.No.: D of C, AP15, p. 252.

Mint. $175.00   Ex. $150.00   G. $95.00   F. $50.00

HIAWATHA

ca.1929, 12 in. (30 cm). All composition, one-piece head and body, jointed hips and shoulders. Painted brown eyes, black line over eye; black mohair wig in braids; open-closed mouth. Mark: on head, RELIABLE/MADE IN CANADA.
Ref.No.: D of C, BY13, p. 253.

Mint. $160.00   Ex. $100.00   G. $60.00   F. $40.00

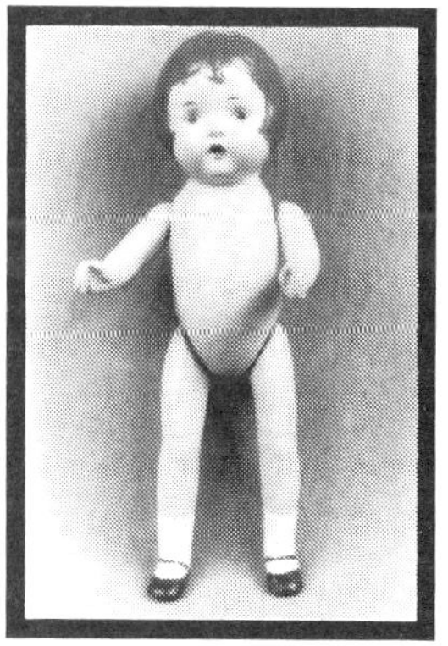

PATSY TYPE

ca.1930, 12 in. (30 cm). All composition, one piece head and body, jointed hips and shoulders. Repainted. Blue eyes, black line over eye, moulded hair, closed mouth. Mark: on head, RELIABLE/MADE IN/CANADA.
Ref.No.: D of C, BW29, p. 253.

Mint. $150.00   Ex. $95.00   G. $60.00   F. $40.00

RELIABLE - 1930

ca.1930. 26 in. (66 cm). Excelsior stuffed cloth body, legs, and upper arms, composition 3/4 arms. Composition shoulderhead; painted blue eyes with black line over eye, painted upper lashes; moulded brown hair; closed mouth. Mark: on shoulderplate, RELIABLE DOLL/MADE IN CANADA.
Ref.No.: D of C, CC2, p. 253.

Mint. $130.00   Ex. $ 75.00   G. $50.00   F. $40.00

RELIABLE - 1931

ca.1931. 17 in. (43 cm). Cloth body, composition arms and straight legs. Composition shoulderhead; blue metal eyes, lashes and painted lower lashes; moulded hair; open mouth showing two teeth. Mark: on shoulderplate, A/RELIABLE/DOLL/MADE IN CANADA.
Ref.No.: D of C, CP3, p. 254.

Mint. $140.00   Ex. $105.00   G.   75.00   F.   40.00

RELIABLE - 1932

ca.1932. 22 in. (56 cm). Cloth body, composition arms and straight legs. Composition head; green tin eyes, lashes, painted lower lashes; moulded brown hair; open mouth, two inset teeth. Mark: on head, A RELIABLE DOLL/MADE IN CANADA.
Ref.No.: D of C, CB34A, p. 254.

Mint. $250.00   Ex.   225.00   G.   140.00   F.   50.00

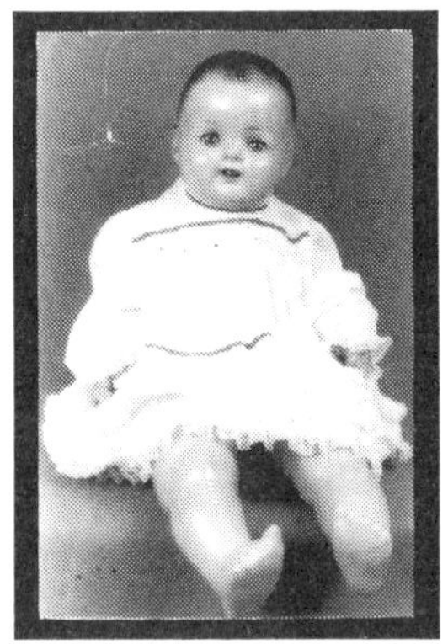

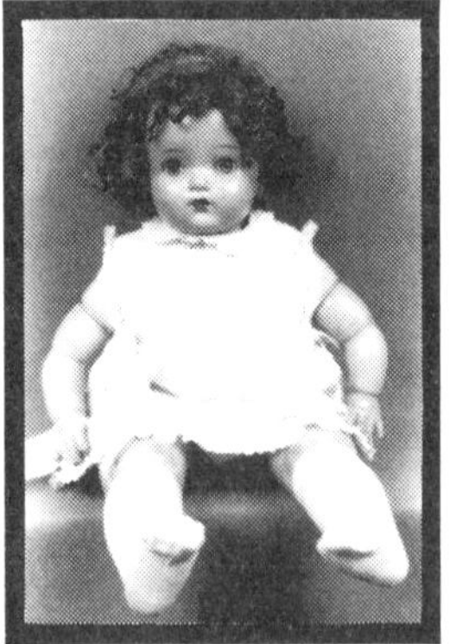

RELIABLE - 1932

ca.1932. 25 in. (63.5 cm). Cloth body, composition arms and straight legs. Composition head; blue glassene sleep eyes, lashes, painted lower lashes; brown mohair wig; closed mouth. Mark: on head, RELIABLE/MADE IN CANADA.
Ref.No.: D of C, BX2, p. 254.

Mint. $250.00   Ex. $225.00   G.   150.00   F.   60.00

BABY FONDA

ca.1933. 25 in. (63.5 cm). Cloth body, composition arms and straight legs. Composition head; blue tin sleep eyes, lashes, painted lower lashes; brown moulded hair; open mouth showing two teeth and tongue. Mark: on head, A RELIABLE/DOLL/MADE IN CANADA. Particularly attractive face.
Ref.No.: D of C, AO10, p. 255.

Mint. $250.00   Ex.   225.00   G.   150.00   F.   60.00

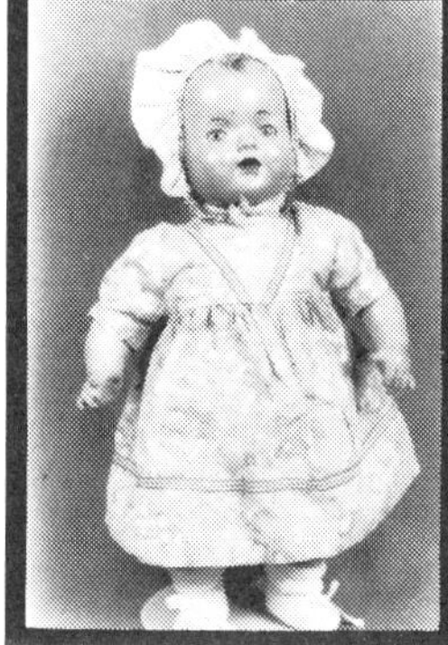

RELIABLE - 1933

ca.1933. 20 in. (51 cm). Cloth body, composition arms and straight legs. Composition head; blue tin sleep eyes, lashes, painted lower lashes; brown moulded hair; closed mouth. Mark: on head, A RELIABLE/DOLL MADE IN CANADA.
Ref.No.: D of C, CR20, p. 255.

Mint $150.00   Ex. $125.00   G.   95.00   F.   45.00

RELIABLE - 1933

ca.1933. 18 in. (45.5 cm). Cloth body, composition arms and straight legs. Composition shoulderhead; blue sleep eyes, lashes; brown moulded hair; closed mouth. Mark: on shoulderplate, RELIABLE/MADE IN CANADA.
Ref.No.: D of C, CH29, p. 255.

Mint $150.00   Ex. $125.00   G.   75.00   F.   40.00

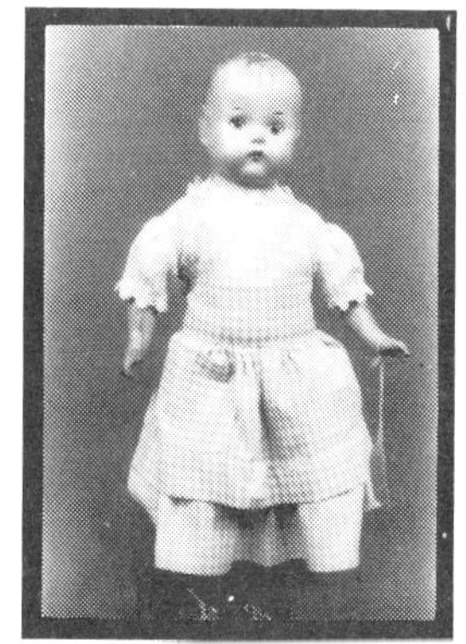

SHIRLEY TEMPLE

1934. 18 in. (45.5 cm). Compostion body, jointed hips, shoulders, and neck. Composition head with dimples; green sleep eyes, lashes, painted lower lashes; blond mohair wig; open mouth showing teeth. Mark: on head, SHIRLEY TEMPLE/COP. IDEAL/N.& T. CO.; on dress, A GENUINE/SHIRLEY TEMPLE/DOLL DRESS/RELIABLE TOY CO. LTD., along the side, MADE IN CANADA.
Ref.No.: D of C, AW23, p. 256.

Mint $650.00   Ex. $550.00   G.   300.00   F.   150.00

RELIABLE - 1934

ca.1934. 16 in. (40.5 cm). Cloth body with crier; composition arms and straight legs. Composition head; blue tin sleep eyes, lashes, painted lower lashes; brown moulded hair, closed mouth. Mark: on head, RELIABLE DOLL/MADE IN CANADA.
Ref.No.: D of C, CR22, p. 256.

Mint $150.00   Ex. $110.00   G.   85.00   F.   40.00

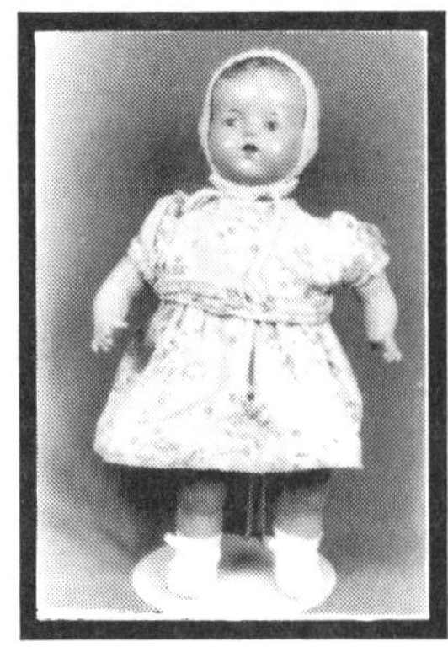

HAIRBOW PEGGY

ca.1935. 18 in. (45.5 cm). Excelsior stuffed cloth body and legs, composition forearms. Composition shoulderhead; blue painted eyes, black line over eye; well- defined moulded hair with a hole for a hair ribbon; closed mouth. Mark: on shoulderplate, A/RELIABLE/DOLL/MADE IN CANADA.
Ref.No.: D of C, BY9, p. 257.

Mint $150.00   Ex. $ 95.00   G.   75.00   F.   35.00

RELIABLE - 1935

ca.1935. 18 in. (45.5 cm). Cloth body, composition bent arms and straight legs. Composition shoulderhead; blue sleep eyes, lashes, painted lower lashes; moulded hair, originally had a wig; closed mouth. Mark: on shoulderplate, A/RELIABLE/DOLL/MADE IN CANADA.
Ref.No.: D of C, CW27, p. 257.

Mint $125.00   Ex. $ 95.00   G.   55.00   F.   35.00

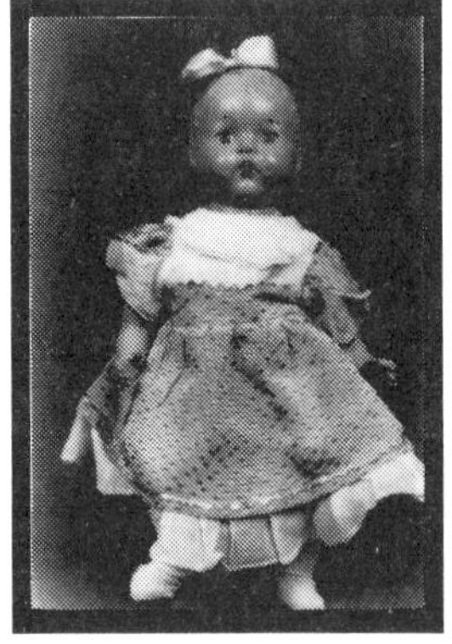

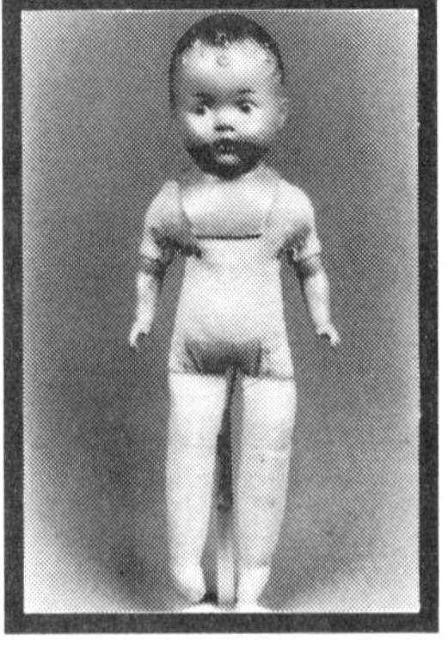

RELIABLE - 1935

ca.1935. 18 in. (45.5 cm). Excelsior stuffed cloth body, upper arms, and legs, composition 3/4 arms. Composition shoulderhead; blue painted side-glancing eyes, black line over eye; brown moulded hair; closed mouth. Mark: on shoulderplate, A/RELIABLE/DOLL/MADE IN CANADA.
Ref.No.: D of C, AP20, p. 257.

Mint $80.00   Ex. $65.00   G.   45.00   F.   30.00

BABY BUNTING

ca. 1835, 14 in. (35.5 cm). Cloth body and bent legs softly stuffed, composition arms. Composition head; blue sleep eyes; brown moulded hair; open mouth with two teeth. Mark: RELIABLE DOLL/MADE IN CANADA.
Ref.No.: D of C, CG11, p. 257.

Mint $120.00   Ex. $85.00   G.   50.00   F.   35.00

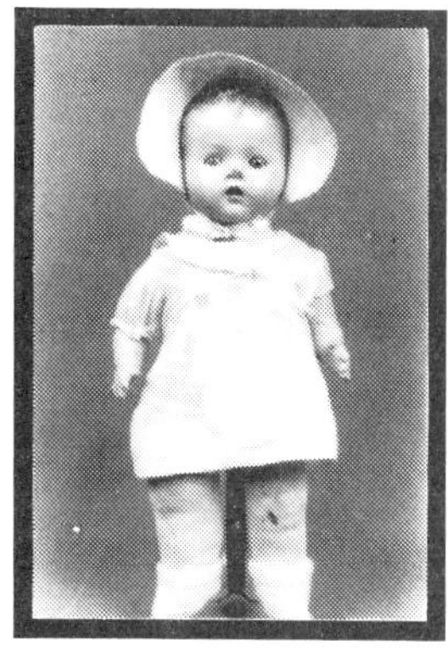

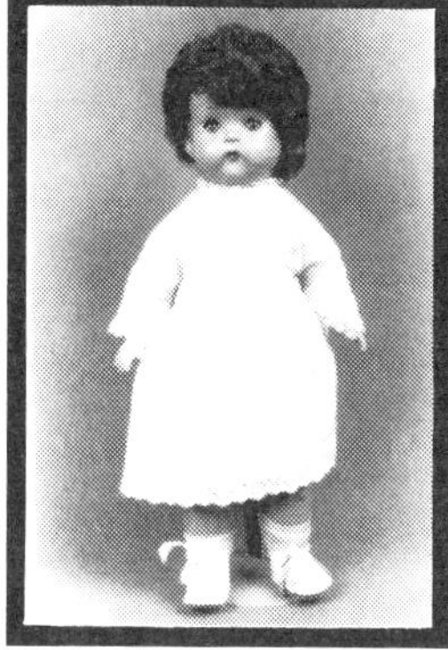

CHUBBY

ca.1935. 17 in. (43 cm). Cloth body, composition arms and straight legs. Composition head; blue tin sleep eyes, lashes, painted lower lashes; brown caracul wig; closed mouth. Mark: on head, RELIABLE/MADE IN CANADA.
Ref.No.: D of C, BF21, p. 258.

Mint $225.00   Ex. $150.00   G.   110.00   F.   75.00

SHIRLEY TEMPLE - 1936

ca. 1936. 25 in. (63.5 cm).Composition body, jointed hips, shoulders, and neck. Composition head with dimples; green glassene sleep eyes, lashes, painted lower lashes; blond mohair wig; open mouth showing teeth and tongue. Mark: no mark on the head or body. Original label on the dress, A GENUINE/SHIRLEY TEMPLE/DOLL DRESS/RELIABLE TOY CO. LTD.; along one side: MADE IN CANADA.
Ref.No.: D of C, AM11, p. 258.

Mint $800.00   Ex. $700.00   G. $325.00   F.$125.00

SHIRLEY TEMPLE LOOK ALIKE.

ca. 1936. 15 in. (38 cm). Composition body, jointed hips, shoulders, and head. Composition head with dimples; green sleep eyes, lashes, painted lower lashes; blond mohair wig; closed mouth. Mark: on head, RELIABLE/MADE IN CANADA.
Ref.No.: D of C, CD20, p. 259.

Mint $150.00   Ex. $100.00   G.   80.00   F.   40.00

RELIABLE - 1936

ca.1936. 14 in. (35.5 cm).Cloth body and legs, composition forearms. Composition shoulderhead; blue painted eyes, black line over eye, painted upper lashes; moulded brown hair; closed mouth. Mark: on shoulderplate, A RELIABLE DOLL/MADE IN CANADA.
Ref.No.: D of C, BN2, p. 259.

Mint $ 85.00   Ex. $ 50.00   G.   40.00   F.   25.00

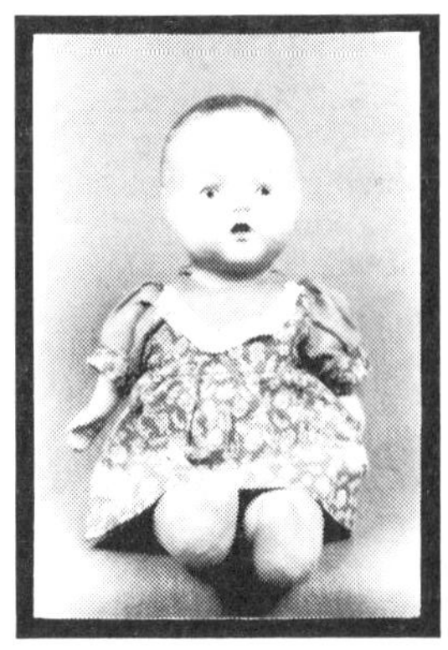

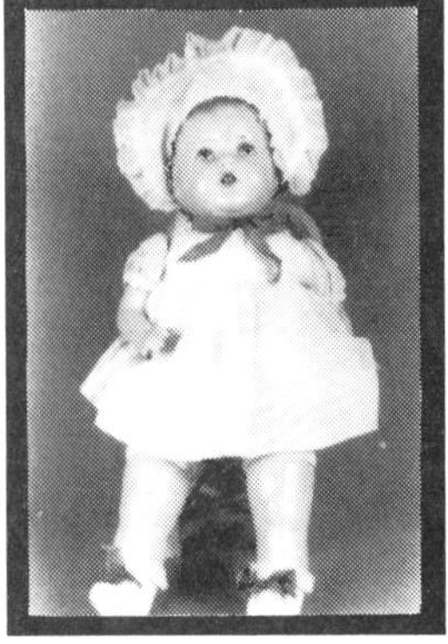

RELIABLE - 1936

ca.1936. 17 in. (43 cm). Cloth body, composition arms and straight legs. Composition head; blue sleep eyes, lashes; brown moulded hair; open mouth showing two teeth. Mark: on head, RELIABLE/MADE IN CANADA.
Ref.No.: D of C, BZ6, p. 259.

Mint $175.00   Ex. $150.00   G.   95.00   F.   45.00

MOUNTIE AND HORSE

1936. 17 in. (43 cm). Excelsior stuffed cloth body and legs; composition arms. Composition head; brown painted eyes; brown moulded hair; closed mouth. Mark: on head, RELIABLE/MADE IN CANADA.
Ref.No.: D of C, AO29, p. 260.

Note: Appears on new issue Canadian postage June 8, 1990.

Mint $350.00   Ex. $275.00   G.   195.00   F.   120.00

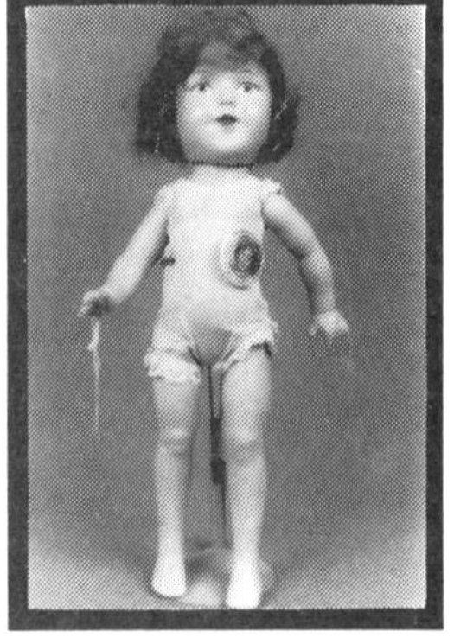

SHIRLEY TEMPLE - 1937

ca.1937. 13 in, (33 cm). Composition body, jointed hips, shoulders, and neck. Composition head with dimples; blue painted eyes with highlights, black painted upper lashes; light brown mohair wig; closed mouth. Mark: on head, RELIABLE/MADE IN CANADA; on body, SHIRLEY TEMPLE. Ref.No.: D of C, CA32, p. 260.

Mint $150.00   Ex. $125.00   G.   85.00   F.   45.00

SHIRLEY TEMPLE - 1938

1938. 19 in. (48.5 cm). Composition body, jointed hips, shoulders, and neck. Composition head; hazel glassene sleep eyes; lashes; blond mohair wig; open mouth showing teeth. Mark: on head, 16 SHIRLEY TEMPLE; original label on dress, A GENUINE SHIRLEY TEMPLE DOLL DRESS. RELIABLE TOY CO. LTD. MADE IN CANADA.
Ref.No.: D of C, BF22, p. 261.

Mint $650.00   Ex. $550.00   G.   300.00   F.   100.00

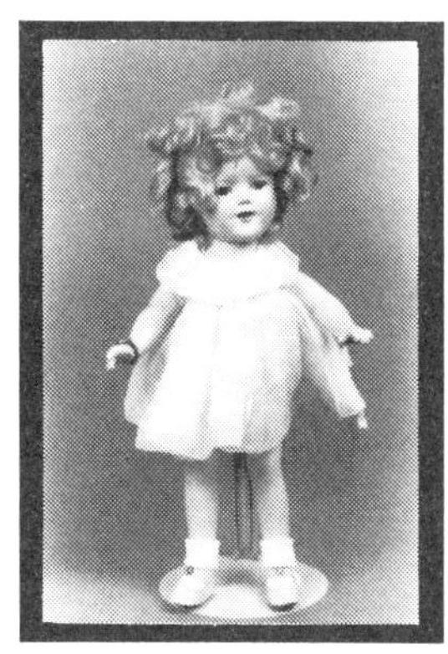

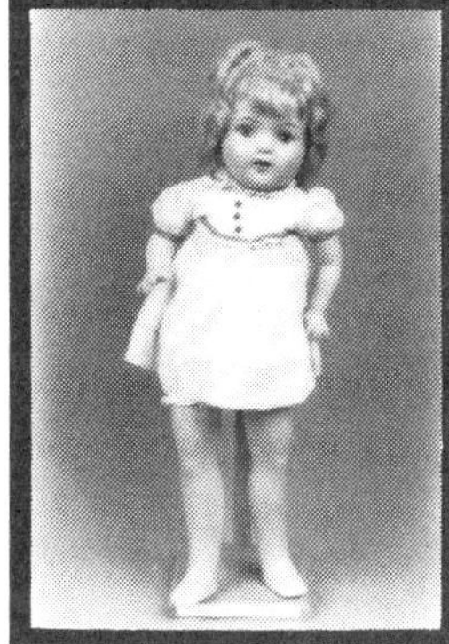

RELIABLE - 1938

ca. 1938. 20 in. (51 cm). Cloth body, composition arms and straight legs. Composition shoulderhead; blue metal sleep eyes; lashes, painted lower lashes; blond mohair wig; open mouth showing teeth. Mark: on head, RELIABLE/MADE IN CANADA.
Ref.No. D of C; CQ7 p. 261

Mint $200.00   Ex. $175.00   G. $140.00   F. $60.00

BABY MARILYN

ca. 1938. 14 in. (35.5 cm). All composition, jointed hips, shoulders, and neck. Composition head; brown sleep eyes,, lashes, painted lower lashes; brown moulded hair; closed mouth. Mark: no mark on doll, original label GENUINE/BABY MARILYN/DOLLS/RELIABLE TOY CO. LTD./MADE IN CANADA.
Ref.No.: D of C, BT4A, p. 261.

Mint $180.00   Ex. $150.00   G. $125.00   F. $60.00

SNOW WHITE

ca. 1938. 15 in. (38 cm). Cloth body and legs, composition forearms. Composition shoulderhead; blue painted eyes, black line over eye; brown moulded hair with hair bow moulded in; closed mouth. Mark: on shoulderplate, A RELIABLE DOLL/MADE IN CANADA.
Ref.No.: D of C, BZ17, p. 262.

Mint $150.00   Ex. $115.00   G. $70.00   F. $30.00

TOUSLEHEAD

1939. 17 in. (43 cm). Cloth body, composition arms and straight legs. Composition head; blue tin sleep eyes, lashes, brown caracul wig; open mouth showing two teeth and tongue. Mark: on head, A RELIABLE DOLL/MADE IN CANADA.
Ref.No.: D of C, BJ7, p. 256.

Mint $225.00   Ex. $150.00   G.   110.00   F.   75.00

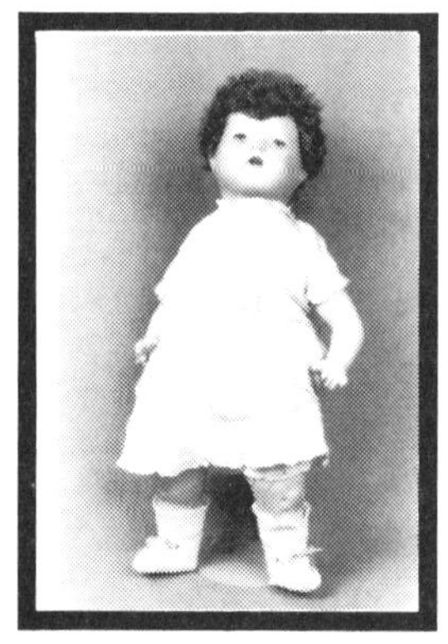

SHIRLEY TEMPLE - 1939

ca. 1939. 16 in. (40.5 cm). Composition body, jointed hips, shoulders, and neck. Composition head with dimples; green sleep eyes, lashes, painted lower lashes; blond mohair wig; open mouth showing six teeth. Mark: on head, SHIRLEY TEMPLE; on arms, 14; on body, SHIRLEY TEMPLE 14; on dress, A GENUINE/SHIRLEY TEMPLE/DOLL DRESS/RELIABLE TOY CO. LTD.; on side of label, MADE IN CANADA.
Ref.No. D of C; BZ18 p. 262

Mint $500.00   Ex. $400.00   G. $250.00   F. $125.00

LADDIE

ca. 1939. 12 in. (30 cm). All composition, jointed hips and shoulders. Composition head; blue painted eyes, black line over eye; light brown moulded hair; closed mouth. Mark: on back, RELIABLE/MADE IN/CANADA.
Ref.No.: D of C, BH29, p. 262.

Mint $125.00   Ex. $90.00   G. $50.00   F. $30.00

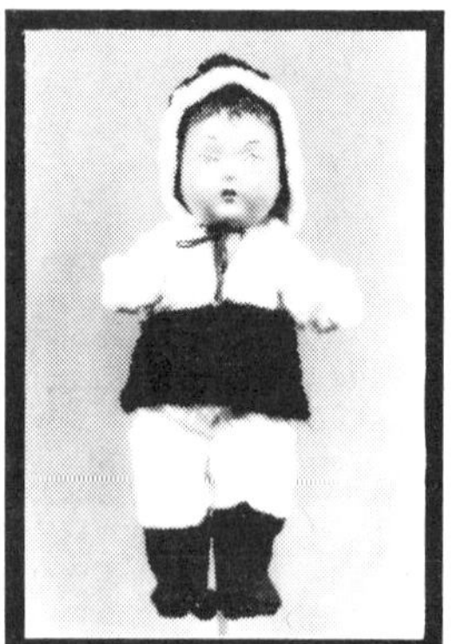

ESKIMO

ca. 1939. 14 in. (35.5 cm). All composition, jointed hips, shoulders, and neck. Composition head; black, almond shaped painted eyes, black line over eyes; black moulded hair; closed mouth. Mark: on head, 1/RELIABLE/MADE IN CANADA.
Ref.No.: D of C, AT12, p. 263.

Mint $130.00   Ex. $95.00   G. $70.00   F. $45.00

BABY MARILYN

ca. 1939. 15 in. (38 cm). All composition body, jointed hips, shoulders, and neck. Composition head; blue tin sleep eyes, lashes, painted lower lashes; blond mohair curly wig; open mouth showing two teeth. Mark: on head, RELIABLE/MADE IN CANADA.
Ref.No.: D of C, BZ24, p. 263.

Mint $200.00   Ex. $175.00   G. $130.00   F. $60.00

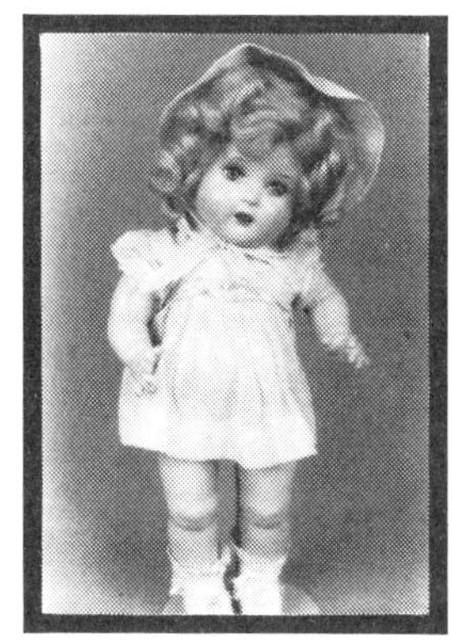

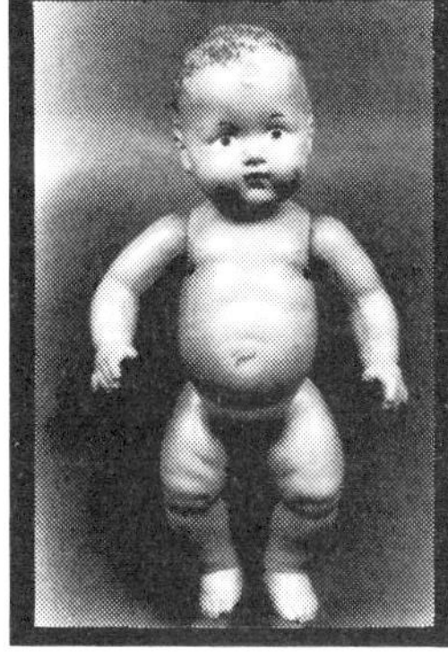

WETTUMS

ca. 1939. 17 in. (43 cm). All composition, jointed hips, shoulders, and neck. Composition head; blue painted eyes; brown moulded hair; open mouth nurser. Mark: on head, RELIABLE TOY/MADE IN CANADA.
Ref.No.: D of C, CW17, p. 263.

Mint $100.00   Ex. $ 80.00   G. $60.00   F. $30.00

PIGTAILS

ca. 1939. 18.5 in. (47 cm). Composition body, jointed hips, shoulders, and neck. Composition head; blue sleep eyes, lashes, painted lower lashes, grey eyeshadow over eyelids; honey blond mohair wig in original braids with curled bangs; open mouth showing four teeth. Mark: on head, RELIABLE/MADE IN CANADA.
Ref.No. D of C; CD13 p. 264

Mint $200.00   Ex. $175.00   G. $140.00   F. $60.00

BABYKINS

ca. 1939. 12 in. (30 cm). All composition, jointed hips and shoulders. Composition head; blue painted eyes, black line over eye, painted upper lashes; brown moulded hair; closed mouth. Mark: on head, RELIABLE/MADE IN CANADA. Original gold label, MADE IN CANADA/BABYKINS/A RELIABLE DOLL/A BRITISH EMPIRE PRODUCT.
Ref.No.: D of C, BW21, p. 264.

Mint $90.00   Ex. $70.00   G. $50.00   F. $30.00

SCOTTISH LASSIE

ca. 1940. 15 in. (38 cm). All composition, jointed hips, shoulders, and neck. Composition head; blue sleep eyes, lashes, painted lower lashes; brown wig; closed mouth. Mark: on head, RELIABLE/MADE IN CANADA.
Ref.No.: D of C, BJ5, p. 264.

Mint $125.00   Ex. $ 95.00   G.   60.00   F.   30.00

RELIABLE - 1940

ca.1940. 14 in. (35.5 cm). Brown composition, jointed hips, shoulders, and neck. Composition head; black painted side-glancing eyes; black braided wool wig over moulded hair; open-closed mouth. Mark: on head, RELIABLE/MADE IN CANADA.
Ref.No.: D of C, BN17, p. 265.

Note: Brown composition dolls are hard to find.

Mint $135.00   Ex. $100.00   G. $75.00   F.$40.00

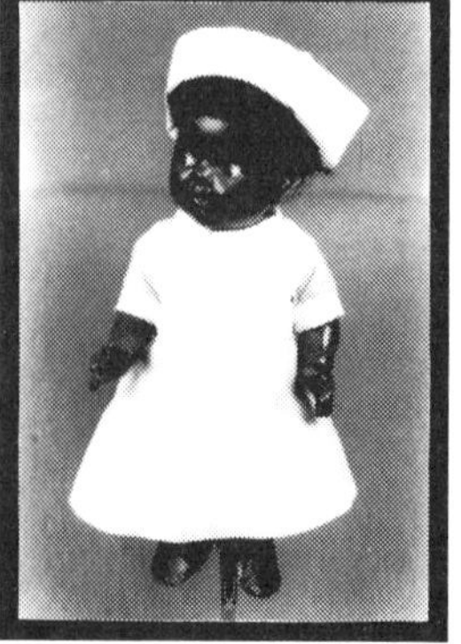

TOPSY

ca. 1940. 17 in. (43 cm). All composition, dark brown, jointed hips, shoulders, and neck. Composition head; black painted side-glancing eyes, painted upper lashes; black moulded hair with three inset wool braids; open-closed mouth with two painted teeth. Mark: on head, RELIABLE/MADE IN CANADA.
Ref.No.: D of C, BH12, p. 266.

Mint $250.00   Ex. $225.00   G. $150.00   F. $60.00

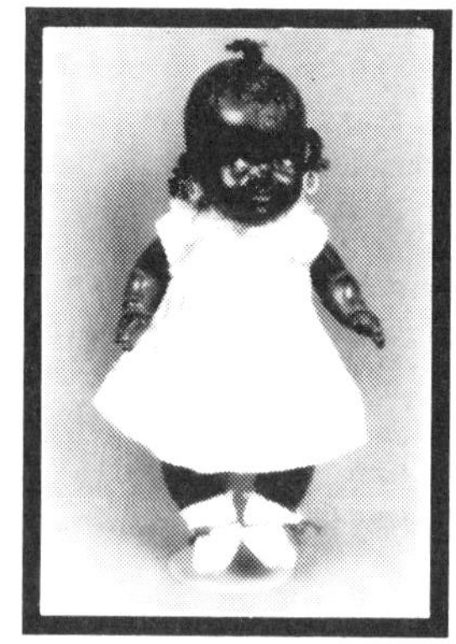

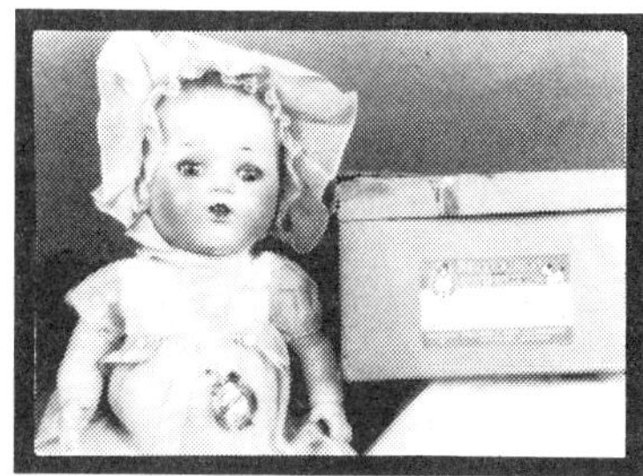

CHUCKLES

1940. 20 in. (51 cm). All composition jointed hips, shoulders, and neck. Composition head; blue tin sleep eyes, lashes, painted lower lashes; brown moulded hair; open mouth showing two teeth and tongue. Mark: on head, RELIABLE/MADE IN CANADA. Original label, MADE IN CANADA/CHUCKLES/RELIABLE TOY CO.
Ref.No.: D of C, CN31, p. 265.

Mint	**$225.00**	**Ex.**	**$185.00**
G.	**$115.00**	**F.**	**$50.00**

KENNY-TOK

1940. 24 in. (61 cm). Sawdust filled cloth body, composition forearms. Composition head with moveable jaw that opens when the string at the back is pulled; painted brown side-glancing eyes; moulded hair painted black; five painted teeth. Mark: on head, MFG. BY/RELIABLE TOY CO/CANADA.
Ref.No.: D of C, BZ2, p. 266.

Note: Regional price differences, lower in the western provinces and the Maritimes.

Mint $225.00   Ex. $195.00   G. $150.00   F. $115.00

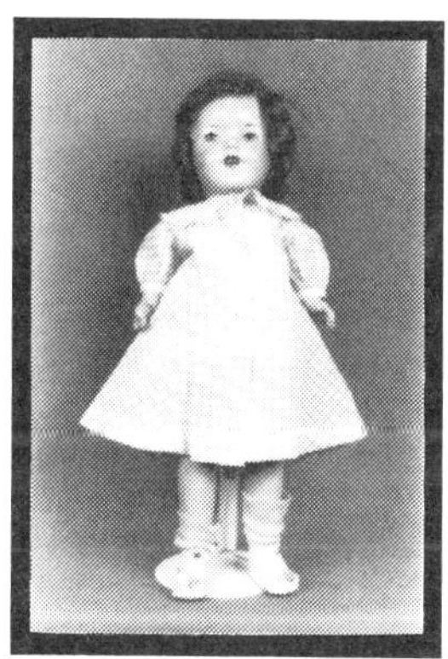

SALLY ANN

1940. 18 in. (45.5 cm). Cloth body, composition arms and straight legs. Composition head; blue tin sleep eyes, lashes; brown mohair wig; open mouth showing teeth. Mark: on head, A RELIABLE DOLL/MADE IN CANADA.
Ref.No.: D of C, BH13, p. 266.

Mint $160.00   Ex. $125.00   G. $100.00   F. $50.00

GLORIA

1940. 18 in. (45.5 cm). Cloth body, composition 3/4 arms and straight legs. Composition shoulderhead; dark blue tin eyes, painted upper lashes; brown mohair wig parted on one side; open mouth showing teeth. Mark: on shoulderplate, A/RELIABLE/DOLL/MADE IN CANADA.
Ref.No.: D of C, CL36, p. 267.

Mint $125.00   Ex. $95.00   G. $75.00   F. $35.00

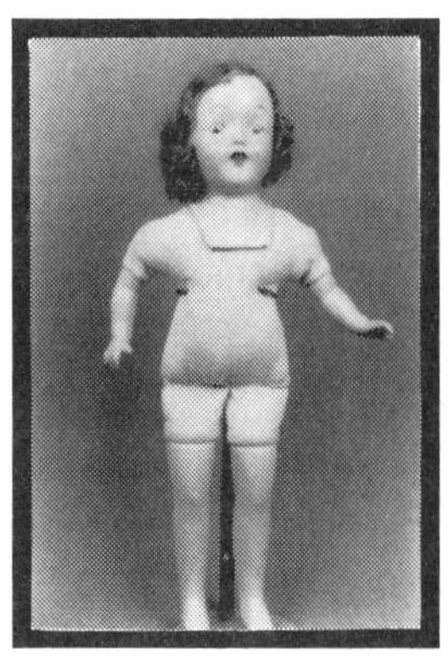

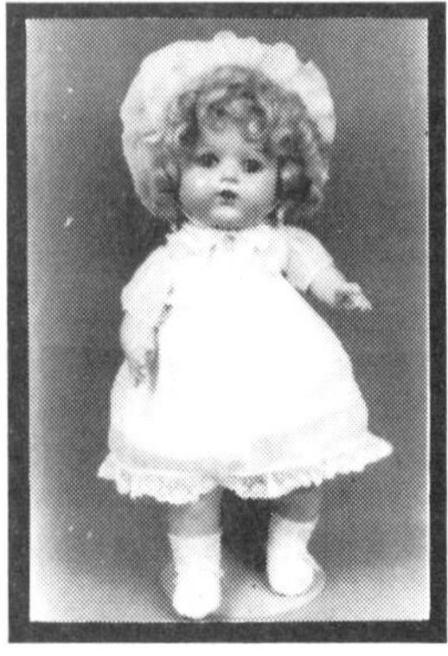

JOAN

1940. 20 in. (51 cm). All composition body, jointed hips, shoulders, and neck. Composition head; blue glassene sleep eyes, lashes, painted lower lashes; blond mohair curly wig; open mouth showing two teeth and tongue. Mark: on head, RELIABLE/MADE IN CANADA.
Ref.No.: D of C, CM11, p. 267.

Mint $230.00   Ex. $175.00   G. $125.00   F. $65.00

BABYKINS

1940. 12 in. (30 cm). All composition, jointed hips, shoulders, and neck. Composition head; blue sleep eyes, lashes, painted lower lashes; brown moulded hair; open mouth showing two teeth and tongue. Mark: no mark on doll but wearing the original tag, MADE IN CANADA/BABYKINS/A RELIABLE/DOLL/MADE BY RELIABLE TOY CO.
Ref.No.: D of C, CG14, p. 267.

Mint $105.00   Ex. $80.00   G. $60.00   F. $35.00

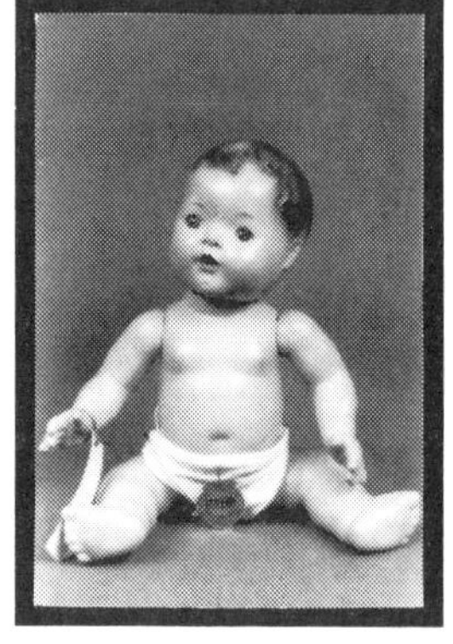

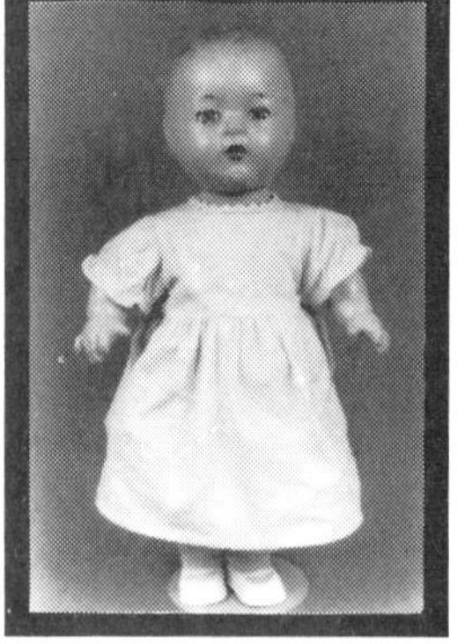

RELIABLE - 1940

ca. 1940 16 in. (40.5 cm). All composition, jointed hips, shoulders, and neck. Composition head; blue sleep eyes, lashes, painted lower lashes; light brown moulded hair; closed mouth. Mark: on head, RELIABLE/MADE IN CANADA.
Ref.No.: D of C, BY10, p. 268.

Mint $115.00   Ex. $85.00   G. $65.00   F. $35.00

WETUMS

1940. 11 in. (28 cm). All composition, jointed hips and shoulders. Blue painted eyes, black line over eye; light brown moulded hair; open mouth nurser. Mark: on head, RELIABLE/MADE IN/CANADA. Original tag, MADE IN CANADA/RELIABLE/A RELIABLE DOLL (in script)/A BRITISH EMPIRE PRODUCT/RELIABLE TOY CO. LIMITED.
Ref.No.: D of C, CD18, p. 268.

Mint $90.00   Ex. $65.00   G. $40.00   F. $25.00

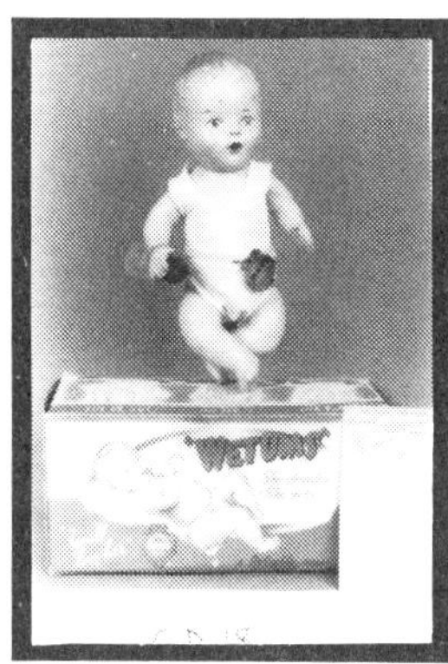

CUDDLEKINS

1940. 19 in. (47 cm). All composition, jointed hips, shoulders, and neck. Composition head; blue metal sleep eyes, lashes, painted lower lashes; light brown moulded curls, originally had a wig; open mouth showing two teeth. Mark: on head, RELIABLE/MADE IN CANADA.
Ref.No.: D of C, CC13, p. 268.

Mint $225.00   Ex. $185.00   G. $115.00   F. $50.00

NURSE

1941. 24 in. (61 cm). Excelsior stuffed cloth body and legs, composition forearms. Composition shoulderhead; blue painted eyes, painted upper lashes; moulded light brown curls; closed mouth. Mark: on shoulderplate, RELIABLE DOLL/MADE IN/CANADA.
Ref.No.: D of C, CT3, p. 269.

Mint $150.00   Ex. $125.00   G. $85.00   F. $45.00

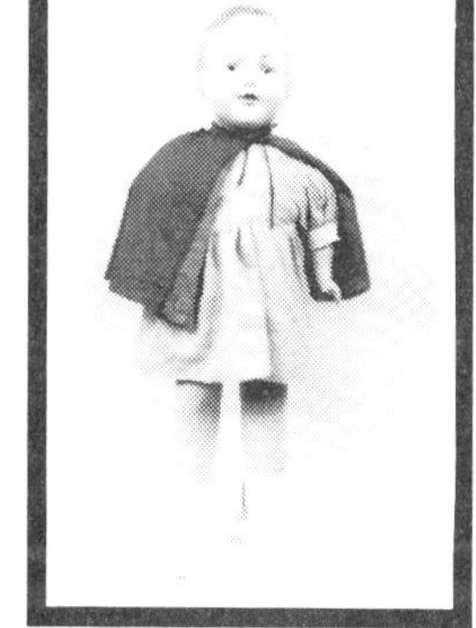

OLD FASHIONED GIRL

1941. 15.5 in. (39 cm). All composition, jointed hips, shoulders, and neck. Composition head; blue tin sleep eyes, lashes, painted lower lashes; blond mohair wig; open mouth showing four teeth. Mark: on head, RELIABLE/MADE IN CANADA.
Ref.No.: D of C, BJ8, p. 269.

Mint $175.00   Ex. $120.00   G. $75.00   F. $5.00

BABYKINS

1941. 20 in. (51 cm). All composition, jointed hips, shoulders, and neck. Composition head; blue glassene eyes, lashes, painted lower lashes; brown moulded hair; open mouth showing two teeth. Mark: on head, RELIABLE/MADE IN CANADA.
Ref.No.: D of C, AM31, p. 269.

Mint $175.00   Ex. $125.00   G. $75.00   F. $40.00

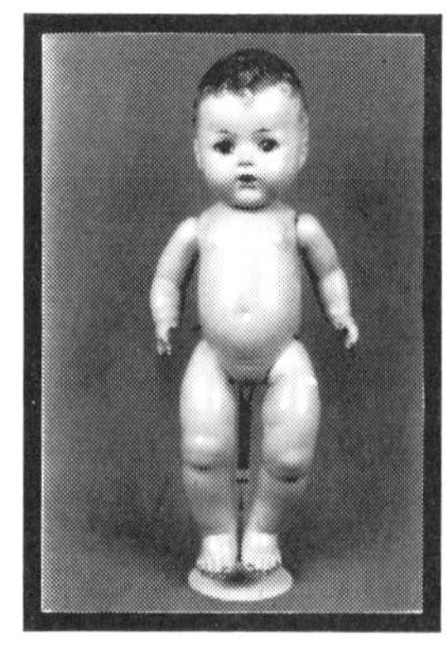

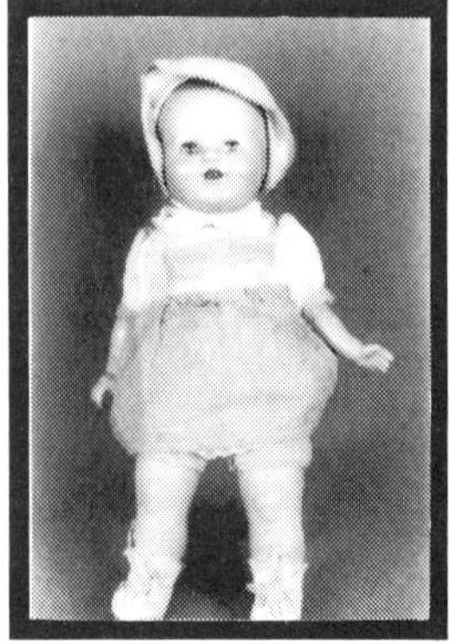

CUDDLEKINS

1941. 15 in. (38 cm). Cloth body, composition arms and straight legs. Composition shoulderhead, dimples; blue tin sleep eyes, lashes, painted lower lashes; brown moulded hair; open mouth showing two teeth. Mark: on shoulderplate, RELIABLE/DOLL/MADE IN CANADA.
Ref.No.: D of C, BZ33, p. 270.

Mint $150.00   Ex. $105.00   G. $60.00   F. $35.00

RELIABLE - 1941

ca. 1941. All composition, jointed at hips, shoulders, and neck. Composition head; blue tin sleep eyes, lashes, painted lower lashes; brown mohair wig, moulded hair underneath; open mouth showing two teeth and tongue. Mark: on head, RELIABLE/MADE IN CANADA.
Ref.No.: D of C, BH35, p. 270.

Mint $185.00   Ex. $120.00   G. $85.00   F. $45.00

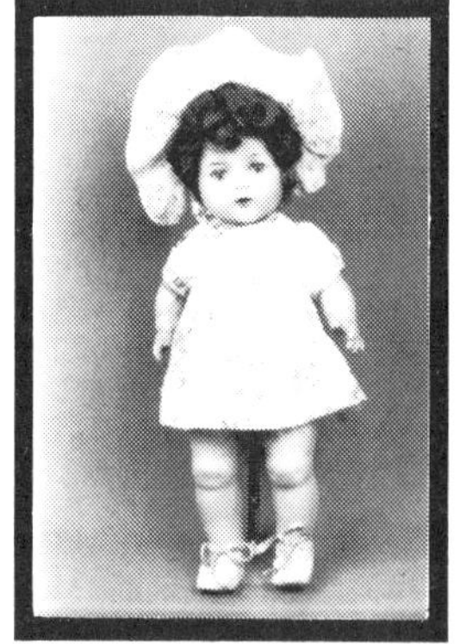

ARMY DOLL

1942. 13 in. (33 cm). Excelsior stuffed body and legs, composition forearms. Composition shoulderhead; blue painted eyes, fine black line over eye; light brown moulded hair; closed mouth. Mark: on shoulderplate, RELIABLE DOLL/MADE IN CANADA.
Ref.No.: D of C, Cl30, p. 270.

Mint $95.00   Ex. $65.00   G. $45.00   F. $30.00

RELIABLE - 1942

ca. 1942. 14 in. (35.5 cm). All composition, jointed hips, shoulders, and neck. Composition head; blue tin sleep eyes, lashes; brown moulded hair, originally wore a wig; open mouth, showing two teeth. Mark: RELIABLE/MADE IN CANADA.
Ref.No.: D of C, CL2, p. 271.

Mint $105.00   Ex. $85.00   G. $60.00   F. $40.00

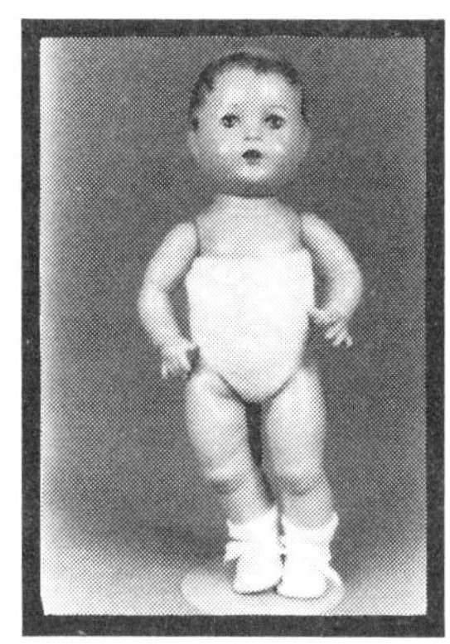

RELIABLE - 1942

ca. 1942. 19 in. (48.5 cm). Composition body, jointed hips, shoulders, and neck. Composition head; blue tin sleep eyes, lashes, painted lower lashes; brown mohair wig with bangs; open mouth showing teeth and tongue. Mark: on head, RELIABLE/MADE IN CANADA.
Ref.No.: D of C, CY5, p. 271.

Mint $210.00   Ex. $185.00   G. $125.00   F. $60.00

RELIABLE - 1942

ca. 1942. 21.5 in. (55 cm). Excelsior stuffed cloth body, legs and upper arms, composition 3/4 arms. Composition shoulderhead; blue painted eyes, black line over eye; brown moulded hair; closed mouth. Mark: on shoulderplate, A RELIABLE DOLL/MADE IN CANADA.
Ref.No.: D of C, CC3, p. 271.

Mint $95.00   Ex. $70.00   G. $50.00   F. $30.00

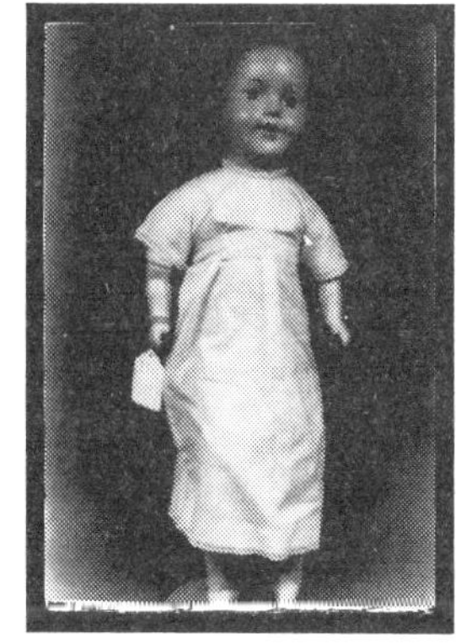

STANDING DOLL, NURSE

1942. 8 in. (20.5 cm). All composition, jointed shoulders. Black painted side-glancing eyes, painted upper lashes; blond mohair wig; closed mouth. Mark: on back, RELIABLE/MADE IN CANADA.
Ref.No.: D of C, BW19, p. 272.

Mint $50.00   Ex. $40.00   G. $30.00   F. $20.00

RED CROSS NURSE

1942. 18 in. (45.5 cm). Excelsior stuffed cloth body, composition arms and straight legs. Composition shoulderhead; blue painted eyes, black line over eye, painted upper lashes; blond mohair wig; closed mouth. Mark: on shoulderplate, RELIABLE DOLL/MADE IN CANADA.
Ref.No.: D of C, Cl34, p. 272.

Mint $110.00   Ex. $75.00   G. $50.00   F. $30.00

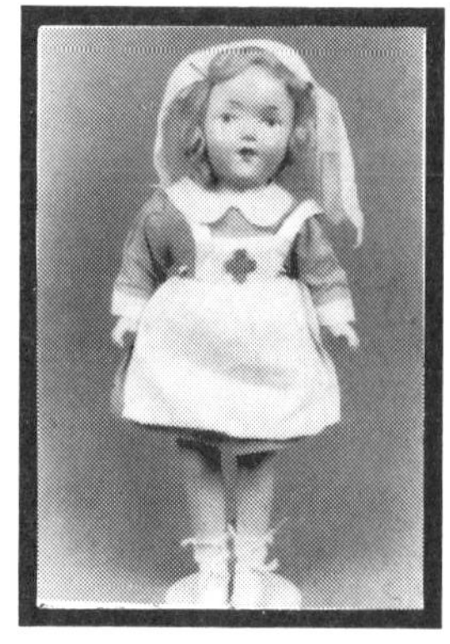

BABY LOVUMS - 1942

1942. 17 in. (43 cm). Cloth body, composition hands and bent limb legs. Composition head; green sleep eyes, lashes, painted lower lashes; brown mohair curly wig; closed mouth. Mark: on head, A/RELIABLE/DOLL.
Ref.No.: D of C, CD4, p. 283.

Note: Listed in the first edition (1986) D of C incorrectly as 1948.

Mint $230.00   Ex. $195.00   G. $120.00   F.   65.00

STANDING DOLL, ARMY

ca. 1943. 8 in. (20.5 cm). Composition body and head, jointed shoulders. Painted side-glancing eyes; mohair wig, closed mouth. Mark: on body, RELIABLE/MADE IN/CANADA. Original army uniform, moulded painted shoes and socks.
Ref.No.: D of C, BM24, p. 107.

Mint. $50.00   Ex. $40.00   G. $40.00   F. $20.00

STANDING DOLL, AIR FORCE

ca. 1943. 8 in. (20.5 cm). All composition, jointed shoulders. Black painted side-glancing eyes, painted upper lashes; blond mohair wig; closed mouth. Mark: on back, RELIABLE/MADE IN CANADA.
Ref.No.: D of C, BW17, 272.

Mint $50.00   Ex. $40.00   G. $30.00   F. $20.00

RELIABLE - 1943

ca. 1943. 18 in. (45.5 cm). All composition body, jointed hips, shoulders, and neck. Composition head; blue tin sleep eyes, lashes; blond mohair wig; open mouth with teeth and felt tongue. Mark: on head, RELIABLE/MADE IN CANADA.
Ref.No. D of C, XH25, p. 273.

Mint $185.00   Ex. $165.00   G. $120.00   F. $60.00

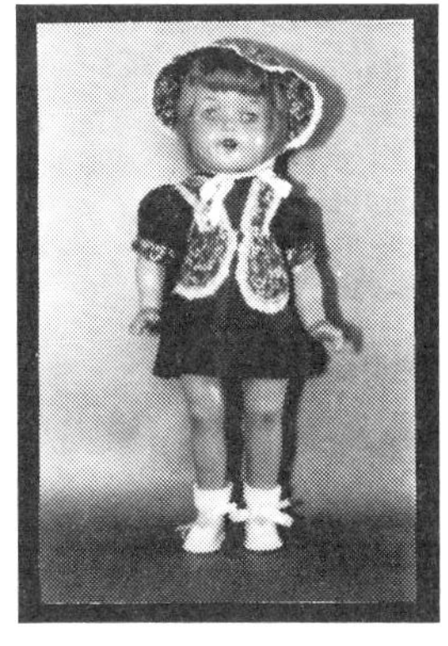

AIR FORCE DOLL

ca. 1943. 18 in. (43 cm). Cloth body and legs, composition arms. Composition head; painted brown eyes, black line over eye; brown moulded hair; closed mouth. Mark: on head, RELIABLE/MADE IN/CANADA.
Ref.No.: D of C, CA2, p. 273.

Mint $195.00   Ex. $150.00   G. $95.00   F. $45.00

BABY PRECIOUS - 19 in.

1943. 19 in. (48.5cm). Cloth body, composition arms and straight legs. Composition head; blue tin sleep eyes, lashes, painted lower lashes; light brown mohair wig over moulded hair; closed mouth. Mark: on head, A RELIABLE DOLL.
Ref.No.: D of C, BN35, p. 273.

Mint $200.00   Ex. $170.00   G. $100.00   F. $60.00

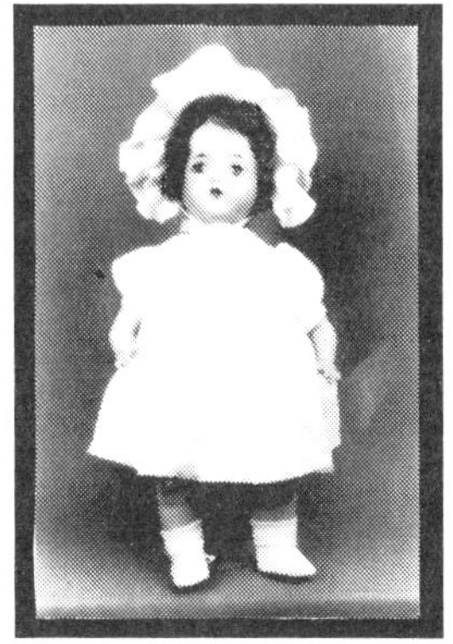

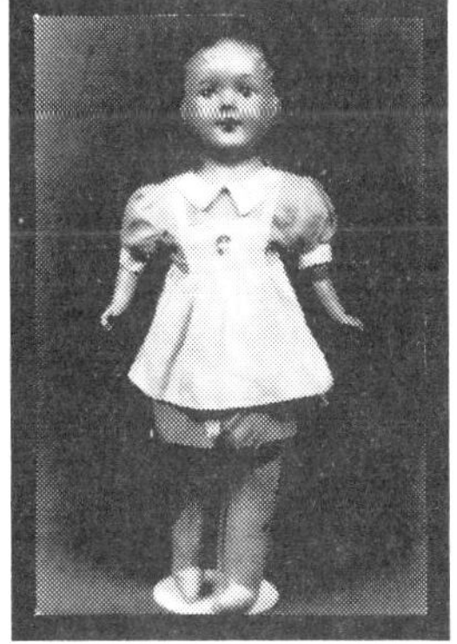

NURSE DOLL

1944. 24 in. (61 cm). Excelsior stuffed cloth body and legs, composition arms. Composition shoulderhead; blue painted eyes, white highlights, fine black line over eye, painted upper lashes; brown moulded hair; closed mouth. Mark: A RELIABLE DOLL/MADE IN CANADA.
Ref.No.: D of C, CW28, p. 274.

Mint $150.00   Ex. $125.00   G. $85.00   F. $45.00

STANDING DOLL, INDIAN GIRL

1944. 8 in. (20.5 cm). All composition, jointed shoulders. Black painted side-glancing eyes, painted upper lashes; black synthetic wig in braids; closed mouth. Mark: on body, RELIABLE/MADE IN/CANADA.
Ref.No.: D of C, CN18, p. 274.

Mint $50.00 Ex. $40.00 G. $30.00 F. $20.00

STANDING DOLL

ca. 1945. 8 in. (20.5 cm). All composition, jointed shoulders. Black painted side-glancing eyes, painted upper lashes; blond mohair wig; closed mouth. Mark: on back, RELIABLE/MADE IN/CANADA.
Ref.No.: D of C, BP8, p. 274.

Mint $45.00 Ex. $35.00 G. $25.00 F. $15.00

MINIATURE DOLL

1945. 11 in. (28 cm). All hard plastic, jointed shoulders and neck. Hard plastic head; blue plastic side-glancing sleep eyes, painted upper lashes; blond mohair wig; closed mouth. Mark: on body, RELIABLE/MADE IN CANADA.
Ref.No.: D of C, CL8, p. 275.

Mint $20.00 Ex. $15.00 G. $10.00 F. $8.00

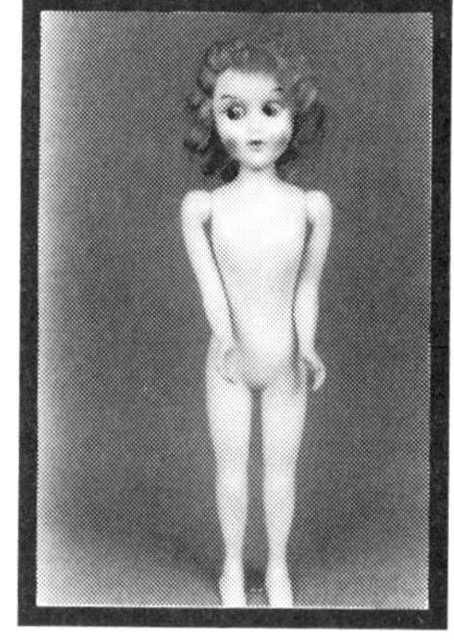

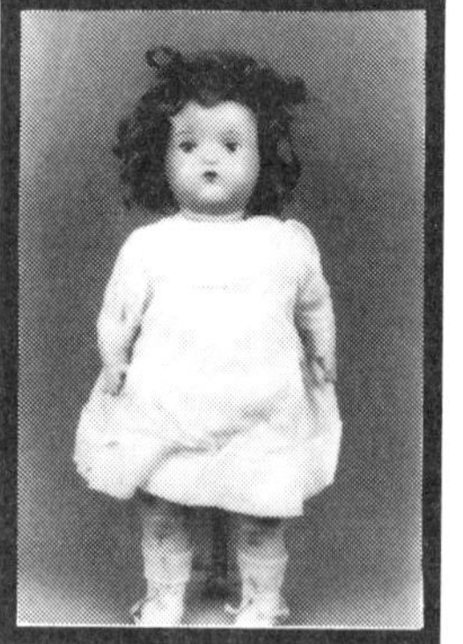

BABY PRECIOUS - 17 in.

ca. 1945. 17 in. (43 cm). Cloth body, composition arms and straight legs. Composition head; blue sleep eyes, lashes, painted lower lashes; light brown mohair wig; closed mouth. Mark: RELIABLE/DOLL/MADE IN CANADA.
Ref.No.: D of C, CJ35, p. 275.

Mint $200.00 Ex. $170.00 G. $100.00 F. $50.00

RELIABLE - 1946

ca. 1946. 14 in. (35.5 cm). All composition bent limb baby, jointed hips, shoulders, neck, and wrists. Composition head; glassene sleep eyes, lashes, painted lower lashes; painted hair; closed mouth. Mark: RELIABLE/MADE IN CANADA.
Ref.No.: D of C, BF27, p. 275.

Mint $120.00   Ex. $90.00   G. $65.00   F.   35.00

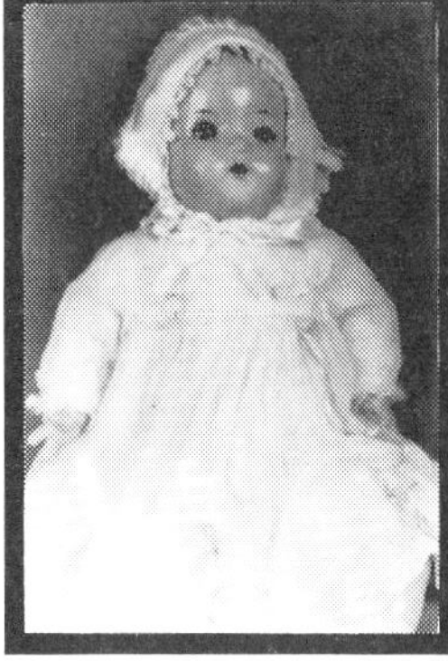

BABY LOVUMS - 24 in.

ca. 1947. 24 in. (61 cm). Cloth body with crier, composition hands and bent-limb legs. Composition head; blue sleep eyes, lashes, painted lower lashes, black eye shadow over eye; light brown moulded hair; closed mouth. Mark: on head, RELIABLE.
Ref.No.: D of C, CB7, p. 276.

Mint $255.00   Ex. $200.00   G. $135.00   F. $60.00

BABY LOVUMS - 26 in.

ca. 1947. 26 in. (66 cm). Cloth body with crier, composition bent-limb arms and legs. Composition head; blue sleep eyes, lashes, painted lower lashes; brown mohair wig; closed mouth. Mark: on head, RELIABLE.
Ref.No.: D of C, BZ22, p. 276.

Mint $275.00   Ex. $250.00   G. $150.00   F. $70.00

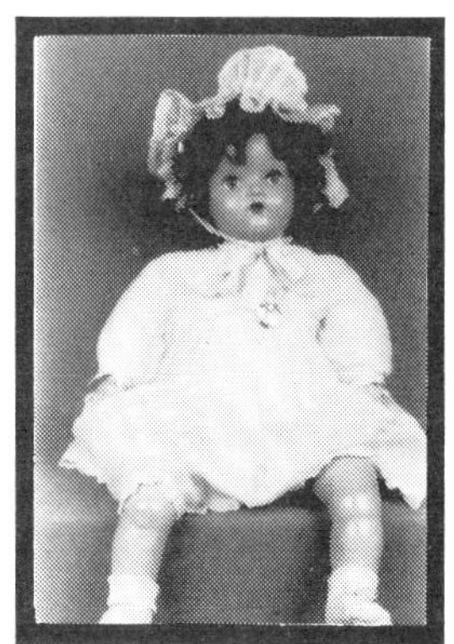

MAGGIE MUGGINS

1947. 15 in. (38 cm). All composition, jointed hips, shoulders, and neck. Composition head; blue sleep eyes, lashes, painted lower lashes and freckles; red mohair wig in pigtails; open mouth showing teeth. Mark: on head, RELIABLE/MADE IN CANADA.
Ref.No.: D of C, AP10, p. 276.

Note: Maggie Muggins is much in demand and very hard to find. Appears on new Canadian postage stamps June 8, 1990.

Mint $350.00   Ex. $275.00   G. $160.00   F. $85.00

BABY PRECIOUS - 20 in.

ca. 1947. 20 in. (51 cm). Cloth body, composition arms and straight legs. Composition head; blue sleep eyes, lashes, painted lower lashes; blond mohair wig; closed mouth. Mark: on head, A/RELIABLE/DOLL.
Ref.No.: D of C, BF28, p. 277.

Mint $245.00   Ex. $195.00   G. $110.00   F. $60.00

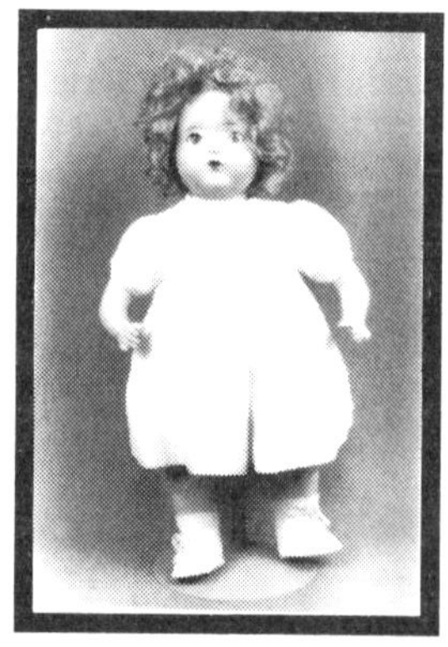

LADDIE

ca. 1947. 12 in. (30.5 cm). All composition, jointed hips and shoulders. Blue painted eyes, black line over eye; light brown moulded hair; closed mouth. Mark: on head, RELIABLE/MADE IN/CANADA.
Ref.No.: D of C, AO23, p. 277.

Mint $125.00   Ex. $90.00   G. $60.00   F. $30.00

BABY JEAN

1947. 12 in. (30.5 cm). All composition, jointed hips and shoulders. One piece head and body. Painted blue eyes; moulded brown curls; closed mouth. Mark: on body, RELIABLE/MADE IN/CANADA; label, BABY JEAN.
Ref.No.: D of C, CX13, p. 277.

Mint $85.00   Ex. $60.00   G. $50.00   F. $25.00

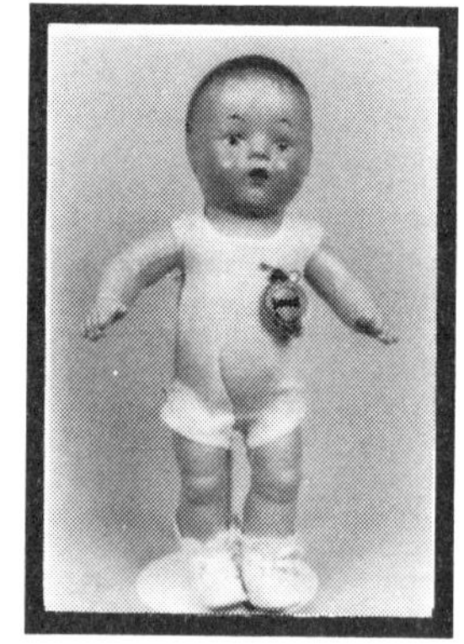

BABY MARILYN

1947. 20 in. (51 cm). All composition, jointed hips, shoulders, and neck. Composition head; blue plastic sleep eyes, lashes, painted lower lashes; blond mohair wig; closed mouth. Mark: on head, RELIABLE/MADE IN CANADA ; original gold name label.
Ref.No.: D of C, CT4, p. 278.

Mint $200.00   Ex. $165.00   G. $115.00   F. $60.00

GLORIA

ca. 1948. 18 in. (45.5 cm). Cloth body, composition arms and straight legs. Composition shoulderhead; blue sleep eyes, lashes; blond mohair wig; closed mouth. Mark: on shoulderplate, RELIABLE/MADE/IN CANADA.
Ref.No.: D of C, CF28, p. 278.

Mint $125.00   Ex. $95.00   G. $55.00   F. $35.00

HIAWATHA

1948. 12 in. (30.5 cm). All composition, jointed hips and shoulders. Brown painted eyes, black line over eye; black wig in braids; closed mouth. Mark: on back, RELIABLE/MADE IN CANADA.
Ref.No.: D of C, BH6, p. 278.

Mint $140.00   Ex. $105.00   G. $55.00   F. $30.00

PIGTAILS

1948. 15 in. (38 cm). All composition, jointed hips, shoulders, and neck. Composition head; blue sleep eyes, lashes, painted lower lashes; blond mohair wig in pigtails with curled bangs; closed mouth. Mark: on head, RELIABLE/MADE IN CANADA.
Ref.No.: D of C, CD26, p. 279.

Mint $125.00   Ex. $95.00   G. $55.00   F. $35.00

SCOTCH LASSIE

1948. 15 in. (38 cm). Composition body, jointed hips, shoulders, and neck. Composition head; blue tin sleep eyes, lashes, painted lower lashes; blond mohair wig with bangs; closed mouth. Mark: on head, RELIABLE/MADE IN CANADA.
Ref.No.: D of C, CY8, p. 279.

Mint $130.00   Ex. $100.00   G. $55.00   F. $30.00

BABY MARILYN

1948. 20 in. (51 cm). All composition toddler, jointed hips, shoulders, and neck. Composition head; blue sleep eyes, lashes, painted lower lashes; blond wig; closed mouth. Mark: No mark on doll. Original Reliable tag.
Ref.No.: D of C, BF32, p. 279.

Mint $200.00   Ex. $165.00   G. $115.00   F. $60.00

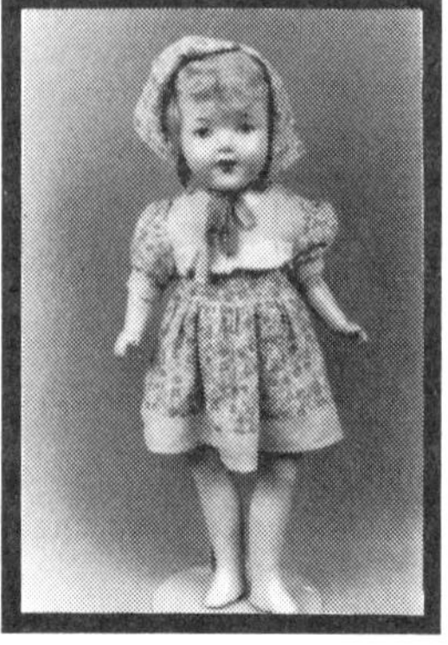

GLORIA

1948. 18 in. (45.5 cm). Cloth body, composition arms and straight legs. Composition shoulderhead; blue sleep eyes, lashes, painted lower lashes; blond mohair wig; closed mouth. Mark; on shoulderplate, A/RELIABLE/DOLL/MADE IN CANADA.
Ref.No.: D of C, CO18, p. 280.

Mint $125.00   Ex. $95.00   G. $55.00   F. $35.00

BABY PRECIOUS - 24 in.

1948. 24 in. (61 cm). Cloth body, composition forearms and straight legs. Composition head; blue tin sleep eyes, lashes, painted lower lashes; replaced blond mohair wig over moulded hair; closed mouth. Mark: no mark on doll. Original tag, BABY PRECIOUS/MADE IN CANADA/A RELIABLE DOLL/MFD. BY RELIABLE TOY CO. CANADA/A BRITISH EMPIRE PRODUCT.
Ref.No.: D of C, CD5, p. 280.

Mint $250.00   Ex. $200.00   G. $110.00   F. $60.00

TOPSY - 17 in.

1948. 17 in. (43 cm). Brown composition, jointed hips, shoulders, and neck. Composition head, dimpled cheeks; black painted side-glancing eyes; open-closed mouth showing two painted teeth. Mark: on head, RELIABLE/MADE IN CANADA.
Ref.No.: D of C, BQ0, p. 280.

Mint $165.00   Ex. $150.00   G. $95.00   F. $65.00

JOAN

1948. 9.5 in. (24 cm). All composition bent-limb baby, jointed hips, and shoulders. Blue painted eyes, black line over eye; brown moulded hair; closed mouth. Mark: on back, RELIABLE/MADE IN CANADA.
Ref.No.: D of C, CL5, p. 281.

Mint $65.00   **Ex.** $45.00   **G.** $30.00   **F.** $20.00

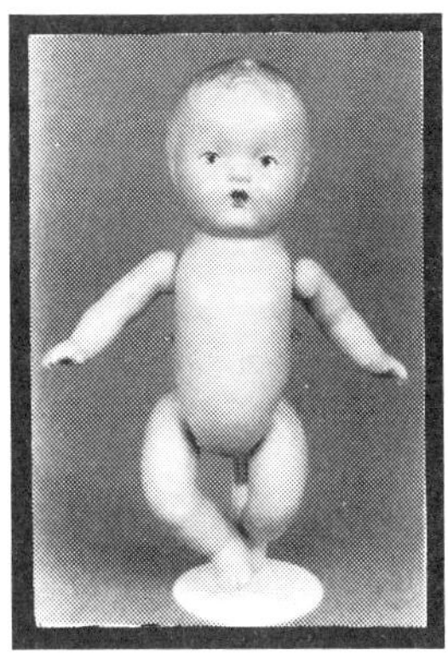

SALLY ANN

1948. 22 in. (56 cm). All composition, jointed hips, shoulders, and neck. Composition head with dimpled cheeks; blue metal sleep eyes, lashes, painted lower lashes; red mohair wig; open smiling mouth showing six teeth. Mark: on head, RELIABLE/MADE IN CANADA.
Ref.No.: D of C, CA34, p. 281.

Mint $225.00   **Ex.** $175.00   **G.** $95.00   **F.** $45.00

PLASSIKINS

1948. 14 in. (45.5 cm). Hard plastic bent-limb baby, jointed hips, shoulders, neck, and wrists. Hard plastic head; blue plastic sleep eyes, and lashes; light brown moulded hair; closed mouth. Mark: RELIABLE/MADE IN CANADA. One of the first hard plastic dolls in Canada.
Ref.No.: D of C, CL3, p. 281.

Mint $130.00   **Ex.** $95.00   **G.** $60.00   **F.** $35.00

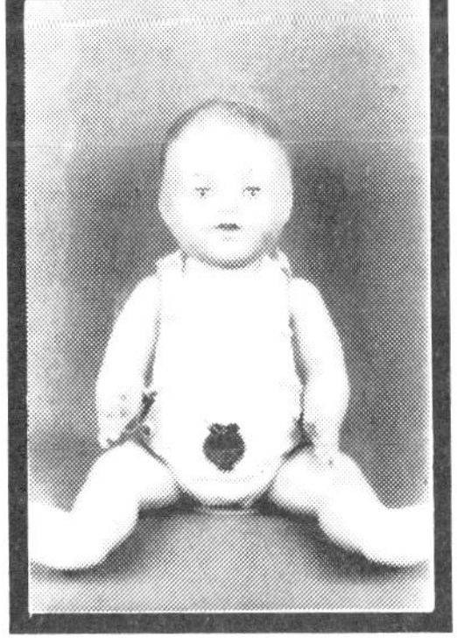

BABYKINS

1948. 17 in. (43 cm). All composition, jointed hips, shoulders, and neck. Composition head with dimpled cheeks; blue tin sleep eyes, lashes, painted lower lashes; reddish brown moulded hair; open-closed mouth, two painted teeth. Mark: on head, RELIABLE/MADE IN CANADA.
Ref.No.: D of C, CJ36, p. 282.

Mint $125.00   **Ex.** $95.00   **G.** $75.00   **F.** $30.00

CUDDLES

1948. 22 in. (56 cm). Cloth body, composition arms and straight legs. Composition head; blue metal sleep eyes, lashes, painted lower lashes; blond moulded hair; closed mouth. Mark: on head, A/RELIABLE/DOLL/MADE IN CANADA.
Ref.No.: D of C, CO24, p. 282.

Mint $245.00   Ex. $195.00   G. $125.00   F. $60.00

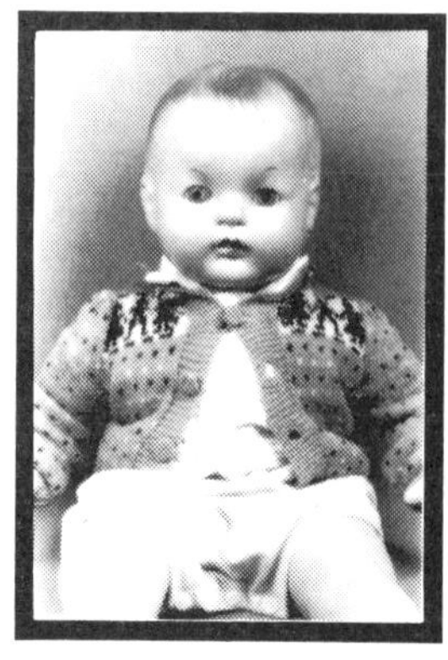

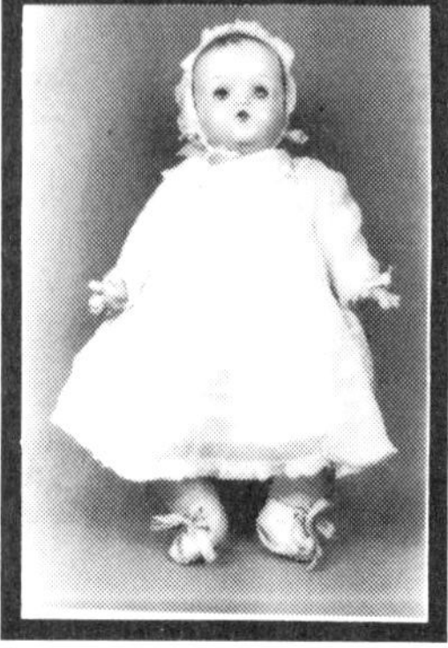

BABY LOVUMS

1948. 17 in. (43 cm). Cloth body with crier, composition hands and bent-limb legs. Composition head; blue sleep eyes, lashes; brown moulded hair; closed mouth. Mark: on head, A/RELIABLE/DOLL.
Ref.No.: D of C, BJ6, p. 282.

Note: Listed in the first edition (1986) D of C incorrectly as Baby Precious.

Mint $215.00   Ex. $180.00   G. $115.00   F. $50.00

RUTHIE

ca.1949. 17 in. (43 cm). Cloth body, bent limb, latex arms and legs, crier in the body. Composition head; brown tin sleep eyes, lashes, painted lower lashes; blond mohair wig; closed mouth. Mark: on head, RELIABLE DOLL/MADE IN CANADA.
Ref.No.: D of C, AW22, p. 283.

Mint $195.00   Ex. $150.00   G. $85.00   F. $55.00

PIGTAILS - 19 in.

1949. 19 in. (48.5 cm). Composition body, jointed hips, shoulders, and neck. Composition head; blue tin sleep eyes, lashes, painted lowers; blond mohair wig in pigtails and bangs; open mouth showing four teeth and tongue. Mark: on head, RELIABLE/MADE IN CANADA.
Ref.No.: D of C, CY6, p. 283.

Mint $210.00   Ex. $185.00   G. $95.00   F. $60.00

SUSIE STEPPS - 15 in.

ca. 1949. 15 in. (38 cm). All hard plastic walker, jointed hips, shoulders, and neck. Hard plastic head; blue sleep eyes, upper lashes missing, painted lower lashes, dark upper eye shadow; synthetic blond wig; open mouth showing four teeth and tongue. Mark: on body, RELIABLE (in script)/MADE IN CANADA.
Ref.No.: D of C, CD28, p. 284.

Mint $175.00   Ex. $135.00   G. $90.00   F. $40.00

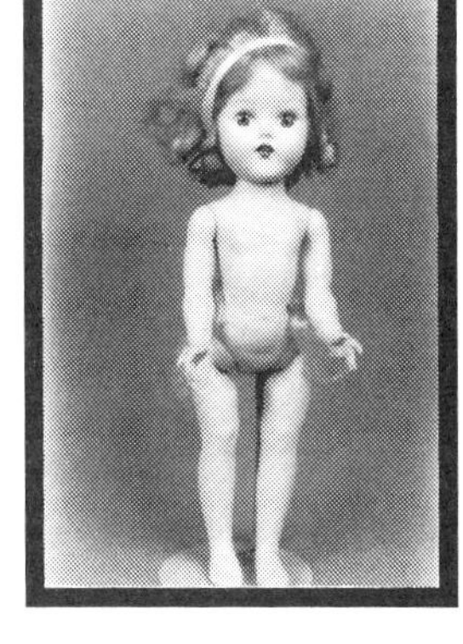

BRIDE DOLL

ca. 1949. 15 in. (30.5 cm). Composition body, jointed hips, shoulders, and neck. Composition head; blue plastic sleep eyes, lashes, painted lower lashes; blond mohair wig; open mouth. Mark: on head, RELIABLE/MADE IN CANADA.
Ref.No.: D of C, BZ16, p. 284.

Mint $150.00   Ex. $110.00   G. $75.00   F. $35.00

BABY LOVUMS - 1949

1949. 24 in. (61 cm). Cloth body composition legs and hands. Composition head; blue sleep eyes, lashes, painted lower lashes, eye shadow over eye; blond mohair curly wig; closed mouth. Mark: on head RELIABLE/MADE IN CANADA.
Ref.No.: D of C, BT22, p. 284.

Mint $260.00   Ex. $200.00   G. $125.00   F. $65.00

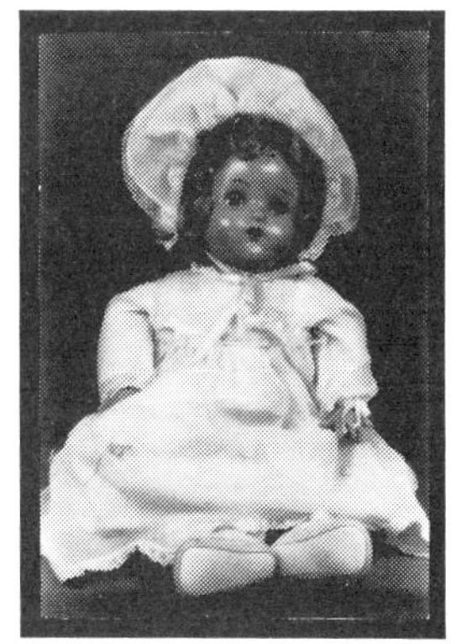

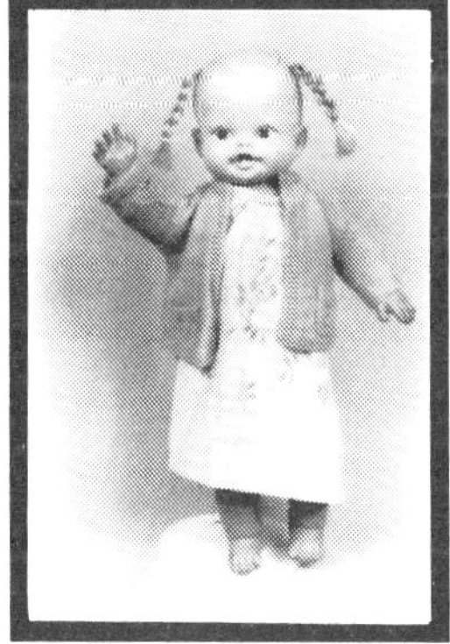

BONNIE BRAIDS

1950. 14 in. (35.5 cm). Magic Skin one piece body and legs, jointed shoulders. Vinyl head; painted blue eyes, painted upper lashes; moulded hair with two inset braids; open-closed mouth. Mark: on head, RELIABLE (in script)/13BVE.
Ref.No.: D of C, CX15, p. 285.

Mint $125.00   Ex. $ 85.00   G. $55.00   F. $30.00

SNOOZIE - 17in.

1950. 17 in. (43 cm). Cloth body and arms, stuffed vinyl hands and legs. Head is an early soft vinyl that feels like sponge rubber; blue painted eyes, painted upper lashes; light brown moulded hair; open-closed yawning mouth. Mark: on head RELIABLE. Also came in 12 and 14 inch sizes with latex hands and legs.
Ref.No.: D of C, AM5, p. 285.

Mint $85.00   Ex. $70.00   G. $45.00   F. $20.00

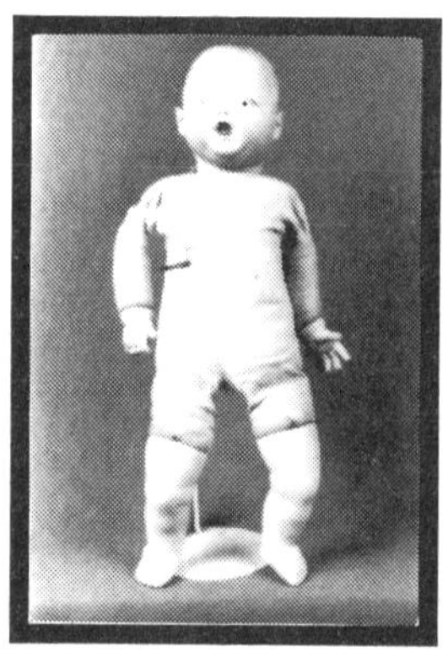

TONI

1950. 14 in. (35.5 cm). Hard plastic body, jointed hips, shoulders, and neck. Hard plastic head; blue sleep eyes, lashes, painted lower lashes; dark brown nylon wig (glued on head); closed mouth. Unmarked.
Ref.No.: D of C, CD10, p. 285.

Mint $185.00   Ex. $160.00   G. $95.00   F. $45.00

SUSIE STEPPS - 20 in.

1950. 20 in. (51 cm). Hard plastic body, jointed hips, shoulders, and neck. Hard plastic head; brown sleep eyes, lashes, painted lower lashes; light brown saran wig; open mouth showing teeth and tongue. Mark: RELIABLE.
Ref.No. D of C; CF33 p. 286

Mint $200.00   Ex. $150.00   G. $95.00   F. $45.00

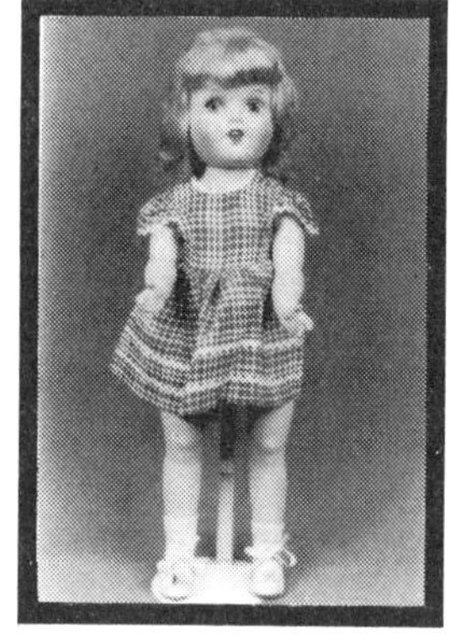

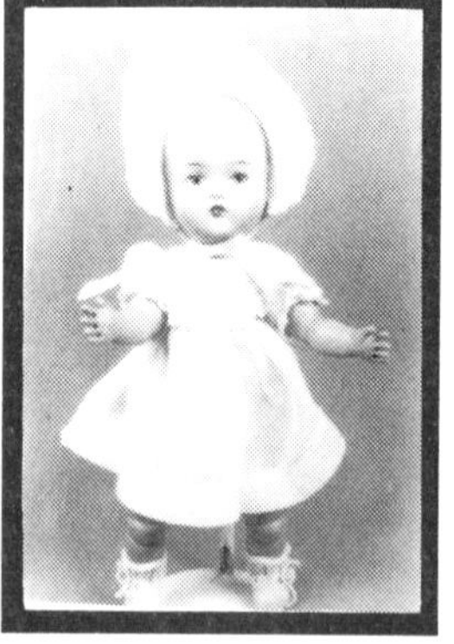

RELIABLE - 1950

1950. 15 in. (38 cm). Cloth body, stuffed latex arms and legs. Composition head; blue plastic eyes, lashes, painted lower lashes; moulded hair, originally she wore a semi-wig; closed mouth. Mark: on head, RELIABLE/DOLL/MADE IN CANADA.
Ref.No.: D of C, CI36, p. 286.

Mint $90.00   Ex. $75.00   G. $45.00   F. $20.00

TOPSY - 10 in.

1950. 10 in. (24 cm). All composition body, jointed hips, and shoulders. Black painted side-glancing eyes; black moulded hair; closed mouth. Mark: on back, RELIABLE/MADE IN CANADA.
Ref.No.: D of C, CH8, p. 286.

Mint $85.00   Ex. $65.00   G. $40.00   F. $20.00

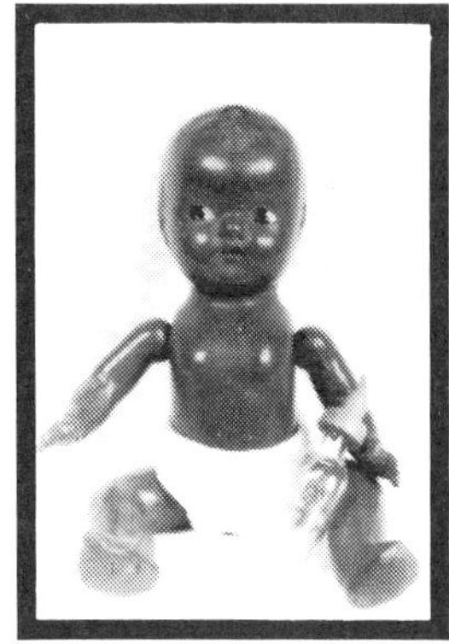

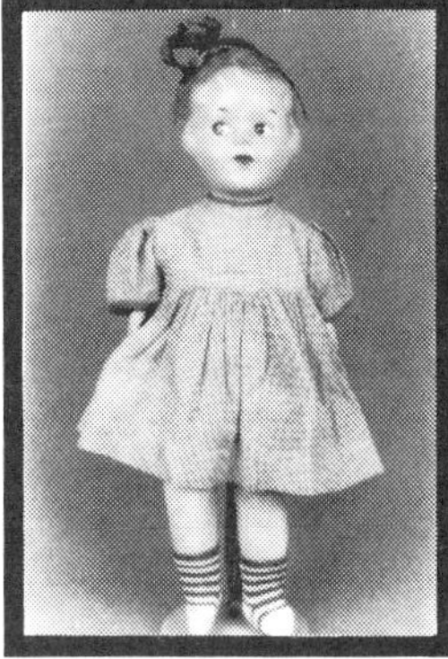

PEGGY

1950. 16.5 in. (42 cm). Cloth body and legs, composition arms. Composition shoulderhead; black painted side-glancing eyes, black line over eye; light brown moulded hair with hole for hair ribbon; closed mouth. Mark: on shoulderplate, RELIABLE DOLL/MADE IN CANADA.
Ref.No.: D of C, BZ29, p. 287.

Mint $95.00   Ex. $80.00   G. $55.00   F. $35.00

PIGTAILS - 15 in.

1951. 15 in. (38 cm). All composition body, jointed hips, shoulders, and neck. Composition head; blue sleep eyes, lashes, painted lower lashes; blond mohair wig in pigtails with bangs; closed mouth. Unmarked.
Ref.No.: D of C, CR24, p. 287.

Mint $130.00   Ex. $85.00   G. $45.00   F. $30.00

PIGTAILS - 18 in.

1951. 18 in. (45.5 cm). Composition body, jointed hips, shoulders, and neck. Composition head; blue sleep eyes, lashes, painted lower lashes; honey blond mohair wig in pigtails with curly bangs; open mouth showing four teeth. Mark: on head, RELIABLE/MADE IN CANADA.
Ref.No.: D of C, BJ13, p. 287.

Mint. $185.00   Ex. $130.00   G. $80.00   F. $55.00

PIGTAILS - 22 in.

1951. 22 in. (56 cm). Composition body, jointed hips, shoulders, and neck. Composition head with dimples; blue sleep eyes, lashes, painted lower lashes; light brown mohair pigtails with curly bangs; open mouth showing teeth and tongue. Mark: on head, RELIABLE.
Ref.No.: D of C, CO22, p. 288.

Mint $225.00   Ex. $190.00   G. $95.00   F. $60.00

BABY SKIN

1951. 12 in. (30.5 cm). Stuffed latex body with coo voice. Composition head with nostril holes; blue plastic sleep eyes, lashes, painted lower lashes; light brown moulded hair; closed mouth. Mark: on head, RELIABLE/MADE IN CANADA.
Ref.No.: D of C, BH11, p. 288.

Mint $85.00   Ex. $75.00   G. $45.00   F. $25.00

DREAM BABY - 20 in.

ca. 1952. 20 in. (51 cm). Cloth body, stuffed vinyl arms and legs. Vinyl head; blue sleep eyes, lashes, painted lower lashes; rooted blond saran hair; open-closed mouth. Mark: on head, RELIABLE/4CV28.
Ref.No.: D of C, BH17, p. 288.

Mint $125.00   Ex. $85.00   G. $55.00   F. $30.00

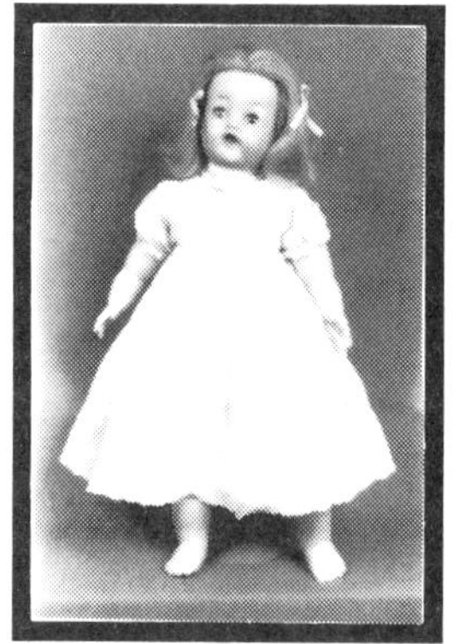

RELIABLE - 1952

ca. 1952. 24 in. (61 cm). Cloth body, stuffed latex arms and legs. Composition shoulderhead; blue sleep eyes, lashes, painted lower lashes; blond saran wig; open mouth showing two teeth and tongue. Mark: on shoulderplate, A/RELIABLE/DOLL/MADE IN CANADA.
Ref.No.: D of C, CF34, p. 289.

Mint $135.00   Ex. $95.00   G. $75.00   F. $45.00

RELIABLE - 1952

ca. 1952. 14 in. (35.5 cm). Composition body, jointed hips, shoulders, and neck. Composition head with freckles; hazel sleep eyes, lashes; auburn saran wig; open mouth showing teeth and tongue. Mark: on head, RELIABLE/MADE IN CANADA.
Ref.No.: D of C, CD23, p. 289.

Mint $110.00   Ex. $85.00   G. $50.00   F. $30.00

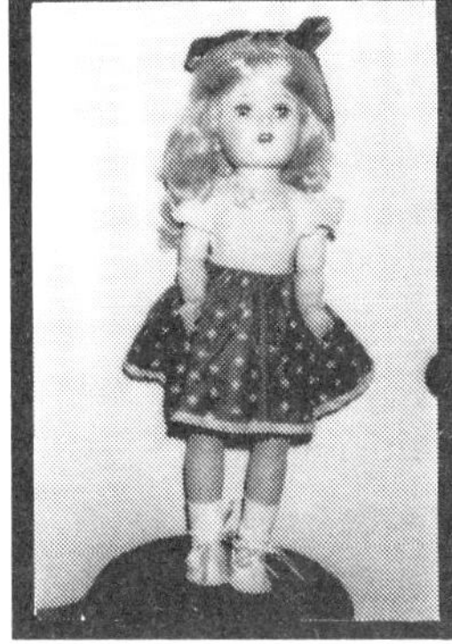

SUSIE STEPPS - 19 in.

1952. 19 in. (48.5 cm). Hard plastic body, jointed hips, shoulders, and neck. Hard plastic head; blue sleep eyes, lashes; saran blond wig; open mouth showing teeth. Mark: RELIABLE.
Ref.No.: D of C, CT24, p. 289.

Mint. $200.00   Ex. $150.00   G. $95.00   F. $45.00

HER HIGHNESS CORONATION DOLL

1953. 14 in. (35.5 cm). All composition body, jointed hips, shoulders, and neck. Composition head; blue sleep eyes, lashes, reddish brown painted lower lashes and brows; auburn wig; open mouth, smiling showing six teeth. Mark: on head, A/RELIABLE DOLL.
Ref.No.: D of C, CA30, p. 290.

Mint $225.00   Ex. $175.00   G. $85.00   F. $30.00

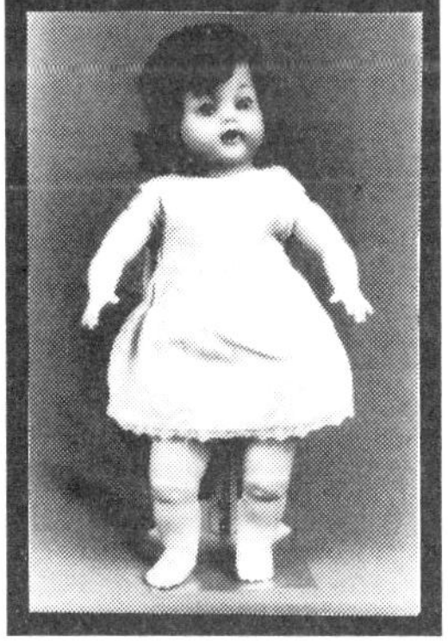

DREAM BABY - 19 in.

1953. 19 in. (45.5 cm). Cloth body, vinyl flex arms and legs. Vinyl head; blue sleep eyes, lashes, painted lower lashes; dark brown saran hair; open-closed mouth. Mark: on head, Reliable (in script)/MADE IN CANADA/V18.
Ref.No.: D of C, AP13, p. 290.

Mint $95.00   Ex. $75.00   G. $50.00   F. $30.00

DRESS ME DOLL

1953. 11 in. (28 cm). Hard plastic body, jointed shoulders and neck. Hard plastic head; sleep eyes; brown wig; closed mouth. Mark: on back, RELIABLE/PAT. PEND. 1953.
Ref.No.: D of C, BQ5, p. 291.

Mint $25.00   Ex. $20.00   G. $15.00   F. $10.00

TICKLE TOES

1953. 23 in. (53.5 cm). One piece stuffed latex body. Vinyl head; blue sleep eyes, lashes, painted lower lashes; rooted blond hair with bangs; open-closed mouth. Mark: on head, RELIABLE (in script)/MOV19.
Ref.No.: D of C, CJ5, p. 291.

Mint $125.00   Ex. $85.00   G. $55.00   F. $30.00

PATTY

1953. 14 in. (35.5 cm). Hard plastic body, jointed hips, shoulders, and neck. Hard plastic head; blue sleep eyes, lashes, painted lower lashes; blond mohair wig; closed mouth. Mark: on back, RELIABLE (in script).
Ref.No.: D. of C, CI12, p. 291.

Mint $130.00   Ex. $90.00   G. $50.00   F. $30.00

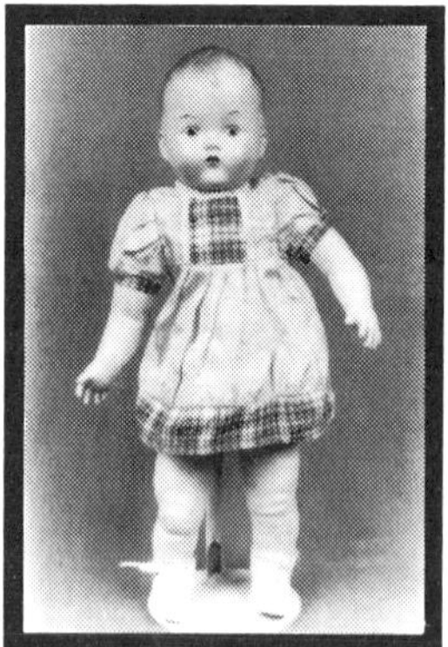

HONEY

1953. 16 in. (40.5 cm). Cloth body, stuffed latex arms and legs. Hard plastic head; blue painted eyes, black line over eye; brown moulded hair; closed mouth. Mark: on head, RELIABLE (in script).
Ref.No.: D of C, CM2, p. 292.

Mint $85.00   Ex. $60.00   G. $35.00   F. $25.00

SNOOZIE - 11 in.

1953. 11 in. (28 cm). One piece magic skin (stuffed latex) body, with coo voice. Vinyl head; blue plastic inset eyes, painted upper lashes; light brown moulded hair; open-closed yawning mouth. Mark: on head, RELIABLE (in script)/121131.
Ref.No.: D of C, CJ23, p. 292.

Mint $85.00   Ex. $60.00   G. $35.00   F. $25.00

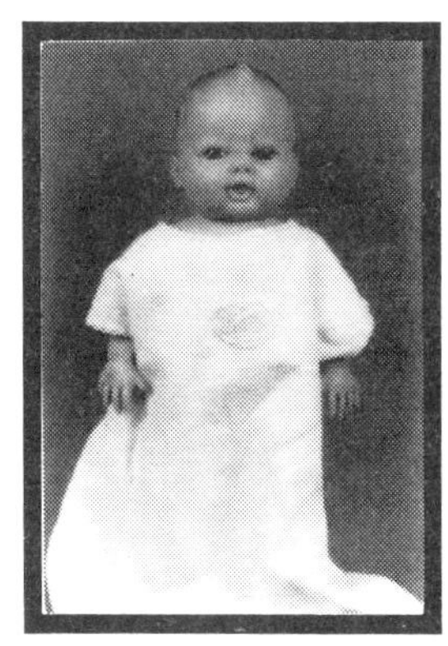

SUSIE WALKER - 1953 - 13 in.

1953. 13 in. (33 cm). Hard plastic body, jointed hips, shoulders, and neck. Hard plastic head; blue sleep eyes, moulded lashes, painted lower lashes; dark brown synthetic wig; closed mouth. Mark: RELIABLE (in script)/MADE IN CANADA.
Ref.No.: D of C, CO32, p. 292.

Mint $105.00   Ex. $85.00   G. $45.00   F. $30.00

SAUCY WALKER - 1953 - Open Mouth

1953. 22 in. (56 cm). Hard plastic body with crier, jointed hips, shoulders, and neck. Hard plastic head; plastic flirty eyes, lashes, painted lower lashes; blond saran wig; open mouth showing two teeth and tongue. Mark: RELIABLE/MADE in CANADA.
Ref.No.: D of C, CG21, p. 293.

Mint $200.00   Ex. $150.00   G. $95.00   F.$45.00

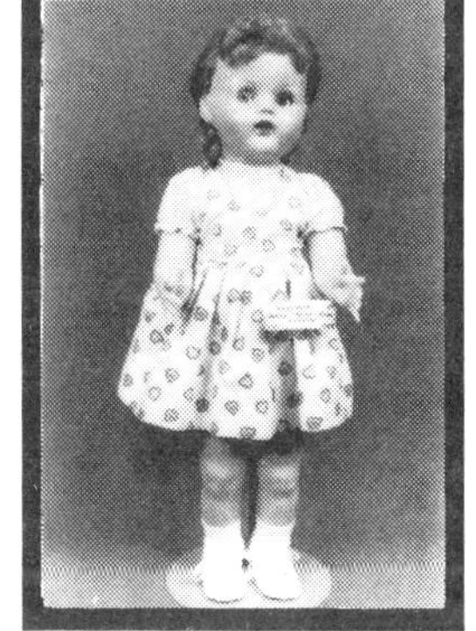

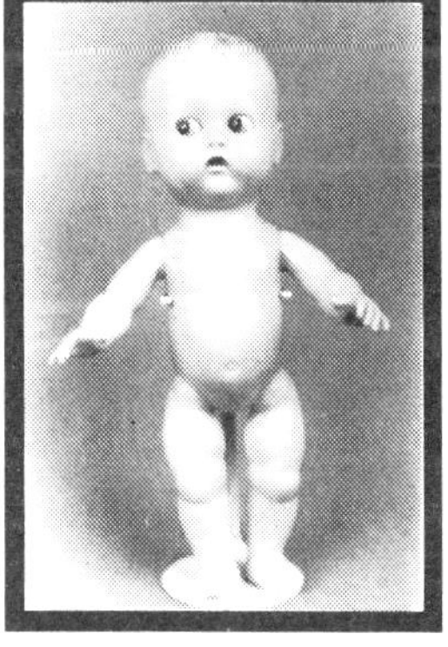

SOUVENIR DOLL

1954. 10 in. (25.5 cm). Hard plastic body, jointed hips, and shoulders. Blue sleep side-glancing eyes; light brown moulded hair; open mouth. Mark: on back, RELIABLE (in script)/MADE IN CANADA.
Ref.No.: D of C, BP16, p. 293.

Mint $45.00   Ex. $35.00   G.   20.00   F.15.00

RELIABLE - 1954

ca. 1954. 19.5 in. (49.5 in). One piece vinyl-flex body. Vinyl head; blue sleep eyes, lashes, painted lower lashes; rooted blond saran curly hair; closed mouth. Mark: on head, RELIABLE/1581.
Ref.No.: D of C, BH18, p. 293.

Mint **$85.00** **Ex.** **$70.00** **G.** **$40.00** **F.$** **25.00**

SUSIE WALKER - 1954 - 15 in.

1954. 15 in. (38 cm). Hard plastic body, jointed hips, shoulders, and neck. Hard plastic head; brown sleep eyes, plastic lashes, painted lower lashes; blond wig in braids with bangs; open-closed mouth showing two moulded teeth. Mark: on back, RELIABLE (in script)/MADE IN CANADA.
Ref.No.: D of C, BX7, p. 294.

Mint **$175.00** **Ex.** **$135.00** **G.** **$90.00** **F.** **$40.00**

SAUCY WALKER - 1955

1955. 22 in. (56 cm). Plastic body, jointed hips, shoulders, and neck. Vinyl head; hazel sleep eyes, lashes, painted lower lashes; rooted blond curly hair; closed mouth. Mark: on head, 1391/RELIABLE (in script).
Ref.No.: D of C, CE16, p. 294.

Mint **$160.00** **Ex.** **$120.00** **G.** **$80.00** **F.** **$40.00**

MARGARET ANN

1955. 20 in. (51 cm). One piece Vinyl-flex body. Vinyl head; blue sleep eyes, lashes, painted lower lashes; rooted blond saran hair; closed mouth. Mark: on head, 1481/RELIABLE (in script).
Ref.No.: D of C, CE14, p. 294.

Mint **$85.00** **Ex.** **$70.00** **G.** **$40.00** **F.** **$25.00**

GLAMOUR GIRL

1956. 15 in. (38 cm). One piece vinyl skin body. Vinyl head; blue inset eyes, painted upper lashes; rooted blond hair; closed mouth. Mark: on back R-15X; on shoes, RELIABLE/950-O/MADE IN CANADA.
Ref.No.: D of C, BC17, p. 295.

Mint **$65.00** **Ex.** **$50.00** **G.** **$40.00** **F.** **$20.00**

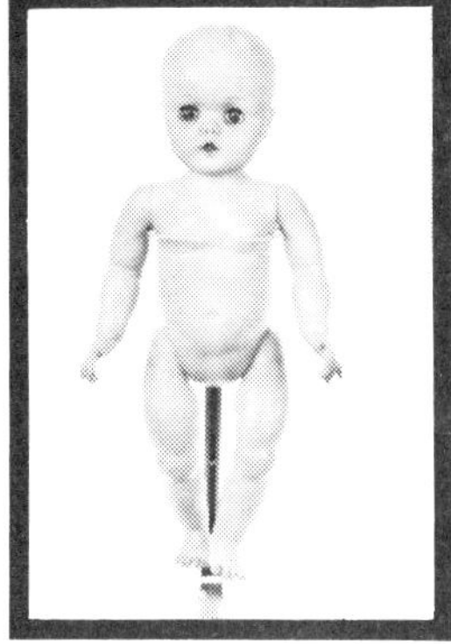

RELIABLE - 1956

ca. 1956. 25 in. (63.5 cm). Plastic body, jointed hips, shoulders, and neck. Vinyl head; blue sleep eyes, lashes, painted lower lashes; light brown moulded hair; open mouth nurser. Mark: on back, RELIABLE (in script).
Ref.No.: D of C, AE8, p. 295.

Mint **$85.00** **Ex.** **$60.00** **G.** **$40.00** **F.** **$25.00**

MAGGIE MUGGINS

1956. 16 in. (40.5 cm). One piece magic skin (stuffed latex) body. Vinyl head with freckles; blue sleep eyes, lashes, painted lower lashes; rooted red saran hair in pigtails with curly bangs; closed mouth. Mark: on head, RELIABLE.
Ref.No.: D of C, CF9, p. 296.

Mint **$150.00** **Ex.** **$120.00** **G.** **85.00** **F.** **45.00**

DAVY CROCKETT

1956. 12 in. (30.5 cm). One piece magic skin (stuffed latex) body with coo voice. Vinyl head; plastic inset eyes; moulded hair; closed mouth. Mark: Original tag, MADE IN TORONTO, CANADA/BY RELIABLE TOY CO. LIMITED./WALT DISNEY'S OFFICIAL DAVY CROCKETT.
Ref.No.: D of C, BH36, p. 296.

Mint **$95.00** **Ex.** **$65.00** **G.** **$45.00** **F.** **$25.00**

BABYKINS

1956. 20 in. (51 cm). One piece Vinyl-flex body. Vinyl head; blue sleep eyes, lashes, painted lower lashes; brown moulded hair; open-closed mouth. Mark: on head, RELIABLE 1590.
Ref.No.: D of C, AN29, p. 296.

Mint $40.00   Ex. $30.00   G. $20.00   F. $10.00

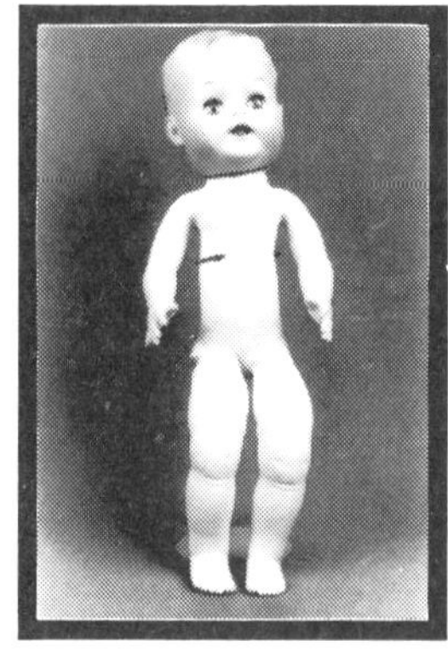

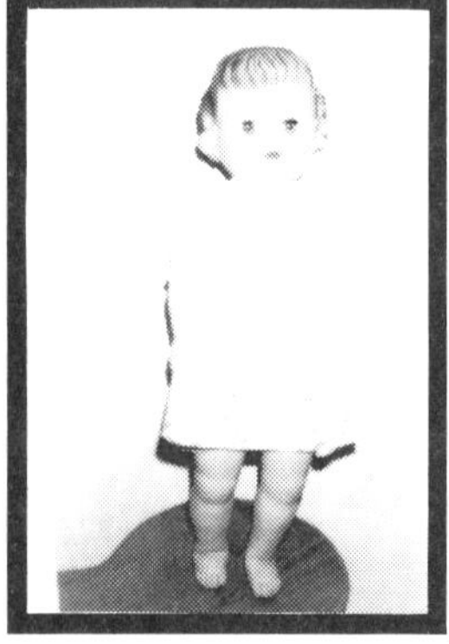

BABY BUBBLES

1957. 21 in. (53.5 cm). One-piece Vinyl-flex body with coo voice. Vinyl head; blue sleep eyes, lashes; deeply moulded blond curls with bangs; closed mouth. Unmarked.
Ref. No.: D of C, CT18, p. 297.

Mint $105.00   Ex. $85.00   G. $65.00   F.$40.00

SUSIE the WALKING DOLL

1957. 9 in. (23 cm). Hard plastic body, jointed hips, shoulders, and neck. Hard plastic head; blue plastic sleep eyes, moulded lashes; blond wig; closed mouth. Mark: on back, RELIABLE (in script)/MADE IN CANADA.
Ref.No.: D of C, BP5, p. 297.

Mint $80.00   Ex. $70.00   G. $45.00   F. $20.00

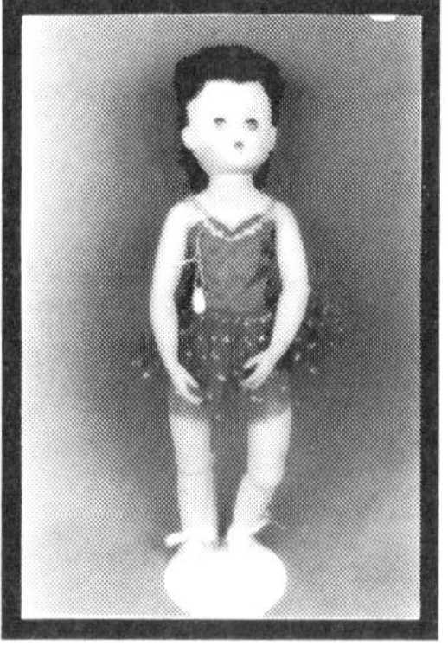

BALLERINA DOLL

1957. 20 in. (51 cm). Plastic body and legs, vinyl arms, jointed knees, hips, shoulders, and neck. Vinyl head; blue sleep eyes, lashes, painted lower lashes; rooted brown saran hair; closed mouth. Mark: on head, RELIABLE.
Ref.No.: D of C, CF26, p. 297.

Mint $130.00   Ex. $95.00   G. $60.00   F. $30.00

POSIE

1957. 23 in. (58.5 cm). Hard plastic body, jointed knees, hips, shoulders, and neck. Vinyl head; blue sleep eyes, lashes, painted lower lashes; rooted blond saran hair; closed mouth. Mark: on head and body, RELIABLE.
Ref.No.: D of C, CF10, p. 298.

Mint $130.00   Ex. $110.00   G. $75.00   F. $45.00

TOPSY - 1957 - 14 in.

1957. 14 in. (35.5 cm). One piece Vinyl-flex body. Vinyl head; golden brown sleep eyes, lashes, painted lower lashes; rooted black saran curly hair; closed mouth. Original tag, TOPSY/RELIABLE/MADE IN CANADA.
Ref.No.: D of C, BQ2, p. 298.

Mint $95.00   Ex. $60.00   G. $35.00   F. $25.00

BETSY WETSY

1957. 14 in. (35.5 cm). Vinyl body, jointed hips, shoulders, and neck. Vinyl head; brown sleep eyes, lashes, painted lower lashes; rooted brown curly saran hair; open mouth nurser. Mark: on back, RELIABLE (in script)/12.
Ref.No.: D of C, AM16, p. 298.

Mint $65.00   Ex. $45.00   G. $25.00   F. $15.00

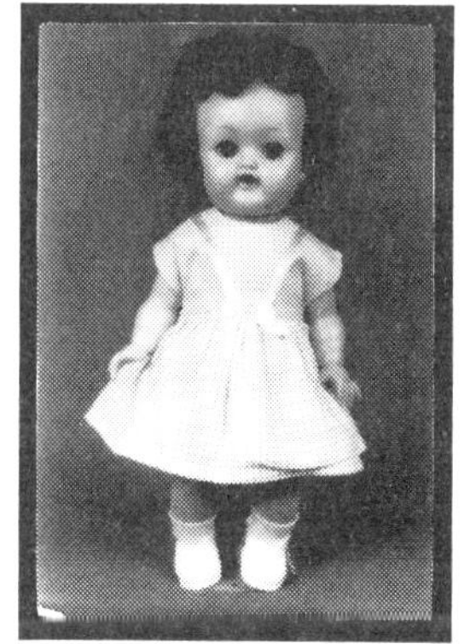

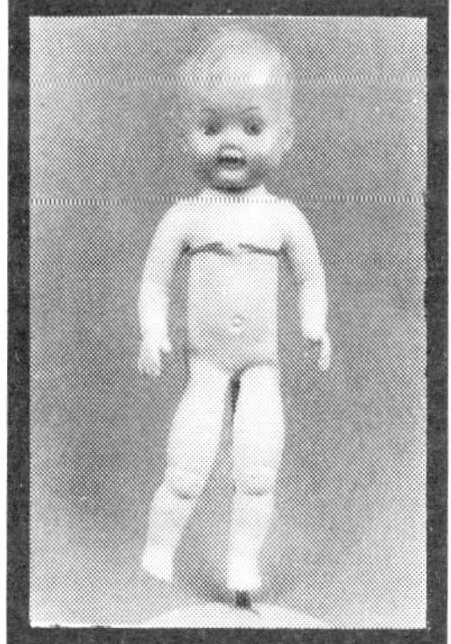

SLEEPYHEAD

1957. 14 in. (35.5 cm). One piece Vinyl-flex body. Vinyl head; inset plastic eyes, painted upper lashes; moulded hair; open-closed mouth. Mark: on head, RELIABLE (in script); on body, R-15X.
Ref.No.: D of C, BU12, p. 299.

Mint $20.00   Ex. $15.00   G. $12.00   F. $8.00

SUSIE the WALKING DOLL

1957. 9 in. (23 cm). Hard plastic body, jointed hips, shoulders, and neck. Hard plastic head; blue sleep eyes, moulded lashes; brown wig in braids; closed mouth. Mark: on back, RELIABLE.
Ref.No.: D of C, CO3, p. 299.

Mint $85.00   Ex. $60.00   G. $40.00   F. $20.00

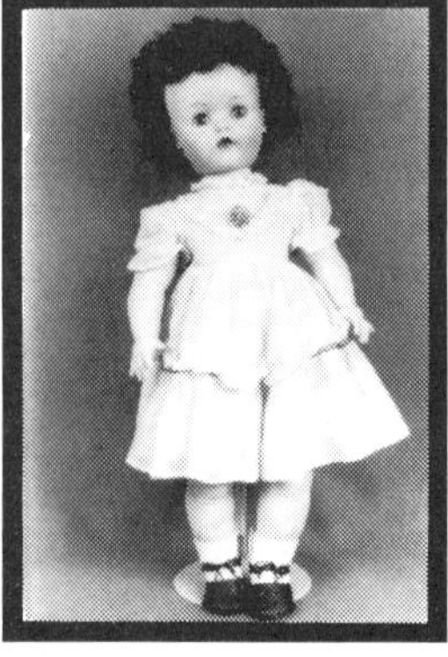

MARY ANN

1957. 23 in. (58.5 cm). One piece Vinyl- flex body. Vinyl head; blue sleep eyes, lashes, painted lower lashes; rooted brown curls; closed mouth. Unmarked.
Ref.No.: D of C, CR14, p. 300.

Mint $85.00   Ex. $75.00   G. $45.00   F. $25.00

BABY TEAR DROPS

1957. 11 in. (28 cm). Vinyl body, jointed hips, shoulders, and neck. Hard plastic head; blue sleep eyes, moulded lashes; brown moulded hair; open mouth nurser. Mark: on head, RELIABLE (in script)/7.
Ref.No.: D of C, CO30, p. 300.

Mint $60.00   Ex. $45.00   G. $30.00   F. $20.00

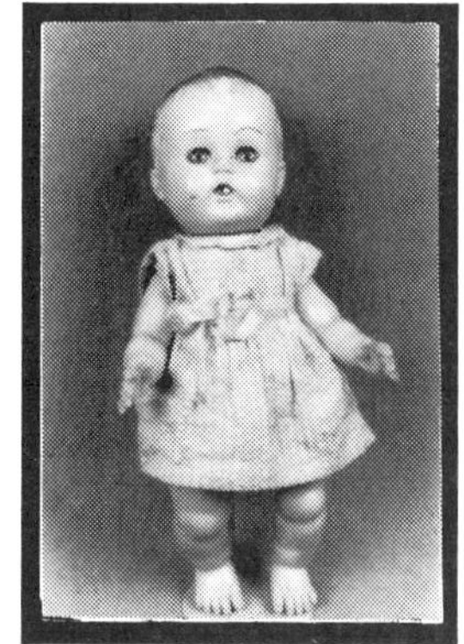

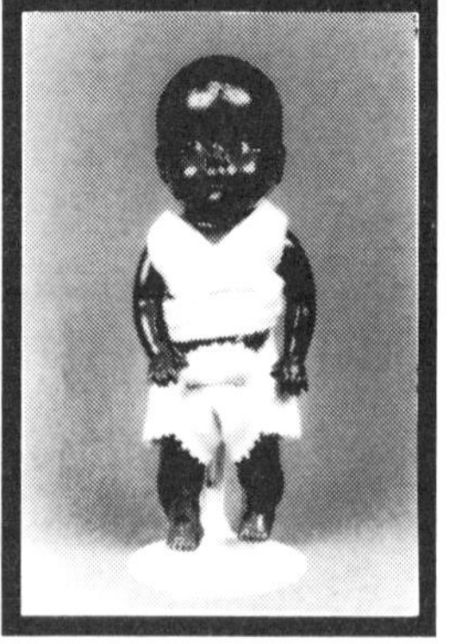

RELIABLE - 1958

ca. 1958. 7.5 in. (19.5 cm). Brown plastic baby, jointed hips and shoulders. Black side-glancing sleep eyes; moulded hair; closed mouth. Mark: on body, RELIABLE (in script)/MADE IN CANADA/PAT. PEND.
Ref.No.: D of C, BM32, p. 300.

Mint $55.00   Ex. $35.00   G. $20.50   F. $20.00

MISS CANADA - 1958 - 10.5 in.

1958. 10.5 in. (26.5 cm). Hard plastic body and legs, vinyl arms, jointed hips, shoulders, and neck. Vinyl head with earrings; blue sleep eyes, moulded lashes; rooted brown hair; closed mouth. Mark: on head, P.
Ref.No.: D of C, BQ18, p. 301.

Mint $115.00   Ex. $90.00   G. $55.00   F. $25.00

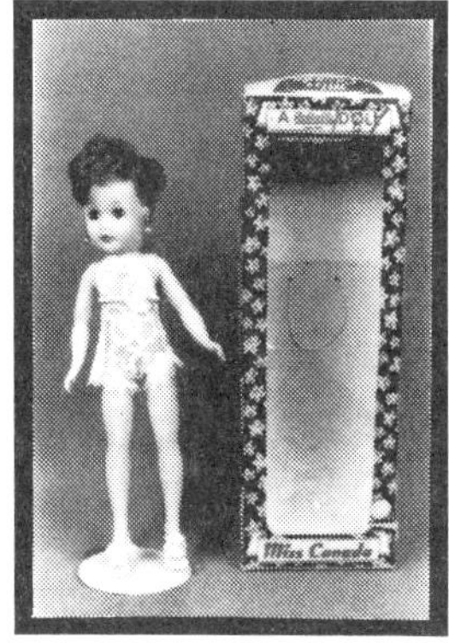

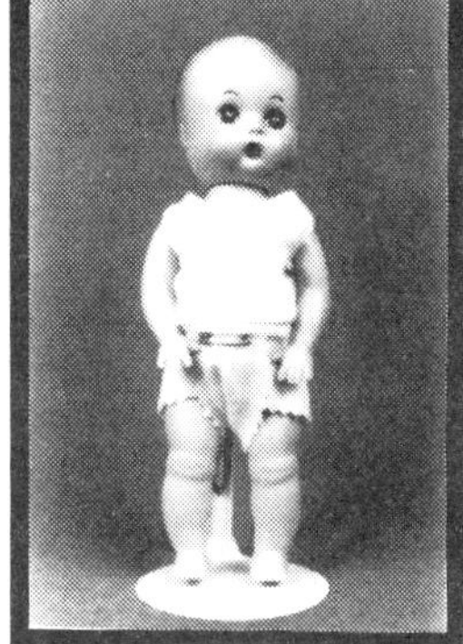

RELIABLE - 1958

1958. 8 in. (20.5 cm). Plastic body, jointed hips, shoulders, and neck. Plastic head; sleep eyes, moulded lashes; moulded hair; open mouth nurser. Mark: on body, RELIABLE (in script)/MADE IN CANADA/Pat. 1958.
Ref.No.: D of C, BM31, p. 301.

Mint $45.00   Ex. $35.00   G. $25.00   F. $15.00

JUDY BRIDESMAID

1958. 17 in. (43 cm). One piece vinyl body. Vinyl head with earrings; blue sleep eyes, moulded lashes, painted lower lashes; rooted black saran curls; closed mouth. Mark: on head, RELIABLE.
Ref.No.: D of C, BU13, p. 301.

Mint $60.00   Ex. $40.00   G. $30.00   F. $20.00

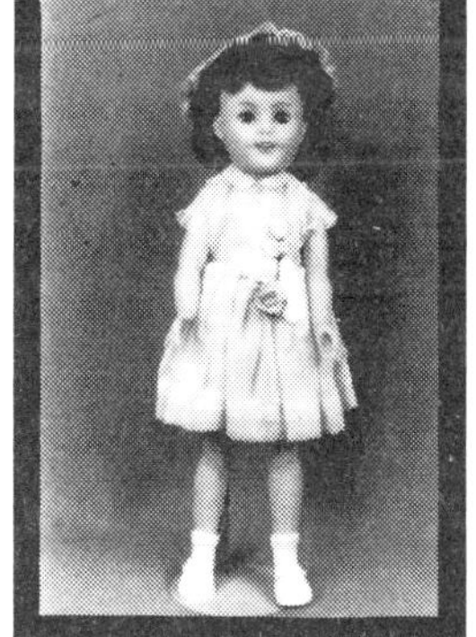

ROSALYN

1958. 18 in. (45.5 cm). Plastic body, jointed hips, shoulders, and neck. Vinyl head with dimples; brown sleep eyes, lashes, painted lower lashes; rooted brown saran hair in curls; open-closed smiling mouth showing teeth. Mark: on Head, RELIABLE.
Ref.No.: D of C, BQ19, p. 302.

Mint $150.00   Ex. $125.00   G. $80.00   F. $50.00

BARBARA ANN -1958 - 20 in.

1958. 20 in. (51 cm). Plastic teen body, jointed hips, waist, shoulders, and neck. Vinyl head; blue plastic sleep eyes, lashes, painted lower lashes; rooted black curls; closed mouth. Unmarked.
Ref.No.: D of C, CT5, p. 302.

Note: Appears on new issue Canada postage stamps June 8, 1990.

Mint $115.00   Ex. $95.00   G. $50.00   F. $30.00

TOPSY - 1958 - 12 in.

1958. 12 in. (30.5 cm). One piece vinyl body. Vinyl head with dimples; black painted side-glancing eyes, painted upper lashes; hair moulded in braids tied with ribbons; open-closed mouth. Mark: on head, RELIABLE.
Ref.No.: D of C, BQ8, p. 302.

Mint $75.00   Ex. $60.00   G. $50.00   F. $30.00

PATSY

ca. 1959. 9 in. (23 cm). Hard plastic body, jointed hips, shoulders, and neck. Hard plastic head; blue sleep eyes, moulded lashes; brown moulded hair; closed mouth. Mark: on back, RELIABLE (in script).
Ref.No.: D of C, BM29, p. 303.

Mint $75.00   Ex. $45.00   G. $30.00   F. $20.00

PEGGY

1959. 9 in. (23 cm). Hard plastic walker, jointed hips, shoulders, and neck. Hard plastic head; blue sleep eyes, moulded plastic lashes; honey blond saran wig in braids; closed mouth. Mark: on back, RELIABLE/MADE IN CANADA.
Ref.No.: D of C, CL7, p. 303.

Mint $80.00   Ex. $70.00   G. $45.00   F. $20.00

MISS CANADA - 1960 - 18 in.

1960. 18 in. (45.5 cm). Plastic teen body, jointed hips, shoulders, and neck. Vinyl head; blue sleep eyes, lashes, painted lower lashes; rooted auburn curls; closed mouth. Mark: on body, RELIABLE (in script)/CANADA.
Ref.No.: D of C, CS8, p. 303.

Mint $110.00   Ex. $75.00   G. $55.00   F. $25.00

PATTY SUE PLAYMATE

1960. 35 in. (89 cm). Plastic body, jointed hips, shoulders, and neck. Vinyl head; blue sleep eyes, lashes, painted lower lashes; rooted blond saran hair; closed mouth. Unmarked.
Ref.No.: D of C, BH9, p. 304.

Mint $135.00   Ex. $95.00   G. $65.00   F. $40.00

TICKLETOES

1960. 18 in. (45.5 cm). One piece Vinyl-flex body. Vinyl head; blue sleep eyes, lashes, painted lower lashes; rooted blond saran hair; closed mouth. Unmarked.
Ref.No.: D of C, BH10, p. 304.

Mint $55.00   Ex. $45.00   G. $30.00   F. $20.00

BARBARA ANN - 1960 - 16 in.

1960. 16 in. (40.5 cm). Plastic body and legs, vinyl arms. Vinyl head; blue sleep eyes, lashes, painted lower lashes; rooted blond curly hair; open mouth nurser. Mark: Reliable (in script)/CANADA.
Ref.No.: D of C, CJ26, p. 304.

Mint $70.00   Ex. $55.00   G. $40.00   F. $20.00

LITTLE SISTER

1960. 30 in. (76.5 cm). Plastic body, jointed hips, shoulders, and neck. Vinyl head; blue sleep eyes, lashes, painted lower lashes; rooted brown saran curls; closed mouth. Mark: on back, Reliable.
Ref.No.: D of C, BQ16, p. 305.

Mint $105.00   Ex. $85.00   G. $60.00   F. $40.00

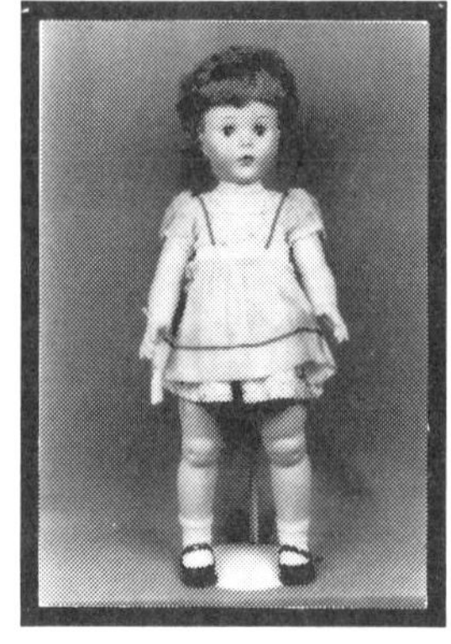

GRENADIER GUARD

1960. 16 in. (40.5 cm). Plastic body, jointed hips, shoulders, and neck. Vinyl head; blue sleep eyes, lashes, painted lower lashes; brown moulded hair; closed mouth. Mark: on back, RELIABLE (in script)/CANADA.
Ref.No.: D of C, BN36, p. 305.

Mint $60.00   Ex. $50.00   G.   430.00   F. $15.00

SOUVENIR DOLL

1960. 16 in. (40.5 cm). Plastic body and legs, vinyl arms, jointed hips, shoulders, and neck. Vinyl head; brown sleep eyes, lashes, painted lower lashes; rooted long black hair; closed mouth. Unmarked.
Ref.No.: D of C, BQ4, p. 305.

Mint $50.00   Ex. $40.00   G. $30.00   F. $15.00

BRIDE

1960. 17 in. (43 cm). One piece Rigidsol body. Vinyl head; brown sleep eyes, lashes, painted lower lashes; rooted brown hair; closed mouth. Mark: on head, RELIABLE; on body, H-17.
Ref.No.: D of C, CW21A, p. 306.

Mint $55.00   Ex. $45.00   G. $25.00   F.$15.00

RELIABLE BOY

1961. 12 in. (30.5 cm). One piece vinyl body. Vinyl head; black painted side-glancing eyes, painted upper lashes; brown moulded hair; open-closed mouth showing tongue. Mark: on head, 1/1104/RELIABLE/MADE IN CANADA.
Ref.No.: D of C, CG30, p. 306.

Mint $60.00   Ex. $50.00   G. $30.00   F. $15.00

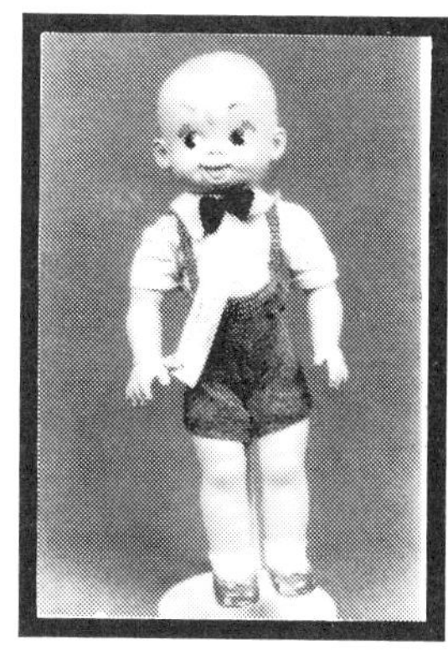

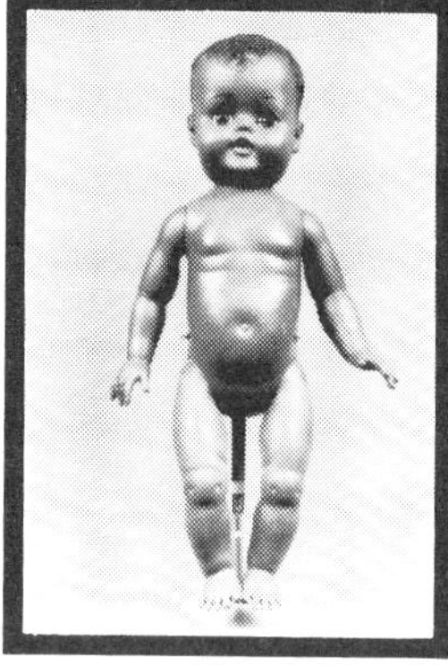

WETUMS

1961. 20 in. (51 cm). Brown plastic body and legs, vinyl arms, jointed hips, shoulders, and neck. Vinyl head; brown sleep eyes, lashes, painted lower lashes; black moulded hair; open mouth nurser. Mark: on body, RELIABLE (in script)/MADE IN CANADA.
Ref.No.: D of C, AT13, p. 306.

Mint $60.00   Ex. $45.00   G. $30.00   F. $20.00

RELIABLE GIRL

1961. 12 in. (30.5 cm). One piece vinyl body. Vinyl head, dimples; black painted side-glancing eyes, painted upper lashes; yellow moulded hair in braids; open-closed mouth. Mark: on head, RELIABLE (in script).
Ref.No.: D of C, CM5, p. 307.

Mint $45.00   Ex. $35.00   G. $20.00   F. $10.00

COLOURED NURSE WALKING DOLL

1961. 30 in. (76.5 cm). Brown plastic body, jointed hips, shoulders, and neck. Vinyl head; brown sleep eyes, lashes, painted lower lashes; rooted black curls; closed mouth. Mark: on head, RELIABLE TOY/MADE IN CANADA.
Ref.No.: D of C, CP17, p. 307.

Mint $125.00   Ex. $105.00 G. $60.00   F. $35.00

SAUCY WALKER - 35 in.

1961. 35 in. (89 cm). Plastic body, jointed hips, shoulders, and neck. Vinyl head; blue sleep eyes, lashes, painted lower lashes; rooted auburn saran straight hair with bangs; closed mouth. Mark: on body, RELIABLE (in script).
Ref.No.: D of C, CW12, p. 307.

Mint $135.00   Ex. $95.00   G. $65.00   F. $40.00

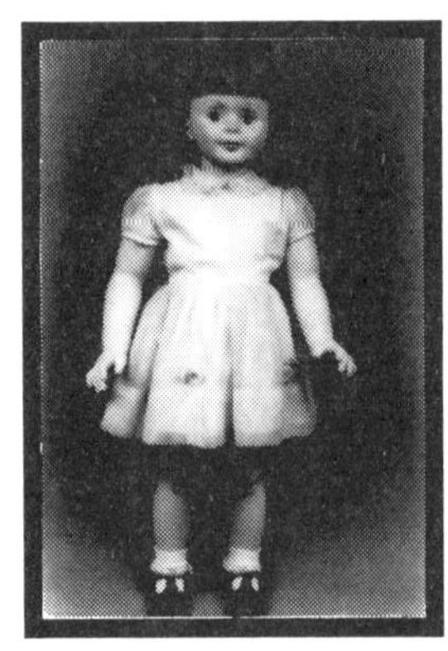

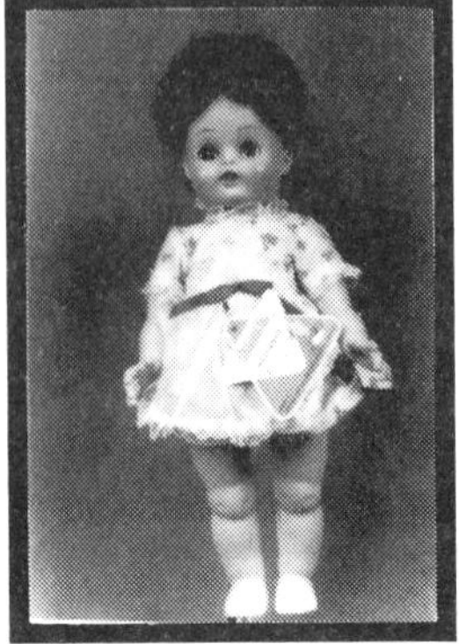

CINDY LOU

ca. 1961. 14 in. (35.5 cm). Plastic body and legs, vinyl arms, jointed hips, shoulders, and neck. Vinyl head; blue sleep eyes, lashes, painted lower lashes; rooted brown saran hair in ponytail and bangs; closed mouth. Mark: on head, RELIABLE.
Ref.No.: D of C, BQ13, p. 309.

Mint $65.00   Ex. $45.00   G. $30.00   F. $15.00

LOUISA

1961. 30 in. (76.5 cm). Plastic body, jointed waist, hip, shoulder, swivel-jointed upper leg, wrists and ankles. Vinyl head; blue sleep eyes, lashes, painted lower lashes; rooted red saran hair; closed mouth. Unmarked.
Ref.No.: D of C, CS21A, p. 308.

Mint $200.00   Ex. $175.00   G. $150.00   F. $95.00

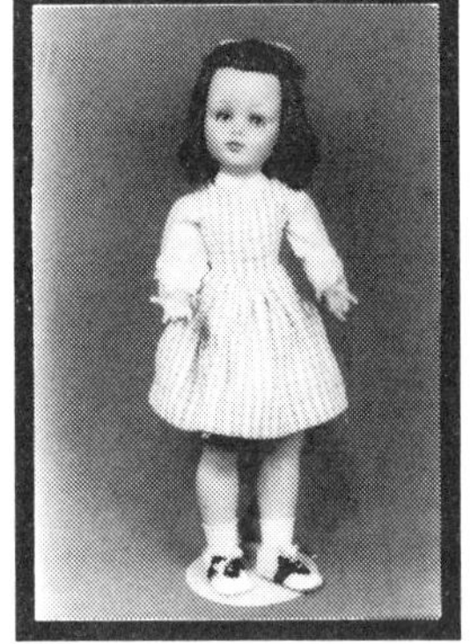

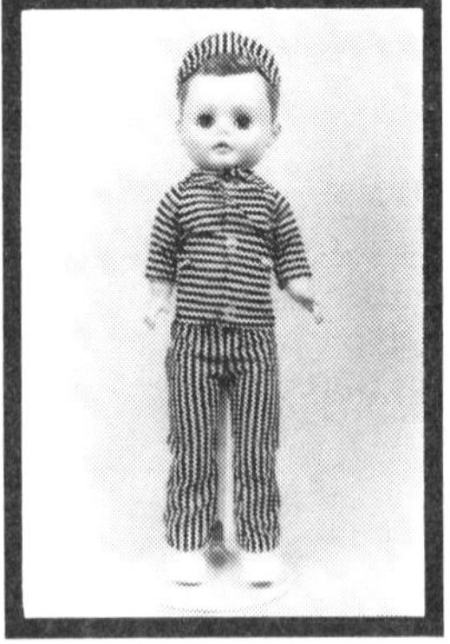

LITTLE MISTER BAD BOY

ca. 1961. 18 in. (45.5 cm). Plastic body, jointed hips, shoulders, and neck. Vinyl head, blue sleep eyes, lashes, painted lower lashes; moulded brown hair; closed mouth. Mark: on body, RELIABLE (in script).
Ref.No.: D of C, CY7, p. 309.

Mint $65.00   Ex. $45.00   G. $30.00   F. $20.00

RELIABLE - 1962

ca. 1962. 19 in. (48.5 cm). Cloth body, vinyl bent- limb arms and legs, originally had a pull cord in the back of the body. Vinyl head; blue sleep eyes, lashes; rooted straight blond baby hair; open-closed mouth. Mark: on head, RELIABLE. *Ref.No.: D of C, CW2, p. 309.*

Mint $40.00   Ex. $30.00   G. $25.00   F. $15.00

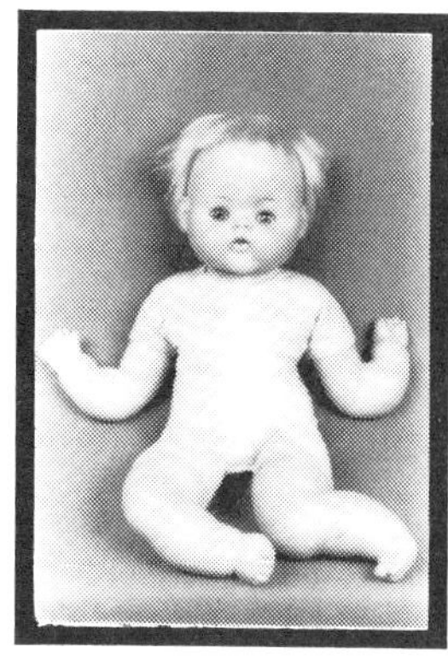

RELIABLE - 1962

ca. 1962. 17 in. (43 cm). Plastic body, jointed hips, shoulders, and neck. Vinyl head; blue sleep eyes, lashes, painted lower lashes; rooted blond saran hair; open-closed mouth. Mark: on head, RELIABLE; on body, Reliable (in script). *Ref.No.: D of C, CW24, p. 310.*

Mint $45.00   Ex. $35.00   G. $20.00   F. $10.00

RELIABLE - 1962

ca. 1962. 16 in. (40.5 cm). Plastic body, jointed hips, shoulders, and neck. Vinyl head; blue sleep eyes, lashes, painted lower lashes; rooted dark brown hair in twin pony tails and bangs; open-closed mouth. Mark: on head, RELIABLE; on body, RELIABLE (in script)/CANADA. *Ref.No.: D of C, CW26, p. 310.*

Mint $50.00   Ex. $40.00   G. $25.00   F. $15.00

RELIABLE - 1962

ca. 1962. 16 in. (40.5 cm). Plastic body, jointed hips, shoulders, and neck. Vinyl head; blue sleep eyes, lashes, painted lower lashes; black moulded hair; closed mouth. Mark: on body, RELIABLE (in script)/CANADA. *Ref.No.: D of C, CG16, p. 310.*

Mint $50.00   Ex. $40.00   G. $30.00   F. $15.00

DOCTOR TODDLER

1963. 15.5 in. (39 cm). Plastic body, jointed hips, shoulders, and neck. Vinyl head; blue sleep eyes, lashes, painted lower lashes; black moulded hair; closed mouth. Mark: on body, RELIABLE (in script)/CANADA.
Ref.No.: D of C, CW20A, p. 311.

Mint $65.00   Ex. $45.00   G. $30.00   F. $20.00

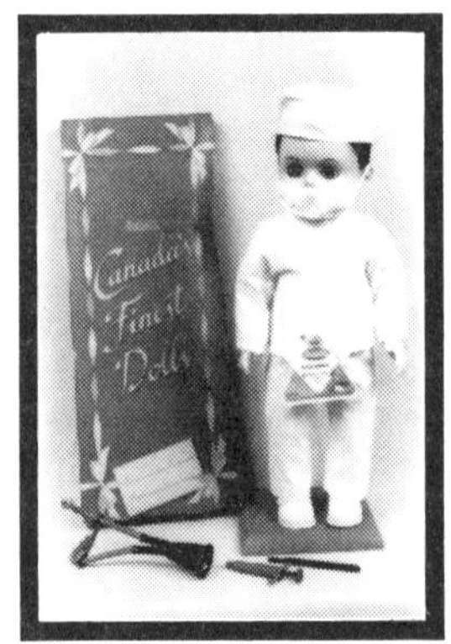

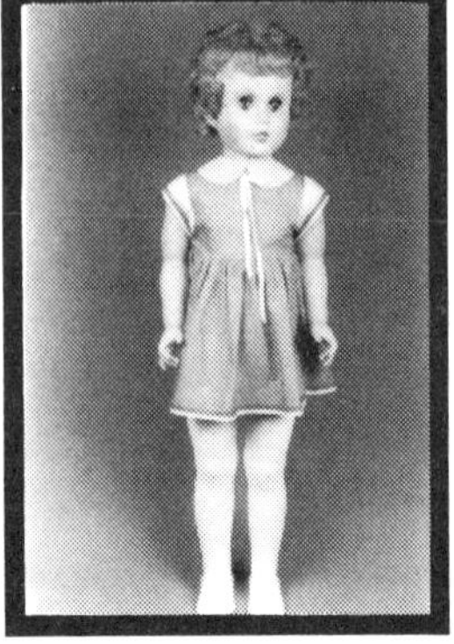

MARY ANNE

1963. 35 in. (89 cm). Plastic body, jointed hips, shoulders, and neck. Vinyl head; blue sleep eyes, lashes; rooted saran honey blond curls; closed mouth. Mark: on body, RELIABLE (in script).
Ref.No.: D of C, BZ20, p. 311.

Mint $105.00   Ex. $80.00   G. $45.00   F. $35.00

MARY, MARY QUITE CONTRARY

1963. 18 in. (45.5 cm). Plastic body and legs, vinyl arms. Vinyl head; green sleep eyes, lashes, painted lower lashes; rooted blond saran hair; closed mouth. Mark: on head, RELIABLE/MADE IN/CANADA.
Ref.No.: D of C, BH30, p. 311.

Mint $45.00   Ex. $35.00   G. $25.00   F. $15.00

BARBARA ANNE, DRUM MAJORETTE

1963. 15.5 in. (39 cm). Plastic body and legs, vinyl arms, jointed hips, shoulders, and neck. Vinyl head; blue sleep eyes, lashes; rooted blond hair; closed mouth. Mark: on head, RELIABLE; on body, RELIABLE (in script)/CANADA.
Ref.No.: D of C, XH22, p. 312.

Mint $55.00   Ex. $40.00   G. $25.00   F. $15.00

RELIABLE GIRL

1963. 14 in. (35.5 cm). Plastic body, jointed hips, shoulders, and neck. Vinyl head with bonnet moulded on the head; blue plastic fixed eyes, painted upper lashes; yellow moulded hair; open-closed mouth. Mark: on back, RELIABLE/CANADA.
Ref.No.: D of C, BC21, p. 312.

Note: This doll is hard to find.

Mint $55.00 **Ex.** $45.00 **G.** $30.00 **F.** $20.00

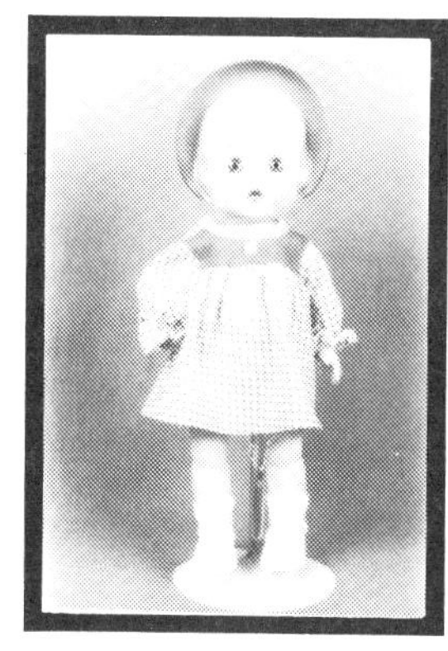

BARBARA ANNE NURSE

1963. 16 in. (40.5 cm). Plastic body, jointed hips, shoulders, and neck. Vinyl head; blue sleep eyes, lashes, painted lower lashes; rooted brown curls; closed mouth. Mark: on head, RELIABLE.
Ref.No.: D of C, BH20, p. 313.

Mint $60.00 **Ex.** $45.00 **G.** $20.00 **F.** $15.00

RELIABLE - 1963

1963. 16 in. (40.5 cm). Brown plastic body, jointed hips, shoulders, and neck. Vinyl head; golden brown sleep eyes, lashes, painted lower lashes; rooted black curls; open mouth nurser. Mark: on head, RELIABLE (in script); on body, RELIABLE (in script)/CANADA.
Ref.No.: D of C, BP26, p. 313.

Mint $50.00 **Ex.** $35.00 **G.** $25.00 **F.** $15.00

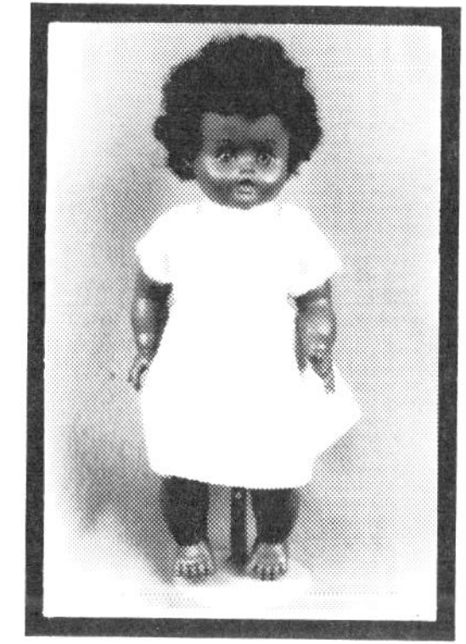

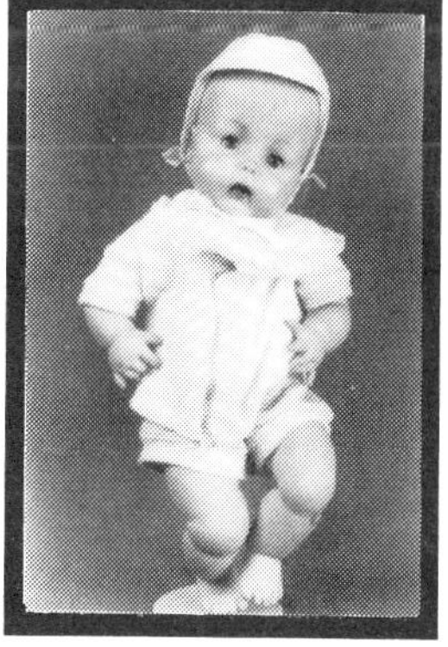

BABY CUDDLES

1963. 20 in. (51 cm). Vinyl bent-limb body. Vinyl head; blue sleep eyes, lashes; rooted blond hair over moulded hair; open-closed mouth. Mark: on head, RELIABLE.
Ref.No.: D of C, CN22, p. 313.

Mint $70.00 **Ex.** $60.00 **G.** $40.00 **F.** $20.00

TAMMY

1964. 12 in. (30.5 cm). Plastic body, jointed hips, shoulders, and neck. Vinyl head; blue painted side-glancing eyes, painted upper lashes; rooted honey blond curls; closed mouth. Mark: on head, C. IDEAL TOY CORP.; on back, RELIABLE/CANADA.
Ref.No.: D of C, BN34, p. 314.

Mint $50.00   Ex. $40.00   G. $20.00   F. $15.00

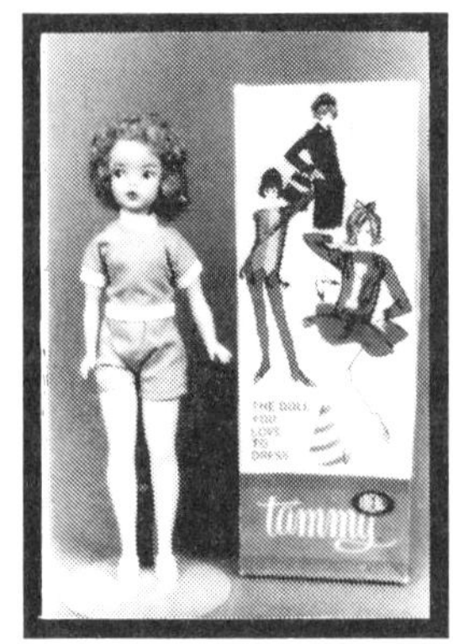

RUTHIE

1965. 18 in. (45.5 cm). Plastic body, jointed hips, shoulders, and neck. Vinyl head; blue sleep eyes, lashes, painted lower lashes; rooted honey blond hair; closed mouth. Mark: on head, RELIABLE (in script); on body, RELIABLE (in script).
Ref.No.: D of C, AO21, p. 314.

Mint $55.00   Ex. $40.00   G. $25.00   F. $15.00

RELIABLE - 1966

ca. 1966. 12 in. (30.5 cm). Plastic body, jointed hips, shoulders, and neck. Vinyl head; blue sleep eyes, lashes, painted lower lashes; brown moulded hair; open mouth nurser. Mark: on body, RELIABLE (in script)/CANADA.
Ref.No.: D of C, AN7, p. 314.

Mint $30.00   Ex. $20.00   G. $12.00   F. $8.00

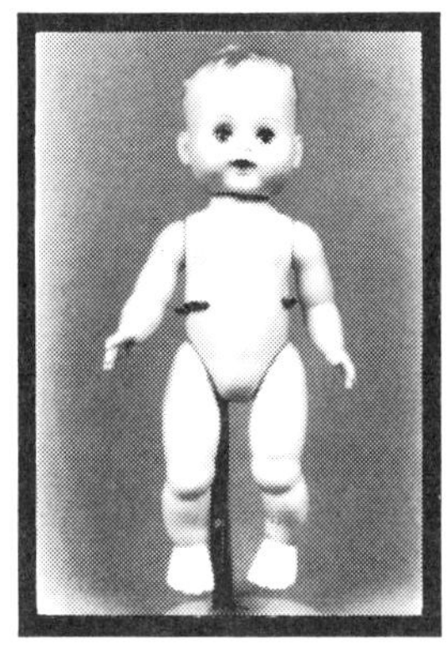

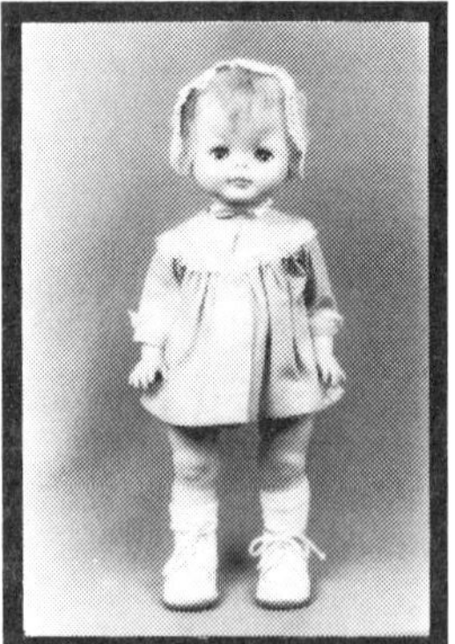

SUSIE STEPPS - 21 in.

1966. 21 in. (53.5 cm). Hard plastic body and legs, vinyl arms, jointed hips, shoulders, and neck. Body has a battery box with an on/off switch. Vinyl head; blue sleep eyes, lashes; rooted blond straight hair; closed mouth. Mark: RELIABLE/MADE IN CANADA.
Ref.No.: D of C, BC14, p. 315.

Note: Rarely found in working condition.

Mint $85.00   Ex. $65.00   G. $50.00   F. $35.00

HONEY TODDLER

1967. 14 in. (35.5 cm). Plastic body jointed hips, shoulders, and neck. Vinyl head; blue plastic sleep eyes, lashes; rooted auburn hair trimmed with black grosgrain ribbon; closed mouth. Mark: on back, Reliable (in script)/MADE IN CANADA.
Ref.No.: D of C, CD21, p. 315.

Mint $45.00   **Ex.** $35.00   **G.** $20.00   **F.**$12.00

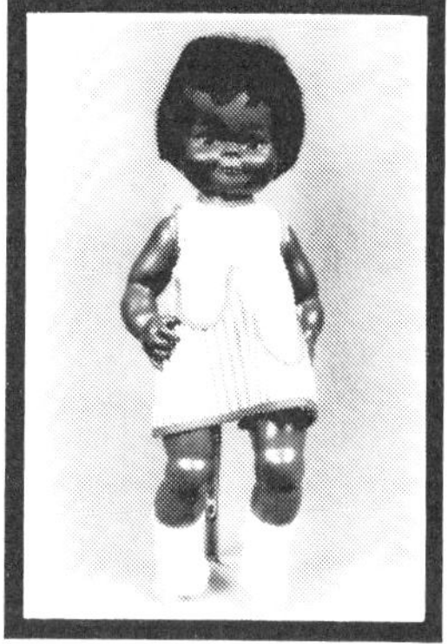

TOPSY BABY

1967. 16 in. (40.5 cm). Plastic body, jointed hips, shoulders, and neck. Vinyl head; brown plastic sleep eyes, lashes; rooted black straight hair; closed smiling mouth. Mark: on head, RELIABLE/MADE IN CANADA.
Ref.No.: D of C, BN22, p. 315.

Note: Unusually nice black baby.

Mint $75.00   **Ex.** $55.00   **G.** $30.00   **F.** $20.00

RELIABLE - 1968

1968. 16 in. (40.5 cm). Plastic body, jointed hips, shoulders, and neck. Vinyl head; blue stencilled eyes; rooted blond hair; open mouth nurser. Mark: on head, RELIABLE TOY CO. LTD./19c68/MADE IN CANADA; on body, RELIABLE (in script)/CANADA.
Ref.No.: D of C, AN18, p. 316.

Mint $25.00   **Ex.** $20.00   **G.** $15.00   **F.** $8.00

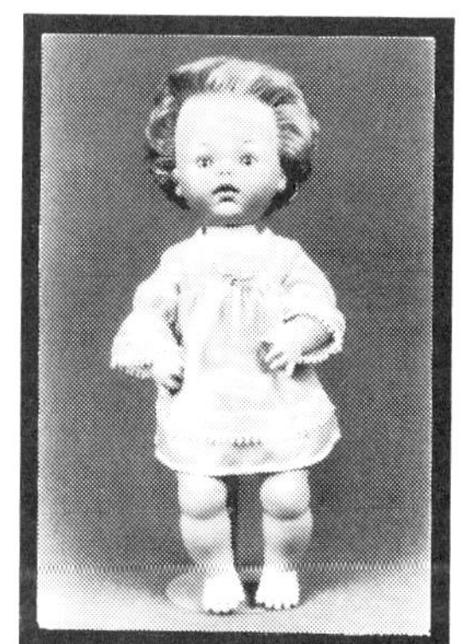

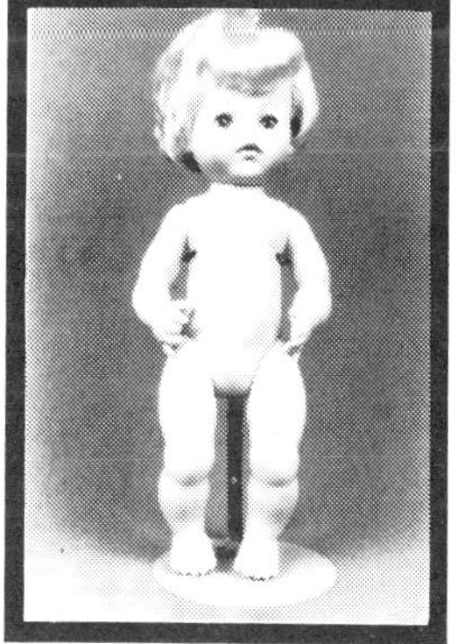

BABY LOVUMS - 1969

1969. 16 in. (40.5 cm). Plastic body, jointed hips, shoulders, and neck. Vinyl head, with earrings; blue sleep eyes, lashes, painted lower lashes; rooted blond hair; open mouth nurser. Mark: on head, RELIABLE TOY CO. LTD./19c68/MADE IN CANADA.
Ref.No.: D of C, AN24, p. 316.

Mint $45.00   **Ex.** $30.00   **G.** $20.00   **F.** $10.00

RELIABLE BABY

1968. 14 in. (35.5 cm). Plastic body, jointed hips, shoulders, and neck. Vinyl head; blue stencilled, side-glancing eyes; rooted honey blond curls; open mouth nurser. Mark: on head, O26914/RELIABLE TOY CO. LTD./19c69/MADE IN CANADA; on body, RELIABLE (in script)/CANADA.
Ref.No.: D of C, AN11A, p. 316.

Mint $35.00   Ex. $25.00   G. $15.00   F. $10.00

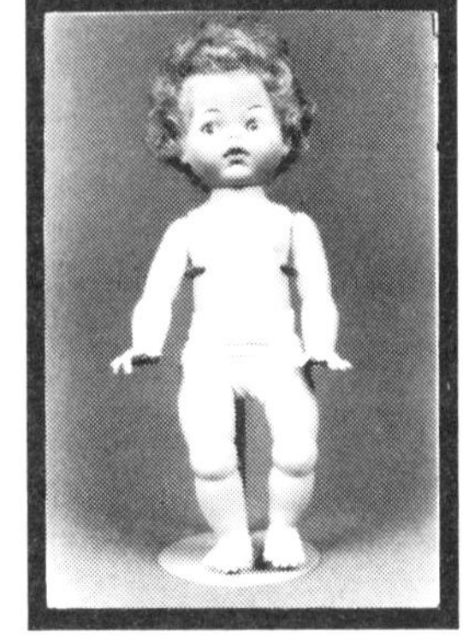

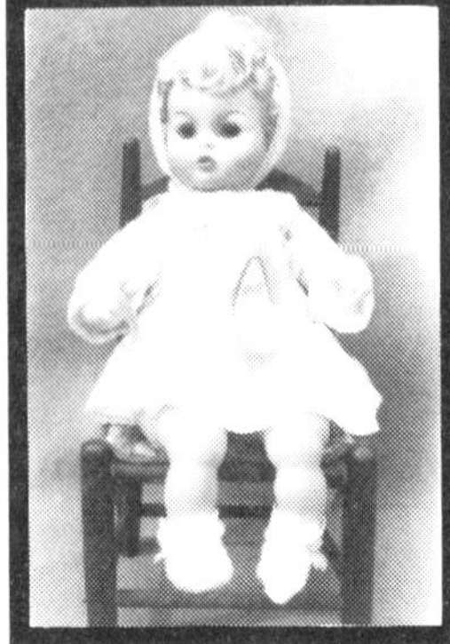

BABY PRECIOUS - 18 in.

1969. 18 in (46 cm). Cloth body, vinyl bent-limb arms and legs. Vinyl head; sleep eyes, lashes; rooted blond nylon curls; open-closed mouth. Mark: on head, RELIABLE.
Ref.No.: D of C, BJ24, p. 317.

Mint $75.00   Ex. $55.00   G. $35.00   F. $20.00

MARY ANNE WALKER

1969. 30 in. (76.5 cm). Plastic body, jointed hips, shoulder, and neck. Vinyl head; blue sleep eyes, lashes, painted lower lashes; rooted blond hair; closed mouth. Mark: on head, RELIABLE (in script)/MADE IN CANADA.
Ref.No.: D of C, BW1, p. 317.

Mint $75.00   Ex. $55.00   G. $40.00   F. $30.00

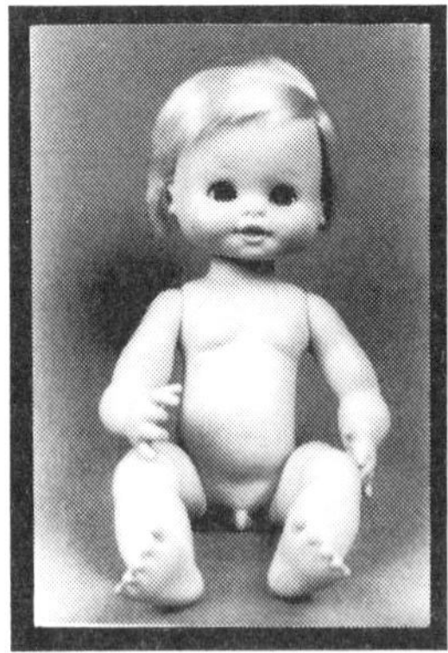

LITTLE BROTHER

1969. 16 in. (40.5 cm). Vinyl body, jointed hips, shoulders, and neck. Vinyl head; blue sleep eyes; lashes; rooted blond saran hair; open-closed mouth. Mark: on head, 2054/15eye/10/RELIABLE TOY CO. LTD./c1967/MADE IN CANADA.
Ref.No.: D of C, BN8, p. 317.

Mint $45.00   Ex. $30.00   G. $20.00   F. $15.00

BABY CUDDLES

1969. 9 in (23 cm). Plastic body, jointed hips, shoulders, and neck. Vinyl head; blue sleep eyes; lashes; three painted upper lashes; rooted blond saran curls; open mouth nurser. Mark: on head, RELIABLE TOY CO./19c69.
Ref.No.: D of C, BX25, p. 318.

Mint $35.00 Ex. $25.00 G. $15.00 F. $10.00

NICOLE

1969. 16 in. (40.5 CM). Plastic body and legs, vinyl arms, jointed hips, shoulders, and neck. Vinyl head; blue sleep eyes; lashes; rooted brown straight hair; closed smiling mouth. Mark: on head, Reliable (in script); on body, RELIABLE (in script)/CANADA.
Ref.No.: D of C, CS13, p. 318.

Mint $55.00 Ex. $35.00 G. 25.00 F. 15.00

ROSALYN

1969. 18 in. (45.5 cm). Plastic body, jointed hips, and shoulders. Vinyl head; blue sleep eyes, lashes, painted lower lashes; rooted blond curls with bangs; closed mouth. Mark: on head, 22/RELIABLE (in script); on body, RELIABLE (in script).
Ref.No.: D of C, CR11, p. 318.

Mint $50.00 Ex. $40.00 G. $25.00 F. $15.00

RELIABLE - 1970

ca. 1970. 12 in. (30.5 cm). Plastic body, jointed hips, shoulders, and neck. Vinyl head; blue stencilled side-glancing eyes with black line over eye, four painted upper lashes; rooted blond hair; open-closed mouth. Mark: on head, RELIABLE.
Ref.No.: D of C, CJ12, p. 319.

Mint $25.00 Ex. $15.00 G. 10.00 F. $5.00

CAROL WALKER

ca. 1974. 24 in. (61 cm). Plastic body, jointed hips, shoulders, and neck. Vinyl head; blue sleep eyes, lashes, painted lower lashes; rooted blond curls; closed mouth. Mark: on body, RELIABLE (in script)/CANADA.
Ref.No.: D of C, AN32, p. 319.

Mint $35.00 Ex. $25.00 G. $20.00 F. $10.00

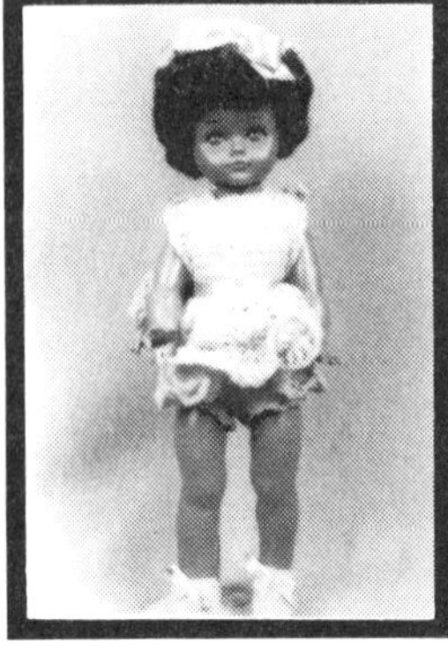

BLACK GLORIA

1974. 16 in. (40.5 cm). Brown plastic body, jointed hips, shoulders, and neck. Vinyl head; brown stencilled eyes, black line over eye, painted upper lashes; rooted black curls; closed mouth. Mark: on head, RELIABLE TOY CO. LTD./MADE IN CANADA.
Ref.No.: D of C, CI13, p. 319.

Mint $25.00 Ex. $20.00 G. $15.00 F. $10.00

RELIABLE - 1975

ca. 1975. 18 in. (45.5 cm). Plastic body, jointed hips, shoulders, and neck. Vinyl head; blue sleep eyes, lashes, painted lower lashes; rooted blond curls; closed mouth. Mark: on body, RELIABLE (in script).
Ref.No.: D of C, CW29, p. 320.

Mint $30.00 Ex. $20.00 G. $15.00 F. $10.00

LORRIE WALKER

ca. 1975. 32 in. (81.5 cm). Plastic body, jointed hips, shoulders, and neck. Vinyl head; blue sleep eyes, lashes, painted lower lashes; rooted black hair with bangs; closed mouth. Mark: on head, RELIABLE (in script)/MADE IN CANADA; on body, RELIABLE (in script)/CANADA.
Ref.No.: D of C, AO11, p. 320.

Mint $40.00 Ex. $25.00 G. $20.00 F. $15.00

BABY LOVUMS - 1975

ca. 1975. 13 in. (33 cm). Plastic body, jointed hips, shoulders, and neck. Vinyl head; blue sleep eyes, lashes, painted lower lashes; rooted straight blond hair; open mouth nurser. Mark: RELIABLE TOY CO. LTD./10c00/MADE IN CANADA.
Ref.No.: D of C, CG32, p. 321.

Mint $35.00   Ex. $20.00   G. $15.00   F. $10.00

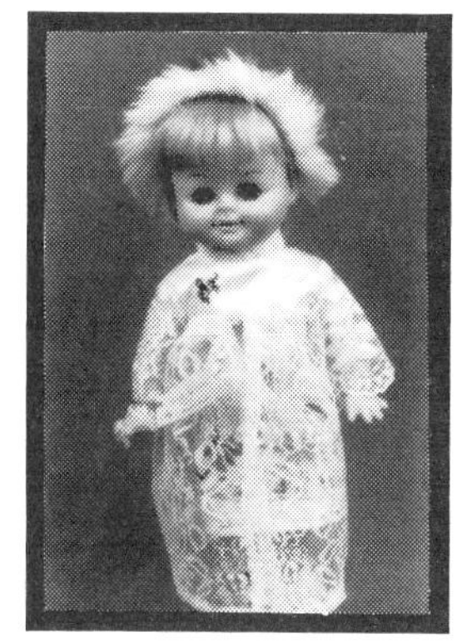

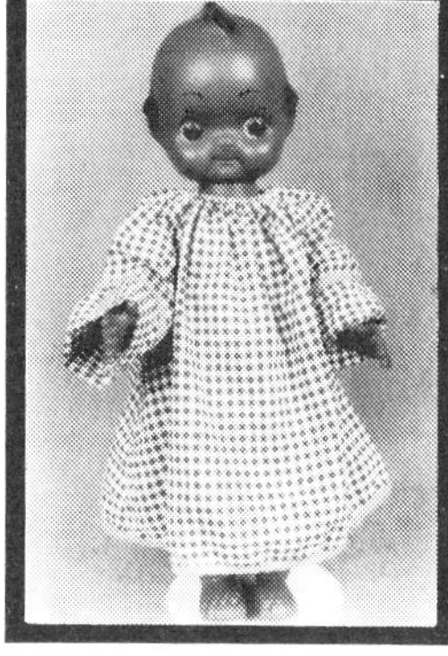

RELIABLE - 1975

ca. 1975. 16 in. (40.5 cm). Plastic body, jointed hips, shoulders, and neck. Vinyl head; black stencilled side-glancing eyes, painted upper lashes; black moulded tufts of hair; closed mouth. Mark: RELIABLE.
Ref.No.: D of C, CA7, p. 321.

Mint $20.00   Ex. $15.00   G.   10.00   F. $8.00

RELIABLE - 1975

ca. 1975. 16.5 in (42 cm). Plastic body, jointed hips, shoulders, and neck. Vinyl head; blue sleep eyes, lashes; rooted blond curls; open mouth nurser. Mark: on head, RELIABLE/MADE IN CANADA; on body, RELIABLE (in script)/CANADA.
Ref.No.: D of C, AN22, p. 321.

Mint $20.00   Ex. $15.00   G. $10.00   F. $8.00

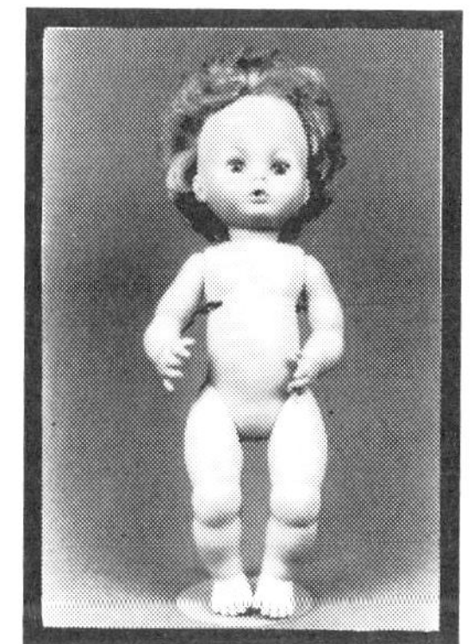

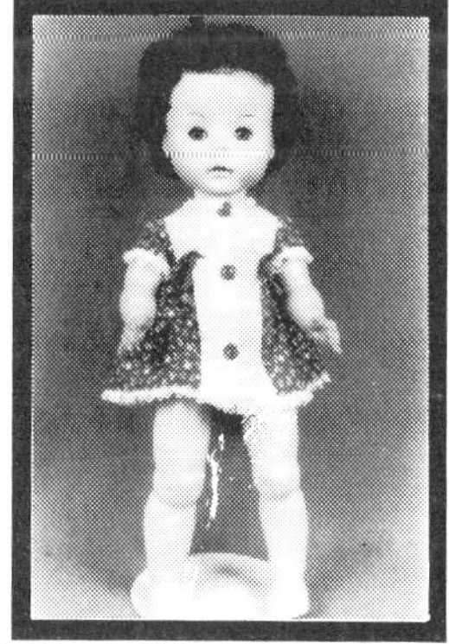

RELIABLE - 1976

ca. 1976. 19 in. (48.5 cm). Plastic body, jointed hips, shoulders, and neck. Vinyl head; green sleep eyes, lashes, painted lower lashes; rooted brown curls; closed mouth. Mark: on head, RELIABLE.
Ref.No.: D of C, CJ28, p. 322.

Mint $30.00   Ex. $20.00   G. $15.00   F. $10.00

CINDERELLA

ca. 1976. 30 in. (76.5 cm). Plastic body, jointed hips, shoulders, and neck. Vinyl head; blue sleep eyes, lashes, painted lower lashes; rooted black curly hair with long hair on each side; closed mouth. Mark: on head, RELIABLE 9 in script)/MADE IN CANADA; on body, RELIABLE (in script)/CANADA; on shoe, CINDERELLA/NO. 5.
Ref.No.: D of C, CH2, p. 322.

Mint $40.00 **Ex.** $30.00 **G.** 25.00 **F.** $15.00

RELIABLE - 1977

ca. 1977. 13 in. (33 cm). Jointed hips, shoulders, and neck. Soft vinyl head; light brown moulded hair; stencilled eyes; open mouth nurser. Mark: RELIABLE (in script) CANADA.
Ref.No.: D of C, CG27, p. 323.

Mint $25.00 **Ex.** $20.00 **G.** $15.00 **F.** $8.00

RELIABLE - 1978

ca. 1978. 18 in. (45.5 cm). Plastic body, jointed hips, shoulders, and neck. Vinyl head; blue sleep eyes, lashes, painted lower lashes; rooted blond hair; closed mouth. Mark: on head 27/RELIABLE (in script); on body, RELIABLE (in script).
Ref.No.: D of C, AN33, p. 323.

Mint $30.00 **Ex.** $20.00 **G.** $15.00 **F.** $10.00

INUIT DOLL

1978. 12 in. (30.5 cm). Plastic body, jointed hips, shoulders, and neck. Vinyl head; black stencilled eyes, eye outlined in black; rooted straight black hair; open- closed mouth. Mark: on head, RELIABLE TOY CO. LTD./19c68/MADE IN CANADA.
Ref.No.: D of C, BU30, p. 322.

Mint $45.00 **Ex.** $30.00 **G.** $25.00 **F.** $15.00

RELIABLE - 1980

ca. 1980. 16 in. (40.5 cm). Plastic body, jointed hips, shoulders, and neck. Vinyl head; blue plastic sleep eyes, lashes, painted lower lashes; rooted blond hair; open mouth nurser. Mark: on head, RELIABLE (in script); on body, RELIABLE/CANADA.
Ref.No.: D of C, CG26, p. 323.

Mint $35.00 Ex. $25.00 G. $20.0 F. $10.00

GLORIA

ca. 1983. 16 in. (40.5 cm). Plastic body, jointed hips, shoulders, and neck. Vinyl head; blue stencilled eyes, black upper lashes and upper eye liner; rooted blond hair tied at each side; closed mouth. Mark: RELIABLE.
Ref.No.: D of C, BX12, p. 324.

Mint $30.00 Ex. $20.00 G. $15.00 F. $10.00

CHUBBY

1984. 21 in. (53.5 cm). Plastic body, vinyl arms and legs, jointed hips, shoulders, and neck. Vinyl head; blue plastic sleep eyes, lashes, painted lower lashes; rooted blond curls; open-closed mouth showing two moulded teeth. Mark: on head, RELIABLE/MADE IN CANADA.
Ref.No.: D of C, BU2, p. 324.

Mint $40.00 Ex. $25.00 G. $20.00 F. $15.00

BALLERINA DOLL

1984. 16 in. (40.5 cm). Plastic body, jointed hips, shoulders, and neck. Vinyl head; blue stencilled eyes with black upper lashes; rooted blond hair; closed mouth. Mark: on head, RELIABLE TOY CO. LTD./MADE IN CANADA; on back, RELIABLE (in script)/CANADA.
Ref.No.: D of C, AO18, p. 324.

Mint $30.00 Ex. $20.00 G. $15.00 F. $10.00

JACKIE

1984. 17 in. (43 cm). Plastic teen body, jointed hips, shoulders, and neck. Vinyl head; brown stencilled eyes with black upper lashes; rooted black curls; closed mouth. Mark: on head, 8/RELIABLE TOY CO. LTD./MADE IN CANADA; on back, RELIABLE (in script)/CANADA.
Ref.No.: D of C, AO20, p. 324.

Mint $35.00 Ex. $20.00 G. $15.00 F. $10.00

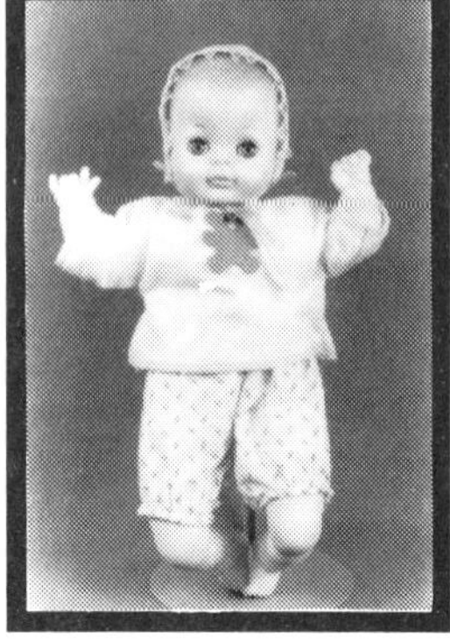

BABY LOVUMS - 1985

1985. 15 in. (38 cm). Plastic body, vinyl arms and legs, jointed hips, shoulders, and neck. Vinyl head; blue plastic sleep eyes, lashes, painted lower lashes; rooted blond hair; open mouth nurser. Mark: on head, RELIABLE (in script); on body, RELIABLE (in script).
Ref.No.: D of C, BW23, p. 325.

Mint $40.00 Ex. $20.00 G. $15.00 F. $10.00

BRENDA

1985. 17 in. (43 cm). Cloth body with crier, vinyl arms and legs. Vinyl head; blue plastic sleep eyes, lashes; light brown moulded hair; closed mouth. Mark: on head, RELIABLE/MADE IN CANADA.
Ref.No.: D of C, BW24, p. 325.

Mint $30.00 Ex. $20.00
G. $15.00 F. $10.00

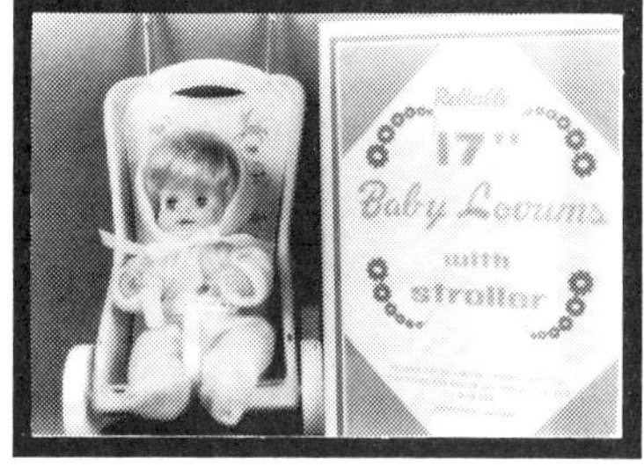

STANDARD TOYS LTD
ca1917

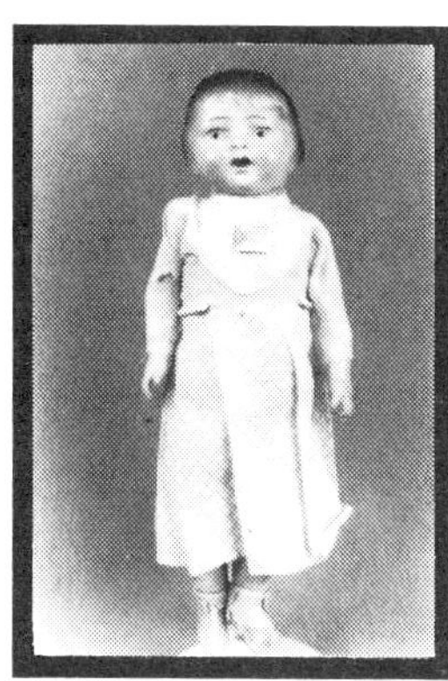

STANDARD

ca.1917. 14.5 in. (36 cm). Excelsior stuffed cloth body, metal disc hip and shoulder joints. Composition head; blue painted eyes; moulded reddish-brown hair; closed mouth. Mark: on head, H.B.CO.; label on dress, STANDARD QUALITY/DOLLS/ MADE/ IN/CANADA.
Ref.No.: D of C, CN14, p. 326.

Mint $200.00   Ex. $175.00   G. $85.00   F. $60.00

STAR DOLL MANUFACTURING COMPANY
1952 - 1970

Star Doll Manufacturing made vinyl dolls for almost twenty years but it is sometimes difficult to identify a Star Doll as the moulds were used by several companies.

STAR DOLL - 1957

ca.1957. 17 in. (43 cm). One piece stuffed vinyl body. Vinyl head; green sleep eyes, lashes, painted lower lashes; rooted honey blond hair; closed mouth. Mark: on head, 14R ; on body, A. Original box marked, Star Doll Co. 7182.
Ref.No.: D of C, XH21, p. 327.

Mint $75.00   Ex. $50.00   G. $35.00   F. $25.00

STAR DOLL - 1960

ca.1960. 16 in. (40.5 cm). Plastic body, jointed hips, shoulders, and neck. Vinyl head; blue sleep eyes, lashes, painted lower lashes; rooted blond hair; open mouth nurser. Mark: on head, STAR.
Ref.No.: D of C, BQ7, p. 327.

Mint $60.00   Ex. $45.00   G. $3500   F. $25.00

STAR DOLL - 1961

1961. 20.5 in. (52 cm). Cloth body, vinyl bent-limb arms and legs. Vinyl head; blue sleep eyes, lashes; rooted honey blond hair; open-closed mouth. Mark: on head, PLATED MOULDS INC./C1961; tag sewn into body, MADE BY/STAR DOLL MFG. CO.
Ref.No.: D of C, BF7, p. 328.

Mint $60.00   Ex. $40.00   G. $30.00   F. $20.00

STAR DOLL - 1963

ca.1963. 18 in. (45.5 cm). Plastic body, jointed hips, shoulders, and neck. Vinyl head; blue sleep eyes, lashes, painted lower lashes; rooted light brown curls; closed mouth. Mark: on head, STAR DOLL.
Ref.No.: D of C, CO16, p. 328.

Mint $40.00   Ex. $30.00   G. $20.00   F. $10.00

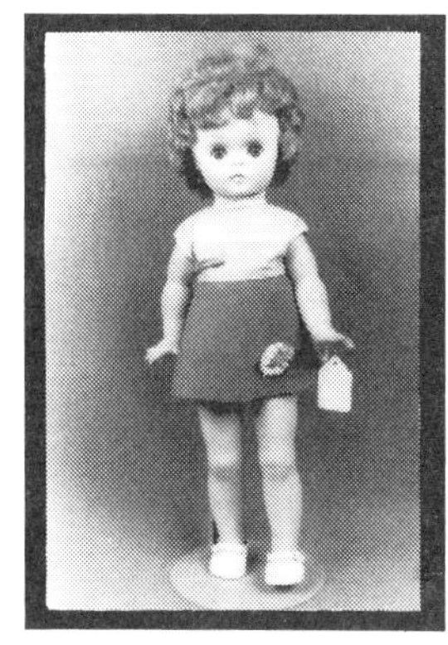

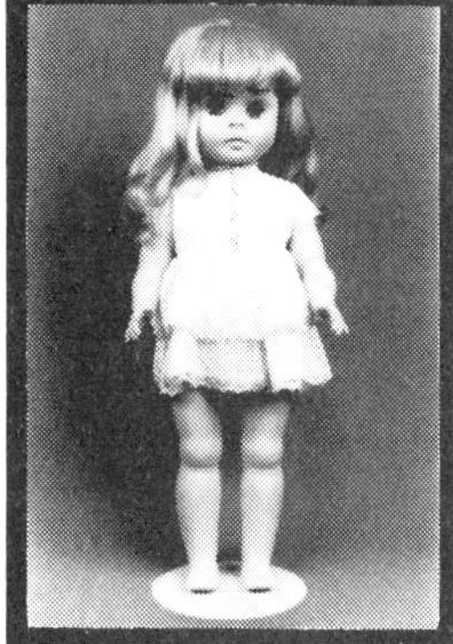

STAR DOLL - 1965

1965. 23 in. (58.5 cm). Plastic body, jointed hips, shoulders, and neck. Vinyl head; blue sleep eyes, lashes, painted lower lashes; rooted blond hair with bangs; closed mouth. Mark: on head, STAR DOLL/c1965 CANADA.
Ref.No.: D of C, AN26, p. 329.

Mint $45.00   Ex. $35.00   G. $25.00   F. $15.00

STAR DOLL - 1967

1967. 18 in. (45.5 cm). Cloth body, vinyl bent-limb arms and legs. Vinyl head; blue sleep eyes, lashes; rooted auburn hair; closed mouth. Mark: STAR DOLL/MADE IN CANADA.
Ref.No.: D of C, CG28, p. 330.

Mint $50.00   Ex. $45.00   G. $30.00   F. $25.00

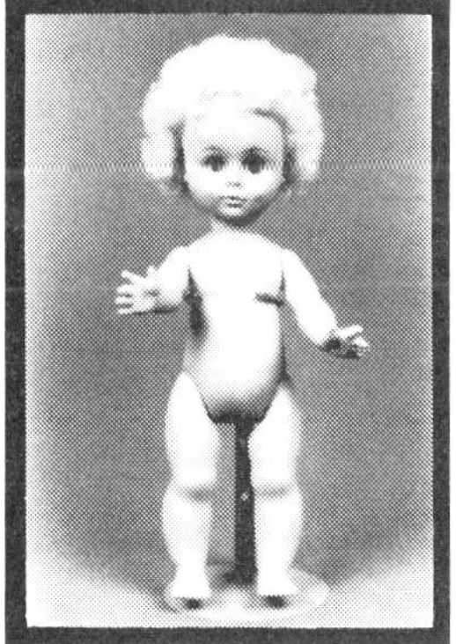

STAR DOLL - 1968

1968. 14 in. (35.5 cm). Plastic body, jointed hips, shoulders, and neck. Vinyl head; blue sleep eyes, lashes, painted lower lashes; rooted platinum curls; closed mouth. Mark: on head, STAR DOLL; on body, 13 G.
Ref.No.: D of C, AN8, p. 330.

Mint $35.00   Ex. $25.00   G. $15.00   F. $10.00

STAR DOLL - 1969

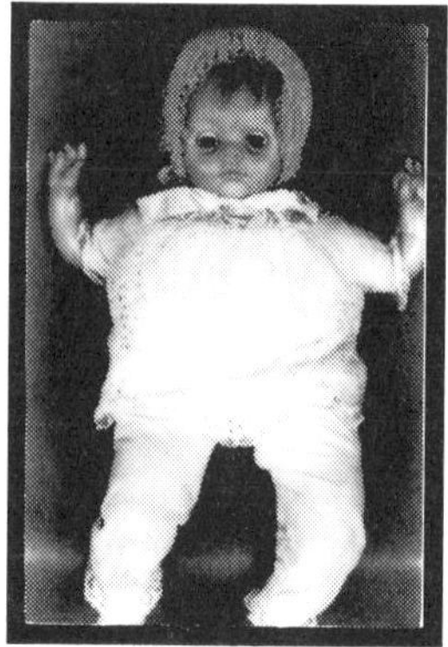

ca.1969. Cloth body, vinyl bent-limb arms and legs. Vinyl head; blue plastic sleep eyes, lashes, painted lower lashes; rooted straight blond hair; closed mouth. Mark: on head, STAR DOLL/MADE IN CANADA.
Ref.No.: D of C, CW15, p. 331.

Mint $65.00   Ex. $45.00   G. $35.00   F. $25.00

The doll prices given in this book are intended as value guides rather than arbitrarily set prices. Each price recorded here is actually a compilation. The retail prices in this book are recorded as accurately as possible but in the case of errors, typographical, clerical or otherwise, the author and publisher assume no responsibility for any loss incurred by users of this book.

STUDIO KUUSKOSKI
Ca1984

Studio Kuuskoski is a family owned business making over one hundred different trolls.

GOLDNOSE

1977. 12.5 in. (32 cm). Stuffed felt body. Felt eyes and nose; horse hair whiskers and hair. Felt hands, feet, and hat. Mark: label, GOLDNOSE BY STUDIO KUUSKOSKI.
Ref.No.: D of C, AE13, p. 331.

Mint $35.00 **Ex.** $25.00 **G.** $15.00 **F.** $10.00

TE-RI PRODUCTS
1972 -

Te-Ri products makes over sixty different trolls representing a variety of characters and professions.

HOCKEY PLAYER

1985. With skates: 17 in. (43 cm). One-piece cloth body and head. Felt clothing is part of body, very large feet with plastic skate blades attached. Black felt eyes, red felt nose, hair and beard are reindeer fur. Mark: label, Fufel Doll collection/Te-Ri Products Ltd.; 2nd label, OFFICIAL LICENSED PRODUCT/NHL/NATIONAL HOCKEY LEAGUE.
Ref.No.: D of C, CM3, p. 332.

Mint $25.00   Ex. $20.00   G. $15.00   F. $10.00

TILCO INTERNATIONAL INC.
1940 - ca1978

Tilco is the parent company of Tilly Toy of St. Jean, Quebec. They made both rubber and soft vinyl dolls.

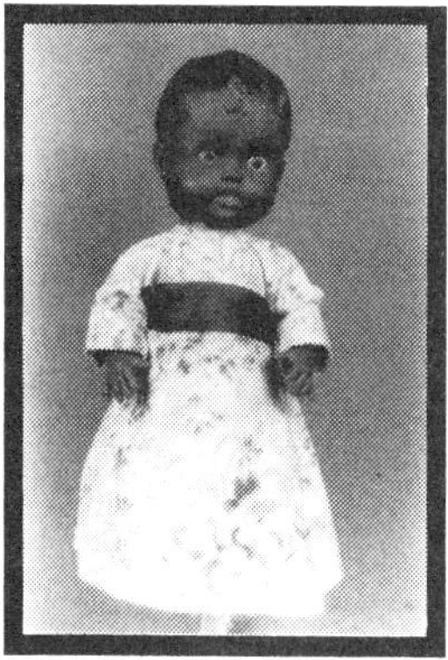

TILCO

ca.1958. 10 in. (25.5 cm). One piece brown vinyl body. Black painted eyes, black moulded hair, open-closed mouth.
Ref.No.: D of C, CQ11, p. 332.

Mint $35.00   **Ex.** $30.00   **G.** $20.00   **F.** $15.00

TILCO

ca.1965. 6.5 in. (17 cm). One piece soft vinyl. Black painted side-glancing eyes, moulded blond hair, open-closed mouth. Mark: on back, TILLY TOY/MADE IN CANADA. Moulded nurses uniform; moulded baby in her arms
Ref.No.: D of C, BX18, p. 332.

Mint $25.00   **Ex.** $20.00   **G.** $12.00   **F.** $8.00

VALENTINE DOLL COMPANY
1949 -1959

Most Valentine dolls were unmarked but some had a small 'V' on the body.

VALENTINE

ca1955. 21 in. (53 cm). One piece vinyl body, jointed neck. Vinyl head; blue sleep eyes, lashes, 3 painted upper lashes; rooted blond hair, closed mouth. Mark: on body, V. Original blue taffeta gown with net over-skirt.
Ref.No.: PGC11

Note: Valentine dolls are hard to find.

Mint $60.00   Ex $50.00   G. $40.00   F. $25.00

BALLERINA

ca1955. 15 in. (37 cm). Plastic body, jointed hips, shoulders and neck. Vinyl head; sleep eyes, moulded lashes; rooted brown curls; closed mouth. Unmarked. Company name on the box. Original blue ballerina costume.
Ref.No.: PGG1

Mint $100.00   Ex. $80.00   G. $35.00   F. $20.00

VICEROY MANUFACTURING COMPANY LIMITED
1935 -

Viceroy Manufacturing made small dolls of rubber or soft vinyl. They are noted for producing the Gerber Baby.

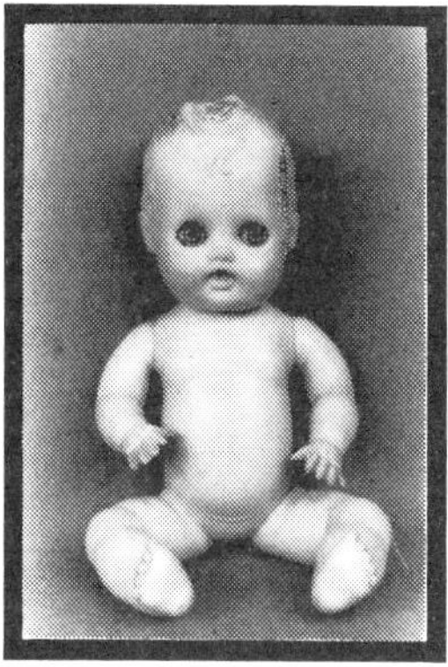

BETTY BOWS

ca.1950. 11.5 in. (29.5 cm). All rubber bent-limb baby body, jointed hips, shoulders, and neck. Vinyl head; sleep eyes, lashes; moulded hair with a curl on top; open-mouth nurser. Mark: A VICEROY/SUNRUCO DOLL/MADE IN CANADA/PATENT PENDING.
Ref.No.: D of C, BX24, p. 334,

Mint $45.00 **Ex.** $35.00 **G.** $25.00 **F.** $15.00

RONNY

ca.1952. 7 in. (17 cm). One piece rubber body and head. Blue painted side-glancing eyes; moulded hair; open-closed mouth. Mark: RONNY/C.RUTH E. NEWTON/VICEROY/MADE IN CANADA/3. Moulded clothing.
Ref.No.: D of C, CH6, p. 334.

Mint $25.00 **Ex.** $ 20.00 **G.** $15.00 **F.** $10.00

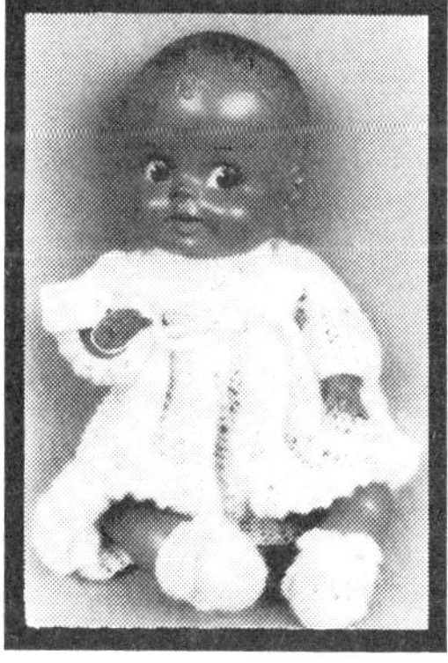

HONEY BABE BROWNIE

1954. 12 in. (30.5 cm). Brown all rubber bent-limb baby body, jointed hips, shoulders, and neck. Brown rubber head; black painted side-glancing eyes, painted upper lashes; black moulded hair; open-mouth nurser. Mark: on body, A VICEROY/SUNRUCO DOLL/MADE IN CANADA/PATENT PENDING.
Ref.No. : D of C, CL29, p. 335.

Mint $60.00 **Ex.** $45.00 **G.** $35.00 **F.** $25.00

TOD-L-TIM

1953. 10 in. (25.5 cm). One piece vinyl body and head. Inset blue eyes; black moulded hair; closed mouth. Mark: on foot, TOD-L-TIM/SUN RUBBER CO./MADE IN CANADA/BY VICEROY.
Ref.No.: D of C, CH3, p. 335.

Mint $45.00 **Ex.** $35.00 **G.** $25.00 **F.** $15.00

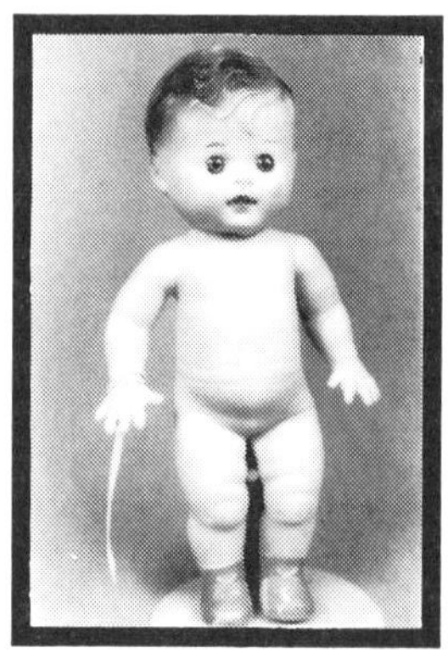

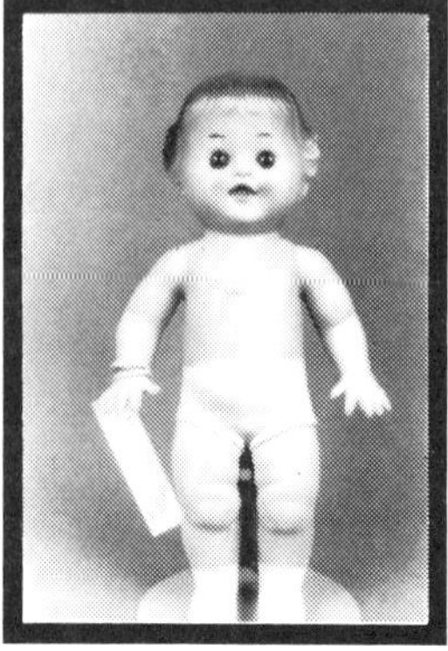

TOD-L-DEE

1953. 10 in. (25.5 cm). One piece vinyl body and head. Inset brown eyes; brown moulded hair; closed mouth. Mark: on foot, TOD-L-DEE/SUN RUBBER CO./MADE IN CANADA BY VICEROY.
Ref.No.: D of C, CH4, p. 335.

Mint $50.00 **Ex.** $40.00 **G.** $30.00 **F.** $20.00

VICEROY - 1954

ca.1954. 11 in. (28 cm). Brown all rubber bent-limb baby body, jointed hips, shoulders, and neck. Brown rubber head; brown painted side-glancing eyes; black moulded hair; open-mouth nurser. Mark: on body, A VICEROY/SUNRUCO DOLL/MADE IN CANADA/PATENT PENDING.
Ref.No.: D of C, AZ3, p. 336.

Mint $60.00 **Ex.** $45.00 **G.** $35.00 **F.** $25.00

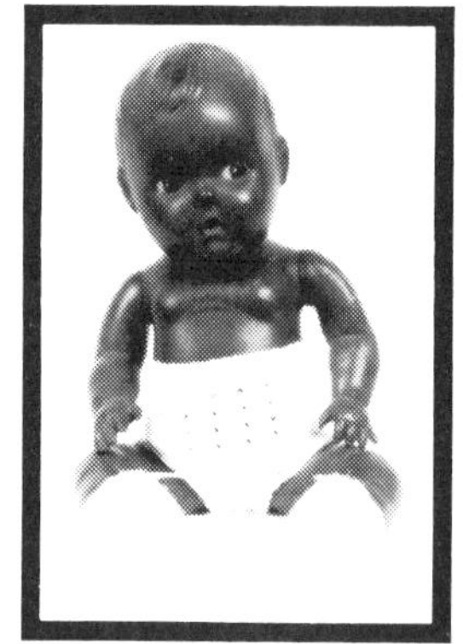

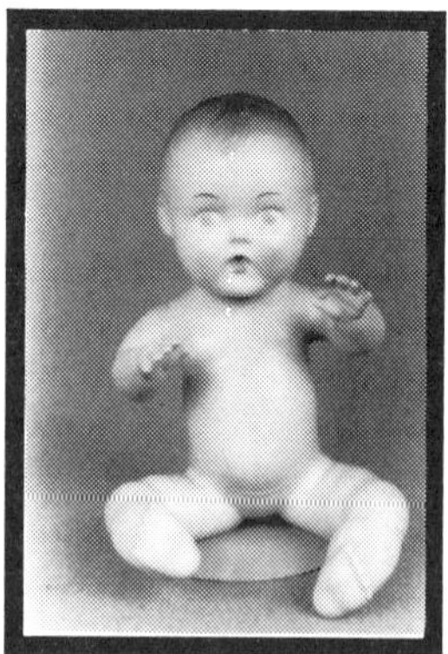

HONEY BABE BLONDIE

1954. 11 in. (28 cm). All rubber bent-limb baby body, jointed hips, shoulders, and neck. Rubber head; blue painted eyes, painted upper lashes; brown moulded hair; open-closed mouth. Mark: on body, A VICEROY/SUNRUCO DOLL/MADE IN CANADA/PATENT PENDING.
Ref.No.: D of C, CL4, p. 336.

Mint $55.00 **Ex.** $40.00 **G.** $30.00 **F.** $20.00

VICEROY - 1955

ca.1955. 7.5 in. (18 cm). One piece vinyl body and head. Black side-glancing eyes; black moulded hair; open-closed mouth. Mark: on feet, VICEROY/MADE IN CANADA. Moulded snowsuit, hood, and boots.
Ref.No.: D of C, BX19, p. 336.

Mint $35.00   Ex. $30.00   G. $20.00   F. $12.00

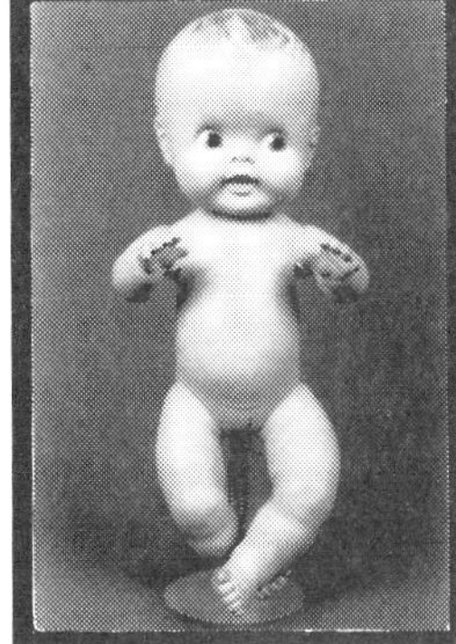

SUNBABE BLONDIE

1955. 12 in. (30.5 cm). All rubber bent-limb baby body, jointed hips, shoulders, and neck. Rubber head; blue painted side-glancing eyes, painted upper lashes; brown moulded hair; open mouth nurser. Mark: on body, A VICEROY/SUNRUCO DOLL/MADE IN CANADA/PATENT PENDING.
Ref.No.: D of C, AB28, p. 337.

Mint $55.00   Ex. $45.00   G. $35.00   F. $25.00

VICEROY - 1956 - 11.5 in.

ca.1956. 11.5 in. (29.5 cm). All rubber bent-limb baby, jointed hips, shoulders, and neck. Rubber head; inset blue eyes, painted upper lashes; brown moulded hair; open-mouth nurser. Mark: on body, A VICEROY/SUNRUCO DOLL/MADE IN CANADA.
Ref.No.: D of C, BX22, p. 337.

Mint $55.00   Ex. $45.00   G. $35.00   F. $25.00

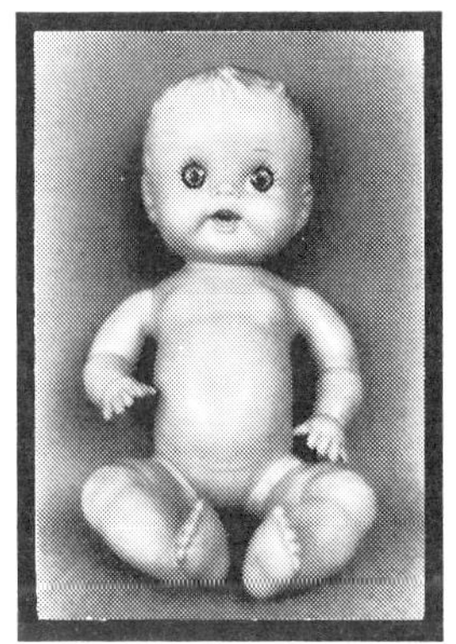

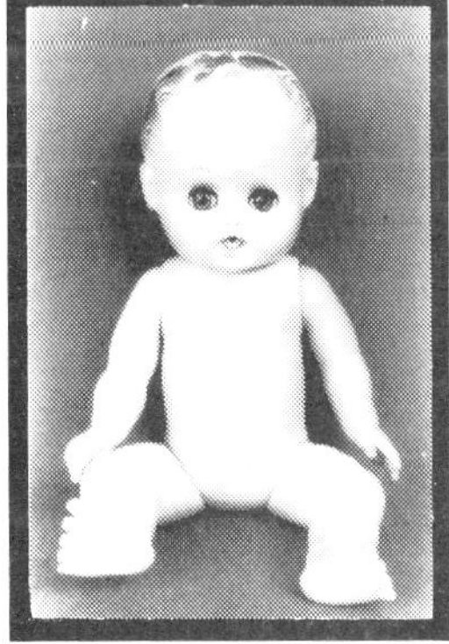

VICEROY - 1956 - 12 in.

ca.1956. 12 in. (30.5 cm). All rubber bent-limb baby body, jointed hips, shoulders, and neck. Rubber head; sleep eyes, lashes, painted lower lashes; brown moulded hair; open-mouth nurser. Mark: on head, W/VICEROY/MADE IN CANADA.
Ref.No.: D of C, BX21, p. 337.

Mint $55.00   Ex. $45.00   G. $35.00   F. $25.00

WIS-TON TOY MFG. CO. LTD.
STAR DOLL DIVISION
1983-

Wis-Ton is owned and run by Sam. Manganaro who began his career in doll-making with the original Star Doll in the 1950's.

Wis-Ton or Star Doll as it is now called is working with Distinctive Dolls of Canada to produce a line of collector's dolls.

MANDY

1986. 32 in. (81.5 cm). Plastic body, jointed hips, shoulders, and neck. Vinyl head; brown sleep eyes, lashes, painted lower lashes; rooted long streaked brown hair with bangs; closed mouth. Mark: on head, C CANADA/33W.
Ref.No.: D of C, CY13, p. 338.

Mint $35.00 **Ex.** $30.00 **G.** $25.00 **F.** $20.00

BABY CUDDLE-SOFT

1986. 17 in. (43 cm). Cloth body with vinyl bent-limb arms and legs. Vinyl head; blue sleep eyes, lashes; rooted blond curls; open-closed mouth. Mark: on head, STAR DOLL/MADE IN CANADA. label on body, MADE BY WIS-TON MFG.
Ref.No.: D of C, CY11, p. 338.

Mint $35.00 **Ex.** $30.00 **G.** $25.00 **F.** $20.00

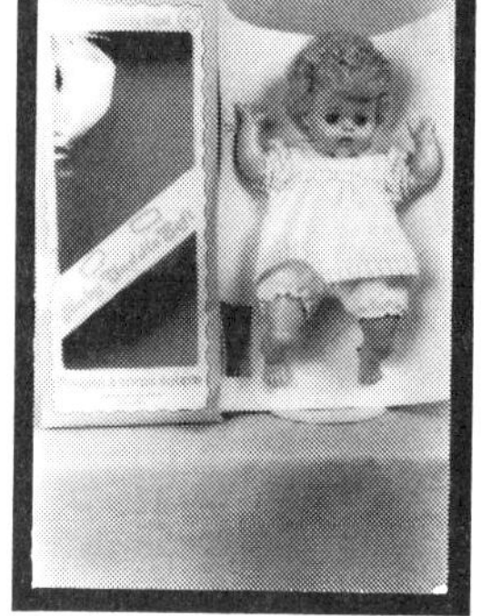

PLAYFUL CHILD

1988. 14 in. (35.5 cm). Cloth body, vinyl arms and legs. Vinyl head; brown sleep eyes, lashes; rooted brown curls; watermelon mouth. Mark: body tag, Wis-Ton Mfg. Co. Ltd./Toronto, Ontario, Canada; on head, Star Doll. Original pink cotton dress with white sailor collar.
Ref.No: 2KA3

Mint $20.00 **Ex.** $15.00 **G.**$10.00 **F.** $5.00

BABY CUDDLE SOFT

1988. 25 in. (63 cm). Cloth body, vinyl arms and legs. Vinyl head; brown sleep eyes, lashes; moulded brown hair; open-closed mouth. Mark: on head, WIS-TON/CANADA ; tag on body, MADE BY WIS-TON/MFG. CO. LTD. ONT. Original pink blanket sleeper with white attached bib.
Ref.No.: DF22

Mint $40.00   Ex. $30.00   G. $20.00   F. $15.00

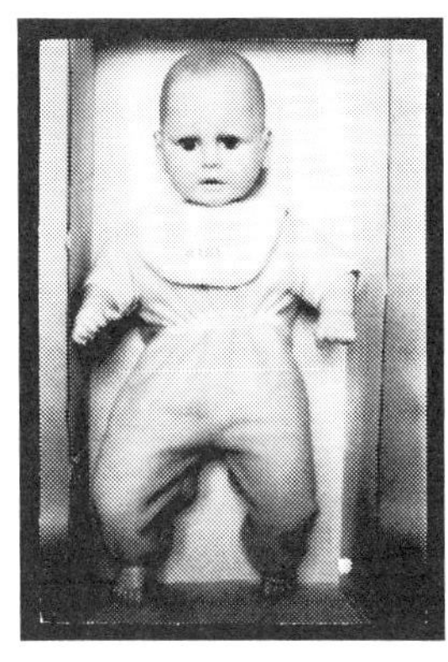

WENDY WALKER

1986. 26 in. (66 cm). Plastic body, jointed hips, shoulders, and neck. Vinyl head; brown sleep eyes, lashes, painted lower lashes, eyeshadow; rooted strawberry blond curls; closed mouth. Mark: on head, C CANADA/26W.
Ref.No.: D of C, CY12, p. 338.

Mint $35.00   Ex. $30.00   G. $25.00   F. $20.00

ELIZABETH MANLEY DOLL

Star Doll and Distinctive Dolls of Canada. 1989. 17 in. (43 cm). Plastic body, jointed hips, shoulders and neck. Vinyl head; brown sleep eyes, lashes; rooted short blond curly hair; open-closed mouth showing teeth. Mark: on head, ELIZABETH MANLEY/1989/STAR DOLL.
Ref.No.: PGA19.

Mint $40.00   Ex. $30.00   G. $30.00   F. $20.00

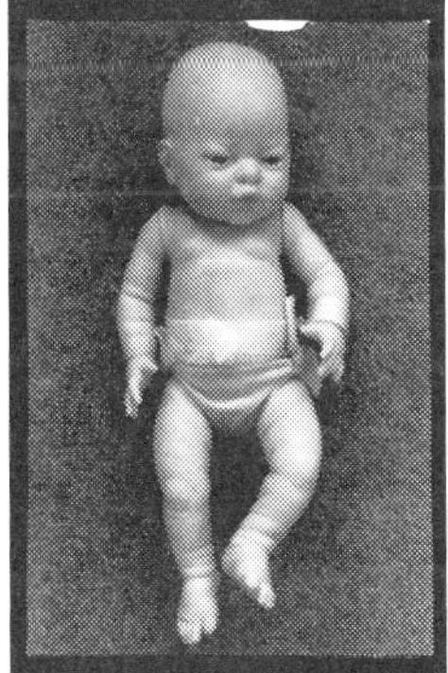

BABY NEW ARRIVAL

1989. 17 in. (43 cm). Realistic wrinkled newborn vinyl body, jointed hips, shoulders and neck. Anatomically correct, boys and girls. Vinyl head; moulded hair; stationary eyes; open-closed mouth. Diaper, navel band and bracelet.
Ref. no. PGD6.

Mint $30.00   Ex. $25.00   G $20.00   F. $15.00

SATIN N' LACE - Short Satin Dress

1989. 22 in. (56 cm). Cloth body, vinyl arms and legs. Vinyl head; sleep eyes, lashes; moulded painted hair. Cries "Mama". Knee-length Satin and lace dress.
Ref.No.: PGE6.

Mint $40.00   Ex. $25.00   G. $20.00   F. $15.00

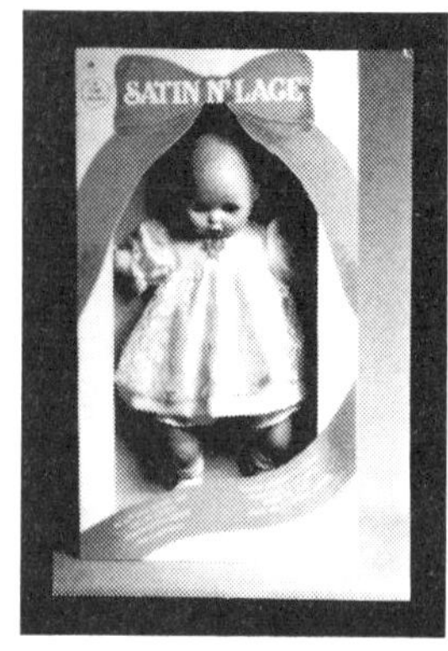

SATIN N' LACE - Long Satin Dress

1989. 22 in. (56 cm). Cloth body, vinyl arms and legs. Vinyl head; sleep eyes, lashes; moulded painted hair. Cries "Mama". Long satin and lace gown and matching bonnet.
Ref.No.: PGE7.

Mint $45.00   Ex. $20.00   G. $25.00   F. $15.00

WENDY WALKER, DOCTOR

1989. 18 in. (46 cm). Plastic body, jointed hips shoulders and neck. Vinyl head; sleep eyes; rooted straight hair; closed mouth. Dressed in Doctors pant suit with two accessories.
Ref.No.: PGE5.

Mint $20.00   Ex. $20.00   G. $15.00   F. $10.00

WENDY WALKER, NURSE

1989. 18 in. (46 cm). Plastic body, jointed hips, shoulders and neck. Vinyl head; sleep eyes; rooted curly hair; closed mouth. White cotton pant suit and matching cap. One accessory.
Ref.No.: PGE2.

Mint $20.00   Ex. $20.00   G. $15.00   F. $10.00

WENDY WALKER, NURSES AID

1989. 18 in. (46 cm). Plastic body, jointed hips, shoulders and neck. Vinyl head; sleep eyes; rooted wavy hair; closed mouth. White blouse and striped apron. One accessory.
Ref.No.: PGE3.

Mint $20.00   Ex. $15.00   G. $10.00   F. $10.00

THIRSTY WALKER, GIRL

1990. 24 in. (61 cm). Plastic body, jointed hips shoulders and neck. Vinyl head; sleep eyes, lashes; moulded hair, open mouth nurser. Nightgown, mobcap, plush dog and nursing bottle.
Ref. No.: PGE17.

Mint $35.00   Ex. $30.00   G. $25.00   F. $15.00

THIRSTY WALKER, BOY

1990. 24 in. (61 cm). Plastic body, jointed hips, shoulders and neck. Vinyl head; sleep eyes, lashes; moulded hair; open-mouth nurser. Cotton print shirt and overalls, plush dog and nursing bottle.
Ref.No.: PGE19.

Mint $35.00   Ex. $30.00   G. $25.00   F. $15.00

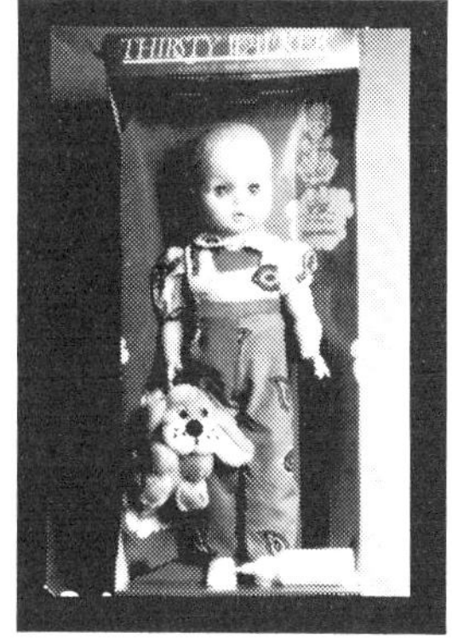

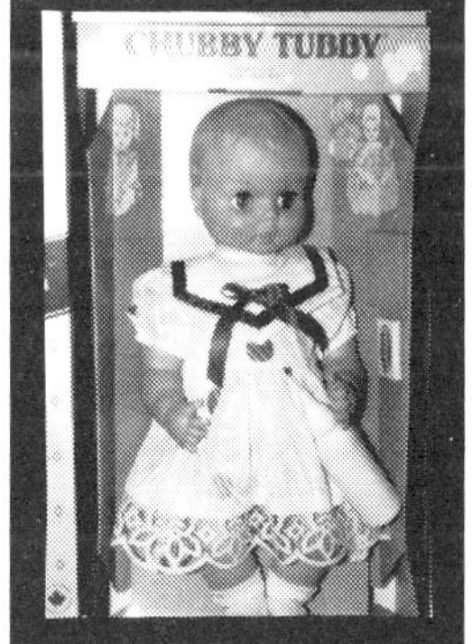

CHUBBY TUBBY

1990. 21 in. (53 cm). Plastic baby body, jointed hips, shoulders and neck. Vinyl head; sleep eyes, lashes; moulded hair; open-mouth nurser. Dress, panties and socks with nursing bottle.
Ref.No.: PGE8.

Mint $40.00   Ex. $35.00   G. $30.00   F. $15.00

CHUBBY TUBBY

1990. 21 in. (53 cm). Plastic baby body, jointed hips, shoulders and neck. Vinyl head; sleep eyes, lashes; rooted straight hair; open-mouth nurser. Dress, panties, socks and nursing bottle.
Ref.No.: PGE9.

Mint **$45.00** **Ex.** **$40.00** **G.** **$35.00** **F.** **$15.00**

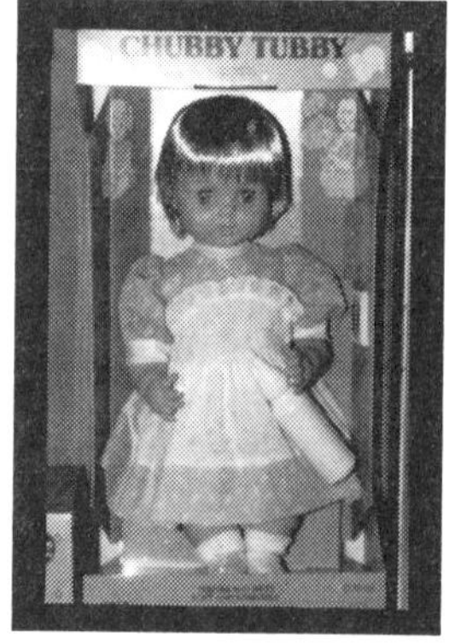

Dolls that are "Mint In the Box" (MIB) are about 10 to 15% higher for vinyl dolls and 40 to 50% higher for composition dolls. The composition dolls in boxes are of course much rarer. For the MIB category the box should be labelled with the manufacturers' name and possibly the name of the doll. A cardboard box with nothing printed on it has very little value.

ORIGINAL ARTISTS' DOLLS

The guidelines for original artists' dolls must include originality, creativity, technique, effectiveness and permanence. It is very difficult to standardise or categorise original dolls because they vary so much in size, structure and materials used, etc. Even artists themselves cannot agree on exactly what constitutes an original doll.

There must, however, be something original about the doll. By originality we mean constructive imagination or significant innovation must be demonstrated. The choice of materials, the techniques with which they are used, or possibly just a fresh and moving new face may be original. Each artist must do something unique that no one else has done. It is acceptable to use some parts such as a wig that are not made by the artist. It is not acceptable to use a head mould designed by someone else. Some dolls, however, are still considered original that use commercial bodies with original heads. The doll would be more valuable if the artist has designed and modelled the whole doll.

The doll must show creativity. By this we mean the artist should have the ability to put her own feelings and passion into her creation producing a doll that is unique. The design of each artist should be distinct. It is not unusual to be able to tell who made the doll just by looking at it.

The technique used or the way in which technical details are treated is extremely important. There is no point in having a creative idea if no skill is evident in the finished product. The technical methods used should accomplish the desired effect; whether it requires sculpting, painting, carving, sewing, finishing or shoe-making skills to produce the planned doll, the artist must be master of all. It is sad to see an excellent idea poorly executed.

Is the finished doll effective? Are the proportions correct? Are there any incongruencies in the doll? Is there balance in the quality of materials used? Is what the artist trying to say portrayed eloquently? Hopefully, the doll gives a message; be it mischief, pensiveness, joy or unhappiness, the intention of the artist should be clear. All these questions should be considered when buying an original artist's doll. Each original doll should give a new perspective, beauty, new meaning and an element of surprise.

Will the doll have permanence? Many things such as a flower can be beautiful but such beauty does not last. If we are considering value and price then the quality of permanence is important.

This book includes artists' dolls made with many different materials, in a variety of sizes and with differing degrees of artistic talent.

After careful scrutiny of a doll we are thinking of buying and with the application of these general standards we can then decide if the pleasure we will have from owning it is worth the price. An original doll with all these qualities is most likely to appreciate in value over time.

A LETTER FROM BARBARA BICKLE ON ORIGINAL DOLLS

Originality and technical mastery go hand-in-hand as basic criteria in an artist's doll. My feeling is that for a work to be original, it must have "originated" with the artist, it requires a creative spark. What lacks its own spark of originality can only be a dull reflection of someone else's creativity.

Along with the creativity must come enough mastery of the techniques required that the craftmanship is unquestioned. Technical mastery is taken for granted, because craft becomes art only in the hands of a master, and not because it is so wished but because it is so done. The mastery of the materials requires that the artist be aware of their capabilities and shortcomings. Creativity may stretch the limits of traditional craftsmanship, but the respect for the materials remains intrinsic.

Craftsmanship is between the hand and the eye, but artistry also involves the mind. Dolls can be regarded as works of artistry on a personal scale. Their size means that we can hold them in our hands and caress them with our fingers. Their size also means that they can be taken in at a glance. What elevates a doll from being merely a crafted object into the realm of being a work of art is that a simple glance is not sufficient to see all that is there to be seen. It must engage the imagination, for surely the mind naturally follows that which it finds most charming.

Although form and function may vary - dolls are used both as objects of play or instruction, as objects of ritual or decoration - what remains constant is the universality of the doll as an important portrait of the human condition. Somehow a doll transcends all narrower classifications of material, form and function and speaks to us of our bonds of humanity. It tells us about ourselves, and above all it meets a human need.

An artist who makes dolls must be aware that this is an activity charged with a certain responsibility. It should not be taken lightly. It is not just a rendition of the human form, but a glimpse into the human heart, and as such should be approached not just with technique and skill, but with grace and sensitivity.

ALMA BEDNARKSKI
Saskatoon. Saskatchewan

MARY JANE

1982. Ball-jointed lady body. Bisque head; blue glass stationary eyes; light brown human hair wig; closed mouth. Mark: artist's symbol which includes the year and number of the doll. Limited edition of 25.
Ref.No.: D of C, CG33, p. 363.

Artist's price: $250.00

BARBARA BETTS
New Brunswick
(deceased)

THE LOYALISTS

Date unknown. 9.5 in. (24 cm). Cloth bodies over a wire armature. Papier-mache heads covered in nylon; painted features; wool hair. Mark: label, BARBARA BETTS DOLLS.
Ref.No.: D of C, AJ25, p. 363.

Resale: $125.00

BARBARA BICKLE
Whitby, Ontario

All Barbara's exquisite dolls are one-of-a-kind, with faces individually sculpted and hand-painted. The bodies are stitched from finely woven silk fabric. Each doll is signed and dated, usually on the foot or on the base. They measure 9.5 to 10 in. tall.

BLANKET OF STARS

ca.1983. The figure of Evening watches over the sleeping child, Morning, under a blanket of stars as they rest on a cloud.
Ref.No.: D of C, XX13, p. 364.

Artist's price: $225.00

WOMAN WITH BIRD'S NEST

ca.1983.
Ref.No.: D of C, XX17, p. 364.

Artist's price: $225.00

SNOWBALL

ca.1984. Little girl holding snowball behind her back.
Ref.No.: D of C, XX15, p. 364.

Artist's price: $165.00

READING

1989. A little red-haired girl with glasses is reading a story and the book's characters are coming to life in front of her.
Ref.No.: PGBB1.

Artist's price: $175.00

FATHER & BABY

1989. A frazzled father with a new baby in his arms. He's wearing his pyjamas; it's the middle of the night, and the bottle is leaking all over the rug.
Ref.No.: PGBB2.

Artist's price: $195.00

FISHING

1989. A little girl is intent upon catching one of the goldfish in a garden fishpond.
Ref.No.: PGBB3.

Artist's price: $175.00

ROWING IN A BASKET

1989. With her eyes closed, the laundry basket becomes a boat and the brooms become oars.
Ref.No.: PGBB4

Artist's price: $160.00

TREE HOUSE

1989. A tree goddess guarding the house.
Ref.No.: PGBB5.

Artist's price: $195.00

SUMMER MEADOW

1989. Earth and sky are depicted as a young woman. At her feet the meadow flowers bloom. Her hair is a soft sky blue.
Ref.No.: PGBB6.

Artist's price: $195.00

CHRISTMAS ANGEL

1989. Fewer than 24 of these are made each year and the faces are truly angelic on each one.
Ref.No.: PGBB7.

Artist's price: $110.00

DEBORAH BRENNAN
Victoria, British Columbia

H.R.H. PRINCESS OF WALES
1984. 24 in. (62 cm).
Ref.No.: D of C, CC29, p. 364.

Resale: $750.00

VICTORIA
1986. 30 in. (76 cm). Human hair wig. Hand-blown glass eyes.
Ref.No.: PGC20.

Artist's price: $500.00

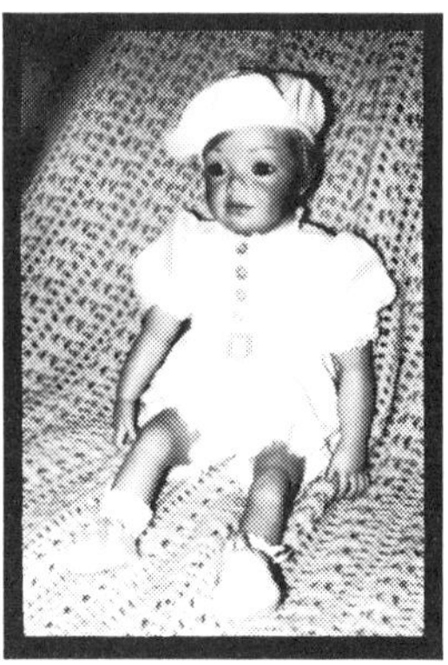

FIRST BORN
1986. 23 in. (58 cm). Human hair wig. Hand-blown glass eyes.
Ref.No.: PGC18.

Artist's price: $500.00

JUDE CROSSLAND
Wilno, Ontario

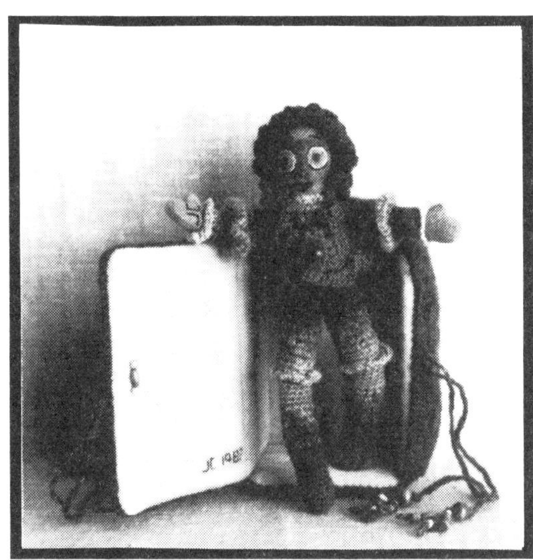

JACK-IN-THE-BOX

1984. Doll is 7 in. (17 cm); box is 5 x 3.5 in. Crocheted with cotton and wool. Box is woven flat in one piece, lines, lightly stuffed, and stitched together. Mark: on doll's hand JC. Edition closed.
Ref.No.: D of C, XH30, p. 371.

Artist's price: $360.00

JUMPING JESTER WITH BELLS

1984. 8 in. (20.5 cm). Crochet and stitchery using mercerized cotton, tapestry yarn, and sewing thread. Mark: JC. Edition closed.
Ref.No.: D of C, XH33, p. 371.

Artist's price: $85.00

CHRISTMAS ANGEL

1984. 10 in. (25.5 cm). Crochet and stitchery using mercerized cotton, tapestry yarn, and silk. Mark: JC.
Ref.No.: D of C, XH34, p. 371.

Artist's price: $160.00

TWIN PACK

1984. 17 in. (43.cm). Crochet and leather pouch, lined. Pouch hangs on the wall and holds twin figures. Figures made with crochet and stitchery. Mark: JC.
Ref. No.: D of C, XH35, p. 372. Edition closed.

Artist's price: $160.00

ANNIE

1984. 20 in. (51 cm). Crocheted figure using cottons, wools, linens, leather, and lace. Mark: JC
Ref.No.: D of C, XH36, p. 372. Edition closed.

Artist's price: $260.00

PRIMITIVE

1984. A primitive piece in both design and materials used; woven and stuffed; hangs on the wall Mark: JC. Edition closed.
Ref.No.: D of C, XH37, p. 372.

Artist's price: $120.00

FESTIVE JESTER

ca. 1989. 12.5 in. (32 cm) .Crochet and stitchery using mercerized cotton, tapestry yarn and sewing thread. Star sequins and metal bells. Free standing on a wooden base. Limited edition.
Ref.No:. PGJC1.

Artist's price: $320.00

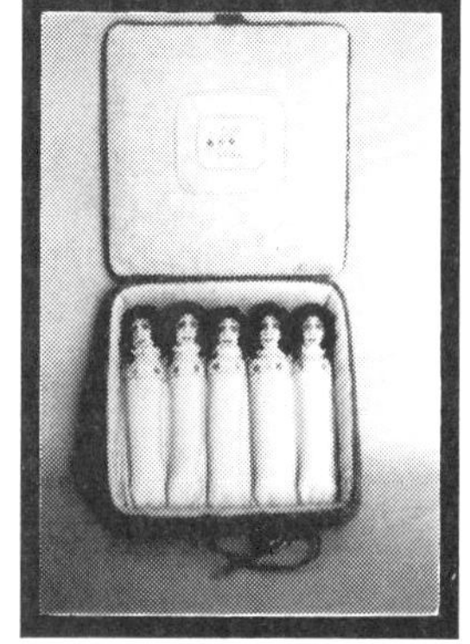

FEMALE FORM

ca. 1989. 12 in. (30.5 cm). Woven using cotton, linen, wool and unspun hemp. Clay, glass and metal beads. Limited edition.
Ref.No.: PGJC2.

Artist's price: $160.00

PRIMITIVE MAN

ca. 1989. 22 in. (56 cm). Woven using cotton, linen, wool and hemp. Stitched and stuffed. Clay and metal beads. Limited edition.
Ref.No.: PGJC3.

Artist's price: $560.00

FIVE STAR QUALITY

ca. 1989. 7 x 14 x 1.5 in. (17.5 x 35.5 x 3.5 cm). open. Crochet and stitchery using cotton, mercerized cotton and wool. The box is woven flat in one piece, lined, lightly stuffed and stitched together. Dolls are stitchery and crochet. Limited edition.
Ref.No.: PGJC4.

Artist's price: $560.00

ROSE DOLHANYK
Beamsville, Ontario

WOOL SELLER

1984. 11 in. (28 cm). Muslin padded wire armature. Head and hands are sculpted clay; grey mohair wig; closed mouth. Mark: label, HANDMADE/BY/ROSE DOLHANYK/ GRIMSBY, ONT.
Ref.No.: D of C, BU29, p. 375.

Doll store price: $195.00

HAT SELLER

1984. 11 in. (28 cm). Padded muslim over wire armature. Head and hands are sculpted clay. Hand painted features.
Ref.No.: D of C, DA2, p. 375.

Doll store price: $195.00

Photo Not Available

BOOK SELLER

1984. 11 in. (28 cm). Padded muslin over wire armature. Head and hands are sculpted clay.
Ref.No.: D of C, BV14, p. 375.

Doll store price: $195.00

JOHN FERGUSON
Victoria, British Columbia

MAD HATTER

1971. 23 in. (58.5 cm). Carved wooden body. Carved wooden head; glass eyes; grey human hair; painted moveable mouth. Mark JKF.
Ref.No.: D of C, XH18, p. 377.

Artist's price: $500.00

PUNCH

1971, 30 in. (76.5 cm). (marionette). Carved wooden body. Carved wooden head; lac bead eyes; painted moveable mouth. Mark: JKF.
Ref.No.: D of C, XH19, p. 377.

Artist's price: $750.00

DORITA GRANT
Vancouver Island, British Columbia

Dorita Grant's dolls are all one-of-a-kind.

WOMAN WEARING CHILKAT DANCING BLANKET and APRON

1983. 12 in. (30.5 cm). Cloth body filled with sawdust; clay hands and feet. Sculpted clay head. Mark: on back and foot, DORITA GRANT/83-5-3.
Ref.No.: D of C, XG9, p. 379.

Artist's price: $250.00

CEDAR BARK WOVEN CLOTHING

1983. 12 in. (30.5 cm). Cloth body filled with sawdust; clay hands and feet. Sculpted clay head; human hair. Mark: on back and foot, DORITA GRANT/83.S.6.
Ref.No.: D of C, XG11, p. 379.

Artist's price: $250.00.

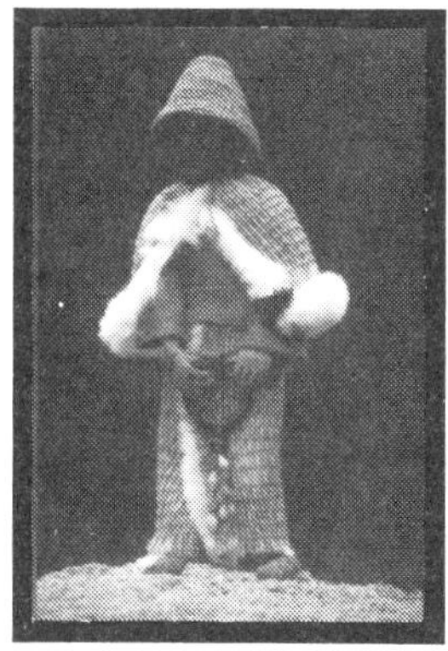

WOMAN in BUTTON BLANKET

1983. 12 in. (30.5 cm). Cloth body filled with sawdust; clay hands and feet. Sculpted clay head; human hair. Mark: on back and foot, DORITA GRANT/83-13.
Ref.No.: D of C, XG14, p. 379.

Artist's price: $250.00

COAST SAALICH FEATHER CLOTHING

1983. 12 in. (30.5 cm). Cloth body filled with sawdust; clay hands and feet. Sculpted clay head; human hair. Mark: on back and foot, DORITA GRANT/83.8.
Ref.No.: D of C, XG20, p. 379.

Artist's price: $250.00

EAGLE BUTTON BLANKET

1984. 12 in. (30.5 cm). Cloth body filled with sawdust; clay hands and feet. Clay sculpted head; human hair. Mark: on back and foot; DORITA GRANT/84-5.5.
Ref.No.: D of C, XG13, p. 379.

Artist's price: $250.00

NEWFIE FISHERMAN

1986. 12 in. (30.5 cm). Cloth body filled with sawdust; clay hands and feet. Sculpted clay head; human hair. Mark: DORITA GRANT/86-12.
Ref.No. DG2.

Artist's price: $250.00

MAN in CHILKAT BLANKET

1987. 12 in. (30.5 cm). Cloth body filled with sawdust; clay hands and feet. Sculpted clay head; human hair. Mark: DORITA GRANT/87C3.
Ref.No. DG3.

Artist's price: $250.00

WOMAN with HAIDA MASK

1987. 12 in. (30.5 cm). Cloth body filled with sawdust; clay hands and feet. Sculpted clay head; human hair. Mark: DORITA GRANT/82M4.
Ref.No. DG4.

Artist's price: $250.00

WOMAN in BUTTON BLANKET

1987. 12 in. (30.5 cm). Cloth body filled with sawdust; clay hands and feet. Sculpted clay head; human hair. Mark: Dorita Grant/87C22.
Ref.No. DG5.

Artist's price: $250.00

COWICHAN INDIAN

1987. 12 in. (30.5 cm). Cloth body filled with sawdust; clay hands and feet. Sculpted clay head; human hair. Mark: DORITA GRANT/87-3
Ref.No. DG6.

Artist's price: $250.00

MANUEL ZUIMPER and PACIFIC COAST INDIAN

1989. 12 in (30.5 cm), 13 in. (33 cm). Cloth bodies filled with sawdust; clay hands and feet. Sculpted clay head; human hair. Mark: DORITA GRANT/895.
Ref.No. DG1.

Artist's price: $250.00 each

MARILYN KILBY
Victoria, British Columbia

Limited editions of 100.

KIM and MIA

1981. 16 in. (40.5 cm). KIM has a porcelain body, MIA has a composition body. Bisque heads; fixed brown glass eyes; synthetic black wigs; closed mouths. Mark: on heads, MARILYN KILBY 1981 THE TWINS #13/85 ON KIM and #20/85 on MIA.
Ref.No.: D of C, CA6, p 383.

Artist's price: $175.00 each.

YEN FU

1982. 25.5 in. (64.5 cm). Composition body, fully jointed. Bisque socket head; fixed brown glass eyes; black human hair wig; closed mouth. Mark: on head, Original by Marilyn Kilby #3, Vic. B.C.
Ref.No.: D of C, CL12, p. 383.

Artist's price: $350.00

NATASHA

1982. 22 in. (56 cm). Cloth body with porcelain arms and legs. Bisque head; fixed brown glass eyes, painted upper and lower lashes; synthetic black braids; open mouth with two teeth. Mark: on head, MARILYN KILBY/1983 2/83.
Ref.No.: D of C, CA3, p. 382.

Artist's price: $195.00

JOKER JACKSON, MINSTREL MAN

1985. 15 in. (38 cm). Porcelain body with musical mechanism, jointed hips, shoulders and neck. Bisque socket head; fixed brown glass eyes, painted upper and lower lashes; synthetic curly black wig; open mouth showing two teeth. Mark: on head, MARILYN KILBY 1985.
Ref.No.: D of C, CA11, p. 382.

Artist's price: $175.00

CLAUDETTE KRISTOF
Hull, Quebec

CLAUDETTE KRISTOF

1980. 20.5 in. (52 cm). Cloth slim lady body. Cloth head; embroidered blue eyes, black lashes, blue eyeshadow; mohair and wool hair; embroidered closed pink mouth. Mark: on slip hem, C. KRISTOF.
Ref.No.: D of C, AE7, p. 385.

Artist's price: $120.00

MALORIE

1984. 23 in. (58.5 cm). Cloth slim lady body. Cloth head; embroidered blue eyes, eyelashes and eyeshadow; mohair and wool hair; embroidered closed mouth. Mark: on slip hem, C. KRISTOF.
Ref.No.: D of C, AO28, p. 385.

Artist's price: $120.00

MOTHER and DAUGHTER

1989. 20.5 in. (52 cm). Cloth slim lady body. Cloth head: embroidered eyes, eyelashes and eyeshadow. Daughter gowned beautifully in lace with a matching hat. Mother with grey hair, elegantly dressed with matching fur collar and beribboned hat.
Ref.No.: D of C, PGCK1 & PGCK2, p. 385.

Artist's price: MOTHER: $160.00   DAUGHTER: $250.00

CLARA

1989. 20.5 in. (52 cm). Cloth slim lady body. Cloth head: embroidered eyes, eyelashes and eyeshadow. The exquisite embroidery gives the doll real feeling and expression.
Ref.No.: D of C, PGCK3, p. 385.

Artist's price: $190.00

ANGELIKA LA HAISE
Lanark, Ontario

Angelika no longer makes the cloth dolls that she was noted for but has begun making a finely crafted wooden doll. These are hand carved from basswood and are painted with acrylic paint with a lacquer finishing coat. Some of her dolls have wooden heads and cloth bodies but most are all wood with jointed hips, shoulders and neck. This hard-working artist can produce about 45 wooden dolls plus 15 wooden babies per year. These dolls are excellent value for the money.

ANGELIKA LA HAISE

1989. 12 in. (30 cm). Cloth baby body. Wooden head; painted eyes; closed painted mouth; blond wig. Mark: on head, 0301 1989. White cotton blouse and blue jumper.
Ref.No.: PGA1.

Artist's price: $250.00

ANGELIKA LA HAISE

1989. 12.5 in. (32 cm). Wooden body, jointed hips, shoulder and neck. Wooden head; painted eyes; closed painted mouth; brown wig. Mark: on head, 073 1989. Green dress with white lace pinafore, stockings, shoes and carrying a basket of cherries.
Ref.No.: PGA2.

Artist's price: $350.00

ANGELIKA LA HAISE

1989. 12.5 in. (32 cm). Wooden body, jointed hips, shoulders and neck. Wooden head; painted eyes; closed painted mouth; honey blond wig. Mark: on head, 075 1989. Flowered cotton dress with pink printed pinafore, white socks and pink shoes.
Ref.No.: PGA3.

Artist's price: $350.00

ANGELIKA LA HAISE

1989. 18.5 in. (47 cm). Cloth body, wooden arms and feet. Wooden shoulderhead; painted eyes; closed painted mouth; brown wig in coiled braids. Mark: burned on head and the soles of the feet, 0201 1989. White blouse, blue jumper, print apron, carrying a basket of pine cones.
Ref.No.: PGA6.

Artist's price: $450.00

ANGELIKA LA HAISE

1989. 23 in. (58 cm). Cloth body with leather at joint connections, wax hands and feet. Wax head, human hair wig.
Ref.No.: PGA5.

Artist's price: $750.00

JOAN LINTVELT
Vancouver Island, British Columbia

AUSTRIAN GIRL

1985. 18 in. (45.5 cm). Felt over wire armature body. Felt over porcelain head; painted eyes; fleece hair; painted mouth. Mark: card with artist's signature.
Ref.No.: D of C, BV28, p. 390.

$200.00

AUSTRIAN BOY

1985. 18 in. (45.5 cm). Felt over wire armature body. Head is porcelain covered with felt; painted eyes; fleece hair; open-closed mouth showing teeth. Mark: card with artist's signature.
Ref.No.: D of C, BV27, p. 390.

$200.00

ESKIMO WOMAN

1985. 16 in. (40.5 cm). Cloth over wire armature body; sculpted clay hands. Head sculpted from FIMO acrylic modelling clay; painted eyes; yak hair wig; open-closed mouth with tongue and teeth. Mark: on back of neck, artist's signature.
Ref.No.: D of C, BZ26, p. 391.

$225.00

LADY IN THE PARK

1985. Cloth over wire armature body; sculpted clay hands. Head sculpted from FIMO acrylic modelling clay; painted eyes; grey wig; open-closed mouth. Red flannelette bloomers, wool dress, fur coat, shawl and hat and boots. Sitting on a wooden park bench, surrounded by her possessions. Unmarked. Original tag.
Ref.No.: PGE24.

$225.00

BETTY MACDONALD
Cornwall, Ontario

Betty was born in Lancaster, Ont. but raised her family in Cornwall. She began making rag dolls for her daughters and later became fascinated by antique dolls. She studied commercial art by correspondence and found that her natural ability ran from portraits to landscapes to advertising layouts.

Betty's centennial project in 1967 was a doll named Laurie of Upper Canada, representing children of the area one hundred years ago. This led to more dollmaking and soon Betty was teaching dollmaking at St. Lawrence College in Cornwall.

During the early 1970's Betty joined the International Doll Makers Association in the United States and attended all the yearly conventions. During this time she won a number of first place ribbons. In 1977 in Florida, she won the Silver Award with a leather doll named Crystal. In 1981 at Milwaukee, a new category called the Diamond Award was created which Betty won with a leather portrait doll of her daughter Marion as a child.

Since winning the top award, Betty has judged dolls in competition for I.D.M.A. in cities such as New Orleans, Las Vegas, Atlantic City, Phoenix, Denver, Houston and Oakland.

Betty has created original dolls in leather, cloth, felt, soft sculpture, bread-dough and low fired clay. The faces are hand painted and the eyes, especially in child dolls, are very expressive. The character dolls, such as bag ladies, grannies, historical figures, both men and women, tell a story. The dolls are usually signed on the upper back by the artist.

ETIENNE BRULE

1975. 16 in. (40 cm). Leather body with wire armature. Head; leather; painted brown eyes; mohair wig; closed mouth covered with mustache and beard. Mark: on back, artist's signature. Dressed in fringed leather suit, fur hat, leather mocassins, snowshoes (from Newfoundland).
Ref.No.: PGB15.

$150.00

CRYSTAL

1977. 15.5 in. (38 cm). Leather one piece body with copper wire armature. Head: leather moulded over sculptured face; blue painted eyes; painted lashes; blond acrylic wig; open-closed painted mouth. Mark: on back, BETTY MACDONALD (in script). Dressed in pink cotton lace trimmed dress, slip, panties, socks and shoes.
Ref.No.: PGB13.

10.5 in. $100.00   15.5 in. $150.00

KLONDIKE KATE

1979. 18.5 in. (47 cm). Leather body with wire armature. Head; leather; painted blue eyes; painted lashes; mohair wig; closed painted mouth. Mark: on back, artist's signature. Dressed in a black lace strapless top with a red satin skirt, black lace stockings, feather headdress.
Ref.No.: PGB16.

$150.00

FLAPPER

1980. 18 in. (45 cm). Leather body with wire armature. Head; leather; painted blue eyes; painted lashes; mohair wig; closed painted mouth. Mark: on back, artist's signature. Dressed in peach embroidered dress, pink beads, headband with feather, stockings and shoes.
Ref.No.: PGB14.
$150.00

MADELEINE NEILL-ST. CLAIR
Nanoose Bay, British Columbia

All of "Maddy's Dolls" are now being sold in the United States by an agent and command $850.00 - 1,150.00 U.S. wholesale.

TOMMITY

1986. 16 in (40.5 cm). Composition body with French jointed knees, hips, elbows, shoulders. Bisque socket head, pierced ears; brown glass paperweight eyes, painted upper and lower lashes; black curly wig; closed mouth.
Ref.No.: D of C, CV8, p. 392.

Artist's price: $495.00

LITTLEMAD BABY

ca.1986. 8 in. (20 cm). Cloth body with wire armature; porcelain hands and feet. Porcelain shoulderhead. Mark: #I/B/13 "TEDDY".
Ref.No.: NS1.

Artist's price: $195.00

VIVIAN

ca.1986. 22 in. (55 cm). Composition body; porcelain hands. Porcelain head. Mark: MADDY III #3 Vivian.
Ref.No.: NS2.

Artist's price: $595.00

MICHELÉ PRASIL
Quebec City, Quebec

This talented doll artist received a grant from the Quebec Ministry of Cultural Affairs and consequently spent four months at the Grevin Museum in Paris learning the techniques of making dolls in wax.

JACQUES CARTIER

ca. 1980. 43 in. (110 cm). Cloth body. Sculpted stone head; painted features; human hair wig and beard.
Ref.No.: D of C, BM12, p. 394.

Artist's price: $2,700.00

GRAND de MAMSELLE

1984. 30 in. (76 cm). Long slim cloth body. Sculpted stone head with painted features; brown wig; closed mouth. Label attached to wrist.
Ref.No.: D of C, BM2, p. 394.

Artist's price: $325.00

MICHELÉ PRASIL

1984. 24 in. (61 cm). Long slender cloth body. Sculpted stone head; painted features, goat fleece wig; closed mouth. Label with the artist's name.
Ref.No.: D of C, BP37, p. 394.

Artist's price: $190.00

CHILD of 1870

1989. 37.5 in. (95 cm). Face of sculpted stone.
Ref.No.: MPb

Artist's price: $675.00

MICHELÉ PRASIL

1989. 18th Century Bourgeois. 16 in. (40 cm). Head of faience.
Ref.No.: MPe.

Artist's price: $150.00

JOANNE PRATT
Forrester Falls, Ontario

Joanne's doll-making has changed since Dolls of Canada was written. She has developed a unique technique and is producing beautiful and unusual dolls. The method she uses is to create a doll using soft sculpture techniques with a wire armature inside so detailed that it has wire fingers. The artist coats the fabric with gesso and paints it with acrylic paint. They are certainly one-of-a-kind and quite outstanding.

GLAD RAGS

1981. 12 in. (30.5 cm). Cotton knit body and head. Soft sculptured head; eyes are seed beads and embroidery; hair is orange maribou feathers stitched to head; mouth embroidered with silk thread. Mark: on bottom, J.Pratt/81.
Ref.No.: D of C, XH13, p. 394.

Artist's price: $125.00

CRUISING

1982. 24 in. (61 cm). Body and head made from beige velour; bosom covered with mother of pearl shells; mermaid tail, overlay of organza, padded, quilted, hand embroidered and beaded with mother of pearl and opalescent beads; eyes have glass iris and pupil. Mark: on botton J. Pratt 82.
Ref.No.: D of C, XH14, p. 394.

Artist's price: $400.00

CELESTE

1989. 18.5 in. (47 cm). Cotton knit fabric coated with gesso and acrylic paint. Dressed in silk, antique lace beads and metallic trim. Persian lamb for hair. Mark: on bottom, Celeste/J. Pratt 1989.
Ref.No.: JP1 and JP2.

Artist's price: $475.00

SHERLOCK HOLMES

1986. 24 in. (62 cm) (standing). Dressed in silk fabrics and suede slippers. His armchair is velvet.
Ref.No.: JP3 and JP4.

Artist's price: $450.00

PATIENCE

1986. 18 in. (45 cm). Dressed in silk with a long strand of the artist's hair as her hair.
Ref.No.: JP6.

Artist's price: $400.00

SNOW QUEEN

1987. 18.5 in. (47 cm). Dressed in white panne velvet, fur, swan's down, beads and silk. Mark: on bottom, J. PRATT/1987.
Ref.No: JP5.

Artist's price: $450.00

FATHER CHRISTMAS

1989. 12 in. (30 cm). Mark: on bottom, J.Pratt/year. These are production dolls made each year for Christmas but each one is a little different.
Ref.No.: JP7.

Artist's price: $120.00

MOTHER CHRISTMAS

1989. 10 in. (26 cm). Mark: on bottom, J. PRATT/YEAR.
Ref.No.: JP8.

Artist's price: $120.00

YVONNE RICHARDSON
West Hill, Ontario

AURORA

1985. 17 in. (43 cm). Cloth over wire armature body, bisque lower legs and forearms. Bisque shoulderhead; two-tone brown painted eyes, brown line over the eye, painted lower lashes; brown short straight wig; closed mouth. Mark: on shoulderplate, AURORA/YVONNE 85   6/10. Dressed in green moire knickers, lace trimmed shirt, brocade vest, shoes are moulded on the feet. Carrying tiny books.
Ref.No.: D of C. CP11, p. 395.

Artist's price: $500.00

AMELIA

1985. 17 in. (43 cm). Cloth body over wire armature, bisque lower legs and forearms. Bisque shoulderhead; painted eyes; moulded hair in a pompadour; closed mouth. Mark: on shoulderplate, AMELIA/cYVONNE 1984; tiny Y on heels.
Ref.No.: BD10

Artist's price: $500.00

ELF

ca. 1985. 8 in. (20 cm). Bisque head. Limited edition of 10. Sold out.
Ref.No.: PGYR1.

Artist's price: $135.00

SIR JOHN A. MACDONALD

1987. 16 in. (40 cm). All porcelain, jointed hips, shoulders and neck. Porcelain head; painted eyes; closed mouth; moulded hair. Dressed in finely tailored wool suit with vest. Gold pocket watch with semi- precious fob and a miniature picture of his wife.
Ref.No. DNa

Artist's price: $625.00

ANNE OF GREEN GABLES - 1989

1989. 16 in. (41 cm). Cloth body with wire armature. Porcelain head and hands designed by the artist. Clothing designed by Martha Mann.
Ref.No.: PGYR3.

Artist's price: $250.00

BABY JEAN

1989. 21 in. (53 cm). Cloth body. Porcelain head; shoulderplate, hands and feet. Comes with a tiny doll and a locket with a picture of Jean Francis inside. Limited edition of 25.
Ref.No.: PGJF1

Artist's price: $350.00

OLD ELF

1990. 8 in. (20 cm). Porcelain doll. Limited edition of 10.
Ref.No.: PGYR2.

Artist's price: $275.00

ANNE OF GREEN GABLES - 1990

1990. 16 in. (41 cm). Artist's proof. Limited edition of 25.
Ref.No.: PGJF2

Artist's price: $500.00

SHEILA ROSE
Toronto, Ontario

All of the Sheila Rose dolls are one-of-a-kind and all are outstanding.

JUGGLING MARIONETTE CLOWN

20 ins. (51 cm). Porcelain and fabric marionette.
Ref.No.: D of C, XH12, p. 396.

Artist's price: $195.00

ELF and INSECT

7 in. (17 cm). Porcelain and silk.
Ref.No.: D of C, XH8, p. 396.

Artist's price: $200.00

GREAT AUNT BETSY

17 in. (43 cm). A character from David Copperfield.
Ref.No.: D of C, XH5, p. 397.

Artist's price: $250.00

WILLIAM LYON MACKENZIE

36 in. (91.5 cm). Stoneware and fabric figure giving an
impassioned speech from a vegetable cart.
Ref.No.: D of C, XH6, p. 397.

Artist's price: $450.00

SNOWFLAKE DANCER

11 in. (28 cm). Papier-mache and fabric.
Ref.No.: D of C, XH9, p. 397.

Artist's price: $175.00

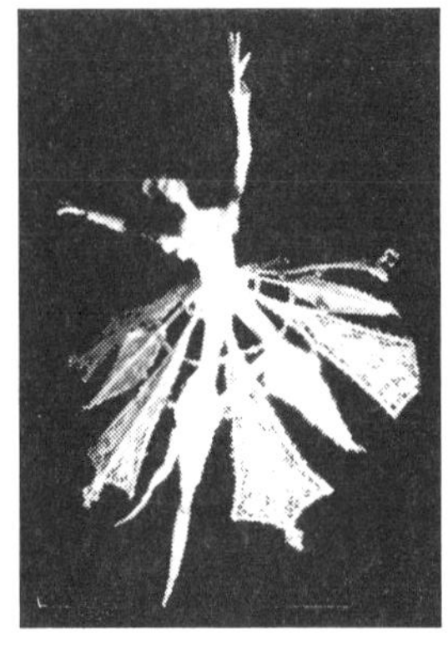

CAPTAIN HOOK

21 in. (53.5 cm). Made of Papier-mache, fabric, metal, wood, leather.
Ref.No.: SR1 and SR2.

Artist's price: $300.00

THE SUFFRAGETTE

15 in. (38 cm). Made of stoneware, fabric, metal, wood.
Ref.No.: SR3.

Artist's price: $300.00

THE PROSPECTOR

18 in. (45.5 cm). Made of Papier-mache, fabric, metal, wood, leather.
Ref.No.: SR4

Artist's price: $800.00

BLUE PIEROT

29 x 20 x 14 in. This is a larger hanging piece. The costume is pieced together in stripes to match the tones of blue in the layered porcelain of the face, hands and buttons.
Ref.No.: SR5.

Artist's price: $250.00

DANCING WARRIOR

30 x 30 in. (76.5 x 76.5 cm). Face and hands are pure white porcelain. The costume is designed by quilting silk which was dyed in the Batik technique. The quilted lines are embroidered with metalic copper thread. The scimitar is copper. The figure hangs so it can turn as if dancing and be viewed from all angles.
Ref.No.: SR6.

Artist's price: $580.00

MADELEINE SAUCIER
Montreal, Quebec
(deceased)

RED RIVER DOLL

1963. 15 in. (38 cm). Cloth body over wire armature. Felt head; brown painted eyes; light brown wool braids; closed mouth. Mark: cloth label on the back, MADELEINE SAUCIER/MONTREAL, P.Q.
Ref.No.: D of C, CP18, p. 398.

$150.00

SWEDISH GIRL

ca.1967. 15 in. (38 cm). Cloth one-piece body. Felt swivel head; blue painted eyes, synthetic blond hair; closed painted mouth. Mark: label inside petticoat, MADELEINE SAUCIER/MONTREAL, P.Q. One of an international series.
Ref.No.: D of C, CT7, p. 398.

$150.00

MADELEINE DE VERCHERES

1967. 15 in. (38 cm). Felt body over wire armature. Felt head; brown painted eyes; brown wool braids; closed mouth. Mark: label, MADELEINE SAUCIER/MONTREAL, P.Q.
Ref.No.: D of C, AP17, p. 399.

$150.00

JUDI THOMPSON
Grand Forks, British Columbia

Judi is a self taught artist who studied books on her own to answer all her questions about sculpting, painting and mould making. The results are stunning. Her dolls are so life-like and the eyes painted so realistically one inevitably mistakes them for hand blown glass eyes of the best quality. Many of her dolls are one-of-kind while a few are in editions of fifty.

PRINCE WILLIAM

1983. 19 in. (48.5 cm). Cloth body, porcelain arms and legs. Bisque head; painted eyes, human hair wig. Wearing silk rompers. Limited edition of 50.
Ref.No.: DJ22.

Artist's price: $1000.00

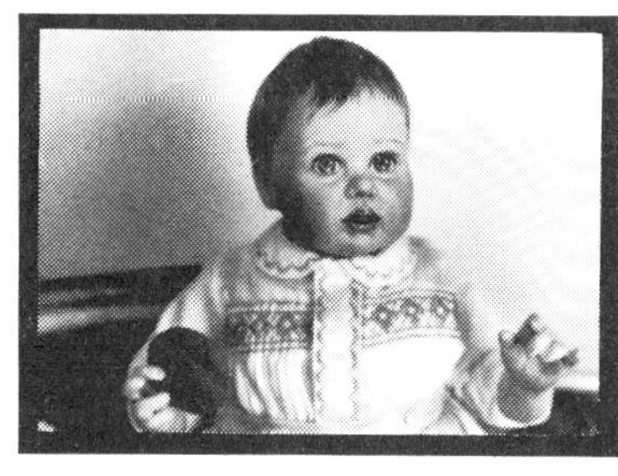

HEATHER

ca.1983. 17 in. (43.5 cm). Courtesy of Helen Durham, Grand Forks, B.C.
Ref.No.: DJ19.

Artist's price: $590.00

DIONNE QUINTUPLETS

1980. 13 in. (33 cm). Each doll has a different expression.
Ref.No.: DJ20.

Artist's price: $1000.00

CARMEN VAIR
Owen Sound, Ontario

GREY OWL

1983. 23 in. (58.5cm). All cloth body, individual fingers. Cloth head; painted facial features; black synthetic hair. Mark: on foot, CARMEN 83/ A circle with a C inside and the number inside the C.
Ref.No.: D of C, AE11, p. 402.

Artist's price: $650.00

CARMEN VAIR

1983. 23 in. (58.5 cm). Cloth body, detailed fingers and toes. Cloth head; painted facial features; synthetic fur wig. Mark: on side of foot, CARMEN 83.
Ref.No. : D of C, AE12, p. 402.

Artist's price: $650.00

LITTLE SNOW FOX

1984. 23 in. (58.5 cm). Cloth body. Cloth head; painted features; black synthetic hair with back in braids. Mark: label, CARMEN/NATIVE DOLLS. Carrying a cloth Indian doll.
Ref.No.: D of C, BO6A, p. 401.

Artist's price: $600.00

YOUNG WOLF

1986. 24 in. (61 cm). Interlock knit body. Needle sculptured features painted with acrylic paint. Synthetic fur hair. Wearing a cotton "ribbon shirt", deerhide leggings, deerhide loin cloth fringed and trimmed in silver coloured cones. A synthetic bone and beaded chestplate. Low-cut moccasins with beaded toes and long feathers in his hair. One-of-a-kind.
Ref.No.: PGCV4.

Artist's price: $500.00

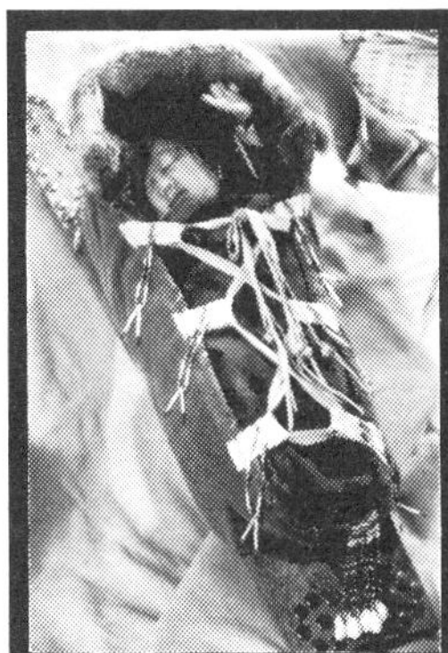

MAY MAY GWAY SHI, (Cree "Fairy")

1987. 15 in. (38 cm). Interlock knit body. Features needle sculpture and painted with acrylics. Synthetic fur hair. Wearing earrings and a bead bracelet. Cotton dress, slip and pants, wool socks. Wrapped in a vintage fabric blanket edged in beads. The doll rests in her papoose carrier lined in muskrat fur. The exterior of the carrier is covered in velvet (vintage) and adorned with beaded rosettes. The carrier is closed with deerhide and decorated with quills, beads, shells and dance bells. The carrier rests on two weathered backboards. One-of-a-kind.
Ref.No.: PGCV1 and 2.

Artist's price: $900.00

TIMID FAWN

1988. 22 in. (56 cm). Interlock knit head, hands and feet, unbleached cotton body. Synthetic fur hair. Wearing a cotton slip and pants, a long cotton dress with a beaded rosette centre front with a long bead and quill fringe. Necklace is quills and beads. Beaded rosettes with leather ties in her hair. Fur cape, and a feather fan in her hand. Low cut moccasins have a felt tongue with quills and beads. Wearing brass dance bells on her ankle. One-of-a-kind.
Ref.No.: PGCV7.

Artist's price: $1,300.00

CHARGING EAGLE

1988. 24 in. (61 cm). Interlock knit head, hands and feet, unbleached cotton body with wire armature in the legs, synthetic fur hair, acrylic painted features. Wearing old denim overalls an flannel shirt with handmade leather buttons. Old quilted long overcoat (vintage). High leather boots trimmed in muskrat fur, snakeskin and beads. He carries a leather bag on his side trimmed in snakeskin, flap closed with a piece of smooth wood. Over the coat is a leather fringed bib with shell, beads, quills and silver cones. He has one long bead earring, long braids tied in leather, feathers in his hair and a very tiny turquoise and silver ring. One-of-a-kind.
Ref.No.: PGCV12.

Artist's price: $1,400.00

STAR LIGHTFOOT

1989. 24 in. (61 cm). Interlock head, hands and feet, body unbleached cotton. Cotton underclothes. Bright cotton dress. Over shirt done in pigskin reverse side to give the appearance of a hand-tanned hide. Trimmed in shells, thongs, feathers and beads. Entire shirt hand tied (seams) with leather. Deerhide leggings decorated on side with beads and deer dewclaws. Moccasins are low cut with head and quill design, soles and upper toes are aged and worn looking. Her headpieces are of deerhide, beads and quills. Holding a hand-dyed rag doll with a leather face. One-of-a-kind.
Ref.No.: PGCV13.

Artist's price: $1,500.00

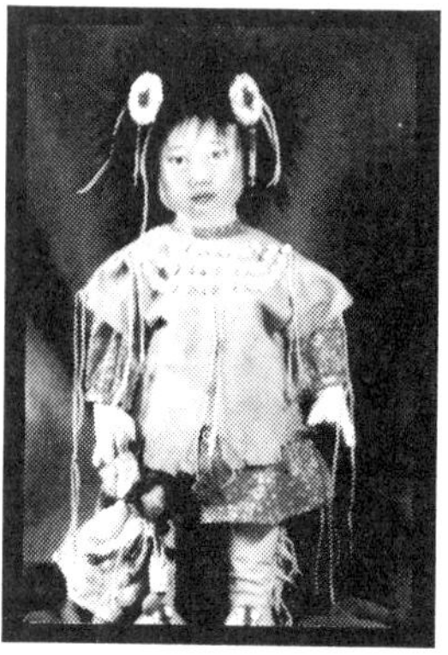

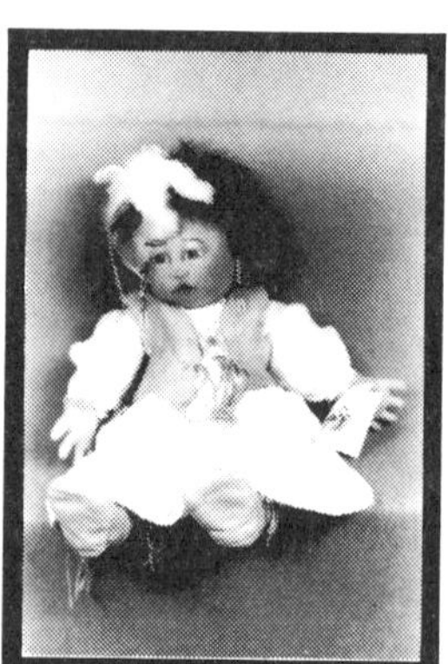

INDIAN BABY

1989. 21 in. (53.5 cm). Cloth body. Cloth head; painted facial features; black synthetic hair. Mark: label, NATIVE DOLLS/BY CARMEN VAIR.
Ref.No.: D of C, AZ17, p. 401.

Artist's price: $450.00

JEANNE VENTON
Victoria, British Columbia

LUCY

1983. 18 in. (45.5 cm). All porcelain reproduction body. Bisque head; brown stationary side-glancing eyes, painted upper and lower lashes; black tightly curled wig; open-closed mouth, showing teeth.
Ref.No. : D of C, CA10, p. 403.

Artist's price: $200.00

PRINCE WILLIAM

1985. 20 in. (50.5 cm). All porcelain body, jointed hips, shoulders and neck. Original bisque head; blue glass stationary eyes; blonde synthetic wig; open-closed mouth. Marks:
Ref.No.: D of C, CA15, p. 403.

Artist's price: $250.00

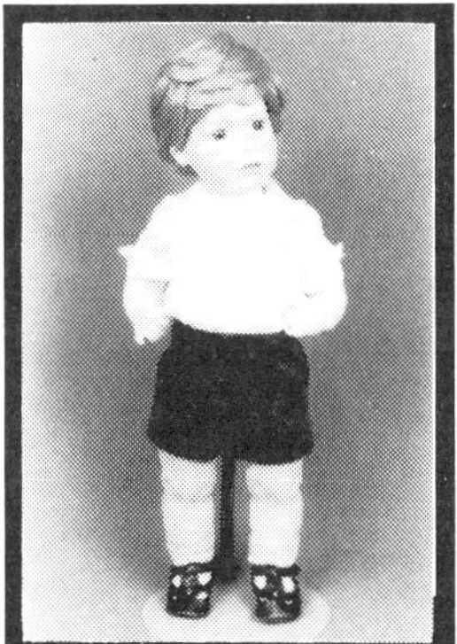

ELIZABETH MANLEY

1989. 16 in. (41 cm). All porcelain body, jointed hips, shoulders and neck. Porcelain head; brown glass eyes; open-closed smiling mouth; blond wig; earrings. Dressed in blue Spandex with silver sequin trim, hand-made leather ice-skates, sterling silver medal on a striped ribbon. Mark: on head, ELIZABETH MANLEY/ JEANNE VENTON/ 1989. #1.
Ref. no.: PGD21.

Artist's price: $495.00

PHILOMENA WALLACE
Victoria, British Columbia

MILKMAID

1983. 12 in. (30.5 cm). Cloth over wire armature body; clay hands. Head sculpted from FIMO modelling clay; painted eyes; mohair wig; open-closed mouth. Mark: on head, P.W. Carrying a pail.
Ref.No.: D of C, BZ4, p. 403.

Artist's price: $125.00

WESTERNER

ca.1988. 15 in. (38 cm). Cloth over wire armature body; clay hands. Head sculpted from FIMO.
Ref.No.: PW1.

Artist's price: $250.00

MIA

ca.1988. 18 in. (46 cm). Cloth over wire armature body; clay hands. Head sculpted from FIMO.
Ref.No.: PW2.

Artist's price: $375.00

ANNE

ca.1988. 18 in. (46 cm). Cloth over wire armature body; clay hands. Head sculpted from FIMO.
Ref.No.: PW3.

Artist's price: $350.00

SAINT NICKOLAUS

ca.1988. 18 in. (46 cm). Cloth over wire armature body; clay hands. Head sculpted from FIMO.
Ref.No.: PW4.

Artist's price: $225.00

BIBLIOGRAPHY

Charlton Press	The Charlton Standard Catalogue of Royal Doulton Figurines. Toronto: Charlton. 1981
Coleman, D.S.	The Collector's Encyclopedia of Dolls. New York: Crown. 1968
Foulke, Jan	9th. Blue Book Dolls & Values. Cumberland, Md.: Hobby House. 1989
Foulke, Jan	8th. Blue Book Dolls & Values. Cumberland, Md.: Hobby House. 1987
Foulke, Jan	7th. Blue Book Dolls & Values. Cumberland, Md.: Hobby House. 1986
Lavitt, Wendy	Dolls. (The Knopf Collectors' Guides to American Antiques). New York: A.A. Knopf. 1983
Smith, Patricia	Doll Values: Antique to Modern. Paducah, Ky.: Collector. 1979
Strickler, Eva	Inuit dolls: reminders of a heritage. Toronto: Canadian Stage and Arts Publications. 1988.
Unitt, Peter	Unitt's Canadian Price Guide to Dolls & Toys. Peterborough, Ont.: Clock. 1988

INDEX

DOLLS OF CANADA REFERENCE NUMBERS

For the collectors who have Dolls of Canada: A Reference Guide, this table may be used as a cross reference between the two books.

D of C Ref. No.	Guide Page No.	D of C Ref. No.	Guide Page No.	D of C Ref. No.	Guide Page No.	D of C Ref. No.	Guide Page No.	D of C Ref. No.	Guide Page No.
2KA3	206	AO11	190	AZ36A	9	BH32	79	BO50	41
AA18	120	AO18	193	BC3	10	BH35	154	BP3	134
AB1A	3	AO20	194	BC4	10	BH36	173	BP5	174
AB2	31	AO21	186	BC5	8	BJ3	51	BP8	158
AB28	205	AO22	114	BC7	4	BJ4	50	BP11	8
AE7	230	AO23	160	BC13	23	BJ5	150	BP14	10
AE8	173	AO25	134	BC14	186	BJ6	164	BP16	171
AE10	60	AO28	230	BC15	56	BJ7	148	BP19	18
AE11	252	AO29	146	BC17	173	BJ8	153	BP26	185
AN11A	188	AO33	140	BC18	52	BJ10	52	BP37	239
AE12	252	AP3	119	BC19	53	BJ13	167	BQ0	162
AE13	199	AP4	115	BC21	185	BJ23	97	BQ1	34
AE14	2	AP5	26	BD10	244	BJ24	188	BQ2	175
AE18	41	AP8	33	BF4	102	BL7	130	BQ4	180
AJ25	214	AP9	77	BF5	77	BM1	127	BQ5	170
AM5	166	AP10	159	BF7	196	BM2	239	BQ6	69
AM11	145	AP11	110	BF13	134	BM12	239	BQ7	196
AM16	175	AP13	169	BF21	145	BM24	156	BQ8	178
AM17	132	AP15	141	BF22	147	BM28	11	BQ11	24
AM19	50	AP17	250	BF25	121	BM29	178	BQ13	182
AM21	66	AP19	79	BF26	130	BM30	6	BQ15	62
AM23	61	AP20	144	BF27	159	BM31	177	BQ16	180
AM24	33	AP21	108	BF28	160	BM32	176	BQ18	177
AM26	107	AP27	125	BF30	57	BM33	36	BQ19	177
AM28	133	AP29A	34	BF31	52	BM35	84	BQ20	100
AM31	154	AP31	19	BF32	162	BM36	132	BQ21	69
AM34	101	AP32	123	BF33	96	BN2	146	BQ24A	19
AN5	74	AR18	4	BF36	49	BN4	37	BS2A	15
AN7	186	AR19	1	BH5	4	BN7	131	BS10	24
AN8	197	AR20	2	BH6	161	BN8	188	BS12	61
AN10	133	AR22	1	BH7	3	BN9	38	BS32	70
AN11A	188	AT12	148	BH9	179	BN10	130	BS36	139
AN15	133	AT13	181	BH10	179	BN14	103	BT1A	28
AN17	135	AW21	33	BH11	168	BN15	49	BT4A	147
AN18	187	AW22	164	BH12	150	BN16	100	BT8A	17
AN20	136	AW23	143	BH13	151	BN17	150	BT17	15
AN22	191	AW28	88	BH14	96	BN19	39	BT22	165
AN24	187	AZ3	204	BH16	84	BN22	187	BT24	83
AN26	197	AZ4	87	BH17	168	BN24	138	BU2	193
AN29	174	AZ5	111	BH18	172	BN25	92	BU3	55
AN31	129	AZ17	254	BH19	37	BN26	99	BU5	70
AN32	190	AZ18	135	BH20	185	BN30	100	BU12	175
AN33	192	AZ25	1	BH23	22	BN32	67	BU13	177
AN35	129	AZ27	8	BH24	22	BN33	104	BU17	72
AO2	138	AZ32	2	BH25	16	BN34	186	BU29	223
AO5	133	AZ33	3	BH26	19	BN35	157	BU30	192
AO7	119	AZ34	9	BH27	20	BN36	180	BU31	74
AO8	118	AZ35	9	BH29	148	BO1	38	BU35	140
AO10	143	AZ36	7	BH30	184	BO6A	252	BV14	223

D of C Ref. No.	Guide Page No.	D of C Ref. No.	Guide Page No.	D of C Ref. No.	Guide Page No.	D of C Ref. No.	Guide Page No.	D of C Ref. No.	Guide Page No.
BV18	42	BZ15	25	CC22	41	CF32	70	CI13	190
BV27	234	BZ16	165	CC29	218	CF33	166	CI15	52
BV28	234	BZ17	147	CD2	137	CF34	168	CI16	140
BW1	188	BZ18	148	CD3	69	CG3	128	CI17	139
BW8	32	BZ19	99	CD4	156	CG4	65	CI18	139
BW11	30	BZ20	184	CD5	162	CG5	120	CI19	139
BW17	156	BZ21	69	CD7	78	CG6	118	CI30	154
BW19	155	BZ22	159	CD8	63	CG7	119	CI31	138
BW20	47	BZ23	97	CD9	72	CG8	125	CI34	156
BW21	149	BZ24	149	CD10	166	CG11	145	CI36	166
BW23	194	BZ26	234	CD13	149	CG12	86	CJ4	66
BW24	194	BZ28	62	CD15	121	CG14	152	CJ5	170
BW27	85	BZ29	167	CD16	35	CG16	183	CJ10	74
BW28	85	BZ30	128	CD17	124	CG17	96	CJ11	73
BW29	141	BZ32	101	CD18	153	CG19	63	CJ12	189
BW34	76	BZ33	154	CD19	67	CG21	171	CJ13	126
BX2	142	CA2	157	CD20	145	CG22	137	CJ17	21
BX5	60	CA3	229	CD21	187	CG23	55	CJ19	17
BX6	68	CA6	228	CD23	169	CG25	118	CJ20	23
BX7	172	CA7	191	CD24	37	CG26	193	CJ23	171
BX8	97	CA8	78	CD25	71	CG27	192	CJ26	179
BX10	74	CA10	255	CD26	161	CG28	197	CJ27	128
BX11	36	CA11	229	CD28	165	CG29	124	CJ28	191
BX12	193	CA15	255	CD33	81	CG30	181	CJ35	158
BX13	73	CA16	37	CE2	5	CG31	131	CJ36	163
BX14	135	CA18	21	CE7	125	CG32	191	CL2	155
BX15	113	CA23	34	CE8	49	CG33	213	CL3	163
BX16	62	CA27	110	CE10	136	CG35	26	CL4	204
BX18	201	CA29	24	CE11	137	CH2	192	CL5	163
BX19	205	CA30	169	CE14	172	CH3	204	CL6	78
BX20	136	CA31	80	CE15	137	CH4	204	CL7	178
BX21	205	CA32	146	CE16	172	CH5	38	CL8	158
BX22	205	CA33	110	CE21	29	CH6	203	CL12	228
BX24	203	CA34	163	CE29	54	CH7	127	CL22	18
BX25	189	CA35	86	CE31	53	CH8	167	CL25	82
BX31	9	CA36	68	CE34	20	CH9	93	CL26	73
BX32	2	CA39	11	CF2	14	CH10	136	CL27	79
BX34	76	CB5	65	CF4	80	CH11	127	CL29	203
BY6	10	CB7	159	CF5	78	CH12	104	CL31	109
BY9	144	CB14	60	CF8	36	CH18	15	CL36	152
BY10	152	CB15	3	CF9	173	CH22	14	CM2	170
BY12	83	CB17	71	CF10	175	CH24	22	CM3	200
BY13	141	CB21	54	CF12	54	CH26	16	CM5	181
BY14	20	CB24	77	CF16	35	CH29	143	CM6	11
BY16	58	CB32	55	CF20	129	CH31	17	CM7	12
BZ2	151	CB34A	142	CF21	72	CH32	21	CM8	82
BZ4	256	CC2	142	CF22	106	CI4	53	CM9	82
BZ6	146	CC3	155	CF25	72	CI6	102	CM11	152
BZ7	81	CC5	81	CF26	174	CI7	128	CN3A	44
BZ8	107	CC6	82	CF27	103	CI8	77	CN7	44
BZ9	131	CC8	80	CF28	161	CI9	64	CN11	107
BZ12	7	CC11	53	CF29	61	CI10	55	CN14	195
BZ13	5	CC13	153	CF30	58	CI11	125	CN18	158
BZ14	6	CC14	51	CF31	56	CI12	170	CN19	76

D of C Ref. No.	Guide Page No.	D of C Ref. No.	Guide Page No.	D of C Ref. No.	Guide Page No.	D of C Ref. No.	Guide Page No.	D of C Ref. No.	Guide Page No.
XH22	184	XH25	157	XH30	219	XH35	220	XX13	215
XH23	45	XH26	105	XH33	219	XH36	220	XX15	215
XH24	44	XH27	119	XH34	220	XH37	221	XX17	215

DOLLS OF CANADA: A REFERENCE GUIDE
By Evelyn Robson Strahlendorf

This book is for doll collectors, museums, libraries, antique dealers. doll stores, and flea market operators. It contains the dates, names, and characteristics to identify about one thousand Canadian dolls from prehistoric times to the present, with the emphasis on dolls of this century manufactured commercially and dolls made by Canadian artists. It may be considered a history of Canadian dolls. Also included are about fifty dolls sold by the T. Eaton Co. Limited labeled as Eaton's Beauties. Many of the Eaton Beauty dolls were made by European companies like J. D. Kestner, Armand Marseille, and Cuno and Otto Dressel. However, they are included because they are an integral part of Canadian doll history. Attention is devoted to the doll industry in Canada and how the manufacturing process evolved from bisque and composition dolls through the various plastics to the dolls of today. Reproduction dolls are not presented, although two are shown as working dolls. With few exceptions, every doll described in this book has been personally examined by the author.

This book is also intended for a special class of doll enthusiast whom we call the closet collector. There are tens of thousands of these doll lovers in North America who have dolls and may also collect dolls, but do not admit this pleasure to others.

Available from University of Toronto Press.   ISBN: 0-9692586-0-7